D0979049

Ernest L. Norman
**Author, Philosopher, Poet, Scientist,
Director-Moderator of Unarius Science of Life**

UNARIUS
UNiversal **AR**ticulate Interdimensional
Understanding of **S**cience

TEMPUS

INVICTUS

TEMPUS INVICTUS

THIRD EDITION

Printed in China

ISBN 0-9724710-5-7

Unarius Educational Foundation
El Cajon, California, 92020

*

TEMPUS INVICTUS

By
Ernest L. Norman

UNARIUS PUBLICATIONS
145 S. Magnolia Avenue
El Cajon, CA 92020

Other works by Ernest L. Norman

The Pulse of Creation Series

The Infinite Concept of Cosmic Creation
Key to the Unarius Science (13 Lesson Course)
(7 Advanced Lessons) Addendum Added 1970

The Truth About Mars
Cosmic Continuum
Infinite Perspectus
Infinite Contact
Tempus Procedium
Tempus Interludium Vol. I
Tempus Interludium Vol. II

The Elysium (Parables)
The Anthenium (Poetry)

These texts may also be obtained on magnetic
recording tape.

Table of Contents

(cont'd)

Table of Contents (Cont'd)

CHAPTER I

The Psychic Anatomy
Development Concept

In a broad and general abstraction, the presentation of the Unarius curriculum, and as an interdimensional science inclusive of all known and unknown factors in the creative interdimensional cosmogony, this presentation was, therefore, in its first form, most necessarily simplified to make it even partially understood and also by necessity certain comparisons and compromises were also included to make this interdimensional conception more easily compatible with existing third dimensional objectivisms.

However, in all aspects and in any particular objective introspection, the presentation of any Unariun concept does deserve a more thorough presentation which will make it more serviceable and understandable in a more progressive intellectual society—particularly the scientific society. The concept of the psychic anatomy is one of utmost importance, as it at once does either directly or indirectly, involve all aspects of planetary and interdimensional life. This concept should therefore be most fittingly expanded into its true perspectives. In the present state of development, all sciences as they are now so propagated, are all strictly third dimensional in their circumferences and, as a consequence, are still completely ignorant of the true basic life factors which are not third dimensional in nature, but which are an expressionary composite of interdimensional energy forms which function immutably according to well defined laws; called in the more familiar idiom of this science, as oscillations or the

1

interchange of positive-negative polarities which carry the idiom of information, and to subsequent harmonic patterns regenerated in this oscillating process which can and do, in this grand synonymy of interdimensional oscillation, link and relink this interdimensional cosmos into the creative effigy of Infinity.

To start with then, let us refresh our minds with this first basic primary law of energy interchange as an oscillating polarity. In a magnetic structure, two north poles repel or north and south poles attract, etc. A negative south pole oscillating to the north pole will, in that meeting, be repolarized and assume the positive polarity as a phase-reversal and as a now existing positive oscillation, will be attracted back to the original south pole to again repeat this oscillation process in the interchange of energy or as information according to its oscillating frequency or, as in other similar wave form transmissions such as television, carry added information.

It is this same basic energy interdimensional phase-reversal-oscillating-condition which is so universally expressed in all adjunctive relationships, such as the earth's magnetic field or the gravitational field. A stone by the road, while seemingly solid and with a certain weight is actually a conglomeration of pulsating atoms; and despite the external appearances, are very far apart and are linked together by a pulsating or oscillating field of force which they (the atoms) radiate. Here again is this same positive-negative oscillating wave-form condition which can and does either strongly link a group of atoms together in molecules or with an inverse proportional reaction, repel other atom-conglomerations. This is the underlying factor and principle which determines the quantitive assessments of the ninety-two atom forms, and as they are, technically speaking, erroneously called mass.

While the stone by the road is, within itself, a complex matrix of oscillating wave forms, there is also another complex matrix of wave forms oscillating through the stone and in a sense, mingling with the total radiated energy-field of the stone. To move this stone, therefore, means that at any given distance or time, we are changing the basic polarity patterns of interchange between this stone atom-configuration and the entire magnetic and gravitational force-fields of the earth, the earth to the sun—the sun to the galaxy, etc.

The energy used to move the stone is therefore inversely proportional to the expressive quanta of negative-positive energy oscillations involved in this intergalactic complex. Equally important, this intergalactic complex of expressionary elements expressed as universes, galaxies, planetary systems, earth-worlds, etc., are in turn, part of the net sum and total of all expressionary agents and elements in the interdimensional cosmos—a scientific explanation of why the fall of a sparrow is noted!

To continue further in our explorations and as it more specifically concerns the human anatomy, the repercussive karma etc: in former discussions, a human being was presented in a simplified manner as functioning according to the same basic principle as does the television. However, in that presentation, in a simplified form it might be much more difficult to technically understand, or that it might be less acceptable to a more scientifically-inclined understanding. The television transmission is essentially radiating a basic sine-wave which has impounded within it two synchronization pulses, plus the pulses of video and audio wave forms. While this was first considered a straight line type of communication, that is, it traveled as a beam of light from transmitter to receiver, this was in reality, a closed circuit condition. The transmitter was grounded to the earth as a negative polarity as was the television set; therefore, the antenna of the transmitter was actually oscillating through the air to the earth in the interchange of positive-negative waveform polarizations. The receiver and its antenna then, in effect, became a parasitic secondary positive-negative oscillator, and from this oscillating condition, through the circuitry of the receiver, finally resolved into the picture on the screen.

Like the television concept, every human—as does everything else—has a transmitter—the psychic anatomy. The psychic anatomy of the stone was the net electromagnetic field generated by the composite atoms. The human also has such an atom energy-field which determines, among other things, the weight or pounds gravitational pull. The concept here is as total as with the stone. Like all other atomic forms of life, the human has a much more highly-developed psychic anatomy than has the stone, and as a human, represents the highest development of the psychic anatomy concept.

It is within this psychic anatomy development concept that we find the true kernel of truth in evolution and which was unknown by Darwin or any succeeding contemporaries! That is, true evolution takes place only within the psychic anatomy, the external or physical body—the expressionary agent.

For example, with a former presentation of Charlie, the amoeba: in his natural habitat, a watery pond, Charlie lives in a temperature of, say approximately 70 degrees F. However, if we begin to raise the temperature of his watery environment, we can in the succeeding weeks, see the progenies of the great, great, great, great-grandchildren of Charlie live in a water temperature which would have quickly killed good old Charlie! Now the tolerance factor was not passed on to the succeeding generation through the DNA molecule, which was only a secondary transmitting or oscillating element. The tolerance factor was information impounded in the psychic anatomy of each succeeding generation of amoebas; energy referring back to the same oscillating polarity exchange and the subsequent harmonic regeneration which impounded these harmonic fractions within the psychic anatomy, to again regenerate under the same closed-circuit conditions into the succeeding amoeba-body, this tolerance factor.

To better understand this closed-circuit condition and how, as in the case of a human, a malformed anomaly (or vortex) is formed in the psychic anatomy, we may refer to the original chart in the second Lesson Course where, as a block diagram, the psychic anatomy was sectionalized in three portions and linked to consciousness with a single oscillation for each portion.

To more properly and clearly define a closed-circuit oscillating-condition, we should substitute a wave-form circle instead of a straight-line wave-form which would connect consciousness with that particular portion of the psychic anatomy. We should also draw a fourth section or portion which would represent the entire physical body abstraction as it was so compounded in the psychic anatomy. These portions, as we have called them, would actually represent spectrums of energy oscillations which, according to their frequency, would automatically relegate or confine them in that particular spectrum. The net sum and total as a configuration or portion would then become its base-plane-rate of oscillation. This base-plane-rate of oscillation would then be oscillating in its entirety with the physical anatomy as a closed-circuit condition wherein all waveform elements containing their respective information would be, through frequency, linked to all cell structures in the anatomy, these cell structures representing specific organs, bone structures, etc.

There are billions of cells in the human anatomy, each one linked through oscillating frequency or as a harmonic frequency, to the psychic anatomy and in a closed-circuit condition; that is, constantly and at all times, the net-total information necessary for a cell to live and perform its extremely complex function, to propagate through mitosis or fission, is so flowing into this cell during its entire life-span. The net sum and total of this wave-form-information again harmonically regenerates a primary or base-plane oscillation. This cellular base-plane-rate vibration is the key in understanding the proposition of rejection in transplanting a kidney from one human to another. These net base-plane-rate oscillations are all different in every human —save identical twins. The leucocytes (or white blood cells) also have a base-plane-rate vibration which must be harmonically in tune with every cell in that particular anatomy, otherwise the leucocytes will destroy by eating any cell or similar organism with which it is not in harmonic attunement!

This is the principle of rejection, as not yet understood by doctors who make transplants of kidneys, livers, hearts, etc., and then over the succeeding days and weeks, watch their patients die as the leucocytes literally eat the transplanted organ! If we speculate, perhaps some day doctors will learn about this most important principle and from this knowledge, build an electronic oscillator which could change the harmonic patterns of these base-plane-rate frequencies to correspond with those of the displaced or transplanted organ. Perhaps too, in that future day the doctors would find the true cause of that kidney failure or any other systemic breakdown.

It is at this point we will conclude our entire presentation with this most important factor: the how and why the different organs break down and become diseased or to whatever other systemic disorder is so manifest, excluding those of pathogenic origin, caused more specifically from germ organisms. As of today, there are hundreds of incurable diseases which beset mankind, any and all of which no doctor, no scientist, no biologist can give the true originating cause!—and which has been so emphatically installed and reinstated in the Unariun concept; and as these causes all originate in the psychic anatomy from previous earth lives wherein certain shocks induced into the psychic anatomy under closed-circuit conditions, the malformed energy information which, in the timeless fourth dimension, and as part of the psychic anatomy could, would, and did repeat their destructive information into the physical anatomy according to the interplay of harmonic patterns stemming into the affected cell tissue areas, to again destructively re-create a facsimile of non-constructive expression which eventually destroyed that part or organ of the human anatomy.

If a person is killed by a bullet, a spear, an arrow, etc., the repercussion at that particular moment of impact from the death weapon creates a tremendous electrical surcharge of energy which, traveling on the composite energy wave-form-matrix into the psychic anatomy, creates an anomaly of unrelated, unintelligent, nonreciprocative elements which, in some future day, will conversely reflect and re-express themselves into the physical anatomy; a consequence that can be relived from one life to the next with an ever-increasing indemnity.

This, then, is karma, but finally taken from the realm of religious or mystical interpretations, the direct and scientific implication is the evolutionary process of life—an implication that immediately demands a complete moral responsibility for all humans; for indeed in the present, in this thought and action which is incumbent with the present, is the future formulated!—a future to live or die as we so choose, either in the throes of some violent incomprehensible death or with torturous years filled with wretched pain and suffering.

In the grand scale of evolution as it is so formulated and as it so manifests in the endless successive inter-change of expressionary elements manifest as polarity patterns, there is always the ever-increasing necessity to constantly re-express a proportional positive bias. Call it inspiration, call it recognition of a higher Intel-ligence, or call it the best attributes of life, it will still be the positive biasing agent—a fuel to propel the human soul into a higher state of consciousness, or conversely, the lack of such bias leaves such a soul flatulent, unresponsive and sinking ever deeper into the negative—a negative which is unrelated and un-balanced by a positive interplay and will, in itself, be destructive!

CHAPTER II

Man, The Electronic Computer

There is no doubt that as of these closing days of 1967, we have truly emerged into an age of scientific miracles; accomplishments which would have, even a few decades ago, seemed utterly fantastic.

About sixty or so years ago, a man named Jules Verne presented a number of stories which, at that time, were utterly fantastic, yet today Verne's submarine, "The Nautilus", has been much more than fully justified in our atomically-powered submarines. Undersea vessels which remain totally submerged as long as three months manufacture their own air and maintain a totally enclosed environment. Many manned satellites have encircled the earth, and in at least two instances remained aloft with their two-man crew for two or three weeks. Also in a totally enclosed, self-sustained environment, unmanned satellites have, figuratively, more than duplicated Verne's "balloon trip to the moon", and have soft landed on its surface, taken thousands of pictures of its surrounding lunar landscapes, and with a claw-like arm, dug holes in the moon's surface.

Satellites, too, have gone to Mars, made many pictures of its surface. Other satellites have attempted to probe the atmosphere and surface of Venus, not too successfully in this case, however, as Venus is not strictly a third-dimensional planet.

All this and much more has been made possible by the rapid development of many kinds of scientific apparatus. The greatest single development has been in the field of computers. Computers made the atomic submarine possible; a computer plotted an around-the-world undersea cruise without ever coming to the surface. Computers plot the course of satellites and computers man the cameras and other systems. Inside the space capsules, astronauts depend on computers for many functions, including getting them back to the ground, etc. Here on the earth's surface computers have already occupied a vast and complex position in our society.

Computers monitor electrical and gas supply systems for many millions of American homes; computers are indispensable in hospitals, in surgery, and watching over critical patients. In industry computers have fulfilled countless thousands of operations which, in turn, have made living easier, given us greater abundance and at less cost.

Computers are even found in the home; electronic computers take over the task of automatically washing and drying clothes, cooking foods, etc. In the state of New York, the schools now use computers to teach in a closed television circuit system whereby students both at home and school may study via the help of computers. Army operations, food surplus, troops tasks, etc., are all done more quickly and accurately with computers. Courses for ships and planes are plotted through the benefit of computers.

Computers play an important part in almost every conceivable field; merchandise is sorted, counted; packaged foodstuffs travel over moving belts manipulated by computers; research depots are computer operated; bolts and nuts are sized and counted through the aid of computers.

In many instances man has succeeded in building a robot computer which walks and talks like a man and can perform on command, a limited number of functions. The movies and television have enthusiastically taken over this segment of man's life, particularly on television, through such serials as "Star Trek", "Lost In

10

Space", etc. Many millions of people nightly view these scientific fantasies, some of which are already here, others yet to be met in the future. In the "Invaders" (a television series), we see humanoids—exact electrical mechanical duplicates of earth people, produced by aliens from another galaxy, who are attempting to conquer the earth. "Star Trek" deals with the future explorations of our own galaxy and a host of incredible life forms found in other planetary systems. "Lost In Space" had a featured character, a robot, which is strangely human, and actually makes corny puns!

Now while man has, at this time, made such amazing progress, has electrified and computerized his civilization, and has even begun to explore space, yet even more strangely enough he knows little or nothing about the greatest computer of all, the human being! Yes, indeed this is so. Man is essentially and in principle, a robot-computer, and one which has progressed in its development to a point far beyond any electronic mechanical contrivance he has invented.

Every human who has lived or is so living, or will live, functions basically in principle as does a computer, except that it is a vastly expanded system of function and which is also bidimensional, or functions simultaneously in two dimensions. Like all computers, man has been fed or feeds himself information which is done on the life experience basis and from life to life. This information is stored in his memory banks—the psychic anatomy. This is a timeless proposition where any such experience as an energy wave form vibrating in a closed circuit oscillates forever.

The Internal Revenue of the United States has the financial record of every American taxpayer imprinted on a piece of microfilm about one-half inch long. A single reel of microtape contains many years of financial records for a hundred thousand people, or even a million!

11

The memory banks of our psychic anatomy function on many levels which could be called base plane frequencies. A very important function is in the supervision, maintenance, repair of the physical body. There are hundreds of millions of cells in a human body and there are thousands of different kinds of cells. Loosely speaking, each cell is surrounded by a micro-thin membrane. Within the protoplasm of the cell, there is a complete chemical laboratory which carries on a chemical synthesis above and beyond any contrived by science. It takes in certain chemicals, remanufactures them, and even converts them into other substances. It even generates an electrochemical charge of ultrahigh-frequency electricity with which it carries on through the nerves, conversation with the brain and the psychic anatomy; and just as in the computer, this conversation is in the form of different sequential signals.

The psychic anatomy, however, is the guiding mandate in all cellular functions and activities. The psychic anatomy constantly feeds into each cell a constant stream of information, even when the cell divides and becomes two; and there are about one and one-half million new cells so regenerated in the human body every minute, principally to replace those which have died or been destroyed; for the cell, too, has a natural life cycle. And so here again is one of the most amazing and yet utterly almost unknown functions of life; in fact, it is this constant stream of energy information fed into each cell, each molecule which composes the cell, and each atom which composes the molecule, which is that mysterious life force which the scientist has yet to discover.

As of this time, the science of biology has relegated this life intelligence as coded information in the DNA molecule. He has not yet divined that the DNA molecule is, in turn, only another coded form and is fed coded information on function, activity, etc., from the infinite wave forms of energy contained in the memory banks of the psychic anatomy. Yes, even the individual atom of that DNA molecule performs its function, radiates its own EMF and is otherwise that certain specific atom from information constantly fed into it through its own psychic anatomy and from the memory banks of Infinite Intelligence.

While we may speculate and even eulogize man on his scientific accomplishments in this third-dimensional world, we can only lament his adamant position in refusing to cross over this invisible line of demarcation which separates him from the Infinite Cosmogony; and perhaps, too, this is one more way in which, theoretically, man could find the kingdom within; and obtain suitable life perspectives and answers to intangibles which are as yet unanswered.

It is almost academic to state that once this line is crossed, the scientist, whoever he is or at whatever time, will then discover not only the true source of life, but the infinite nature of this great, intelligent, constructive, life-force which radiates in a coded computer-like fashion according to frequencies, not only into DNA molecules of the animal life on this planet earth but into all other forms; yes, even hard rock which composes a mountainous landscape is held, atomically speaking, in its own time-space dimension, (sermons in stones), for truly as atoms form all seemingly solid substances which comprise the third dimensional world of man, so it is that each of these atoms, whole or subdivided, are a part of form and energy substance of Infinite Creative Intelligence.

And as such, each atom, in its respective cyclic motions within itself, beats harmoniously with the heart and mind of Infinite Intelligence; and in this beat, recreates for man, his material world and the unfathomable future to come.

CHAPTER III

Man - A Living Television Mechanism (1956)

Perhaps it may serve a purpose if we discussed further and point up other similarities or analogies of these energy principles to help convey to you these all-important interdimensional relationships and concepts.

For instance, you can see how electricity going through the light filament, the molecules of tungsten or the filament offers resistance to the oscillating current. Direct current would not pass through it because it would be too highly resistant. The tungsten won't burn up because there is no oxygen, but the molecules can get so steamed up and agitated about the whole thing that they go white-hot. When they begin to get white-hot, they give off six or seven different kinds of frequencies. The molecules are all banded together and churning around. There are big wide open spaces between the molecules. You may think the substance is solid because it seems that way. Everything in this third dimension, as far as atomic structures are concerned, between the various particles called solid, the parallaxes of the waves or the cycles in an atom are so far apart that they are comparable to: if you had 100 acres of land and you took a dozen eggs and put them evenly all over the 100 acres, that is about what an atom would look like in comparative size. So you think that everything is either hard or soft in comparison with your body which is made up of the same type of substance—it is resistant to another substance in direct ratio and proportion according to the atomic scale. That merely means that there isn't anything actually solid.

14

We have 5000 ray particles going through us every minute of 24 hours, and few of them ever hit us in a lifetime—and only very rarely, when they do; some scientists think it's the contributing cause for cancer. When one strikes, it produces a chain reaction of split atoms in some portion of the body. Also, there happens to be things linked there too in the psyche which would continue the chain reaction process into breaking down the natural carrier frequency of intelligence to the atom. That's where the scientists of materiamedica have missed the boat today in their various treatments of incurable diseases—because they have not continued on into the defects and broken down transmissions between the psyche and the atomic structures of the outer body. When they continue and see the life process carried back into the psyche, the spiritual self, then they will have a place to start in the solution of all incurable diseases. Every atom in the body that does not function properly according to the scale of life in which it learned to live in the process of evolution, as we call incarnation, is diseased and non-functional. This is simply because the transmission of intelligence that was developed through incarnation and made that atom possible to exist in the human body in its relationship, that carrier of intelligence has been broken down, been disrupted to a certain degree. It is out of alignment.

Every atom in the human system is linked to the higher or psychic body; just like we had a bunch of small beads lying on a table and every one of those beads had a little string on them that went down through the table and were connected by a wire to a battery underneath the table, and they were all activated by that battery. We could have the same similarity in an iconoscope or some similar piece of electronic apparatus used in television for picking up the picture, which is another development of the iconoscope. They resolve in the same thing—they have light which comes in focus by lenses, goes on to a mosaic screen which is a series of very finely planted pattern of chemically active cells. Those cells are very small, we can liken them to tiny little beads, and when those cells are activated by light or darkness according to how the lens focuses the picture upon them, they in turn are all hooked up by wire and circuitry into various electronic circuits into transmitting apparatus. In that way, they go out onto the ethers and the synchronized picture.

The process is absolutely the same with the psychic body in the human being except, of course, we don't have the orthocon (picture) or the iconoscope and we don't have the mosaic. We have the physical body as the image of the television; we have the psychic body, and the subconscious which is really the picture which picks up the imagery of not only the physical expressions from the exterior but also pictures from the higher plateaus of relationship. The process is very similar and an exact parallel to that used in television transmission. Science unknowingly has struck a very close parallel in the television as in the process of life as far as the human body is concerned with the psyche, except that in the higher dimensions of relationship instead of having metal, glass and other material substances created in various different forms and circuitry or envelopments or configurations, we have frequency relationship, harmonic structures and various other different things which exist in pure vortexal patterns and wave forms in a spaceless dimension. We call this the psychic body and that is our television transmitter, because that is transmitting to us synchronized with external appearances.

We are stimulated from the outside with light, heat, smells, sounds, etc., various other physical stimuli, and they in turn are retranslated into the psyche and they cause stimulation back into the conscious again.

16

That, of course, orients the whole thing in less than one-tenth of a split second. We derive certain extractions in that process of oscillation as comparative value. We have the same process in these great brain machines called Univac. In constructing Univac, they have done exactly the same thing that the Infinite did with the psyche in the human being. They put little cells in the Univac, literally hundreds of thousands of them, and they are able to store up for a short time a certain amount of energy of a certain frequency. Whenever certain circuitry connects them with a punched card, they will store up a frequency. Then when other things happen and correlation is brought about in the machine, they will discharge back into the circuitry again which activates another type of mechanism which prints something on a card. That's the sum and total of it.

(Will you tell me something more about the mirror reflection?)

Well, it's a very simple allegorical picture that a person can create for himself. If we take what we call the Holy Triad—Brahma, Vishnu or Shiva, we always have the three points, the Holy Trinity—Father, Son and the Holy Ghost. What we actually have is the Superconsciousness, the subconscious and the conscious; as far as human beings are concerned, we are either functioning from one or the other at all times. Very few people function from the Superconsciousness and then only in moments of spiritual transcendency or in very special and very highly improbable circumstances; or only very old souls who have been trained in clairvoyance, the function from the Superconsciousness. When we do have moments where the mind is coupled directly with the Superconsciousness, a person can see ahead into the future and behind into the past in many ways and respects. Ordinarily most people function from the subconscious, which is merely that portion of

17

the psychic body which we call the cellar or the basement. It has collected all the reactionary bits because in the psychic body everything has to be dimensionally related. The psyche is in itself composed of an infinite number of various vortexal structures, which in their basic frequency relationship, are related to different planes or dimensions. The closest one to the physical body is the subconscious.

In using the mirror, we can hold the mirror up in front of us and we can tilt the mirror so that we can look at any object on the ground—a pile of rubbish or sticks or stones. That is comparable to the subconscious, or we can turn the mirror upward and see a beautiful tree, a mountain, or many other much more inspiring sights in that same mirror. That is comparable to the conscious mind. When we turn the mirror upward into the reaches of the psychic self or even into the Superconsciousness itself, then of course, all the mysteries of heaven and the Infinite Cosmos will open up to us. That is clairvoyance in its true sense.

When I say clairvoyance, I am not associating it with the common type of spiritualism which we see today manifest in the séance rooms, etc., because that really isn't clairvoyance to my way of thinking. That is the pattering of small feet and children playing with mud pies, so to speak. They really don't understand what is behind these things; they cannot conceive the one basic fundamental element of all creation which is energy. There isn't anything else either here or hereafter that isn't in some form or another a relationship of energy. There is no such thing as a solid, because it would be absolutely impossible for even the Infinite to create anything of a solid substance because it would be foreign to the nature of the Infinite. The Infinite is the sum and total of all abstraction, dynamics and never-ending, ceaseless, interchanging dimensional relationships. In order for the Infinite to be creative, It must be dynamic. Dynamic means of course that there must always be a ceaseless, never-ending movement of energy—a relationship of energy, interdimensional, infinite and finite. It is foreign to the Infinite to have anything solid or stagnant, or static. Even in cases where we have energy supposedly static, we only find that this energy, instead of traveling in a straight line frequency, is only gyrating but it is still moving, even on the plates of condensers moving in never-ending, ceaseless patterns of harmonic structures across the face of the metal. It is like ten thousand birds in a room all trying to escape out of the window at the same time. The little electrons will be called solid particles but are not solid at all, for they are tiny little solar systems of pure energy. Those little solar systems, that we call specks, are in turn more little solar systems and so on into infinity.

It is very hard for the human mind to picture energy until you go right into what scientific apparatus we have, such as the oscilloscope. If you can first get an oscillator, signal generator and oscilloscope, you can gain a very comprehensive idea of how and what energy is, but it takes even more than that. You have to live with it a long time before you can even conceive it, because in the first place it travels at such inconceivable speeds. There is nothing in the human anatomy that could even keep up with it because any energy, even sound, will travel much faster than the human eye can see. It can travel six or seven thousand feet per second. All the other forms of energy of an electronic nature, such as radio waves, light waves, etc., travel at about 186,000 miles per second. Between that and sound, which is the slowest of most of the energy movements, we have numerous different spectrums where energy moves—fringe-line spectrums that are on the end of our visual spectrum which lies in between.

As far as the human brain is concerned, it is simply

a thing which is a development of reincarnation through many lifetimes, and whether we want to admit it or
not, man is in a comparatively low state of evolution as
far as this world is concerned—speaking of at least
ninety-nine percent of the people on the earth. They are
really only about half-way on a scale between an animal and a human being and still struggling in the mire
and the pits, the primeval ooze from which they sprang
many thousands of years ago. It is only recently, in the
last 25 or 50,000 years, that they have succeeded in
maintaining the ego or id from one lifetime to another
as their reincarnative pattern of life. That is what dis-
tinguished them from the animals. In the animal, the
ego or id is not sustained for any length of time after
the animal passes into spirit. The various harmonic
structures, as far as energy is concerned in the other
dimensions which are concerned with the psychic body
of an animal, are related in other interdimensional
relationships and go into other creative patterns, and
come back into other egos or ids of other animals of a
similar species, or even an evolutionary species. That's
the way the pattern goes.

That is the part that Darwin didn't touch because
he did not understand. He could not see into the universes and see how energy in a vortexal pattern of harmonic structures and frequency relationships were
always finding ways and means to seek each other out
on compatible frequencies to regenerate into other
intelligent forms of another nature and re-portray a
particular pattern of life into some materialistic dimension. This is a secondary translation as far as the old
gyrative culmination of energy wave forms were concerned. There we get into more complex and deeper
secrets of life, and they are properly understood only
when we can transcend beyond the barriers of our
physical mind and get "upstairs", so to speak, and get
into the higher mental reaches of the psychic self and

closer to that Superconsciousness which is so completely abstract in nature that the scope of vision is infinite. That is what Jesus meant when He spoke of the Father within, or the Kingdom of Heaven within— one and the same thing. The Father is not a personal being; when he said Father, He meant that it was the creator of all form and substance infinite and finite. Therefore, the Kingdom and the Father were one and the same, because in the Kingdom we find all things finite and infinite and the Father was the creator of all those things—so they are one and the same.

Many people, of course, are badly mixed up on these things because they don't understand the mechanics of the creative form and substance of energy. The only reason we have a physical body is simply because we have incurred the idea and form of association of this physical form through countless ages of time and successive bodies. These energy formations which are associated and formed into the human body have been built up through hundreds of thousands of years until the time when they arrived at the sufficient cohesive element known as the id or ego and more or less kept the thing together passing from one life to another, when a person began to associate himself with the higher structures, because this id or ego was directly connected with another vortexal pattern which is called the Superconsciousness.

These things are very complex. They require a lot of thought and concentration to a person in a position like our dear little sister down here (speaking of Ruth). Those things are very difficult because she is on the threshold of something that even the greatest and most intelligent of our thinkers today have only the faintest inkling because they have refused to transcend the barriers of the physical dimension. They are afraid of their position and impedimenta that they have accumulated through being coached through school and college or academic position or social structures, censorship of their colleagues, etc. They are afraid, even though they may have the inner intuitive sense of the knowledge in the ability to link themselves up with higher ideas, forms and consciousness. Very few of them have had the courage of their convictions to come out and risk all to work these things out. Einstein is one of the mental geniuses who managed to survive, and in surviving he became a hero of the scientific world, along with Isaac Newton and many of the others, but there are very few of them who have that courage.

A few hundred years ago, they burned people at the stake for thinking things like that. Now they have more subtle means of destroying. As far as the average individual is concerned, he is much like the Chinese or Japanese—he hates to lose face with his fellow countrymen, especially if he is in the position of a scientist in a college when his very livelihood depends on his prestige in holding to certain conformed trails of mental relationships or mental paths which they have to follow. After all, back of every great college and institution and back of the fabrication of our scientific structure of this country, we have a very pedagogic and despotic group of tyrants who rule these things and hold the purse strings; and those tyrants are extremely narrow-minded. They are just as narrow-minded as they were back in the Victorian Age. They refuse to accept things beyond their own limited sphere of introspection. In every college we have a board of trustees, and they are very conscious of the prestige of that college. The only time we don't find this is in a new civilization that is young, growing and green, like a new tree. There is no time for that rotten wood to form. It is only after the tree reaches a certain circumference and growth that deadwood starts setting in. This is but bigotry that we have among those who hold key positions and hold the purse strings of the financial backing of the various

22

colleges and scientific institutions of this country—and there are very few places in the land today where a scientist is permitted to go ahead and experiment on his own. Even though they may say so, yet the scientist is very conscious of certain lines over which he dare not pass.

One of the greatest and strongest of these lines is that line which marks the material world from the spiritual. Very few dare cross that line. It is an invisible line, but it is there just the same. As far as the scientist of the world is concerned, anything which is called spiritual is "pseudo". He doesn't believe in anything spiritual the way a person of a more orthodox sense would believe, such as the soul, or spiritual worlds, or man existing on other planets under conditions similar to that of the earth. He could not possibly conceive that a man could live anywhere else unless he had oxygen to breathe the same as here, and a compatible temperature and living environment. That thing, in itself, is one of the most idiotic suppositions that man has ever labored under in the past thousands of years. Even now it is even much more stupid and much more narrow-minded than it has been in the past because the scientist is practically surrounded with proof, imperishable and invulnerable proof that life exists in an infinite number of forms without oxygen under extreme temperatures. In fact, he is confronted with the fact that the very thing he calls life is energy and can exist under any and all circumstances. In fact, there is no place where there isn't energy, even what he calls an impenetrable void of space, a so-called vacuum.

There is a swing-back now to the theory among many of the prominent thinkers of the world that there is no such thing as a vacuum and a void out there. It would be impossible for nature to form a vacuum. Now he finds out that the atmosphere of the earth extends twice as high into space as he formerly thought. With the Palomar telescope, he finds that he has to alter his concept of space and expand it at least two and a half times. If he makes another telescope twice that size, his space will go out that much further, etc., etc.

What is meant by the whole thing is that man has simply refused to admit that he is extremely ignorant and knows absolutely nothing about anything at all beyond a hundred atoms that he can hold in the palm of his hand. He may know something about them and perhaps some of the chemical reaction processes, and has even succeeded in exploding two or three.

I went around year after year in various spiritualist churches and other churches. I was looking, not particularly forming any alliances beyond that which served a purpose of preparing for a day and time when I would have to speak intelligently. I wanted a little practice to overcome a complex I had. I found that most people who called themselves teachers—whether they were ministers or priests or rabbis, etc.,—were comparatively very ignorant and unlearned men in spite of the fact that occasionally I found some with a little academic background and some who had read considerably along certain lines. But I never found one of them in my whole search for fifteen years who knew anything about life. That is a strange thing to say in spite of the fact that they were simply spouting language about life, but there was not a thing in what they said that meant anything. They didn't have the knowledge or know-how; they didn't know anything beyond the grave. To me, that wouldn't add up because I could not see on any ending where there was a beginning. The old adage—which came first, the hen or the egg— was applicable here. As far as the world was concerned, this is only the beginning; and if this is the beginning, then certainly there had to be an ending—and the ending was not here. It had to be out there somewhere. But they did not know and there was no one who could give me any information. In fact, that was one thing that I searched for most—the answer to that riddle that I knew had to be answered before I was satisfied. I didn't find it in any church. I found it at the workbench in a television shop. I found what I was looking for. It wasn't really hidden from me at all because I had known all about it for thousands of years.

I found that man, as far as the earth life is concerned, is stumbling blindly along a path. He does not have a spiritual eye but at the same time through various relationships such as life previously lived, as well as intuitive guidance from higher planes and channels, and his own ability to travel in his sleep state and other human factors—even though he does not acknowledge these things and doesn't know anything about them—he has succeeded in creating some of the greatest miracles of life—like television. The people don't seem to realize the tremendous thing that really is, the various electronic gadgets and appliances they are surrounded with—the radio and communication system—and how far science has gone into perfecting these things for the material world. These are made possible only because somehow he manages to reach through into the higher reaches of his spiritual self. In getting the answer, he has struck a very close parallel with the true creative principle of life.

It would not be possible for any man or any group of men to construct a whole new group of physical laws here on this earth that were different or contrary to those created by the Infinite Mind. Man does not create anything; he only becomes conscious of something that has been there all along! He calls it discovering or creating, but he does not. He has only brought something into existence in another form or state that has been there all the time. He goes around patting himself on the back: he deifies himself—he is the highest form of creation on the earth. If he had a little insight or vision, he would be very ashamed of the comparison, because he is not much higher on the scale of life than the cow he milks or the dog that barks at his door, not so when you start comparing him with things you can see in the Infinite Cosmos which lie beyond the grave —the so-called grave or the loss of the physical form.

When man succeeds in awakening himself as far as his personal ego or id is concerned so he can carry himself into these infinite spiritual dimensions, in the course of time of evolution and reincarnation or whatever evolutionary pattern he wants to follow, he will realize these things in a future day. He has had people, men who have lived on this earth and gone to places like that and who came back to tell about it, but he couldn't understand them and he destroyed them in one way or another. Jesus was one of them, and there have been others. It is one of the primeval laws under which man lives and functions. It guarantees in a sense of the word that he is going to be saved, as far as this world is concerned, for the future generations that he spawned on the earth and followed the same evolutionary pattern. That, in itself, is a direct tribute to the long-range intelligence of that Infinite Mind, for how else could man attain mastership and individual stewardship of the Infinite Mind as an individual without passing through all of the infinite planes of consciousness?

It's a wonderful thing to think about. In spite of all the stupidity, the ignorance, all the things in the ramifications of material life involved, yet behind it there is a wonderful and very beautiful Infinite plan, for man, in spite of all the sins and iniquities and stupidity, is gradually climbing the scale. He destroys himself, sometimes he slides back down, but he always manages to recreate himself and bring himself back up. It would be contrary to conceive anything else. Jesus said that even the sparrow that falls by the wayside is accounted for. He meant that nobody kept records on sparrows but simply that the very atoms of that sparrow's body was part of the Infinite Mind. The loss of form and change of energy from one form to another is always a manifestation, even when it is so small it isn't noticeable. It is all accounted for as far as the Infinite Mind is concerned.

The lowest content of any man's personality is one way that he can live through all, to attain mastery over it. You cannot say that there is no evil, for evil does a good thing for everyone. It becomes good by having conquered evil. How else could man become good if he has not conquered? He would not have anything to go by, no basis, no platform. He would simply be an inert, vibrating mass of electronic protoplasm, without identity. He has to retain the idiom of every circumstance, every experience, every shock he goes through, every evil; even though it is conquered or cancelled out as far as any repercussive effects or any continuity to future life is concerned, the idiom of that is retained. That is all part of the progression. After he has attained mastery over these things, you can say it is a reciprocating polarity pattern which forms the structural patterns of the spiritual self and enables a man to maintain and live in the higher spiritual realms of consciousness.

This principle is very deep and only for that person who has the way and means of reaching through from the reactionary thought process and who turns the mirror of his mind upward to see the reflection and creation with all its grandeur, its magnitude and infinity. Man can live and breathe in it; he can manifest it through his consciousness, and that is the true way of life. Then his mind does not become something that is a slave to the objectivism of this material world— manifestation, the power to concentrate, to realize some gain or appurtenance or particular possession of the material world. He only becomes creative when he tunes himself up and turns the mirror upward into the vast infinity. When he does that, that mirror not only shows him all things as far as the conscious mind is concerned, but somehow or other, those things come to life in his own life, into the lives of others. That is the way he regenerates himself. That is the true truth.

Always does there exist the oscillation through what we call the mental processes of the physical mind— what we think is right for us. We attain power and mastery over the physical dimension to the extent that we can realize the gains and acquisitions of some material wealth. We have not asserted mastership over anything but have become slaves! The true creative process of life simply means that when we turn the mirror of our minds upward, we become something like the wire that brings electricity to our house or pipeline that brings the water into our home. We become a channel for the Infinite Mind to oscillate to the people around us, and that is the true way. That is the only way. That is called, "finding the Father and Kingdom of Heaven Within". It really is the ultimate goal of everyone even though he knows nothing at all about it —and perhaps won't for thousands of years. Yet there is something there that is part of the Christ-Self that Jesus called the Comforter, that guiding ray, that beam that always draws him on from one life to another, with all kinds of sins, iniquities, sorrows and terrors. He becomes a coward or a hero; it makes no difference, because always that guiding light goes ahead to show him the way.

CHAPTER IV

Man — Progressing Or Reverting?

The famous "monkey trial" of John T. Scopes was the result of an anti-evolution law passed by the State of Tennessee in 1925. A year after this law was passed, John T. Scopes was brought to trial, found guilty for teaching evolution in a public school, as it was so compounded by Darwinism.

Here in April of 1967, the Tennessee State House of Representatives just voted 58 to 27 to repeal this law and the following day, a twenty-four year old biology teacher at Dayton, Tennessee was fired from his teaching position because he purportedly was teaching evolution. Now, the awful bigotry which is immediately apparent in this situation is matched only by the colossal ignorance and stupidity of the religionist and religious factions which instigate these and countless other witch hunts, both contemporary and historical, wherein even the casual observer can see the fanatical insanity which revolves within the cloistered minds of these religious fanatics. And paradoxically, their very religion is supposedly based on the context of teachings of their Christian Savior who was violently crucified for teaching evolution two thousand years ago. Evolution, as it is believed by the religionist, is simply the descent of man from monkey, which is extremely repugnant to this religionist, who likes to believe he was created either from mud or ribs; or perhaps these religionists don't like the idea of sexual reproduction and have built up some sort of guilt complex which they try to mitigate in their so-called "holy" matrimony.

It might also be said that when the monkeys look at the religionist, they don't like the idea either. Any self-respecting monkey would feel very badly if his progeny developed into one of these religious fanatics. The asinine, egotistical ignorance of these Christian fanatics is apparent in every facet of life. It is quite apparent they do not understand creation or Infinite Intelligence which they worship as an emotional god-being. Despite the ever-changing, evolutionary world always about them, they have walled themselves up within the limited confines of some ancient superstitious beliefs which lived through legends down into the first origins of the Bible and perpetuated as a tomb within the covers of that book.

The religionists have not one single factual substantial bit of evidence to support their nebulous "supreme being"—a re-adaptation from Jehovah, that well-known ancient god of Babylonia. Quite the contrary, there is overwhelming evidence to disprove the whole insanity of their Christian superstitions; for indeed it is insanity and to those who have succumbed to this fantasy, these unfortunates are completely blind to reason, logic or evidence.

Evolution is not necessarily the descent of man from an ape, nor should it be confined within the strict circumstance of any physical material appearance. Rather, evolution should be solidly placed as the complete and entire background which involves all known and unknown aspects of life. The stone by the road may be made of calcium, and through erosion becomes plant food, the plant food then eaten by some human to become part of his bone structure. That is evolution; likewise, of all other sixteen elements found in the human body. Man, therefore, was not created but arrived at his present time and place through evolutionary metabolism. Metabolism of the human anatomy, as in all other forms of life, is reducible to molecular and atomic structures and in this synthesis, we can therefore see that evolution does not take place in any physical material form, but that this evolution is the ever-changing, regrouping and recombining of atomic and molecular structures.

The evolution of the hydrogen atom into helium is well-known and is said to be responsible for the great radiation of energy from the sun. Likewise, in all other atomic structures, there is a constant, ever-changing evolution within the dimension of our physical material world. There is, likewise, a never-ending, ever-changing evolution which constantly expresses itself in an ever-changing form-structure. Every religionist, whether he likes it or not, is evolving. He is going through many different states of evolution. From the moment of his conception, all through his life, he is physically, mentally and spiritually involved with many kinds and forms of evolution, and his neatly "tied-up package of religion" does not and cannot explain even the simplest creative concept which is part of the expressionary, net-sum and total of infinite creation which he has abrogated into an emotional god.

Worse, far worse, is the obvious fact that these religious fanatics can superimpose and inject their fanaticism into the laws and statutes of this great nation. Despite the Constitution and the Bill of Rights, no man can worship as he sees fit, nor can he sublimate any code of ethics, any constructive provable science as the mandate of his life without eventually running afoul of this fanaticism. Neither can the ethical question of "free speech" be propagated; especially in a classroom, as this young professor found out. He had merely to hint of the parabolistic nature of the Bible to bring the wrath of this fanatical heaven down about his ears. The gross hypocrisy, the awful bigotry is beyond any adequate means of explanation or interpretation.

The people and the nation of America have constantly tried to superimpose the effigy of their democracy on the rest of the world, its superiority, its great compassion, its great freedom, human rights, etc.; yet, as of today, it is torn and rent asunder and there are many schisms of racial hatreds, great poverty, anti-war demonstrations, "hippies", and "beatniks", millions of drug addicts, soaring crime rates and sex perversions; and to cap off the whole horrible, ugly mess is the scab of religious bigotry. And they point proudly to it and say, "What a beautiful country—the land of the free!" etc.

In the final analysis, if any can be made, perhaps we can glean one small grain of truth or that we can find a thread of justification; perhaps we, too, can say, "It was evolution which brought man to his present state and his apparent destruction." Then, in this destruction he could find the necessary desire and fortitude to evolve from this earth-world pit-of-clay and climb this evolutionary ladder into the far-off starry skies.

Finally, in retrospection, we can only muse upon the past, of the three million or so persons who died during the Middle Ages, condemned by the Courts of Inquisition. They died on the rack, the stake and the wheel from the same great religious fanatical bigotry. They died while some fat priest waved a cross in front of them and chanted mantrums, all in the name of the "savior" of mankind. Today the Courts of Inquisition have gone; so have the stake, the rack and the wheel, but in their place and as a form of evolution, there are other ways to express this fanatical bigotry. Through the courts of this land, little old ladies are persecuted, put in jail for their religious beliefs which are contrary or different to the Father-Mother church which spawned all Christian religions. Yes, even these fanatics are not above persecuting their own kind! Through legislative bodies they seek to enact laws which govern the beliefs and methods of expression of millions of people and contrary to their constitution.

Professor Gary L. Scott, (graduate of the University

of Tennessee), has discovered one of the ways and means these religious bigots persecute their fellow-man. His death sentence was, being fired from his position as a teacher and he will, for the rest of his life, be tied to the stake, subject to public censure and ridicule; and unless he is publicly reinstated, it is quite unlikely that he will ever teach again or that he will ever be able to live his life as he sees fit and so desires.

And here again, we can only muse in introspection whether it was John T. Scopes, Gary L. Scott, or millions of others who bore different names—each one has borne his cross to Calvary; each one has been crucified by these religious bigots and all in the name of the "cause", (so they say), of He who is the "savior" of man—His blood that washed away their sins (so they say). And we again speculate and ponder, who will it be in the future,—if there is to be anyone—who will come and wash away the bloody stains from the pages of religious history.

We can also muse upon the fate of Madelyn Murray; after her crusade in 1962 and 1963, which was largely responsible for the Supreme Court banishing prayer in public schools, how a squadron of twenty-one policemen broke into her home and with clubs, severely beat her and her aged mother, so much that her mother was unconscious in a hospital for two weeks. To escape continued persecution, Mrs. Murray was then forced to flee to Hawaii, then later to Mexico. Her crusade is now presently being revived by efforts of these religious bigots through Congress to repeal the anti-prayer decision.

Meanwhile here in California the old "pledge to the flag" and its "under God" quote fight is being renewed by those objecting to the infringement of Constitutional Rights.

*   *   *   *   *   *

33

(Note On May 12, 1967, a television newscast announced that Gary L. Scott had been reinstated into his teaching position. Also, just three days later, this former law against the teaching of Darwinism was repealed.)

CHAPTER V

Abstract Equations

Recently, one of our dear students wrote and expressed the desire to talk to his superconscious. Now this is a typical attitude and desire which has been, to some degree, more or less expressed by a number of other students. Perhaps this would be a suitable place and opportunity to reassert and re-explain just what the superconscious is, as it has, to some degree, been so adequately postulated in other Unarius liturgies. Everything that you can see in this physical world has a psychic anatomy and a superconscious. Trees, houses, articles, animals, birds, even a stone by the side of the road has a psychic anatomy and a superconscious. In the stone this psychic anatomy and superconscious is the net sum and total of the electromagnetic fields which are radiated by the atoms which comprise the stone, and the superconscious part is the cyclic pattern of energy transmission which harmonically links this stone, its net sum and total of atomic constituents to the great interdimensional cosmic universe and to Infinite Cosmic Intelligence. The psychic anatomy of the stone, however, is basic; it has no "personality" developed to a more complex degree, with a number of other constituents and embodiments which would enable it to be, for instance, a bird.

Like the stone, a bird has a psychic anatomy because the bird, too, is composed of atoms and within the bird's psychic anatomy, there are a number of vortexes of energy wave forms, harmonic patterns, etc., which could be loosely called the superconscious because these are more directly linked, harmonically speaking, to Infinite Intelligence. As Infinite Intelligence is an absolute constant which, according to law or principle, never varies or changes in its infinite expressions, this bird's superconscious therefore, will constantly reflect the bird form and the bird life within the psychic anatomy which again is the re-creative intelligence in the physical dimension. In other words, the superconscious is the link between the psychic anatomy and Infinite Intelligence. It is the governing or biasing agent which controls the psychic anatomy and which, in turn, through oscillation, re-creates any particular form, thought or action in the physical mind and body. There is not a single moment in any person's life which is not affected by the superconscious. Every act, every particle, every facet is made possible and is governed by the superconscious. Even the life force, the libido, the inspiration, the desire, etc., are all made possible by the biasing wave forms from the superconscious as this net sum and total of the superconscious oscillates with Infinite Intelligence.

Now this superconscious should not be misconstrued as being some sort of a genie or a god in our lives. It should not be set upon some altar or superimposed as a substitute for former gods or deities. It arrived at its present condition and state of development through evolution. Every moment of your many former lives was, in essence, polarized in a certain level of reference with Infinite Intelligence. These polarized experiences, life movements, etc., are oscillating wave forms of energy and according to their shape, frequency, etc., they can and do convey a certain bit of information, and this they will do unto eternity because they are fourth-dimensional in nature, (or cyclic) and also, as they are oscillating with Infinite Intelligence, they are constantly sustained by this life force (harmonically speaking). That is why in the ancient religions it is said that you take your sins to heaven with you and are judged accordingly. Your book of life is, therefore, more specifically your superconscious, and it might be well to remember that your present and former lives, as well as your future lives, will compound this book of energy wave forms.

Every minute of your life you re-create over a million new cells in your body and each one of these cells is made according to a certain pattern of energy information contained in the psychic anatomy; and in essence, therefore, this psychic anatomy is a robot functioning endlessly and ceaselessly according to the information which you have fed into it from countless life experiences and life itself. Through the many thousands of years and a hundred or more lives you have lived, the reason and desire for this, as well as all other attributes necessary for life are the biasing agents reflected from the superconscious which, in turn, are re-biased from Infinite Intelligence. This can be called the creative facsimile of life, of harmonic regeneration and of evolution which is expressed in all the material forms of the third-dimensional world. And this same principle likewise functions in higher worlds re-expressing evolutionary forms according to dimensional lines of reference.

Do not, therefore, try to talk to your superconscious or even talk to Infinite Intelligence, using it as an interpreter. The desires as they are expressed in wave forms from the conscious mind and instigated, as they are, by different psychic, physical and material pressures, have no emotional meaning or rapport with either superconscious mind or Infinite Intelligence. If you sincerely wish to, and dedicate your life to becoming a better person, then start to develop your psychic anatomy and your superconscious by aligning your conscious mind in a creative manner and in a creative attitude. Re-education is the keynote, and re-education not from unintelligent reactionary emotion which is the product of the third-dimensional jungle-world and the jungle-law which people live by in this world. Instead, learn and re-learn constantly and endlessly, from each moment of life, from each experience, the creative principles which engender your life and all other life forms which you may become conscious of, not only in this world at this time but in the many worlds to come.

CHAPTER VI

The Evolutionary Continuity of Life

From time to time in our mail received here at the Center, there appears certain kinds of literature published and distributed by certain individuals or groups who might be called adventists, in a sense, who are constantly predicting dire catastrophes, racial extinction, etc., for mankind from various causes, principally atom bombs and radiation. Some of these adventists or doom-mongers have even gone so far as to describe various escape devices such as a great space ship appearing at the last moment and rescuing the believers; or the sudden opening of underground caverns and tunnels by unknown races of people who are supposedly living underground and who, being keenly aware of the predicament of mankind, offer the believers the sanctuary of their underground homes.

This propaganda is in all respects quite similar to the kindergarten story of the newly-hatched chick who, when he experienced the fall of a leaf upon his tail, became hysterical, and thinking that the piece of the sky had fallen on him, ran to the mother hen who, in turn, became caught up in the chick's hysteria and ran to the duck. And successively, the duck, a goose and a turkey were likewise caught up in this hysteria, and in running madly about, encountered a fox, who capitalized on the situation, offered them the security of his cave which they gladly accepted and quite naturally were never seen again.

It is amazing to see the almost countless thousands of people who are constantly being duped and victimized by these wild hysterical stories peddled by the doom-mongers, and in the process of being so duped, are not only parted from their hard-to-come-by cash, but are led down the garden path, which will, in the future, become only another great frustration. If these people would only stop and think for a moment—how would all of these escapees live indefinitely in the closely confined quarters of space ships, or upon new and strange planets, or in great subterranean caverns without the conveniences and familiar forms of their everyday life? They would be in even more straightened circumstances than would be the straggling remnants of decimated humanity.

Psychically speaking, the effect of their new environment would be much worse than if they had died in the holocaust. At least, in the spiritual worlds they could have had help, training and preparation for a future incarnation on an earth planet similar to the one they had left. There is nothing logical, realistic or tangible in these various catastrophic and escape stories. They do not prepare the individual for a constructive and progressive future. Apparently, none of these doom-mongers can scientifically describe life or prove its continuity, through science, beyond the grave. In some instances, there may be a few grains of truth scattered among the chaff, but these small grains are only indications and are never presented scientifically in a manner or way which could be acceptable in logical straight-forward reasoning.

If any person is tired of the physical, material life, if he is overwhelmed by the apparent decadency of civilizations, if he is constantly stressed by incurable diseases and conditions and wishes to alleviate these various mental and physical tensions, there is only one logical course to pursue. Only through the doorway of constructive evolution can he hope to aspire to a better life. He must envision the future millions of years as his great opportunity, whereby in successive lifetimes he can learn to live in a higher state of consciousness and which can be assumed to be more and more freed from insoluble conditions.

Throughout the works of Unarius, this straightforward constructive plan of evolution is presented in factual, realistic and scientific concepts. The possibility of constructive evolution is presented as a certain reality which can be obtained by any individual who completely dedicates himself to the task, who is willing to give up the old self, its emotional vicissitudes, etc., and to progressively reconstruct his entire psychic anatomy or spiritual self in a manner and way which will enable him to live in a better world.

It would do no good for any person to temporarily escape death by running into a cavern or by going out into space. Sooner or later he would die the physical death anyway; and finding himself in the spiritual world, he would be even more confused than he would have been had he "died" in the catastrophe.

Yes, and even in the light of analyses, Christianity is, without doubt, one of the greatest of all these dispensations of doom which has been dispensated to countless millions of people in the past two thousand years —those who have gone to the grave believing in the false promises of resurrection and eternal life without proper preparation—preparation which can be attained only through thousands of lifetimes lived progressively, which will prepare the individual by expanding his consciousness beyond the third-dimensional earth life.

If you would like to live a better life, if you would like to live beyond the grave, and in higher realms of consciousness, then you must prepare yourself for the better life in the higher world. Belief in a religious system or an intercessor will get you nowhere. These promises are as hollow as are the tombs of the men who have repeated them throughout the centuries. The actual existence of life is possible only as the present conscious moment of reality, and this reality is almost

41

always entirely compounded from the past.

To most people, the future is not reality; they live only by the sheer necessity of survival. Like plant and animal life on this planet, this survival necessity is only the first step in evolution. Man becomes different from an animal only when he begins to recognize, and through recognition, the possibility of a future beyond the grave and an existence in a higher plane of consciousness is possible—and incidentally, a life which will be lived far more actively than is any earth life—for as consciousness is expanded, so does consciousness increase in its activities whereby various factors of existence are being constantly correlated in the pattern of life.

There is no Utopia in the spiritual worlds. There are no lives lived in indolent ease, playing golden harps while floating about on pink clouds. Above the material plane, life is far more actively integrated in consciousness than on the material plane; moreover, conditions are different. There are no contentions in various differences of mass and energy, for in these higher worlds, all is energy.

The physical processes of sustaining the human body, such as food, drink, elimination, etc., are supplanted by a more direct life-giving principle—the absorption of cosmic energies which are constantly radiating in saturated intensities throughout the great, so-called voids of space. Various forms of consciousness will also undergo metamorphoses. In the first stages of spiritual life, there is a constant attempt to integrate various earth life forms into this new spiritual atmosphere.

The first few million years of spiritual life may be lived in mind-constructed energy formations which to some degree represent the earth life. Various buildings, such as houses, auditoriums, etc., will be constructed of pulsating, radiant-hued energy, held in its existing form as a constant effort of consciousness. Gradually, as thousands of years pass, the necessity of these forms diminish and consciousness will assume a much more infinite perspectus. Mental consciousness will be an extremely widely-diversified relationship with the Infinite in an oscillating manner, whereby consciousness is sustained in a way quite similar to that of the Infinite Creator Itself.

However, this concept is so completely abstract as to be beyond the comprehension of your present consciousness. This is the unknown future—at least unknown to almost all earth people—and because it is unknown, it is not taught in our educational or religious systems. Mankind, therefore, lives constantly in dread of his future. The shadow of death always hovers over him, a death which is as unrealistic as are the many false attitudes of life which result from the coercive fear of death.

CHAPTER VII

Science on Evolution
Lecture March 8, 1961

Good evening, Friends. It is wonderful to have you all here this evening, and I feel sure that there are many of us who have met before in the long, long ago in the shadows of temples or in great halls and places of history. That is one reason that has made this all possible, for this is today the millennium. This millennium started actually in 1945 with the explosion of the first atom bomb. That explosion ushered in not only the atomic age, or even the space age, but it was much more important in many other aspects to an interdimensional cycular junction wherein, we will say, that in a sense there are, astrophysically speaking, interdimensional agencies and other different forces in effect, certain peoples of the world who would of this time and of this place and in this age, enter into what could be more specifically defined as personal liberation—liberation in a sense that each and every one of you have been karmically involved in various lifetimes in the past hundreds or perhaps thousands of years.

The mere fact that you breathe air, you are able to sustain life, you are part of an organized society in some respects is an overwhelming testimonial that you are products, in a pure and simple sense, of a certain evolution—an evolution which is part earth life and part spiritual. Actually, as far as all humanity is concerned—and in fact it is also true with every organic creature which is so sustained with some life process on the planet earth—the various continuities in life transpositions are interdimensional in all aspects; that is, these things are only made possible through a certain junction, a certain principle or element, a dynamic creation.

I believe that we are all very consciously aware this evening that the earth, in its present state, is in a very chaotic condition. Man is raising his voice against his neighbor; nations are raising their voices against each other. We are seeing daily the rise and fall of different systems and different ideologies, and it all bespeaks very eloquently of a great transition and a great metamorphosis which is taking place among the peoples of the world. You as individuals should be very vitally and very consciously minded not only for your own welfare but in respect to the fact that you are also an integrated element of humanity—not only of the planet earth but of a sustained system of planetary systems which evolved in the spiritual dimensions and that each one of you are, in yourselves, a definite element, a definite participle of expression of a great Infinite Intelligence.

Today in our space age science and, in fact, other denominations of life as they are so specifically outlined in our society, are acutely and consciously aware that there is much more to life than that which has heretofore been supposed and that life, in itself, can be extended on to include the infinities of not only our own particular galaxy in its position to the universe, but the universe itself and the many universes extending beyond this one; yet these, in themselves, are only small fractions of the whole because tightly woven, interconnected and in-between, this seeming space is very solid. It is solid in respect to the fact that there are many dimensions, as was pointed out by Einstein, and they are becoming generally recognized in this scientific age. Today, only the very hardened, shell-back, reactionary person maintains a position which he reluctantly and grudgingly admits—that life is possible on other planets or in far-off solar systems. Our science of today—in its rocketry, in its program of satellites, and various different interplanetary probes—is

45

trying to seek out ways and means to establish communication or contact with any possible life in any other planetary systems.

We have at this time a very fortunate position in respect to our own selves personally. We can, in common denominators and in nomenclature which is familiar not only to yourself but to the scientist, define life in so many more dimensions than heretofore has been possible. Life, in itself, now is not earthbound but seeks to escape the trammels and vicissitudes of this earth life. The principle of evolution itself as a dynamically sustained ingredient in your own personal development demands constant and successive extensions of knowledge into unknown dimensions. You, yourselves, within the dimension of your own mind are spiritually quickened; you are cognizant of the fact that here on this earth you are still a spiritual creature and embodied in a physical body, reacting to a certain set of reactionary elements. But always, the sustaining principle of spirit as the dynamic principle of life comes through. It is the ever-prompting, the ever-motivating, the ever-wise and the all-inclusive intangible that gives each and every one of us our motivation, our purpose for life.

And so, as we look back into the past histories in the ages, there have been certain personal Avatars who have entered into this earth world and tried to explain certain intangible or spiritual elements of life as they were begun to be lived in their own particular time and place. Socrates was asked how to become wise and he said, "Know thyself". Jesus put it another way. He said, "Seek ye first the Kingdom of Heaven which is within, and all things shall be added unto you". And so, as of this present day and of this time in the turmoil and strife which is ever about us in our everyday lives, and which has been constantly expressed in what appears to be complete contradictions to all known principles, Christian or humanitarian, we, in ourselves, must be firmly rooted on the rock—the rock of understanding.

And what is understanding? What is it to know thyself? How are we to find the Kingdom of Heaven which is within? These are fundamental principles which must be learned by the individual. They cannot be extracted from any known philosophies or sciences as they so exist on the earth today, because these are the intangible, spiritual elements which have sustained us through our evolutionary course—spiritual elements which fortunately now can be, to some extent and to some degree, verified by our present-day science. In this respect and in respect, too, to those who are probing the hundreds of billions of light years into our unknown cosmic universes, to those who are probing with satellites into the unknown and to you, as individuals, seeking your own way, your own destiny and who are always imbued with the spiritual motivating principle of life within, you must all form definite conclusions within yourselves. You must all take a certain definite constructive pattern of thought and action; and these things, in themselves, are not found within the domains of earth-life dispensations. They are within the Kingdom of Heaven.

And what are these sustaining spiritual principles? Fortunately, we do have the science of today; we do have certain particular definite dispensations of science wherein we can set forth into a constructive plan of learning whereby we shall find out about the Infinite. We shall find out what is the principle and what is the purpose, at least to some feasible ultimate—an ultimate which you perhaps cannot envision within the dominion of your own present-day consciousness as it is sustained in this earth life but will in the future eons of time and in countless reincarnations which you will survive as definite human beings. You will attain certain perspectives and certain unknown dimensions which now remain as merely intangible.

We can begin first by realizing that this earth as a whole is neither the place for cause nor is it the starting place and that whatever happens on this earth is a direct result of something happening in a higher dimension. It is an interpolation and an integration of certain junctions of psychic consciousness or cycles of transpositions and which always have their effect in the lower or the atomic structures which compose the material world. And whether they are composed within such familiar objects as surround you in your community life or with various associates or with your own personal life dispensation, the activation, the motivation is always originated in the higher dimensions.

To understand this more properly, we must approach the Infinite as something more tangible and realistic in our consciousness. We must use the Infinite not only to supplant all age-old customs of religious systems of which certain deistic configurations assumed godlike proportions, but we must visualize the Infinite as the Supreme Consciousness, the Supreme Intelligence, the Infinite Expression which not only makes life possible in the atomic form and which constitutes your body (which is really energy in another form) but which also makes evolution possible for you in the higher planes of consciousness. What is the Infinite? The Infinite, for practical purposes, can be described as the sum and total of all known and unknown substances, the visible and the invisible. The Infinite is a constant, ever-expanding perspective of consciousness which makes its own personal realization in our daily lives, in our acts of consciousness toward our fellowman in our associations in our community life. This is the Infinite and in this respect, you as individuals, always have your face turned toward the Infinite. There is always some new horizon to be explored, a new vista to be circumscribed within the consciousness of your own mind; and so the Infinite does always expand. We must realize the dynamic, ever-expanding and progressive principle of the Infinite, for in order to be Infinite, it must sustain itself constantly in an infinite number of forms and in a constant and never-ending, regenerative fashion.

The Infinite is neither good nor evil, but is only associated in our personal relationships in comparative values as to whether these particular transpositions are following straight-line courses, neither reactionary, or that they are assumed reactionary in our various viewings of these happenings. So good and evil are created within the mind of each one—necessarily so, because we must have a point of equation. The Infinite must always compose itself in consciousness as two diametrically opposed polarities and in which consciousness is sustained in an oscillating process, a transposition of thought which levitates itself from one dimension and from one sphere of consciousness to the next.

So life becomes a reality, not in the sense that you, yourself, are a personal being in respect to this life, but as you are in respect to the Infinite, a recreative entity of consciousness with the Infinite. This, in itself, is sufficient to deflate any false ego structures which most people have erected about themselves and found necessary to sustain a reactionary course of existence on planet earth. However, the reactionary principle is neither valid nor effective in worlds which are somewhat more spiritual in nature than the planet earth—worlds in which we become living objects or entities, living forms of consciousness, human beings, or whatever we wish to call ourselves, in direct ratio or proportion as to how well we can incept Infinite Intelligence and radiance within our own minds, our own bodies.

You who are of the earth as of this day are learning

certain basic fundamentals in these principles—principles which can be considered in this particular time and place as reactionary in nature simply because your mind is, consciously speaking, singular, you must extract from time to time singular attitudes and aptitudes for these attitudes to manifest themselves. You must, in a sense, imbue them into your psychic anatomies so that they become conscious realities for your future. This is necessary, inasmuch as every individual has within himself not only great fear of the future but also has great fear of death. Perhaps this is not so; at least, I hope not among you who are sincere truth seekers, and I am assuming that whatever you have studied and whatever you have pursued, and especially with your contact with Unarius, you are now sufficiently levitated to enable you to obtain a constructive perspectus of Infinity. But life will become an ever-increasing, an ever-expanding dimension of consciousness, not necessarily sustained from the reactionary principle of singular, selective reactionary purpose as it is contained in the earth world dimensions but as it is a universal function of Infinite Principle, constantly regenerating itself, constantly assuming new forms, new manifestations; and you, in yourselves, becoming such conscious entities, conscious participles in Infinite Expression, do so continue your evolution in a much more constructive fashion.

For here, this terrestrial world is still, in effect, a jungle; and you have heard it called as such, a jungle in which it apparently seems that each man survives simply by the old reactionary principle as it was explained by Darwin, the "survival of the fittest", a competitive way of life against your fellow man. And even though he is your friend and you can shake his hand, yet it is so, that the very substance of your life and the very substance of his life are reactive components in which you extract from each other.

Mankind as a whole in an earth dimension can be considered parasitic to himself simply because he has not yet succeeded in expanding the dimension of his consciousness to include that ever-expanding supply of Infinity, Infinity which, as consciousness, can regenerate and constantly regenerate within the dimension of his own consciousness. It can give him complete mastery over the old self, the old carnal law of the jungle, where he survived back in the long ago in the dim past as some creature born in a primitive terrestrial earth; and in a sense, you are now functioning with the Infinite, and as an entity of Infinite Consciousness, you are traversing those great spiritual dimensions.

As Jesus said, "In my Father's house, there are many mansions," and you, each and every one of you, are destined to find these various mansions; yet you shall never come to the end of them, for such is Infinity. It always presupposes; it always interjects and it always sustains itself in a never-ending and unceasing dimension of expansion of consciousness, for such is the purpose of the Infinite; and it could not be sustained otherwise. It could not ever be envisioned that there would be a terminating point, for this is a constant, cyclic progression which sustains the individual entity of consciousness through infinite dimensions.

And yet, these things need not be repetitiously spoken; they can be scientifically explained in the modern nomenclature of the scientist. Each one of us can begin to learn to understand the Infinite, first, by transposing our consciousness as an exterior or outer configuration where we see reactions upon reactions as they are superimposed upon the consciousness of the earth minds. We must see and realize the ultimate purpose, the infinite expression behind all things which remain either intangible or reactionary to us.

And what is this sustaining, ever-regenerating principle? It is the great invisible worlds as they are composed of a vast and unending sea of energy—energy in vortexes, energy in great cyclic manifestations, energy in hundreds of millions of different atomic constituents—not merely the 98 odd elements that are known to the earthman but energy in an infinite manner and form, energy which is constantly recreating, regenerating itself according to principle—principle which sustains it as the Infinite Substance of all.

And so the sine wave will become a very vital and a very necessary starting point in your evolution. You can see the sine wave as an expression in your various daily life transpositions—a sine wave being a simple up-and-down wave form of energy of which there are two opposite polarities, carrying between them the conscious entity of expression. These are the sine waves which you find in your daily life—the reflections of light from various objects which are focused from the lens of your eye to the retina. There they are transposed to the transistor brain cells into the psychic anatomy to again react; and in the conflux of harmonic regeneration, the sine waves sustain certain chain-like reactions through other centers of the psychic anatomy to suitably render biases with your past, and to also include in times most necessary other biases which can be considered more infinite in nature, more inspirational —those things which you have had in your darkest hours. Those biases which, in themselves come from the great Infinite Intelligence, have been the principles which sustain the earth life. They have made it possible for you—unknown by you—to regenerate within your body every minute of your life one million five hundred thousand new cells, a feat which cannot be duplicated by science.

You will find as you journey into the future that the world is not solid. You must become infinitely minded in the sense that now you must abandon the old reactionary principle of man against man, element against element. Instead, we will supplant this concept with a much more logical assumption of consciousness which is supremely self-explanatory in every detail. It is magnificently portrayed in all things of which we are conscious. It lends its secret meaning to a vast implosion of Infinite Consciousness within ourselves. It levitates us from the mundane sphere of material consciousness and literally hurtles us through unknown dimensions of consciousness into the infinite vistas of space; for man, in truth, does in such manner and means become an integrated element with Cosmic Consciousness, with those countless billions of people who inhabit other planets in far-off solar systems, with those who live in higher dimensions or who live in spiritual planets, or with others who have gone on into even greater and more far-reaching vistas of infinity.

This is the message; this is the purpose of Unarius, to explain these things to you tangibly, realistically so that you can incept them and use them into your daily life. It will explain to you all of the hidden and unknown elements, the psychological principles behind the unknown psychology of our time, the causes and the cures of all incurable diseases. It will explain to you the purpose and the realization because Unarius is infinite in its science, in its dimensional aspects. It is neither a religion nor, in itself, a terrestrial science, but is an interdimensional science. It is, in effect, a restoration of the Gospel preached by Jesus two thousand years ago, who explained it so simply and so harmoniously that even the barbaric savage could understand it. He taught self-emancipation from the empirical, dogmatic, rhetorical systems of the world, and yet for this, he was crucified, and he and others like him— some less, some even greater in stature, perhaps—all laid aside the mantle of human flesh as a token of submission to those who would still live by the law and

53

the sword—submission only in the fact that in this submission they became supremely wise and demonstrated the continuity of life beyond any question of doubt.

Two thousand years ago at the crucifixion, they took the philosophy of Jesus, the simple psychology of life, and they warped it; they distorted it; they created of it the effigy of a church system, and they forever defamed its purpose. They forever destroyed its utility for mankind. So Jesus lives today in the churches throughout the world as a symbol, not as a purpose and not as a principle in which people—you, I, and everyone—could realize a much greater, a much more abundant and a more peaceful life on this planet.

Jesus said, "Do not pray as does the heathen, on street corners nor in public places, neither in temples nor in synagogues but retire into thine own secret closet and seek out the Father who is within that He may reward ye openly." If you will think for a moment, that in that principle how could it be that any church system could be sustained? It could not! It was for that purpose that those who followed after succeeded in warping, distorting and confusing the whole concept of personal spiritual emancipation into a dogmatic, rhetorical system of effigies and symbols, a system which has held mankind enslaved for almost two thousand years. And yet, here again man is only reliving the old symbology of the past, for this, in itself, is proof of his reincarnation—that out of these old symbologies in the distant ages in which man was spawned from the mud of the earth, he learned of the deistic forces and configurations which confronted him; the unknown elements became gods, spirits, demons, ogres, and he relegated them into their own mythical dimension of consciousness and endowed them with his own particular personal vicissitudes. And he also gave them his long dreamed-of, hoped-for powers of personal emancipation; but the gods could never become any more or less than those who believed in them.

And so it is as of today. How many Christians know that Jehovah or Jehowah is the old Chaldean god which was worshipped by the Babylonians more than three thousand years before Father Abraham, who led the first Israelites out of this forgotten land? How many know that the Koran is the first five books of the Old Testament? How many people know that the stone in the citadel of Mecca is the meteorite which fell at the feet of Abraham in the Evangelistic mission through ancient Chaldea before he started the migration? And yet Jehowah is perpetuated into Christianity and became known as Jehovah, a god which was the fiery furnace of Nebuchadnezzar, a huge bronze image with a hollow stomach and a big door heaped high with a fiery furnace used to liquidate political prisoners and other malcontents in the kingdom.

It was Jesus who tried to destroy Jehowah, or Jehovah. It was Jesus who tried to destroy all the mystical and mythical rites which had been sustained by the Jews throughout their history more than two thousand years since their migration—things which had led them from out the land of Egypt in the forty years of wandering through the wilderness. And how successful was he? Yet you and I as individuals are also vitally concerned, not only with our own future but with the future of mankind in general, for we are never more or less than those with whom we associate. Our associations are, in themselves, the denominators of our plane or elevation of consciousness. In our associations with our fellow man, we find human companionship, not in the gregarious sense that human companionship is necessary in a physical mannerism customarily displayed in community enterprises but that common elevations of consciousness must always be reached and maintained throughout a general intercourse of society.

This, too, is part of the pattern of evolution, something with which you will always be confronted; and in itself, knowledge of humanity, knowledge of or knowing thyself gives you the choice. It is automatically selective in itself; and as you learn of yourself, you learn of the humanity with whom you associate, and you are automatically and consciously selective in the process of when and where and how you will live, for in the Infinite you will never become any more or less than that which you can conceive within the secret closet of your own mind. And if these things are conceived within the limited dimension of the reactionary earth-life, then indeed you will find common consort with the materialist, the criminal and the various other different resurgences. You will find common living patterns with all those who are striving against life yet wishing and hoping for a better life. You will find common companionship with those who are trying to dominate, to coerce, to express all the various reactionary elements in which the materialistic world finds common expression.

Conversely, when you begin to attain a more infinite understanding of your place in the scale of evolution— what you are, where you came from and where you are going, what the Infinite is in proportion to how this knowledge is acquired—so you will be levitated into these different dimensions. I have attempted in some way to describe these places to you in the various books of Unarius—the spiritual planets—which I have given various names merely for purposes of identification. People must always have a place; they must have a name until they arrive at that dimension of consciousness where they can conceive the Infinite in its more universal entirety where names are superfluous, as are places. Instead, there is consciousness, an integration of consciousness universally, which makes names and places superfluous and which are used only as a means in which we can communicate with one another and we can sustain communication within the consciousness of our minds as we incept such various forms of communicative devices throughout our evolutionary history.

So life must be lived differently if we are to find those higher spiritual mansions of which Jesus spoke. We must learn to picture the Infinite infinitely, that the earth is, as I have said, neither the starting place nor the cause. It is only the effect and is only one of the countless places where so many different configurations of the same form of consciousness are transpired, not only instantaneously; but so far as time and space are concerned, they have always been so expressing themselves in different forms and in a different consciousness, and they shall also continue to do so eternally.

You, as an element of consciousness, are selective only on the basis of past experiences, and these things in your psychic anatomies are reactive to you in the sense that you are harmonically attuned with them. You are repeating day by day, in new forms and in new ways, old manners of consciousness, old forms of consciousness. You call them by different names, yet they are basically and essentially the same things which have been with you throughout the ages; and yet, as of tonight, this may be the breaking point. This may be the place where you officially terminate that particular form of oscillating consciousness, that is, as far as practical purposes are concerned in respect to a personal evolutionary future which is both progressive and constructive in nature. This terminating point is complete dedication, the complete resolution within yourself that from now on you can become and you will frequently be your own worst enemy—the old self— from the dogma, the creed, the rhetoricism which was impounded in your past lives. The necessary mandates of your evolutionary flight into the present will now become the ogre which will haunt you, which will always tempt you—the devil with the horns and the tail —which will constantly try to superimpose itself in your daily life. It will find innumerable ways and disguises, and always you must come to your own personal rescue. Your knowledge of the Infinite will become your life preserver, your lifeline. You will always be able to level off these various differences in mental temperaments which come to you from out of this past.

You will always find there is an equitable answer which can be fully and completely justified, not in the sense that it is reactionary but that it is all-inclusive and is part of that ever-expanding, resurgent, regenerative Infinite; this is vastly different than when you were so personally concerned with the same situation which was the same reaction as a principle of survival on the planet earth.

Now this has become a problem of survival in a spiritual evolutionary flight, shall I say, into time and into space, for time and space are synonymous; they are part of the Infinite. There are no means of differentiation between time and space as it concerns the Infinite but only resolves itself into cyclic manifestations as they are concerned with you in your personal consciousness.

Many years ago, Einstein presented to the scientific world the space-time continuum theory in which he mathematically proved that the speed of light was theoretically fictitious, it was nonexistent, and light could and did accelerate to several hundred times the known earth speed in interdimensional flights; yet, this was puzzling to Einstein, just as it has been to all those who have studied space and time. The simple answer to all this is this: we cannot equate these things in third-dimensional realizations and consciousness, they must be integrated in a fourth-dimensional state of consciousness. This fourth-dimensional state of consciousness is called by some clairvoyance, the sixth sense. You all have it; there is no one on this earth who does not have it. In fact, no one could live on this earth without it, for it is actually the manifestation of a great principle within each and every man which is sustaining him in his evolutionary flight.

The paranormal or the clairvoyant aptitude—if I can use this phraseology as it is relative to any person—is only the first beginning, the first stages of consciousness when man really becomes consciously aware, in a material world, of something which is an extended concept of consciousness in another dimension. That dimension has neither time nor space and therefore, so far as the speed of light is concerned, time is nonexistent simply because instead of a sine wave, which has a beginning and an ending point, all things are cyclic in motion. They contain themselves as a cycle, a definite entity of consciousness in their own particular oscillation. They convey to Infinity their own particular and subjective attitude and they are harmonically interlocked through harmonic regeneration with all forms of consciousness throughout the Infinite. It is not possible for anyone to think a thought without it being directly linked to the great Infinite, to all of the dimensions, to all of the many mansions. There is a direct relationship harmonically attuned with every living human, with every living thing on this earth, with any other living thing on any other planet and with any other higher world than this. Your thoughts are not private. Interdimensionally, they are common property to those who, like a radio set, can tune into your thoughts.

And what do your thoughts become? Your thoughts of the moment will become your tomorrow—your future—because here again we have destroyed the illusion of time and space, for the future is here now. You will never have any other moment than that which you have in the immediate present. What you do at this particular moment will be vital to you throughout your entire evolution, just as what you have done is vital to you now.

This is the common harmonic interplay of infinite, resurgent regeneration which some people call God, and which, as was explained by Jesus, is the Kingdom —the Father which liveth within, the Kingdom which was the activating Principle, the purpose and the continuity of expression throughout Infinity. The regenerative All—the Father, which is the Creator—created all forms and substances.

How, then, can any man set himself over another? How, then, can any man say that he is vested in some holy raiment, he must dispense spiritual virtue and guidance to his fellow man, and he is his brother's keeper when the very keystone in the arch of evolutionary progression is self-emancipation and freedom from all rhetorical systems, pedantic attitudes and dogma? Jesus taught it two thousand years ago, so did Buddha, so did many others—personal freedom of thought and mind. Only in this personal freedom can we find an interrelationship with the Infinite—not guided by the dictates of some subversive mind which may be psychotic or even obsessed to dominate and influence—and can we find a purpose, a scientific realization in cause and effect, not as it concerns the earth but as an interdimensional aspect, a part of that Kingdom.

So the reestablishment of the gospel of Jesus is beginning to take place in this world today. There are many who are free thinkers. There are many who have yet not dared to take that first all-important step. They have longed to but as yet, they have not had the fortitude where they can completely dismember themselves as far as their own practical position to the Infinite is concerned with the various rhetorical and dogmatic systems of the earth.

Emerson said, "Be thyself; imitation is suicide", yet every day you are constantly confronted with the never-ending, repetitious, emotional attitudes of people around you who are like sheep following each other; and like sheep, if they continue to do so, they may in the night run off the precipice. Jesus said, when asked where he had been in the three days and nights, "I have been in the pits of hell teaching to the lost souls, yea, some who have been there even before the time of Noah." Dante gave an immortal poem about hell. Hell is a configuration of personal concept in which the human mind or the entity of consciousness so becomes embroiled within the nonsensical elements of its own consciousness that it creates a veritable hell for itself. Hell is no more or no less than is heaven and yet, heaven is not sustained as a principle of uselessness; no more so than hell could be sustained as a destructive, never-ending, torturous, abysmal form of consciousness.

So these things again prove, in themselves, what Jesus meant—that within your own mind is the Kingdom of Heaven. Conversely, if you so desire, you can find also the kingdom of hell. The choice is yours, and that is irrespective of whether you are a member of any church, of any organization, whether you belong to the Elks or whether you are a Republican or Democrat. These things are, in themselves, only outward manifestations or attributes of what you believe as conformity, or form consciousness, in your daily life. Yet from all these things, each one must extract for himself, infinitely speaking, the principle and the purpose behind all of this seeming nonsensical, never-ending succession of interplays of the emotional natures of mankind, for each man is on the threshold.

He is developing from a carnal, carnivorous beast as he prowled the jungles; he is developing in the entity of his consciousness to where he is becoming spiritually minded. You people present, to some extent, have all gone much further than this. You have become spiritually conscious and quickened to the degree that you would gladly lay aside all of these emotional vicissitudes in which the earth man is so involved. You would gladly make for yourself a world which is more constructive, which is more passive and which is, in itself, a much more joyous place to live, a place where everything could be more rationally justified.

What this all means tonight is simply this: that you have all reached that place where none of the systems of the world are going to sustain you for any particular given length of time into the future, no more so than with the thousands of others out in the world tonight so minded as yourselves. This is part of your evolutionary progress. You are destined for higher worlds if you so desire this to be, if you are willing to put forth the necessary constructive effort, if you are willing to sacrifice upon the altar of your own personal life the past—the past in its implications that it has made you an emotional creature, a creature which was dependent parasitically on a community and the life in which you live. The freemasonry of the infinite world is compounded as a direct infraction of intelligence which we incept much the same as a radio incepts the signal from the transmitter.

The universal supply is the Infinite. We live in that world, not by food but by our ability to absorb into our consciousness, into our psychic anatomies, the necessary spiritual substance which is everywhere about us. Even as we breathe the air at this moment, so will we breathe the energy of the higher life and we will be sustained by it, because we know what it is. We realize it just as we know about the air we breathe or as we know about food—in direct proportion to our understanding and its inception. We also become constructively minded and expressive in ourselves in proportion to our understanding to this Infinite. We become regenerative; we become psychokinetically projective in consciousness and so we assist materially in the scale of evolution.

Part Two

Science on Evolution
Questions and Answers—Lecture March 8, 1961

*T - Now if you have some questions, we shall try to answer them for you.

S - What does Communism have to do with the turmoil in the world now?

T - You have to look at the world in this state; this is a very fundamental principle of creation, because you take the sum and total of people as they have lived lives. Now this is not just a simple act of consciousness. I have partly explained this in the lecture. What it means is that we have an ever-resurgent chain-like reaction of cycles which extends on and on and on; we shall say for practical purposes, into infinity. And yet in a sense, there are times, harmonically speaking, when we reach a certain point in a development of any ideology or any civilization or any community or any group of people, or even individually; this is a cyclic junction. This means that according to certain consonants of timing which are involved in these cyclic patterns, they regenerate either as a sum and total of the past in a negative dispensation or conversely, in some much greater and more constructive evolution.

Now as far as Communism is concerned and in the ideology supposedly which fostered Communism and its greatest exponent who was Lenin, we find Marx explaining a philosophy of life which was, in most aspects, very material in nature; and yet we shall say it did form, at the time, a cyclic junction in the lives which were lived by the people of Russia in that time and era. There was the Revolution; there were the vari-

*T - Teacher
 S - Student

64

ous other different things which happened to Russia but yet as of today as we know Communism, there is a conflux of ideologies or principles which were expounded interdimensionally and which were harmonically attuned. This, of course, is the more abstract viewpoint of this concept. But what all these systems of government really boil down to is this fact: as I said in the beginning, we are constantly turning our faces toward Infinity; the various ideologies, the many systems of community life, of governments, etc., are only in themselves various levels which we have found in our evolutionary flight from the beginning. If you did not have some connection with Communism, you would not be conscious of it because in Communism there are common ideologies which all people express in themselves which they have developed in their own particular systems.

S - I was wondering if there is any danger of it growing throughout the world?

T - You should be concerned only in this respect, in your own personal way, because that is why we have Unarius. We want a higher science of life; we want a higher understanding of life because that puts us above the dimension of influences of Communism or any other kind of "ism". If we understand what the Infinite is, what our purpose is as regenerative entities of consciousness of the Infinite, then we are above Communism; we do not have to subscribe to any kind of a system. We are only subscribing to one system itself and that is the life-giving principle of Infinity itself. Up until now, you have symbolized that as some configuration in a deistic sense, but now, it is getting to a point where it is going to be your own moral responsibility. Whether you say it is Communism or whether it is any other particular "ism" or "osm" in the world, you're going to have to be selective on this basis— when you understand or when you are beginning to understand the Infinite and when you can sustain your evolution, you can put yourself above the coercive or the dominating influences of these various dogmas or ideologies. Whatever they are, and in living above them, you automatically become more creative. You can lend your hand, so to speak, to others who are struggling through the same maze that you went through, the same catacombs, the same labyrinth.

S - May I change the subject, Dr. Norman?

T - Of course.

S - Please refresh me on something given in the lecture in regard to the Jehovah of the Old Testament.

T - Yes, this happens to be one of my pet crusades, along with many other persons', but it is historically very well known; it is common knowledge available to everyone. You can find it in the encyclopedias or various books in the library that Jehovah is Jehowah, an old pagan god. He was worshipped in Babylonia and Ancient Chaldea more than four thousand years before the time of Abraham.

S - Is there not another word for this same concept —Jobela?

T - Yes, there are several derivations. The name has changed through common usage in various dialects and various different languages but actually, the same god is synonymous. We say the Near East was actually the birthplace of all religions which are known on the face of the earth today; that is, all the big religions including Mohammedanism, and in a sense it had its effect on the Hindu world as well. There we find the Parsee, for instance. Zoroaster is synonymous with Jesus; so is Osiris. We find the same configurations throughout all the basic or main religions of the world today. They all have Immaculate Conception which had its origin back there in the fertility rites. The virgin maidens were prepared by the priests for their life in marriage and occasionally, they became pregnant in the process. This is as old as history itself. It is still practiced by many of the aboriginal tribes in the world today.

S - May I ask a personal question?

T - Yes, surely.

S - I am a music teacher, and in my effort to teach others, I seem to be able to bring music out of others. I, personally, have great blocks and cannot express music myself. Why is this and how can I rid myself of these psychic blocks?

T - That is a very big problem but it is also very easily recognized if you study especially our more advanced lesson course. It is explained very realistically and scientifically to you. You see, what you have been doing for thousands of years is taking all these little energy wave forms in your daily life and weaving them into this psychic anatomy. Sometimes there was a great inharmony in them or there was psychic shock which created a malformation in this psychic anatomy. It is like having big lumps in your body; you did not know where they came from or how to rid yourself of them. All of these things are constantly oscillating into your consciousness. That is what forms the blocks because they are not harmonically attuned with the present; they are out of tune. So the way to get rid of them is simply to realize what they are—that they are harmonically attuned to some particular experience of the past —they belong to a block, a psychic shock which you incurred in the past; and with this realization, you can rid yourself of them. It is simple psychosomatic medicine, only that you can carry it on back a few hundred or a few thousand years instead of only back to conception of this present lifetime.

It is very important to destroy the illusion of mass in the consciousness. We must realize the Kingdom of Heaven is merely this oscillating process that you have with your psychic anatomy in its connection not only with you consciously but, in a sense, it is also consciously oscillating with the Infinite within itself. It would be well to endeavor to uncover what motivated the interest in music; what it really was that was motivating this desire and what it was that was causing the particular blocks in your efforts. You have not yet arrived at the point where you can create the entity in consciousness in the pupil's mind. Communication is important there. The reason is that one must understand that you must be harmonically attuned with another person's mind before anything can transpire between you, because mere word forms are only conveyors in a sense that they polarize exterior configurations of consciousness; but the main portion of consciousness is a psychic rapport which people have between themselves, just like radio stations. That can be a transcendent quality. It can actually lift you, in a sense of the word, out of a place where you might be very emotionally or dogmatically superimposed as something which is in opposition and yet, you can be temporarily levitated or transcended and become receptive to a new conformative or a new ideology.

We must realize that we have within our minds a great power. This is the power of psychokinesis. It is a projection of mind, a psychic rapport. It is all in that particular dimension of paranormal consciousness which is called clairvoyance, clairaudience or extrasensory perception. They are all one and the same thing. It is a psychokinetical extension of consciousness. In other words, it is developed by first knowing and understanding completely what it is that you wish to convey to that person, then you tune to its frequency just as you tune your dial to whatever station it is that you wish to receive.

Basically, all these blocks are in the psychic anatomy. These are all elements of which a psychologist might say, "Well, you have certain submerged insecurities and they block you because you have not the positive approach." You are not on the positive end of the sine wave that I have spoken about. When you understand the subject thoroughly, when you understand human nature somewhat better than you presently do, then you can communicate with them more rapidly and much more strongly than you are thus able to do at the present time. That is all development, however.

T - Do you have sort of antipathy for beating up eggs in a bowl and being afraid of spattering them on your dress, Vivian?

S - Yes.

T - Because I saw this big yellow bowl and you seemed afraid to beat the eggs with the beater. Someone here in the front row came from a place where they burned coal—you, Helen (Moore). There is an old-fashioned coal stove with a coal scuttle beside it. Do you remember that when you were a little girl? It has four lids on the top.

S - Could be the house I was raised in. Yes, I remember that stove. It sloped in like so at the bottom.

T - Yes, it has a handle or lifter which was made with heavy wound wire which was kept stuck in one of the lids?

S - Yes, I remember that. It was my aunt's house when I was about four.

T - Also about that time, you had a front tooth which was very loose; it was dangling about and was quite a problem to you. Remember that?

S - Yes, I sure do.

T - There was a gentleman with a big mustache (handle-bar), who tied the string to the doorknob to pull the tooth.

S - Yes, that's right.

T - He used to chew tobacco?

S - Yes.

T - A Norwegian?

S - Yes.

T - The man beside her—you have a secret project that you have been wanting to do for years; haven't you?

S - Yes.

T - Have you been to Alaska?

S - I was near Dutch Harbor—within a few miles of it.

T - This trip you have in mind—you are wondering when it will take place?

S - Yes.

T - It will happen in-between the third and fourth years in June—to be more exact, June 24th. You want to make the first stop in the South Sea Islands?

S - Yes.

T - Burma next?

S - Yes.

T - Tahiti?

S - Yes.

T - I am seeing these various places and could give you the dates when you will land on each. You have had trouble with your left foot?

S - Yes.

T - Not too serious but there is trouble. It is the longitudinal arch, the second bone from the main part of the arch. There is a dislocated bone. It seems to slip sometimes.

S - That is right.

T - Gladys, was your husband in a turmoil four days ago?

S - Yes.

T - A bit of trouble with some man?

S - Yes.

T - We shall get a little power on the problem and clear it out. The gentleman on the side there—are you connected with the medical profession?

S - Yes.

T - For I see so many doctors and people of that nature all around you.

S - That's true.

T - Have you been to Germany?

S - No, but my father was born in Germany.

T - I was getting a very strong German influence there.

S - My mother was pregnant with me when she came over.

T - Are there fears of drowning with either you or your wife?

S - We had some narrow escapes with drowning.

T - Was not your wife concerned with the accident?

S - Yes.

T - I see where these drownings actually took place in former lifetimes and you were here trying to work them out. It was in the 1700's on a journey from England to the U.S. There was a shipwreck. You have a rapport with the water, either fear or love.

S - Yes, I love the water very much.

T - There was the drowning and you tried to reenact it. In the sense of science and as far as karma is concerned, we are always the picture of these past psychic shocks. They are always resurgent; they are always coming back. They are locking in the conditions or are reconstructing them for us and we are actually, in a sense, passing through them again so that we can prove that they are not dominant or necessarily destructive to us, because we are trying to work them out. Of course, there is a much better way, a much more comprehensive way to approach these things. If we have the knowledge of them and can look back at them psychokinetically and see several hundred years in the past, we can ferret out these little insecurities and shocks and pinpoint them down; and when we do that, we generate an out-of-phase wave form with the present which cancels out the old past fear. You can still remember it in a sense that you may have a rapport with it but it does no longer dominate you to the point where you will again re-create it for yourself, or that it will still cause you fear. Like the little lady here with (as she says) the many blocks which she has not cancelled out and which are from thousands of years in the past that now exist in this out-of-phase condition.

With your wife here, I assume this is your wife.

S - Yes.

T - Do you recall some relative, an aunt perhaps, who used to bake raisin cookies for you?

S - Yes.

T - There was an old-fashioned wooden table there. The cookies were often kept on this table and you are just about big enough to peer over the top of the table.

S - Yes, I remember that. I did so often. What was the table like?

T - It had heavy round legs with heavy flanges, a yellow color?

S - That is right.

T - Now, you were frightened by a large shaggy dog.

S - I remember a time later when a dog attacked me from behind and scared me terribly.

T - That was a large shaggy dog?

S - Yes, it was.

T - The one that you do not remember happened in a past lifetime and here you were repeating it, as he killed you before. It was a psychic regeneration. Are you interested in Swiss culture, Swiss mountains?

S - Oh, yes, very much so.

T - Snow-covered peaks?

S - They do impress me, yes.

T - This life with the shaggy dog was lived in Switzerland. There is a strong connection with you there. If you saw a large loaf of hard brown bread, you would have a feeling for it; would you not?

S - Oh, yes, I certainly would.

T - That is all connected with that life back there too.

S - Would you kindly develop further the sine wave which you mentioned in the talk?

T - It is a simple derivation of our electronic science, actually, the expression of anything. We can carry that into some sort of a frequency or sine wave transposition. We say light; what is light? Fundamentally, there are three different light vibrations to which the retina of your eye is sensitive. There is the red, the yellow and the blue and beyond that, all color is a matrix or a fabrication of various sine waves which are reflected to your eye. When we get into the differences of how these things are incepted, for instance, we see red. It merely means that we have a substance, atomically speaking, which absorbs all of the various light spectra within itself except the red ray and due to the fact that it is so harmonically constituted that it can refract or reflect—or throughout the electromagnetic fields of the atoms themselves as they compose the substance—they can reflect back the red ray.

The electromagnetic field is very important to remember when we are dealing with atoms, because all of these so-called atomic or solid substances as atoms have very strong electromagnetic fields around them. The earth itself is a huge atom in the sense of the word that it has a great magnetic field. Now, of course, they are finding out about the Van Allen radiation belts and all these principles, which only substantiates what we have here in the lesson course. This was given many years in advance of what they are finding out in our present-day technocracy with their satellites. We are concerned with the sine wave in this respect—that it must become the all-important basic equivalent of every life transposition that we see about us. We are

73

lost until we master that concept. We cannot ever equitably form a very comprehensive evaluation of anything that happens until we can justify it in the sense that it is interdimensional in nature. Follow?

S - Yes, and how do we go about this?

T - First, we take the basic concept of the transposition of energy as a sine wave, and it can be built up to the concept of the universality of the Infinite in a sense that all of these many mansions are the many dimensions of which Einstein was conscious. They are merely ways in which we will say certain junctions were made, harmonically speaking, with a large number of transpositions. Actually, the boundaries were nonexistent and what he meant was that we were harmonically attuned or harmonically justified with any given set of dimensional frequencies. But basically, we must be concerned with the idea or the concept that there is the sine wave which carries the structure of consciousness; whatever the ideology is, whatever the confirmation of an idea, or the conformative of the idea, it has to be basically carried between the two polarities of a sine wave, because a sine wave is either harmonically attuned or harmonically out-of-tune with various impedances in your present-day life. An impedance means your own present evaluation of all life, its own particular consciousness as you express it. In other words, impedance is reactance or resistance. Your ability to visualize the content of a sine wave depends upon the impedance which it stressed in its journey through your consciousness, because in the principle of impedance, we find that here impedance becomes harmonic attunement or becomes harmonically out-of-tune with the particular thing which is coming to us; and on that basis, it can regenerate a form of consciousness on the basis that we have had some similar form of that consciousness before.

That is in your psychic anatomy. If you say, for instance, you see a chair, how do you know it is a chair? You have seen hundreds of chairs in the past; have you not? Back to the time when you were a child, and beyond that, were also chairs—chairs back in many, many lives lived in the past; and so the association of chair-consciousness has been built up to you to the present time in all its forms. We will say that we go back, for instance, three or four hundred years when you were tied in a big carved-oak chair and were tortured to death in this chair. If you went to a museum or to some home and you saw a similar chair, you would have a psychic rapport with that chair. It would immediately subconsciously attune you to the time when you died in that chair three or four hundred years ago. You would have some sense of a vague fear or premonition about it.

That was what I was trying to relate to the lady before in regard to the drownings. These fears are not necessarily strong, impulsive emotions; they can be only very vague insensitive psychic rapports, vagaries or whatever you wish to call them. But sometimes they are very dominant. Cancer is caused by such malformation. A woman who had cancer of the breast came to me several years ago and I explained to her that in a previous lifetime, she was involved in the country of Normandy with the soldiers of Napoleon, who, as was customary among those soldiers, had nasty little habits of whittling off various parts of a lady's anatomy and this was how her psychic shock came about. Because of the sword thrust in her breast at that time, she developed cancer in this life. When that was explained to her, the lump with which she had been bothered and which had been diagnosed as cancer, disappeared, because she had (in this realization) generated an out-of-phase sine wave energy which eliminated the psychic malformed vortex and which re-created itself on the surface of her physical body and healing resulted. In

75

other words, your body is only the image of what you were in the past. She had to know spiritually, we say, that she was preconditioned for this healing in the higher life.

We all live lives in the spiritual worlds in between lives when we pass from one dimension to another; and when we are in these higher worlds, even though we are not specifically conscious of them as they really are, yet we are to some extent vaguely conscious of them. I am speaking, of course, of people who are passing through some of the more lower states of their evolution. These people are conscious of principle and action; they are conscious of the higher organizations, the spiritual forces, etc., so they come back into this life from when they were over there with the avowed purpose that they are going to do better this time; they are going to work it out this time or else, with a firm determination.

True conception, their conscious memory, vanishes simply because a certain part of the psychic anatomy called the subconscious mind is only a temporary part of the psychic anatomy that has developed from life to life. It is there that we get memory consciousness specifically for this life. However, in your mental psychic anatomy you find the continuation of psychic consciousness from previous lives. We have it all down in the lessons, very simply taught in diagrams so that anyone can understand them, and just how we have these various integrations of consciousness which are concerned with interdimensional relationships with our spiritual life in between earth lives and with past lifetimes.

S - Is it necessary to place them exactly, that we know precisely of each experience from the past?

T - No, it is not necessary, in a sense of the word, to re-create the exact image. Now if you think for a moment, if you go back in memory to yesterday and try to describe a particular incident, even though it was a very prominent outstanding incident, you could not describe that accurately, no matter how hard you tried. That may sound a bit far-fetched but it is the truth and has been psychologically proven many, many times. That is the reason that no two people who witness an accident can describe it alike, even though they intend to do so; and though it be but a few moments after it happened, no two persons would describe it precisely alike. The reason for that is because you have this constant resurgence of various harmonic patterns of energy which are stemming from out of your psychic anatomy. These are all formed from out of the past. They are very influential in the sense of the word that they are constantly regenerating harmonic patterns with the present. Therefore, they can influence your position to yesterday to the extent that you were slanted or that you were stressed to be selective on certain basic happenings which happened way back in some distant past. Like many other things, it is only relative; it is only your ability, to some degree, to tune into the past. That is true also with the past lives.

If, for instance, you had been bitten by a snake three or four hundred years ago that would be causing some condition in the physical anatomy today which the doctors could not explain as to what was happening— you would only have to know, in a sense of the word. With a person like myself who can peer back into these past lives, we could bring this experience into focus. This is what Jesus meant when he said, "When two or more are gathered together in My name." "My name" is consciousness; it is not the entity of the conscious self of Jesus; it is the consciousness of Principle. It is the conscious knowledge of the Infinite of which Jesus spoke. This is a practical, workable science which will give the sure solution to every unknown disease and condition which is in existence today. And we have thousands of testimonials in our files to prove that statement.

No, you do not have to actually reconstruct, in a sense that memory is a part. When you come to such a person as myself (with psychic attunement ability), I can automatically suggest to you certain instances, as I did with the doctor's wife a moment ago. We form a rapport with the past sufficiently strong so that the image of that happening, even though it is only vaguely similar, is similar in principle to the experience which caused the malformed vortex; then we are regenerating an out-of-phase harmonic which—in conjunction with the psychokinetic projection which I can also influence or direct in this process—forms a very strong positive force which cancels out that negative vortex in your psychic anatomy. Then your condition will clear up just as sure as night follows day, or vice versa. Just as the little plants come out of the seeds in the ground, you will be freed from these conditions and the diseases when you find the true causes of them. The true cause is seldom in this lifetime. You are here to work it out. That is why you came to earth in this particular cycle.

S - Do we work some out unconsciously?

T - Yes, you can to a certain degree. If you like to keep butting your head against the wall life after life, you can and might, too, reach a point where their effect is considerably diminished, but you have not really gained anything constructive by that process. You have not known either the cause or how to eliminate it and on that same basis, you can also "come a cropper" again. You can regenerate a whole new set of psychic vortexes which are malformed. It is only because you possess the conscious knowledge in your acts of everyday consciousness that you can eliminate them. Not only can a psychic shock cause a malformed vortex but you can also cancel out those which are already in existence. Then you are on your way up when you have learned to do that.

Disease is never caused in the physical body. There are certain pathogenic bacteria which cause disease; that is granted, but I refer to the true disease in the sense of the word where we find an incurable condition such as multiple sclerosis, diabetes, cerebral palsy, heart disease, any kind of thrombosis of the heart, hardening of the arteries, cancer, etc. Regardless of the name, there is always the scientific solution to any of these conditions and the reason why they exist there. The doctors do not know that the cause is in the past, not in the present. You have the condition; now that is proof enough that you incurred a condition way back there when you incurred the sustaining, originating cause which followed you through your evolution. That is the sum and total of it. Some day the science of this world will be developed to that point. They are already doing it on planets like Mars and many of the others throughout the infinite universe. I can name dozens of planets which are living this science—planets which are unknown to the earth man. In fact, on my own planet of Lemuria, people have lived that kind of science for over four hundred thousand years and I can remember that. Sounds a bit far-fetched? Yet I can prove that, too, on the basis that there is no time or space in the next dimension where memory really exists in our psychic anatomy.

It is the same with flying saucers or anything else which poses a seemingly insoluble or impenetrable condition to modern science. We can find a very constructive and a very scientific answer if we can lift the horizon of our thinking from this third dimension and find the true cause, the sustaining motivating action in Infinity itself, as it is compounded from an infinite number of dimensions.

S - How do flying saucers work?

T - They work on exactly the same principle as that

79

which holds the earth in its orbit around the sun. They are an independent regenerative entity; they generate their own gravitational field or anti-gravitational system. They are repulsive to certain lines of magnetic force. The various atoms in the hollow of the structure of the ship itself have been so changed in their atomic relationship to the universe as a whole. The changing can be varied to the degree that these various atomic structures are impelled or repelled by certain magnetic lines of structure which exist forever throughout the infinite universe. Therefore, space travel to that kind of a human being is feasible and possible.

What is meant by good and evil flying saucers is merely the thinking on that matter. Good and evil— one is just as necessary as the other. We could not have one without the other. That is the sum and simple abstraction of it. They are necessary to each other— the part of the infinite plan of understanding, if we can say that there is an infinite plan. It is in the principle of understanding good and evil that we can regenerate constructive principle in our own lives.

If you would like me to quote some history, I could quote you not only personal but various other historical aspects from some of the most degenerated convulsions of history that have regenerated some of the greatest civilizations, some of the greatest purposes, or even that which comes from out of human individual emotionalism. We can say, in a sense, that the deeper we sink into some apathetic or emotional experience we find the greatest, strongest resultant to do something better. I could quote you a little interesting story on this concept that would be helpful to you, as it is part of what we call supernormal phenomena.

This concerns a certain very cultured and refined gentleman of Castilian descent who lives in Beverly Hills and who held a position in the political field in the administration of that city for a number of years.

He was an elderly gentleman who had married a woman somewhat junior to his years. There came the time of the parting of the ways and being rather one of the conniving females, she was taking him for all he was worth, if I can resort to the vernacular. He was very broken up over it as he was emotionally a poised gentleman. In fact, he was so deeply emotionally involved even to the point of committing suicide. And so he came to me as he had heard something of my philosophies of life and I had previously given him little points occasionally. So I invited him over to share my Hi-Fi music one Saturday evening. During the course of our talk, I said, "When you go back to work at the office Monday morning, you will find on your desk a paper, a folded paper, and there will be a message on it which will be very important to you." I stressed it emphatically two or three times.

During the following week, he made a trip especially back to the house with a copy of this notation and explained the circumstances as to how it came to him. He said that the office which he occupied in that building at the time was a new office which had been constructed in front of an old one which he had used previously for many years. The only access to the rear office was through a little passageway right past his desk. He told me when he went in there Monday morning he looked for the paper on his desk which I had described to him and could not find it, so he sat down to try to get into his work but he could not get interested in it. He kept thinking about this paper. After about forty minutes, he arose and went back to this little rear office which was used for nothing but storage space, and there on his old desk was the folded sheet of paper. He opened it and read the message. Part of that message read, "from the dung heaps the fairest lilies grow." Now that man was so astonished and curious, he asked everyone in the office building. He spent several months trying to find any person who had written that letter and he could not. In fact, he could not even find the make of paper in the United States or the typewriter on which it was written (as types vary) but that piece of paper was the turning point in that man's life because of that supernormal phenomenon. It was able to impress him with the insoluble continuity of life and then, suicide was mathematically impossible with him. It was psychologically unsound—and he still talks about the phenomenon.

How are these things done? I could quote you many such instances. I had a gentleman phone me one morning—a Mr. Beasley. I am sure he'd not mind my mentioning his name at all. He is an opera singer and was at one time a devout Christian Scientist. He had spent several years singing opera in Europe in the great Italian opera halls. At the time I knew him and his lovely wife, he was teaching voice in Hollywood, and the time we first met was at the home of one of his students. I had succeeded in describing to him the interior of his home even though I had not been within miles of it. I described the various vases and artifacts about his house. His wife collected art and antiques such as paintings, vases, etc., and was a connoisseur of objects d'art, so I described some of these various vases and pictures which they had about the house, and they were very impressed. So I spent one evening as he took me all about the house showing me the many things which I had described previously to him. But that was very instrumental to him later on in his life; it brought about a turning point in his life, too.

One morning a year or so later, he telephoned me, as I had been quite valuable to him on different occasions in counseling. At this particular time, he had two imported English hunting dogs which were very valuable and he was quite proud of them. They were great roamers and had gotten out of their kennels and wandered away. Of course, he was very frightened for fear of losing them. He said, "I have searched for three days for those dogs. Where are they?" I said to him, "Mr. Beasley, that is very easy. Now you get in your car, go directly up Vine Street (Hollywood) and you will come to a turn in the road. You wind around it, making an S-turn and after passing the S-turn, you will see a little white house with a small picket fence in the front. If you go into that house, you will meet a little man with white hair. He has your two dogs and he has them in a little doghouse which he had built." I told him when he returned with them to call me so I could get off the hook with it. Forty-five minutes later, he called and said, "Dr. Norman, I found my dogs! They were exactly where you said they would be!" He said, "I found the S in the road, the white house with the little white fence and the little white-haired man with my dogs. He had even bought vitamin pills for them. "But," he said, "how did you guide my car around that hill?" Now we see a conjunction here, psychokinetically speaking, where there is a joining or a union of forces in different dimensions. This is a form of consciousness.

I can tell you of many other instances—one which comes to mind. In this same gentleman's house in Hollywood, California, one evening his wife's mother was there, visiting from Denver, Colorado, a city in which I personally had never been, up until this time. She asked me a question as there was a group similar to the one this evening. Could I locate two watches which had been lost for about ten years? One was quite valuable being, . . . "worth about fifteen hundred dollars," she said, "as it was studded with gems." I told her, "Yes, I know right where they are and when you get back home to Denver, go down into the basement, go over to the north wall but before I point out specifically where the watches are, I am going over to the south wall. In the corner is a wet spot; there is a water faucet on the outside but that is not where the water is coming from. Have a man 'step off' twenty steps from the front of the house and six steps to the left; and if he will dig, you will find a cistern under there. That is what is causing the constant dampness and leakage into the basement."

"Now I will tell you about the watches. You go to the trunk that is stored there and dig down into the bottom. You will find a handbag. In that handbag, if you look you'll find a slit or tear in the lining. In between the lining there is a little coin purse containing your watches; but because you will have difficulty in finding this, I will direct your hand while you are looking for them." So she did what I had instructed and she wrote after finding them, "Do you know—I felt something take hold of my wrist and poke my hand in the hole in the lining and I found, just as you said it would be, the coin purse with the two watches in it. But do you know that I have looked in that purse several times before. They had been lost for ten years. I also had a man step off the ground, as you suggested, and sure enough he found the little cistern. I have traced that back for twenty-eight years before anyone knew about it, long before I lived there."

The point I am trying to make here is the fact that when we understand energy, when we get into the next dimensions, we find that all these things will be paranormal activity. (I heard your thought, Ruth; I know time is up.) Extrasensory perception is strictly normal, everyday function. Ruth and I use it daily. There is not a thing in which we do not use it. Velma can vouch for that and so can Bess here. Isn't that right?

S - Yes, indeed.

T - To Velma, I have described intimate happenings in her life that only she knew about. This has happened hundreds of times; has it not?

S - Sure has.

T - The point that I am getting at—I am not trying to eulogize myself or place myself in any sense of the word that I am better than any of you, because I am not. I am only trying to tell you this: that when you become so consciously-minded with the Infinite—as I have so become in the past and developed a personal entity of consciousness as an oscillating polarity with the Infinite—then all of these things are possible. They are a perfectly normal function of your everyday life.

Mental telepathy is a cinch. Ruth and I have an intercom there, a communication system. We never use it. Mental telepathy to us is just as real and expressive as vocal expression—and much handier. And this is the point I am trying to demonstrate to all of you people because I know it is the difference between life and death for you. It is not a problem of whether or not you can accept it but a problem of whether you are going to live or die, because when you have taken this first step —and we will assume that you have taken this first step, otherwise you'd not be studying Unarius—you want to find out about these things. When you have taken these first steps, you have automatically placed yourself in a relationship with the Infinite, so that if you do not dynamically progress in your understanding of the Infinite, you can only go backwards. And "Dante's Hell" is nothing compared to the maze that you may find yourself in if your evolution is continued downward or backward in a retrogressive fashion. That is the pure and simple substance of it.

S - Would you explain further about the person who you mentioned as intending suicide? You say it was mathematically impossible. What was meant by this?

T - I meant it was impossible in this sense of the word that we can say, we add up everything that you are as a sequence of evolutionary factors and they are going to harmonically regenerate themselves on the multiples of two. It is a fundamental electronic principle and you can no more escape the perditions of the present moment by committing suicide than you can hope to escape anything else, because these things are going to multiply themselves in intensity and in manner and in form. Conversely, the good things will also remanifest themselves by the same ratio of incidence. These are mathematical laws and formulas about which I am speaking. It is not merely idle philosophy or supposition; it is a science—a real science.

S - Dr. Norman, I have not rid myself of the itching fingers.

T - You have not gotten to the keystone. The little vortexes haven't been cancelled out. Any improvement?

S - No, it seems even worse.

T - Then you have not conceived it from the other side or recognized from whence the cause as I explained to you. When we dissolve the originating condition of these things, they automatically dissolve the present circumstance. The one is synonymous with the other. There cannot be one without the other. The cause is back there when you used to weave this flax and cut your fingers. You are constantly picking off bits of skin or nails that this strong flax fiber cut into your fingers. When you can realize this past and form a complete junction with yourself and regenerate this out-of-phase motion about which I have been telling you, then that cause will be gone and the sensation will also cease.

S - How can I think this way?

T - You just go along and try to remember what I have told you. We must be harmonically attuned to these things. There is a very important principle involved in these dischargings. There must be a cyclic junction. Remember that everything moves in cycles when it comes to fourth dimension and we have a complete entity of consciousness. It has a certain wave length, a certain frequency. When we reach that frequency in our thoughts, we may do it accidentally. By conjunction of thinking of many other things, all of a sudden you may find yourself harmonically attuned to the past and in that moment we regenerate an out-of-phase wave form which changes our relationship to it.

Gladys, there is a little child here who says she never knew an earth life; that you would have named her Genevieve; is that right? She was unborn?

S - Yes, could be.

T - You like the name, Genevieve?

S - Yes, it's beautiful.

T - There is also a lady here who says she would sit by the window and brush your hair by the hour. You remember that?

S - My mother.

Well friends, I've kept you long overtime. May this evening serve as a new turning point in each of your lives—a new and higher cycle in a regenerative, progressive evolution.

CHAPTER VIII

Group Lecture on History
Of Religion, May 23, 1957

Greetings, Dear Friends: As you all know this is the Spring season, and one of particular significance to all races and classes of people living on the earth today, just as it has been from time immemorial until the present day. Since the beginning or before the written histories of man upon this planet, Spring, in itself, has had a great deal of spiritual meaning. This week represents many things to many people of the world. To the Jewish people, it is the week of Passover, which dates back more than three thousand years to the time when the Angels of the Lord supposedly passed by the door of those who were marked with the bloody cross. To more than seven or eight hundred million people who denote themselves Christians and who follow the way of the Bible and the cross, they too, in some large or small way, will pay tribute to a custom which started almost two thousand years ago; and yet, even that custom, in itself, is older than antiquity itself.

Inasmuch as peoples of the world can be said to be approaching some millennium, some great period of transition, there are many indications in the present day wherein many of the age-old prophecies biblically written or otherwise inscribed in tombs, on stones and various places upon the surface of the earth are about to be fulfilled.

With all of this, it is an age of highly-developed technocracy, and there are numerous pressures, internal and external, which have subjugated people to stresses far beyond the capacity for human endurance. Looking for ways and means of relief and surcease from these particular vicissitudes of the twentieth century and to be enabled to foresee and point to the future a more directed course that is both logical and will bring to conclusion some of the problems with which man is now beset, it is quite evident that with the superficial examination and agreed by laymen and people who are more vitally concerned in humanitarian efforts, there is great need for an understanding, for a development of a spiritual way of life in which the plan supersedes and fills in various and obvious gaps which are presently existing.

In ages old and days gone by, people were not too concerned with the technocracy of the times. Religion in itself is a development which encompasses the daily life of every individual. There are races and countries on the earth today who still manifest some closeness in their relationship of spiritual values to their daily life. Webster's dictionary defines religion as a code of ethics whereby the individual conducts himself in these days. Upon examination of such a concept, one is impressed that this gives each individual considerable latitude, and it may be responsible to a large degree in the more abstract derivation of such ethics and principles that the individual, and especially the Christian, has long since come to the parting of the ways with the spiritual way of life, and that he has relegated such spiritual attributes to a one-day-a-week affair, sitting in front of some pulpit and vaguely remembering or disremembering words uttered which were meant for inspiration and perhaps for courage. While the hundreds of millions of Christians are praying in the churches this following Sunday in commemoration of an advent which we know as the crucifixion, yet all the praying and all the hymn singing will not cover up the growlings of the dogs of war which are now fighting and contesting for some superficial issues upon the very ground hallowed in tradition and which nourished the roots of Christianity!

It is quite obvious to the thinker and to anyone particularly interested in the destinies of man, in an observation or course back into the pages of history, that the particular fault or particular attributes of any religious system was only valuable to the point at which they could be interwoven into daily life. Likewise, such concepts were obviously only tailored and intended in some way, through some governing agent, shall we say from spiritual dimensions, which was of the most value to the people of that particular era. Going back further and examining religion in its basic and its most inceptive or beginning process, we find that man had lived in the first elemental stages of his life upon the planet earth, and whether he was a caveman or some primitive type, that man here first became cognizant of certain unknown, unnamed forces which moved about him in his daily life. He began to recognize these forces of the lightning in the sky, the movements of the storms, the floods, the winds, the fires which sometimes swept across the hills, and all these things he tried to explain in his own particular way.

So it came to pass that as he externalized and began to develop concepts within his mind, these forces of nature began to take on personality. To him, the common derivative of his limited knowledge gave him such vicissitudes and temperaments of human nature as he himself portrayed. Thus it came to be that in the evolution of spiritual consciousness the various governing forces of that ancient man's world were more or less concerned with spirits, demons, and ogres. As a direct spiritual outgrowth for such spiritual transitions man, in the growing-up process of spiritual evolution, began to develop a finer-grained concept of his spiritual concepts. They took on such personifications as gods and goddesses such as was exemplified in Greek mythology which was borrowed by the Romans and developed into a highly-exploited pantheology of those particular eras and times. It is doubtful—if we were to approach either the layman or the Christian or priest and ask him to define to us in a casual way what he considered God to be—that we would get a very logical explanation; for the meaning, the knowledge and the exact portrayal of God cannot be contained in such ideosophies which may be associated with personality or such particular environmental influences with which we may now be in contact. To describe God is like describing everything! Further, if we were to develop our inquiries along these lines into the origin of our present-day Christian orthodoxy; we would find that here again there were certain strange parallels which were drawn and which would lead us basically to the conclusion that there were really no religions in the world except one basic religion. And in some sense of the word the Christian today is worshipping exactly as his ancestors did hundreds of thousands or even millions of years ago, and that there is really, basically, very little difference except in the manner of clothing he may wear and the place in which he worships; for God is still the apartness, God is still the unknown, God is still the embolical force which represents not as a pantheology of demons, ogres, spirits, gods or goddesses but only a particularly centralized force of spiritual expression.

The Christian too—especially in the latter development in the last few hundred years of his expression—has attempted in various ways to go into numerous countries and persuade—into his way of thinking—the various tribes of aborigines or people who live in that particular area, not being conscious of the fact that the people themselves who he was trying to convert to his own way of thinking were much more ideally suited in their spiritual concepts, perhaps closer even to the secret of life itself than he, the Christian missionary. The Christian, too, is apt to be found to be extremely ignorant of his own religion. If we were to ask these questions superficially here and there, where we may find opportunity to do so: what is the background of our modern Christianity? What is the background of all of these things in which a person is supposed to relegate his own personal spiritual ethics?—it is doubtful logical answers could be supplied. Perhaps he does not know that all of the customs, all of the various observances of Christianity itself are derived from concepts interwoven and are infiltrations from age-old customs which basically had their origin in some almost forgotten civilization that has left behind it only the traces of stonework, masonry or other remnants and fragments.

We have much to consider in an effort to analyze Christianity and the origin of our customs; for instance, the festival of Easter itself is linked back into Egypt ten thousand years before the time of Jesus to the concept of Osiris who went out—and as he was the God of all, considered to be worshipped as we would worship our Father in Heaven—and that Osiris slew the black bull which symbolizes all of the evil with which man came in contact and has its direct counterpart in our modern Christian theology and thinking. Now Osiris was wounded beyond the point of death but being immortal, he dragged himself off to his couch and after three days, arose refreshed, revived and able to carry on.

Other concepts, too, from the Hermetic sciences or understanding from ancient Egypt are carried on through our modern Christianity. We may start with Paul, in understanding the Christian church, and while some of these concepts in themselves may be rhetorical, yet we can refresh your mind and perhaps pass on this information to others, for becoming wise is becoming the way into spirit. Paul, who was known as Saul of Tarsus—half Roman, half Jew—built up, in his lifetime, a tremendous frustration and hatred for Christianity, and under the Roman emissary, persecuted the followers of Jesus after the execution. It was Saul, attired in the armor and regalia of a Roman soldier, when making a journey to Damascus, who was overcome by the heat of the desert and suffered sunstroke. As in the case of all psychotic phobias, sometimes an inversion suddenly takes place in the human mind, and so likewise with Saul. The inversion from a persecution complex became one of a humanitarian effort, so Saul deserted the ranks of the Romans and went to Greece and Corinth and there began setting up what was to become two of the world's greatest religious expressions, the Roman Catholic Church and the ancient Byzantine Empire.

Paul had considerable competition. There were two religions in that era of time, around the Mediterranean countries, which had attracted large masses of people; in fact, everybody worshipped one way or the other, the Roman or the Grecian pantheology (Minerva, Apollo, Juno and others too numerous to mention) or the other concept which was Mithraism, a strange mixture of Zoroastrianism and the ancient Hermetic sciences. Paul realized that if he were to draw converts from both, he must express some great degree of attraction to them, and as people are, in some way, like little children—they love parades, they love the regalia, they love various things which can be considered fiestas, or religious observances—so Paul began hunting about for various ways and means to attract people into the new church. The doctrine of Jesus itself offered a very strong attraction, inasmuch as it was considered that it offered eternal life. Yet there had to be other things added to the Christian doxology, and so there came into being and interwoven much of the observances and customs of that time.

About 550 B.C. in the ancient land of Persia, there was born a man who was later known as Zoroaster.

93

According to history, he was one of the first of the immaculate conceptions. He was born in a shepherd's hut on a hillside and witnessed by the shepherds. His father was the Father of all, and the son's name was Mithras, or the son of Light, and his mother was a virgin, the mother earth. So it was that finally, in the derivations of that particular concept, Zoroaster actually became Mithras. Going back, too, into Egypt, this particular conception of the immaculate was further fortified by the Osirian derivative. Osiris, who overshadowed Isis, mother of earth, who begat Horus, the interceder; and even ten thousand years before the time of Christ, Horus stood in picture form before the throne of Osiris and interceded for all those who believed he had the power to intercede in their behalf. And so it was borne into the Christian doxology some of the concepts which have given rise to great conflict.

We can imagine, if we will, if we're in the position of some savage aborigines or some person who lives in a country which has no contact with civilization, what a struggle it is in his mind to accept in full content the Bible as we know it. The two diametrically opposed doctrines pose great problems of compromise. We can hardly imagine accepting the one god who gave the strength of arm to Samson who slew the thousands of soldiers with the jawbone of an ass. We could hardly imagine, too, that it was the one God, the God of Jesus, who stood the earth still so Joshua could kill another thirty or forty thousand Philistines, or that he would burn the cities of Sodom and Gomorrah because he was angry at the people. The Old Testament is a derivative of the ancient Chaldean concepts in the time of Father Abraham more than two thousand years before the advent of Jesus.

Father Abraham, as a revivalist in that time, and dissatisfied with the ministry of various sects and cultisms which existed in that ancient land, decided to do something about it, which he did. During one of the revival meetings, a great meteor crashed to the earth near the encampment. Today this meteorite resides in the central citadel in the city of Mecca and every true Moslem must go to Mecca and walk seven times around the stone and then kneel and kiss it before he is admitted to heaven.

The average Christian does not know that the context of the Koran, as it was written by Mohammed, is based on the first five books of the Old Testament, the Books of Moses, as they were written in bibliography and that it was the purpose of Mohammed five hundred years after the crucifixion to reestablish the old concepts of Abraham and Moses back into Arabia and the ancient land of Chaldea. And so we can go on, and we can arrive at one particular place of introspection after another where we will see the similarity and the parallel of not only our modern Christianity and doxologies as we know them today, but which link us with the past ages and epochs of time.

Buddha, who was born about five hundred years before Jesus, taught a simple way of life, a simple psychology, the enlightenment, the contact with the inner self, Nirvana. Two hundred and fifty years later, until the time of the reign of King Asoka, Buddha was a failure and his religion had not, in any sense of the word, permeated farther than the county in which he lived. Buddha had traveled all over the Malayan Archipelagos and left behind him the basic points of future infiltration for the coming of the new religion. During the reign of King Asoka, Buddhism was established in India, and with it came the usual watering-down process to which all great movements, great Avatars and their truths, have been subjected. Buddhism in many respects retains parallels with modern Christianity. The ennobled form of enlightenment is an exact counterpart of the Ten Commandments. The three Pitakas or baskets of bread again exemplify the Holy Trinity. Even though such derivatives are impounded today, there is in their present form of Hinduism, the old Brahministic concepts which came down from the transcripts of the Aryan race from the planes of Mongolia many, many thousands of years ago—Brahma, the Father of all; Vishnu, the preserver and interceder of life; and Shiva, the devil. Today in India there is a pantheology of more than thirty million gods. It is estimated there is one god for every ten people in India. Everyone worships according to how he sees life. He has constructed his own spiritual code of ethics, and he revolves automatically to such plateaus of expression as he finds in the neighborhood; and as the neighborhood is literally festooned with temples and shrines, there is little difficulty in India to find the level of your understanding.

Man, too, is slow to change. Back some thirty years before the birth of Buddha, another man was born in a northern province of India named Mahavara, who later became known as the genie. It was he who established the genieistic concepts which too are woven into the concepts of modern day Hinduism and gives that particular pantheology not only a very fantastic external appearance, but is very bewildering to the layman and student alike to attempt to probe beneath the surface. Resolving all of these things as we do into what we might call a potpourri of concepts, ideologies, theosophies, religions, cultisms and extractions and derivations of many and varied ideas in the world about us and in the way in which we find man living on the planet earth, we begin to wonder, we begin to search and we begin to think—does man have a way to satisfy the future needs, the generations which are to follow; are the age-old prophesies of the Bible to be fulfilled, and how?

To further confuse and conflict the present-day investigator's mind, another pressure has been brought to bear—pressure from what we might call the scientific technocracy of this day and age. But at least we can say of the scientific technocracies that they have produced very tangible results. In attempting to equate what we consider the evolution of man in future spiritual dimensions in what is commonly called the Aquarian Age, the Golden Age, the age in which God is supposedly ruling the earth, the heart and mind of mankind, as the common denominator of the Golden Rule, "Do unto others as ye would be done by," Jesus said, "Ye have heard of the laws of Moses and of the Ten Commandments, but I give thee one greater than all these—that ye should love thy neighbor as thyself and love thy God with all thy heart and soul." Jesus did not tell us how we should come about these things, no more than when he said, "Seek ye first the Kingdom of Heaven which is within, and all things shall be added unto you." Nor again was the implication the direct knowledge as to what the Kingdom of Heaven was like and how we should arrive at that point; and so we have arrived in our modern Christian doxologies with many strange interpretations of what this particular state of consciousness may be. Some people have envisioned it as riding around on a pink cloud and playing a harp. Such things are not only laughable but can be fatal if they are pursued long.

We should visualize first that if we are to draw anything from our analysis and our equations as to what man will be in the future ages, we must have a very basic and tangible point, a sort of pivot place where we can place the fulcrum or leverage which we will use to pry away the encrustation of the accumulated ages, to arrive at the nutshell or core and kernel of truth. Strangely enough, we cannot revert into the age-old pantheologies of the past for they do not contain what we need. We must seek directly into the field of what we call physical science as it is expressed in the world today.

Back in 1919 Einstein gave to the world a simple mathematical formula based upon the concept that there was no such thing as a solid, and that solids were easily converted into energy and vice versa. We today know the scientists of the world have built up a whole great atomical science. We now know that in the more abstract way there is actually no such thing as a solid. The walls of this room, the earth that we walk upon, all substance and form, the very bodies that we possess are nothing more or less than the accumulation of countless untold millions of small planetary systems of energy called atoms—atoms held in a certain particular way in a dimension which is called time and space. When we have begun to master this concept, then the secret of universal creation begins to unfold before us. We can pyramid upon this concept of energy in its various dimensional forms and transpositions, the true equation, the true answer to everything in life —and there are no exceptions. We do not resort to some book which is mythically compounded—and which is composed—as one Dutch philosopher of the 16th century said, "The Bible is composed of many lies, derelictions, fabrications, and omissions, and there are parts filled with murder, and some of the things are filthy and not fit to be read."

Go back again into our equation of energy and the building up for ourselves a substantial platform whereby we too can join our brothers over the seas of interplanetary distances to distant horizons, to other solar systems, and to planets which are far evolved beyond the dimension of consciousness of our own. What is the Golden age, the Aquarian Age? Will Jesus come, as some adventists believe, upon a great blazing cloud? And man will be destroyed in his entirety, and that only 144 thousand shall be saved? Among the 800 million Christians living today, they all believe they belong to the 144 thousand. We must resolve our equation into more factual and to more demonstrable equations which will give us the true values of life. When we have mastered the concept that the world is not the materialistic, solid, reactionary way of life in which it is commonly supposed to be, we need not become mere creatures which sprang forth from a genetical reaction, to live only in one time and in one place, that we must die and wait a thousand years to spring forth in some vague way at the call of the trumpets. When we begin to understand energy and all of its implications and all of its magnitudes, its grandeur and its glory, we begin to probe directly into the mind and heart and soul of the Infinite Itself.

You and I and everyone in this room—or the countless millions of people who have come and gone upon this planet and every other planet in this and any other universe—are cells in that great Infinite Mind. We are spiritual creations, and outwardly we manifest only in the external countenance of the physical body such idea and form as have been brought to us in the way of our evolutionary path. As cells in the Cosmic Infinite Mind and concerning ourselves as we do, that we have been created not from the mud of the bank of the river but from the energy substance of the Infinite Mind Itself. If God is Infinite, He must maintain infinity by also being finite in all consciousness, in all forms and in all substances. So therefore, the Infinite has placed in each and every one of us all of the condiments, all of the elements, all of the knowledge and wisdom which the Infinite Itself possesses. It is you and I who resolve ourselves as spiritual embryos into the material world to become oscillating polarities; and through the worlds of experience, we multiply the agents of wisdom which build within ourselves the necessary structure which will bring us higher and higher in the evolutionary path of spiritual progress to the time and place when we shall become direct reciprocating polarities with the Infinite Consciousness.

Every atom in your body exists simply because it is internalized by a direct dynamic driving force from another dimension. If you care to, you can envision these things as spiraling, radiating forces of energy, cascading on up and up into infinite vistas and horizons or great and multiple cosmos of these whirling energy forms. They all assume in their own proper relationship, in their own dimension the transposition of their own frequency relationship, governed by inexplicable and the strongest laws which supersede any which are known to man, because the Infinite functions without law, for the Infinite is the Law; It—in the functioning from the Source or Fountainhead—multiplies, recreates into infinity and into all finite forms a direct counterpart, a transposition in some form but primarily as energy.

We, therefore, in our concepts have now arrived at the time and place where we are no longer protoplasmic creations as in a theory on the Darwinian evolution. Darwin was concerned only with such metamorphoses as could be discerned in the physical dimension, and he would have been out of his time and place had he known that all evolution takes place in the spiritual planes; and any creature, fish, fowl, or man himself is only manifest in such form in direct proportion to the energy context of the psychic self of that particular form.

What is the spiritual soul of man? What is it that determines the various reactionary life-sustaining forces which are necessary to carry us on from one day to the next? Every human being creates for himself, every sixty seconds, one million five hundred thousand cells in his body. You have no conscious knowledge of this, nor do you have any direct participation of it as far as your conscious mind is concerned. What is the conscious mind that the doctors of today are struggling with to determine the secret of its energy, the brainwave machine which determines certain forms of resident frequency which stem up and down the pulsating nerve energy? Energy itself is a direct transposition of life in all of its form and substance. You and your five senses—touch, smell, hearing, sight and taste only transform these particular things, as they are energy wave forms, into some meaningful derivation as an oscillating polarity with the subconscious which is a part of the psychic self.

Man, therefore, as a spiritual being, is resolved into an energy body composed of millions and millions of vortexes of energy and have, as counterparts for themselves, externalized into the form of flesh the direct counterpart of their intelligence quotient. These wave forms have been inflected into the psychic self through many, many lifetimes of experience, through countless thousands of years of evolution, all taking place in spiritual rapport with the psychic self—for the substance of the psychic self in the countless billions of wave forms, each portraying its own I.Q., determining what you are today and what you shall be in the future, every thought and action; and as the switchboard of your mind links you with the subconscious, so you inflect into yourself, into your psychic structure the quotient of experience. And that, in itself, explains to you that casting your bread upon the water, so it shall return.

There is not a man or person living upon the earth today who is not manifesting in some direct ratio and proportion all that he is today, what he has been yesterday, not the yesterdays of tomorrow, not the yesterdays as we have concerned them with life upon this present earth, but the yesterdays of ancient Egypt, India, yes, Atlantis and Lemuria.

Customs as old as the written history of man himself—he brings them down from age to age and generation to generation, inflecting and reinflecting into his conscious structures, reliving the consequences of karma, the psychic shocks, the death of a loved one, whatever it is that you care to conceive or name, you will find the answer directly and clearly given when you understand the relationship, the form of energy, the transposition of energy in our everyday life. You and I cannot see or hear the hundreds of radio and television stations which are portraying both sight and sound invisibly into this room at this moment. The instrument in the corner was designed for such interpolation. It can—by simple component parts which resonate in direct frequency to the transmitter—resolve in the pulsations of energy across the screen of the tube, the picture as it is being exactly portrayed from the iconoscope in the television transmitter. You are exactly like that television set. You are.reflecting consciously in every way, in every movement, in every walk of your life, in a direct counterpart of an energy wave form which you have implanted in your psychic body in some way, in some manner, in some form, and your very body is a direct evolution and a development, a form and substance, in an intelligent way, from the comparative values of experience as they were resolved from one dimension to the next, from one lifetime to the next.

That, my friends, will be the future religion. As to whether that circumstance will ever arrive upon this planet earth is a matter which is open to debate for the world and the planet earth in itself was intended, conceived and created for the purpose as a plane of relationship of interpolation for various millions of untold souls who have come and gone through the world of experience and created for themselves the necessary evolutionary substance in their psychic selves which enabled them to go into other planets and to other solar systems, into other worlds which have gone beyond the time and place of their own world. Will our own world ever develop such a time and place that we will be completely rid of all of the old false ideosophies and pantheologies of the past? Will we be able to outlive the fanaticism of our present day-religious systems? Will we ever be able to evade the self-delusion of chasing the will-of-the-wisp, the false materialistic concepts? As far as the majority or bulk of the people upon the planet earth today are concerned, the answer would be a strong, strict and emphatic "no"; they, like you and I and everyone in this room and all truth seekers, who have passed that point, that fork in the road, will—in some way, some place, on some earth—remain in such subjugated materialistic concepts until they, too have imbued within their psychic self the necessary elements which will enable them to live in a higher dimension of consciousness.

We cannot be pacified in any sense of the word by adventism. The false concept is, in itself, that of a preacher who will stand on the platform and scream to the congregation, repentance, and ye shall be damned into eternal hell, and in the next breath, say that you need not worry, Jesus died for your sins; Jesus will even wash them away and you will be white as snow. Such things are unfactual, unrealistic, and should be avoided at all costs. Perhaps they are necessary stepping stones in the evolution of the more primitive minded people of the earth, but you and I—we are the seekers; ahead of us, and in the superconsciousness of our own selves, is the Christ self of which Jesus spoke. "Of myself I can do nothing, but with the Father within. . ." —and what is the Father within? It is that of which I spoke, that immortal cell of eternal life; all of those things of infinity that is the Christ self. Within you, within myself, every one of us—large or small, fat or thin, sick or well, whoever he or she is, on the face of this earth, or in any other world which we care to imagine—has that same Infinite cell, the same infinite number of wisdom quotients, the same necessary condiments known which will enable him to live beyond the time when he again needs the physical coil of flesh to express his way, his understanding of the experience dimension.

It is wonderful, indeed, for many of us to envision to ourselves interplanetary communication with other worlds. To old souls, such things can be relegated to the horse and buggy days; and even though people themselves who fly the flying saucers can likewise be said to be in the horse and buggy days, there comes a time and place, even beyond the need of flying saucers. Interplanetary relationship, residing on a plane of universal introspection—call it mental telepathy, astral flight, or whatever you wish—it is being done consciously and it is being done by many people in our present-day and from other worlds. If the question resides in your mind, as it still may do, will these biblical prophecies be fulfilled? In the second epistle of Peter, "The Lord cometh as a thief in the night, and the earth shall be consumed and even the elements burned with a fervent heat." The old prophet, Peter, looking into the future, saw the explosion of an H-bomb, and knowing nothing of these things, could well misinterpret the meaning—and so it was brought into the New Testament. Yet, it does not mean that this world will be consumed by atomic fire or nuclear heat. There are other ways in which man will destroy himself much more realistically and much more factually than any H-bomb could ever do, for the death of a human being merely means the transposition of the ego consciousness from one dimension to another; but the slow death of spiritual retrogression will revert the cell's life, the infinite cell, the infinity of God, back into the abysmal cosmos, back into the lower orders of the astral world, back beyond even the time and place where redemption is possible.

The ultimate meaning of these things in themselves are complete abstractions and beyond the realm of conception from the finite mind, and possibly the Infinite alone knows the answer; but to you and I as truth seekers, can begin today and bring into our consciousness a true conscious realization of infinity and the motivating forces, these tremendous things which are ever about us. God, or the Infinite, is the energy of life. Historic works in many places will bring to the conscious realization that many scholars, avatars and philosophers have reached that point of introspection in their past lives; men like Plato, Leonardo da Vinci, and a host of others have all reached a place in their own introspection when they have begun to conceive inwardly the "Kingdom of Heaven which is within", and they have begun to place themselves, as it were, to realize that it is the Father within, the great titanic forces of the mind, the capabilities of man to express himself universally and constructively into such dimensional concepts of interpolation that help lift up the less fortunate being from out the abysmal swamps of ignorance and despair.

We rest our case with you.

CHAPTER IX

The Elder Brother Discussing
Energy To A Student — 1958

Throughout history man has been aware of some outside or external force, but he has been given no scientific knowledge of this important truth. He may call that the Supreme Being or Brahma or God or Allah, but the difference is they have not yet evolved to the level of their reference to be able to place it beyond the level of human personality because they still endow whatever this god is with human propensities. And when they do that, they have to do another thing. They have to divide that Absolute, after they personified it to some degree, into two opposing forces—good and evil. Then when they do that, they have to take the evil and call it Satan or they call it Shiva, or they call it something else—Beelzebub, or whatever particular denominator they take—and there, you see, they are back again into paganism.

Christians do the same thing they have always done for past countless ages of time. They have separated the Absolute into two divisions, Satan and Christ, and you cannot divide these things into human personalities whatsoever. If you do, you are lost. Some of the teachers of Christianity know that these things do exist but they do not have the knowledge of the mechanics. Getting into the Absolute—what is the Absolute and the reason it is not divisible in common terms of reference so far as human personalities are concerned? We have to first completely abolish the idea that there are any human propensities with the Absolute whatsoever. What they call God is Infinite; it is the sum and total of all things, and it is infinite only because it becomes finite in all forms and substances—visible and invisible, tangible and intangible. That is the second necessary step. So we have to understand it in an entirely different way.

Now there are plenty of our twentieth century physical scientists—as well as our dynamics—who understand those things that can give us all the necessary information that we want on that subject. We first start with the common equivalent as far as this world is concerned, which we call the sine wave, and that merely means energy going from one point to another as a positive and negative polarity pattern.

We toss a pebble into the pond and we see waves stemming out from the impact. That means that energy is being dissipated and in a way, it forms a pattern which is positive and negative transference of energy as a polarity pattern. Now we begin to understand that there really isn't anything in the world that is solid in the commonly accepted term. What we call mass is atomic energy substance; in other words, they are tiny little planetary systems of energy, like our own planetary system. The space in between the electrons, the neutrons or between the atom is just as great in comparison as it is in our own solar system in between the planets. What they think is a solid substance, an electron, is in reality another sub-atom. They will see it in the future but do not at present. It is another tiny and infinitely smaller solar system of energy.

Now the whole thing means that as far as the atom is concerned, it is connected to another dimension through a vortexal pattern. It is only an outside or an external appearance of something that is going on in another dimension. That little vortex that holds the atom in its own particular periphery or its own particular dimension is a vortexal pattern of energy which is interlinked with an infinite number of dimensions. Now we must visualize these things as traveling polarity patterns and not only within the structure of the vortex itself from positive to negative, but we can liken those forces to centrifugal or centripetal forces which are in the circular motion of energy; but we also find that through harmonics, within harmonic structures, it is interconnected with all of these different infinite number of dimensions. Therefore, we see that the Absolute now has become finite. It is only divisible when we can learn to view these things as dimensions in which a certain given number of frequencies are compatible to each other in a certain way, but all things are interlinked with harmonic structures.

So now we have abolished good and evil. We see that things are maintained only as perspective as positive and negative. What man calls evil is only an opposite perspective; it is the other end of the polarity of something good, and in that way, we can explain everything, no matter what it is. What people call evil is merely their own position, their relationship to a given dimension or force or expression traveling in a certain way.

And so by going from one life to another as we do from one day to another, we obtain in some way or another an infinite number of these different perspective positions of comparative equations; and that is done—and it has been established as far as the personal being is concerned—because it was part of infinity or what we call the superconsciousness of each individual, in other words, the aggregate or the matrix of intelligent wave forms or dynamic structures which are infinite in nature. It contains all of the elements of the Absolute. It is the Absolute personified in a given perspective or a given dimension which becomes eventually the human being, because oscillating down into the outside or the third dimension that way, it obtains an opposite end of the polarity, an infinite number of abstractions from the physical experiences. Therefore, it has constructed for itself the personal ego or the id. It is all very factual; it is all very provable.

S - I can understand you up to a point, but you lose

me.

T - We are getting these things all down in print so you all may learn and study them in your own homes. But I am not at all concerned about these things because they will be the bibliography of the future. It will help man in his future evolution to destroy this illusion, this maya that has been confounding him for the past countless centuries. You see, all religions, all cultisms are basically and essentially the cause for man's greatest distresses because they are forming even in the most liberal perspectives an escape mechanism at best. That is all that religion is in its present status. Man is only obtaining a temporary form of relief, a sort of safety valve situation with a great number of different pressures which have been built up within himself, because he has not understood the common equations with dynamic polarities, the movements of any given form or appearance of substance as it is called, or form of substance through a certain perspective as a certain polarity pattern.

When a person obtains that perspective, he is not subjective to these things in the common sense because they always have a different way of equalizing these things and leveling them off. He does not have to go off on these mad rat-race vacations; he does not have to seek out the priest and obtain this temporary moral opiate that he calls a confession or some religious observance or go to church to ease his conscience because that is all just a form of a tranquilizer, a moral opiate, and that is all that it is.

S - And perhaps to recharge the battery?

T - Well, that is something else that they do not understand. This recharging of the battery is a natural thing which follows through a certain process and depletion of the psychic or depletion of the magnetic aura.

T - Denotes Teacher.   S - Denotes Student.

Actually, we have seven basic auric structures, that is, seven different dimensions of relationship within the psychic from the magnetic into the pranic aura, but subdivisible as they are, they are all interlinked in frequency relationships and harmonic structures. And when we come into a condition where we will say that we are connected as a positive pole with a negative field, we have a tendency to discharge ourselves, and vice versa, we will connect ourselves up in an understanding way; not in a negative way but in an understanding way, we become receptive to a higher degree of positive polarity. And many people—with their differences in these cultisms and the ages of the various religious associations of the past, and the degree that has to be done in a means and a way of supplication—have not understood it; and it has to be done in an intelligent fashion as an understandable way.

I think that some of the past Masters could give very definite information on that. Jesus, in particular, said we have to seek out the Father who is within the closet of our own minds—we make the internal contact. It is not in the churches or synagogues and it is not done in other places; it is not done through prayer. He said very specifically about that, and He knew that human weakness and He gave them this prayer which is common property or part of the New Testament. But He advised them against praying, but to seek out the Father within your own mind that He could reward you openly.

S - And how could we do it otherwise?

T - That is exactly why we are giving this very valuable information. When people will learn or understand the dynamics as I have just gone through it here —more or less of a thumbnail situation—first starting with the sine wave and understanding that these concepts are not personifications in any sense of the word; but they are very definite forms of energy, interdimensional relationships, etc.; when it can be understood that way, they have an entirely different perspectus. They have a way and a means of going over the threshold, and in the future they are going to evolve into lifetimes where they will no longer be pagans in the sense where they have to supplicate or to pray to personalities. Instead, they look up to these things, or look into them and they see how the Infinite—what they call God—is manifesting and remanifesting inwardly and outwardly, up, down and all ways simultaneously. Therefore, he is able to use the kind of mechanics which the scientist is using to construct the radio—to turn the dial of his own mentality—and when he does that by looking into this properly, he immediately attunes himself into it.

It is a very simple thing. Whenever you think about anything, for instance, if you are thinking about looking at that plant over there on the table, you automatically tune yourself into it. You have to because it is a common law of dynamics; you could not escape it if you wished to see it. So therefore, first you place yourself in a susceptible fashion to the rays of light which are being reflected off that plant. Now if that plant was also something which could give off other different kinds of rays (say for instance, vibrations of thought) that, in turn, would place you in a condition whereby you were connected, just as the radio was, with that plant. Whether or not you were conscious of it, you would still be in some sense or way vibrating with whatever emanates from that plant in a way of vibration.

Now that Principle is true if you hold consciousness in any form or in any other different direction. You do not have to externalize it because you have to realize also that energy is stemming into you from a number of other different dimensions. In a sense of the word, the Infinite has become the plant in a number of different ways. Now, by your becoming conscious of this and seeing the Infinite come into you from numerous other different ways, by linking yourself up in the thinking manner, you have consciously activated all of the whole psychic with these thoughts. In other words, going back to the original concept of ringing, as it is called in applications of electronics or physics, you have stimulated all of these centers with an activation, an oscillating condition there with the higher inflows of energy—the influxes of energy from the higher self, or more correctly, through the higher self. It is absolute; it is infallible. You cannot fail once you have attained the idea behind it all. It is absolutely so inviolate you could not go wrong even if you wanted to. The minute you become conscious of these higher things that are vibrating or radiating into you, you do not have to say words, you do not have to utter prayers or burn incense, or go to the altar or the temple. It is vibrating internally with you at all times, twenty-four hours a day —every second. You could not escape it: if you did, you would cease to exist. It's been a part of you ever since you began that evolution of life way back there, heaven only knows when, and it will always be with you. You can't escape that either because of the mere fact that immortality is a part of you, because you have sustained the idiom or the personal ego for countless thousands of years and because that, in itself, is an act of remanifestation of the Infinite Consciousness.

Now as far as the more primitive forms of life so far as man on the earth is concerned, whether it is the aborigine or what we call our modern civilized man in this country, he is still comparatively on a very low rung of the ladder in his scale of evolution. But what it all means is that when he becomes a man, he has sustained a certain set of thought patterns of polarity transferences from one life to another. Psychic shocks and various other malformations are quite naturally carried into this thing. That is the psychic body which is expressing outwardly in its physical form, and that is what causes him to continually reincarnate into a physical form. That is proof of that, in itself, because even primitive man as an aborigine has definite memories of previous lifetimes. He will either consciously memorize it or he will come back into succeeding lifetimes with certain definite and pertinent knowledge which helps him to sustain his life in that particular environmental circumstance. Whichever way we look, we have proof because even the youngster a year or so old that is born into the jungle can survive much more easily than the white man could, because that child is still very closely linked to his former life as a jungle inhabitant.

S - How do you feel about cannibals eating humans?

T - You must understand how we have a certain set of what we call affinities. Affinities merely mean that we have a given set of energy wave forms which are compatible to each other as a definite vortex of consciousness. Now it has a definite frequency and it becomes gregarious to the extent that it begins to form another relationship with a similar vortexal pattern. Through evolution of time, they collect into a matrix which forms a certain definite sphere of interrelationship which can form the id or the ego of the personal being. That contains all the necessary elements as far as the expressive content of these wave forms in the vortexal patterns is concerned, all of the necessary elements for this creature when he reincarnates into a physical life to not only have the necessary physical equipment as a body but also the instincts, as they have been called by psychology or by Darwin or various other scientists. An instinct means that they have recognized the fact that from the previous lifetimes that person has a definite psychic knowledge through the subconscious of doing some particular function, performing a certain function, a certain relationship.

S - What about dogs, horses, etc., then?

T - So far as their id or ego is concerned, it is still not formed completely, not in itself so that it maintains these definite characteristics of self from one life to another because it lacks a certain particular element.

S - You believe we emerged from them?

T - We emerged from these lower forms of animal life in this sense: that these various different evolutions from the lower scale are evolutions in which these various wave forms of energy as idea and form and consciousness of sustaining life is concerned, are forming vortexal patterns of energy which segregate or go together as a gregarious element from which it forms a certain psychic body. And as quickly as this becomes large enough in its own perspective or horizon to attain a definite libido or drive as a personality, in other words, to express its likes and its dislikes to the extent in which a human being does, it expresses a certain creative element. It expresses a great many things which are sometimes lacking in the lower animal forms or which are not quite as strongly personified.

There really is not any dividing line there. We do not wish to make the same mistake the anthropologists have made and say that there is a missing connecting link; there never has been a connecting link in this sense. He has dug out of the past certain primitive forms of man which are the Neanderthal man or the Java man or Pithecanthropus Erectus, or whatever there are which he thinks that, due to certain bone structures, could have given this person a certain status or level of life. And it is all very confusing, because if you take that as a common denominator you are going to become lost.

Actually, we have had so many countless thousands and millions of centuries of time in which man has existed in an infinite number of ways and in an infinite number of forms as far as the physical is concerned, because as far as cranial space is concerned the number of brain cells man has is no denominator of his intelligence, no more so than how many hairs he has on his body or what his tooth structure is, because if we study anthropology today, we find that in many ways the savage of the jungle is much more intuitively and much more spiritually minded than the white man or the Christian is. Many of our so-called primitive savages exhibit a much greater degree of creative instinct in making artifacts and things for him to live with or survive by than a white man could. The white man has evolved away from these instincts. But back in the jungles they were very clever about carving and weaving and doing various other different things, and even into the more recent civilizations, the women and men were much more creative in a general sense than they are now. Now everything is automation, and that in itself is one of the proofs of reincarnation that takes place on a spiritual side of life—the fourth dimension—because that is where evolution takes place anyway. We are only bringing it out here or externalizing it in a sense, or becoming conscious of it on the basis of polarity patterns. But factually, it all takes place on the inner anyway. Everything would have to resolve into spiritual or energy formations before we get anywhere with it at all.

Above all, if we quit trying to determine these aspects as personalities then we have made a big step. The creative forces of life are not in any sense of the word connected with a personality form or personality expression. When we stop praying, we cease to be pagans. We must supplant that with a much more tangible and realistic concept of the dynamics of life, not as they are expressed in the physical forms but how they are moving internally in a different number of dimensions.

S - These jungle people sometimes seem to have

prayers answered.

T - We will refer again to the two polarity patterns. It makes a much closer affinity to that at the present moment of consciousness, because it does this: they are energizing or ringing a certain set of energy formations which link them back through many past lives of consciousness where they prayed and prostrated themselves in the temples or before the priests, and various other different things which is a closer affinity to them and only because they do have that affinity. There is something else that has been entered into which most people are not conscious of and this is in the realm of psychokinetics.

Now most people do not know that the mind in a common term of reference is actually a generator; that is, when the subconscious is oscillating outwardly, we can generate a certain force. A mind reader can sense this and he can read this force and translate it into terms of thought. Now if we realize that when we are energizing the various centers of the psychic we are generating great forces either positively or negatively, according to how they are generated in reference to polarity patterns. That is psychokinetics. Dr. Ryan of Duke University has proven that the mind can produce energy, however, this psychokinetical energy actually comes from the psychic anatomy itself—the spiritual being—which is connected to other dimensions of consciousness!

S - Is he still active?

T - It seems to me I read something about him recently, that he is working with his wife in the university getting thousands of letters a month, and they are still sorting them out and still working on this ESP. Dr. Ryan has not gotten over the threshold of the unknown yet with it, but when he does, he will have made a great step in his own evolution, because he is still trying to confine it according to the slide rule and

116

according to the various other third dimensional equivalents, which is absolutely impossible. It is foolish and childish to do because all of these generative or generic forces of life come from other dimensions. These are only the externalizations of them, so we must face psychokinetics. A person is a transmitter and he is a receiver; he is always transmitting in a certain given set of frequency formations which is compatible to his own dimension of understanding. That is the reason I can tune into a person and go back into his past lives. I can do it whether they are present or whether they are ten thousand miles away from here. I do not have to have any connection with them other than the connection which they have expressed in some way—either with me or even through a friend. And that is the way these things work because they are very scientific principles.

Now let us take this thing as it is contained in any idea or form of consciousness so far as the Infinite is concerned in what some call God (or the Infinite). We can compare this to the wheels of a watch—cycles, large, small, all linked together—but they form a big pattern. Now this is what Einstein was trying to get— the Infinite complete in itself; each cycle is connected to the next through the principle called frequency relationship. It generates according to multiples of two and one half times its own frequency, a harmonic structure. If we vibrate a cello string which vibrates at one hundred cycles per second, it also regenerates harmonics up to the thousand cycles per second or down to nothing. Harmonics as multiples are part of frequency relationship as well as the basic cycle at whichever this idea is vibrating. Now we have an expanded space-time concept here. We have an infinite perspective. Now if we want to we can go a little farther along the line, and our next step is to take any given set of these cycular patterns and divide them, in a sense of the word, according to how they are compatible to one another in a certain relationship into a dimension. That is why the third dimension becomes an external appearance of all that goes on internally because it is now divided into time and space. Now you can begin to understand what Holmes and Bailes and the other metaphysical teachers do not know.

Now let us take this original topic, the third dimension here and the sine wave, and show what it means in terms of reference, for instance, what it means to you when it goes into the subconscious. We take this and call it the psychic body because we have formed a number of cycular patterns in that psychic body from many, many past lifetimes. If we draw a vortex, now we have three or four very active forces going on there as far as that is concerned and which are fourth dimensional, because it is also going out and it is coming in, and it is also coming up and down. Now a huge vortex comes from another dimension, containing an infinite number of these wave forms or structures as they concern the lines of forces which I have drawn as a circular path. Centripetal or inward forces are regenerating from positive to negative structures downwardly at all times, down to the point that comes out into a third dimension as the sun, or the earth or an atom, and which is again expressing a certain relationship of wave forms or emanations of energy out into this dimension.

The psychic body is composed of millions and millions of these different circular patterns of consciousness or idea in a cycle or a vortex, and there are literally millions of these vortexes, large and small, which are all formed of experiences of past lifetimes. Now you see what they do not understand about these things? But they are all contained as a definite pattern in this manner, as one or more of these little cycles and each of these little cycles beat. It has as a whole its own basic rate of frequency. In other words, it beats or oscillates, and when it does, it is also connected with other vortexes of the Infinite in these same patterns of relationship with the Infinite as this one is.

S - I thought everything would get larger.

T - Not necessarily. It would only get larger in this sense: that it transfers its consciousness through harmonic relationship to other particular dimensions.

S - What has polarity to do with the vortex? I do not get the vortex idea.

T - Because here the apex of the vortex would be the negative end, and the positive would be the coming-in forces as they are related to outside or different vortexal patterns to which it was related. They were transferring its consciousness to it through harmonic relationship.

S - For instance, in instances where we catch the sun's rays with the glass, is that a vortex?

T - No, that is not necessarily a vortex because you are only doing something in a third dimension, which means that you will always have a certain given set or lines of force which is this: all you are doing, as the sun is above and it is radiating these same basic sine waves, so when they come down to you and you have a glass, you have a given number of these wave forms which are built into the center and focus this way—or from outward to inward.

But in the fourth dimension, it is much more difficult to understand because we have hurdled the common denominator of our own intelligence, which is the comparative relationship value basis with all other third dimensional substances. Now to equate these things, I have used the word 'vortex' as only the closest approach to something which may not exist actually that way when you get to it; but as far as our mind is concerned, we have to visualize it that way because it is the closest approach we can get to these abstract equations.

S - Let me see if I have understood you. Does each one of these cycles make other vortexes or many vortexes?

T - That could make a vortex as they are linked or relinked to each other according to frequency relationship, and a vortex can contain an infinite number of these smaller vortexes or cycles. All these lines of force of the vortex are an infinite number of cycles, similar to putting a great many pearls on a string and then putting them on a circular path and each little pearl is an idea or consciousness or form of expression that you previously lived. And they are all revolving around each other because they each have a definite frequency relationship. They are spinning very rapidly; there is a common frequency relationship there. Now you are beginning to learn what these so-called teachers do not know. You have been on this path for many thousands of years trying to learn these concepts.

S - Oh, no, I have not; I am no old soul.

T - Oh, yes you have, otherwise you'd not be sitting here asking these questions. How many people would be able to do that?

S - I would think most anyone would be so interested.

T - Listen, I have had professors of the university that could no more get this science than they could fly. I have had one who was the head of the technical department of Douglas Aircraft who was taught out here at UCLA; his name escapes me at the moment, Dr. Louis took me out and introduced me to him in Santa Monica. I explained this thing to him for two hours and finally he said, "I give up; the man has got something but what it is, we do not know." That was in 1944, and since then we have exploded the atom bomb and I have been completely vindicated.

S - But where in relationship to a vortex does the

atom bomb come in; I would not know.

T - Well, any atom, if we take a very simple atom, we will take one positron or proton which is the nucleus, then we take one electron which forms the opposite polarity; one is negative and the other is positive. Now that is going to vibrate or oscillate around it; that is a common hydrogen atom. That merely means that there are only two definite lines of force in the vortex that supports that atom. From here, where the proton is, we go on up into another dimension; the atom is the apex of the cone because it is expressing from the inner that which is oscillating into it. And when they explode the atom bomb, they destroy the vortex; the power comes from the vortex. There is no power in the atom because the atom is the end result of the inner; it has been expressed into the third dimension then.

For instance, if we take a pail of water and throw a few chips in there and we start stirring it around with a spoon, the chips are going to fly around and around in a circle; aren't they? Some of the chips will go down into the center and others will go out to the rim of the bucket. That is exactly what an atom is, in a crude sense of the word, because all of the water that is in there is the vortex which makes the atom; the chips only make the positive and negative relationship to the lines of force of the vortex and which is internal in another dimension. That is what the scientist does not know.

Now when he explodes the atom or implodes it in the case of the hydrogen bomb, that atom collapses. It means he has collapsed the whole vortex internally into itself instead of blowing it apart, as in the case of the atomic bomb, but either way, he has liberated energy from another dimension. But the atomic explosion explodes the atom because they have a complex atom there, which they have stretched out. It contains over two hundred and thirty-five different electrons

121

and protons. They push it out so that it looks like a dumbbell. They change its shape, stretch it until it becomes very unstable; and when they explode it, it merely means that they have separated it right in the middle and one part goes one way and the other another way. The thing that held that together originally is one neutron which buzzed around and around that nucleus and held it together. That is what they think, but actually what they have done in stretching that is they have produced another stable condition with the vortex which supports that atom. This one electron that spins around merely means that that is an aid in helping to disintegrate the vortex by releasing it. It is all very simple when we understand it.

S - I don't quite understand the imploding.

T - If you drop an electric light globe on the hard cement, it implodes. If that television tube were to implode, it has the equivalent of about twenty-five or fifty pounds of dynamite; it would destroy the cabinet, the television set and it might, if you were in the vicinity, very easily injure you or even kill you. That is a simple condition of mechanics in the case of the hydrogen bomb; it is extended on into the atom. There we have molecular implosion, and in the hydrogen bomb we have atomic implosion. In the case, whichever it be, as far as the atom is concerned, implosion or explosion is also exploding the vortex which supported it. That is where the force comes from. So you see how far we go —and this is but the beginning.

An Informal Discussion

S - May I report that since I have ceased to pray for things I want—since I've stopped making conscious effort to persuade God to grant me favors, and have instead, begun to practice Unarius Principle—all things seem to be so much better with me in so many ways! I'm so much more at peace within!

T - This is putting the horse at the right end of the wagon where it belongs. You do not try to make God subjective to you through the will and dominion of your mind, which is taught by all so-called teachers of Truth and who, in a sense of the word, are always trying to tell God what to do instead of tuning themselves in and letting God "reward them openly" the way they should do. But they cannot know how to do this until they understand the very essences and nature of God—which is the sine wave, which is energy. Everything around you here is proof of that. There is no such thing as a solid substance; everything resolves itself into one or another tangible elements of energy—living, dynamic, moving energy which is related and interrelated to the Infinite Cosmogony. That is the absolute and we cannot divide that. We cannot subtract that in any way and say that: this is Satan and this is Jehovah, this is Beelzebub, this is Brahma, this is Shiva, this is Vishnu. That was all for the elementals, the little children who were playing in mud pies. They had to personify these things because that was the struggle within themselves in their own minds. They could not visualize that anything could live except in the external form of a human being just like themselves, in spite of the fact that they themselves, either

S – Denotes Student
T – Denotes Teacher

123

physically or mentally, or any other way were merely a conglomeration, a matrix of energy formation, all expressing the common idiom of its own particular structural energy content as it was superimposed in it by an energy wave form, an oscillation, an up-and-down motion, a forward movement, a positive relationship of an idea, positive or negative from one pole to another.

And that is why I say you are absolutely lost, you are still in the woods unless you understand these dynamics of life, the electronic principles as energy or electricity, whichever way you care to put it. It makes no difference to me but it has to be something which you bring into your own mind. We know we have traveled the path and we have been with these things for hundreds of thousands of years, and we know that no one gets anywhere with himself. He cannot cease to be a pagan and quit worshipping on the street corners—as Jesus warned them against doing—until he begins to get these structural concepts; and nowhere have we found it as yet. I would be very happy to find some others with this knowledge. I don't care to be out here on a limb all by myself, so to speak.

We are always conscious that whenever anyone touches this consciousness, this Channel which we have, that there are immediate and miraculous differences in their lives. Conditions are healed; cancer leaves; all kinds of incurable conditions are corrected; things which they have been stalemated with and locked in for maybe thousands of years disappear. The world changes to them.

Student - I do not see how these things could relate to physical disabilities.

Teacher - Well, we will go back to our original concept of the sine wave. Now we are oscillating here with what the psychologist refers to as the subconscious. He does not know that is part of the matrix of this subconscious of which I spoke before. Now the thing we have to assume in all cases is that any wave as it is superimposed in the psychic anatomy has a certain vibration. Now if that vibration is in harmonic unison with all other vibrations within the psychic, then it is constructive in a general sense. It means that it can go on and regenerate itself into whatever form of consciousness it was originally superimposed or with which it oscillated.

Well, now suppose that we come along here and suddenly someone sticks you with a big dagger. That oscillation that goes into that subconscious is immediately going to have a lot of jagged lines on it. The frequency is going to be upset. When it gets into the psychic, it is going to say to this vortex and all the energies within this vortex what it is; it is going to change all its relationships. It is going to form dark non-regenerative vortexes to the extent that now it is "out of tune" with all of the other particular energy formations in the psychic. And so in the sense of time as a reflex into future consciousness, your future life, it is going to reflect the same negative energy back into the consciousness which is the exterior surface, the physical, so it becomes a cancer. All of the cells in which it is supposed to regenerate or have a controlling influence over have now lost their directive sense.

S - How do you correct this?

T - By simply going back to the person and tuning him back to the time when it happened. For instance, as I would see, this particular person came along and stuck you with a dagger. The person already knows of this internally but they just have not had a way and a means of getting it out into their conscious mind. When they do that, they can immediately bring it out into conscious mind; and that does another thing, which Jesus called the Divine Intercessor—the Father Within which doeth all things. They immediately begin

125

oscillating upstairs here with the superconsciousness and when they do that, there is an inner power and a radiance which zips into this negative vortex which was formed by that dagger thrust and all of those energies are immediately changed or re-vibrated so that they are no longer negative in nature and so the person is then cured of his cancer.

Jesus, we know, healed many of them in his mission, but many people do not know that this healing had already taken place first in the spiritual world before they ever came to the earth. All they had to do was to come to the world and meet Jesus and do the thing which they had already done in the spiritual world and seen done to them. In other words, he served as a definite polarity. We have to resolve these things down so that every person has to express them out because he was a creature traveling through a time cycle—his reincarnation. He always has to come back here to this earth and because this is a negative polarity, he must always start from this end to regenerate those conditions so that they can become a definite part and structure of the psychic; but it has to be done on a polarity basis. They have to come back here and relive in consciousness, as it were, the exact identical situation which formerly superimposed that negative stance in them. They relive it consciously. That is the acknowledgment of what some people call sin and evil —repentance.

This is a conscious reliving or an acknowledgment that there is something very definitely wrong with them —that there is what people call sin or evil within them, and even though they may not be able to describe it at the moment, yet their subconscious is reflecting it outwardly to them, or that they are linked to it, because of their admission to it. They have established a continuity of frequency relationship there with it to the conscious mind. Therefore, when they say to Jesus, "I

have so and so or such and such a condition and I
need healing," Jesus says, "Believest thou this?" This
strengthens whatever purpose they already know inwardly within themselves as they have seen it in the
spiritual worlds when they were there just a few years
before. That starts this ringing motion. That means
that from the transmitter up on the hill to the television set, it will express outwardly onto the screen a
certain picture. They do the same thing because now
they have Jesus to centralize this form and motion
there with them so that they will link up as a superconsciousness; this flood of power comes in, changes
the negative vortexes and they are healed.

S - How do they change it or kick out the negation?

T - Well, you will need to go along in your analysis.
It would be impossible to give you all the answers here
in these few moments, and too, they are in the books
and lessons if you carry on in this seeking. You are
conscious of these things inwardly or you'd not be sitting here asking these questions as you are, but you
know these things exist. You are expressing to me the
same thing or way in which many of the people expressed to Jesus when they came to him for healing.
In your case, your coming to me means that you know
all of these things exist but you like to be told by someone else who also knows them, so that catalyzes or
polarizes what you already know internally. Now you
know that in common terms of reference we must go
back to the sine wave, and when you gain this energy
science, you will realize that all corrections must be
made from and on the inner dimensions and consciousness.

S - How would you explain, for instance, a falling
star or some other things that are not common or
would not come under the general law of natural harmony, etc.?

T - You are only looking again at the external appearance of a lot of physical appearances. Now if you could see all of these things clairvoyantly, you would not see the chaos and disorder that the astronomer sees through his telescope because you see you are actually on the inside of something and looking out, in a sense or degree. If you are sitting in the room here, you cannot see what the outside world is. You are only seeing a few appearances, and that is the same thing when you look through a telescope. You are only seeing just a few superficial things; you cannot possibly envision what the whole thing is.

Now let us get back to this original concept—going back to our sine wave here where we have a positive and a negative. All we are concerned with in any sense of the word is changing the rate of vibration of any wave form as it is contained in the vortex. That is all we're concerned with. When we change the vibrating rate of it, we have changed its intelligence and, in a sense, we have changed the whole thing in its entirety. So when a very strong positive polarity comes in, in direct proportion to a weaker negative one, we have changed its polarity and now it is living in a different expression. It is very simple but also, very scientific because we have taken religion out of the realm of the pseudo into the laboratories where it can be proven in the common denominators with which man is familiar. We are only going on into other dimensions with it.

This is the struggle—and nothing personal is intended—with most of the present metaphysical teachers who have reached a certain threshold of understanding but can go no further because they do not understand the mechanics as I have expressed them to you by starting with the sine wave, polarity patterns as they are expressed by the sine wave, and interdimensional relationships as energy patterns. They cannot possibly conceive what they are talking about until they too understand this Science. They know no more about these things than those whom they are trying to teach. All they are doing is reestablishing what the student in their class already knows exists as a symbolism but not as a reality, because it does not become a reality until the Truth student sees in the common terms of tangible realistic knowledge what he has learned in higher dimensions. And that, too, is part of his progressive evolution.

Prodigies such as were expressed in some of the musical geniuses (Mozart, Mendelssohn, many others) who wrote symphonies even in their childhood, came into the world with all of that even before they expressed it. They learned of these things in the higher Centers of Unarius, as we like to call it. The ancients called it Shamballa and which is a plane of relationship closest to the earth. The same is true with the scientist; the differences are as to how far we can go into the extension of mind when it has to be compromised with our own personal sense of values or the ego, as it is expressed toward our fellowman—pedestals in other words, or losing face as the Chinaman calls it. But anyone who goes out of his depth as far as the other person is concerned and starts postulating concepts and theories which the other person does not understand, he is exposing himself to an old Freudian concept which is very basic in common psychology, which means we always try to destroy that which we do not understand. It is one of the most primitive instincts that we have, instincts which we have carried over from the days when we were aborigines in the jungle.

Our procreative instinct too is one of the last remnants of our physical life on earth because procreation in spiritual planes is what the spiritualist calls materialization. We have it in the Venus book how they construct the actual spiritual bodies for people to come and live in, in that particular dimension of frequency transferences which are around them and which are compatible to them and how, too, they can go out of those worlds just as easily without this thing of laying aside the physical body. This merely means the dissolving of their energy body and traveling on into a higher dimension of consciousness, because again, we are reverting back unto our original concept of the superconsciousness which is our own structural form, our own counterpart of the Infinite. These things are all abstractions of the Infinite as they are personified through each individual existing in that timeless and spaceless dimension, or interdimensional relationships which are connected as polarities with the Infinite. And when you get to that, you have really gotten to somewhere! You will have gone maybe ten, twenty, thirty thousand years into the future as far as the level of life on the earth is concerned.

So many people talk about the New City of Jerusalem, the Second Coming, etc., and they have not the slightest realization of the meaning of what these things are; they are merely rehashing some of the old symbolisms of the pasts, these old things which the Ancients have not properly understood, what the Avatars, the Masters have given. The return of Christ merely means that the person is returning on this particular point in his cycular pattern of life to where he becomes conscious of the Father Within—the Christ self. It does not happen in any given world under any particular condition. It is an attainment in his own personal evolution. His own City of Jerusalem will be erected around him when he begins to live by corresponding advancement in his relationship to the Infinite. By the realization of the internal connection, he will naturally advance into dimensions with which he will be compatible. He will find that City of Jerusalem already built because it will be the externalization of all that he is and connected with internally. It is simple.

The idea that anyone can come from Heaven and touch you on the shoulder and say, "You believed in me and so you are saved," is another form of paganism; it is an escape mechanism. It was never taught by Jesus nor taught by any of the others. He taught you that your own intelligence in connection with your super-consciousness, when you have found the Father With-in, will save you. You will become immortal only when you realize that. That is where you could rise from the grave. When Jesus spoke or made references to Him-self, He was only speaking as I might speak, in mo-ments of transcendency for the sum and total of the Infinite. He did not speak in the personal idiom what-soever. He spoke of the relationship of that which every man attains with the Infinite. And that, too, has been compounded, subtracted and divided and become a personification.

And so you see the swamp, the miasma, the pit of clay that the so-called Christian has dug for himself. We have history, too, to bear out these things, because St. Jerome, the father of all liars and prevaricators of 400 A.D., came along and was actually banished in exile for changing the Bible around in such drastic ways; and later he was excommunicated, and as he stood before the pope he said, "Well if we do not do these things, the church will disappear; it cannot stand," and the pope knew he was right, and what had been written in the scriptures by St. Jerome, stayed! And we have 8000 versions of the Bible, and it has been translated and retranslated; and they were orig-inally parabolical, and legends and were handed down from father to son. And that is the thing in itself which has confounded many of the Bible students because as far as the book itself is concerned, we can go back to Spinoza who said that the Bible is a fabrication of lies and derelictions; it contains murder and prostitution and that there are many parts which are unfit to be read. And it is true—we heard Bible students speak on the radio and tell of the early periods of the administration of Moses that God slew so many people! That is not my idea of God.

The average Christian does not know when he reads the Bible that the God of Moses, Jehovah, is an old pagan god who was brought out of Babylonia by Abraham; he was old Beelzebub. He was erected in gold and bronze and stone many thousands and thousands of years before Abraham. They do not know that the Koran was written on the first five books of the Bible by Mohammed. They do not know that Buddhism is a direct counterpart of Christianity. The Christian does not know that his own religion—what he calls Christianity—is a mixture of the old Egyptian hermetic sciences and the Mithraism of the Mediterranean (as they existed before the time of Christ) which came out of Zoroastrianism 500 to 100 years B.C.—Mithras, the son, Ahuramazda, the father. And he had an immaculate conception, just as Jesus was born on the hillside and witnessed by shepherds, so the story goes. Osiris, father god of all Egypt; Isis, mother of earth, had an immaculate conception and bore Horus, the intercessor 2000 B.C. Horus stood before the throne of Osiris and interceded, and it is written on the temple walls in Egypt.

The Christian does not know that at Christmas time when he brings a fir tree into the house that he is doing just as the Druids did a thousand years B.C. He went out into the woods and offered up a maiden, a human sacrifice at the winter solstice, the 21st of December. The fir tree was the only living thing in that bleak wintry forest—and the virgin was the mate—the god who was to resurrect Spring for them, as they hung the body of the virgin upon the tree after she had been sacrificed for that purpose. And the Christian does not know that. I gave a lecture on that one time in a church and it aroused so much ill-feeling with the minister of that church that I had to leave, but it is common knowledge; it is in history.

S - Quite a well-known person in the metaphysical field once told me not long ago that it would make little sense for a person to return to earth after leaving, that would not be progress to come back. He felt man would go on.

T - Well, you see that person does not know the elements of dynamics. That is my, I will call it, personal quarrel with all of them, because they cannot get into these essentials. He should have known that he cannot polarize any kind of a thought or form of consciousness unless it is done in an infinite number of expressions. He will not only come back once to polarize an idea but he will return a number of times, a great number of times because he is coming into an infinite number of dimensions and into an infinite number of perspectives to carry the whole idea of polarization of consciousness into infinity. And anyone who makes any contrary assertions does not know the dynamic principles of life. And I can prove it—prove it all around you in a thousand different ways. I can take him into the laboratory and prove it.

S - If there are millions and billions of earths or worlds, why then would we have to return here to live again?

T - Simply because these are the conditions under which the original experience was incurred. This is the maya, the realm in which they first incurred, the opposite polarity of what has already been impounded in the abstract as the psychic self, the life cycle. The superconsciousness, the Christ self, contains all of these things, but it has to be known in an infinite number of ways because this then is God recreating himself as a personal being, so the personal being can become a Master or a Supermaster or an Archangel,

133

whichever you wish to call it. And so a definite polarity with the Infinite God or the Archangels is again expressing outwardly into infinity all of the things which it is infinitely and inwardly.

I do not care where you go or what you ask; we can give you very sensible, realistic and tangible answers.

S - I do not know where it comes from or where I get it; I have never studied what you talk about but I do understand and know what you say. It is all very familiar.

T - Yes, you have been on the path of Truth a long time and do know these things, and only need to polarize them in this dimension. Now I am going to bring something to your consciousness: if you saw a beautiful white tower out on the plains that rose a thousand feet into the air, it would look familiar to you (wouldn't it?)—a great white tower with a golden dome on the top?

S - Well, yes!

T - That was the tower or temple that stood on the plains in Lemuria 156,000 years ago. They had a counterpart of that in Atlantis too.

S - I always see cobblestones.

T - That is from your life in the Elizabethan time. You vibrate to that time. We could go back to Egypt with you. I knew you in the temple of Isis there—you were a priestess in that temple. You have an affinity for Egyptian culture, too. When you get to a parallax of cycles, what we call a conjunction of relationship with a number of cycles, we become vaguely conscious of these things.

Do you have a fear, for instance, if you heard a loud thump like an axe or guillotine, would that give you a sense of fear? If you saw a movie of say, Joan of Arc being burned at the stake, would that do something to you?

S - Oh, I could not stand it! I could never watch a

war picture with any violence in it. I would leave.

T - How about red uniforms?

S - No, I do not like them.

T - That goes back to the period of the Napoleonic wars, etc., about one hundred years ago, or the last part of the 1700's and into the 1800's. That is where the cobblestoned streets come in, the plumed hats, Empress Eugenie styles, red uniforms and all that. That is very close to you and that is where the greatest psychic memories come to you from that time. There is an affinity with France and with England. It seems like I am going across the water here with you in two different countries.

You have a little sensitivity on the soles of your feet?

S - Some.

T - That, too, is from burning, fire. You were burned at the stake here in one lifetime, back about 1400— one of the three million that suffered in the courts of inquisition at that time. Yes, it is always a wonderful thing to meet one of the friends from out of the past.

S - My daughter seems precocious and picks up music so readily!

T - So your daughter goes into Muse in her life in between lives and she lives all of these things. She is taught and teaches and comes back with her psychic or retentive memory of all of these different things, and whenever they are played against her in this dimension, they immediately ring—in the common terms of reference of energy translations—so that they are actually a part of her. That is because now she has a realization because they are a part of her. This is why she seems to grasp music or art so readily.

Many thousands of years ago, a great philosopher was asked by a group of friends how they, too, might acquire wisdom, and he answered them thus, "Know thyself". And again the great Master teacher said, "Seek ye first the Kingdom of Heaven which is within". So it might be said that through the ages of time it has always been that those who were most concerned with man and his destiny always arrived at the conclusion that the greatest of blessings which could befall him were not those which come with the acquisition of wealth or of power or of other things of this earth, but the peace of mind which comes to him who has sought and found that greatest of blessings from within himself.

Hysteresis Explained

S - It is understandable about the hysteresis of the energies from the sun to the earth in the daytime but it is not clear to me in regard to the nighttime energy activity. Would you explain further?

T - The earth, the atmosphere, etc., act as a reservoir; the earth holds the energies, so to speak, as a hot water bottle would for a short length of time. We are in a directly opposite position at nighttime to where the energy comes into the earth's atmosphere. For instance, if we take two coils of wire and have electricity going through one and the second one is pointed exactly the same as the first one, then we get a transference of energy going from one coil to the other without any connection whatsoever and you will have voltage in the second coil. At night we do not receive the same amount of transference through the magnetic lines of force. The energy as it comes from the sun is transformed into what we call light and heat through these magnetic lines of force. It is quite different when we get out into what they call space away from the earth. When they learn what the sun really is, then the sun's effects can be felt before it has been transformed into these other frequencies.

For instance, what happens when light strikes any object, such as a green leaf? There are actually several different colors that strike that leaf, and this can be proven with the prism, but we can see only one—yet basically, there are only three colors; the rest are transformed to what we term green, orange, etc., and are only combinations of the three. The prism will separate the rays of the sun into all of the colors of the rainbow. The molecules and atoms of the prism have only done what anything else around the earth does—it takes picture colors and reflects them so that you can see the particular frequencies as they come out on the other side of the prism.

When you are seeing anything, it means that you are seeing only a certain reflected portion; as in the green leaf, the certain number of the molecules and atoms which compose the leaf—chlorophyll especially—absorbs all the other colors and reflects back according to a certain amount of intensity and proportion of blue and yellow. It absorbs the red and reflects back a mixture of blue and yellow. You do not actually see green at all, but only the mixture because there is no green light coming from the sun. That which they believe to be color coming from the sun means that these energies have certain wave lengths and when these wave lengths come in junction with the magnetic lines of force around the earth and the ionized layers of gas and various other frequencies, they are transformed—they are changed in frequency and wave length.

This is the only way that it could be transported, you might say, around 93 millions of miles of space and it would be in that way; it does not pour in, in straight lines, but comes from another dimension which is quite close to the earth but yet not of it. It is formed in cycles which are regenerated from the chromosphere. The same situation exists as with the coil containing electricity in right angles to each other; there is no transduction. The same is true when you turn the earth away from the sun; then the conditions with the cycles which are transforming the energy there are not complete but only in part. In effect, you have turned the earth (as in nighttime) like you have turned the coil. It may seem a bit confusing and is apt to be so until it is thoroughly understood.

For instance, when you turn your face towards the sun, you get the greatest amount of light. This only means that through the purpose for which we are getting energy transformed from the sun from this other dimension is quite close to different actions which take place. It would be impossible for the energy to come from the sun through that 93 million miles to the surface of the earth as the scientist thinks it does. That would be utterly impossible according to physical laws. There are tremendous fields of force around the earth —the vast belts of gas which are highly ionized due to the electrical charges of the static fields of magnetic lines of force which extend not only from the earth itself but with the entire universe.

Under those conditions and due to the fact that heat, for instance, is not transferred through a vacuum; heat will not even penetrate vacuum, let alone carry it through 93 million miles. This was the idea with which Planck was wrestling (his Quantum theory). Einstein was on the right track—but the present-day scientist believes that we get heat and light from the sun; he still holds to the idea that the sun is hot. All that we are doing is using the base level of reference when we say that anything is made hot when energy passes through it, but it is only because it is a resistive element to the energy which went through it.

Actually, there is no such thing as heat and light. It only means that we have tried to catalogue these things in the spectra of wave-lengths which the scientist thinks exists. In your body, when you become warm to the (so-called) rays of the sun, this means only that, due to the transference, lines of force and hysteresis, the various atoms in your body are absorbing a certain amount of energy; it is not heat at all but is only being absorbed; and when it is being absorbed, it means that the little atoms and the electronic fields of force of which the atoms are so composed, changed their frequency to a certain extent. They begin radiating outwardly in a frequency spectra which they ordinarily do not do. That produces the sensation of heat.

We have learned through the thousands of years of

evolution to orient that feeling of heat. If it becomes too intense, there is a feeling of pain. And to prove how true that is, you can do the same thing in reverse by rubbing a piece of dry ice over the skin, which would have the same feeling as would a hot piece of iron. This is true simply because the oscillation in the force fields of the ice atoms is causing carbon dioxide to oxidize and is solidified, and being cold that way, the atoms of the carbon dioxide have dropped down to their normal rate of vibration until they are in an entirely different frequency. When they come in contact with the skin, they immediately absorb and take into themselves the bits of rays of magnetism that the atoms throw off. When they do so, the force fields of the atoms are again changed from their former relationship or oscillation, to the extent that they are destroyed and the skin tissue is burned. The same process is true if you were burned with a hot iron.

In the case of the hot iron, the atoms have absorbed energy to the point that they have been thrown off or out of their natural vibrating frequency and therefore destroyed; and you are burned on that area because a certain number of cells have been destroyed by the impact of that hot iron. The heat of the atoms has been thrown out of alignment with the cell structures and molecules of which they were formed.

We can prove that all these things are true by what the scientist today actually admits that he finds—that actually the "quanta" and the entire fourth-dimensional theory as posed by Einstein could not be possible if this were not so. Mass is an illusion in itself. That, in itself, is the biggest proof that we have had because it only exists because of certain relationships of one atom with another. An atom takes the place of what is termed the dynamics of free moving energy. In other words, atoms contain within themselves the energy and orbit of a certain quantum of energy which comes from other dimensions.

This also explains why it is there can be so many shades of green in the plants because some plants absorb more than others. Each thing has its own particular property of absorption and what it means is that the atoms are stimulated to a certain point, like the action; for instance, if you step upon a worm, the worm is stimulated by the impact of your foot, while an atom is always stimulated to some degree by an outside source of energy. When it is stimulated in a certain way, it regenerates or changes frequency to a point where it will radiate outwardly as that which we call color. It acts as a transducer, in other words.

The sun's rays as they fall upon an object are composed of what you might call red, green and yellow, although there really is no green even though you see green in the prism; but it is not that way, for we have definite basic spectra of energy rays which are transformed from the sun's spectral chromosphere into the various differences with which we are familiar on the earth. There is the transduction or changing just as in anything else. These things could not exist if it were not true; you could not see anything if there were not the transduction. Nothing would have color.

The scientist knows that the moment one of those cosmic particles comes in contact with any electromagnetic field of force, like the gravitational field around the earth, it changes. He knows that, so why would it not change when it comes in contact with any one of the other different bodies such as stars or suns? Why should he think he can bat it around like a pingpong ball? It isn't that way at all.

First, it must be realized that a particle of energy such as a cosmic ray is a form of consciousness. We must realize first that it is complete in itself; it contains at least twenty-seven different kinds of cosmic ray particles according to the charges. The scientist thinks when they come into the force fields around the earth, they bend either right or left, so he has this all doped out himself—which is very crude. Now, if he could only realize that (if he could just get upstairs mentally, so to speak) everything is transferred from the top down—not from the bottom up, like the scientist believes. The earth, our dimension, is one of the last places on the scale of Infinity on the way down (if you can imagine such a thing) where the form of consciousness expresses out into the third-dimensional form or equation.

Have you ever seen mud flying off a wheel while it was revolving? Now let us take a vortex and those forces that swirl around on the inside. There will be tiny particles of energy that will, through different positive and negative repulses and reactions within that vortex, separate themselves, as an entity of consciousness, and from that vortex become a cosmic particle of energy; and in so doing, it loses its relationship to the Infinite. When it loses its relationship to the Infinite, then it automatically becomes subjected to what the scientist calls time, so that here again is an entity trying to gain consciousness by traveling through the third dimension because it is actually a fourth-dimensional particle which is unrelated to the third dimension. But the scientist is merely seeing it in either one place or another in regard to Infinity. That which he calls the screen means only that he is interpreting the entity of energy in relation to any one particular given time.

S - Is this the same principle as is used over the telephone wire?

T - When you speak over the telephone wire, your voice does not travel in a wave over the wire from one end of the wire to the other; all that it does is connect the various syllables that are modulated in its own orthic constituents, in positive and negative reactances or as an already existing charge of force on that wire. The wire is previously charged up with about 30 volts of electricity in the different static fields. While the voice agitates one end of the static field, then vibrates in unison, the energy is transferred. It is not that the voice crawls along the wire, so to speak.

CHAPTER X

The Inescapable
Evolutionary Pathway

It should be realized, after reading the following texts, that the process of life is quite complex and, indeed, far more so than is presently known in any of the liturgy of our sciences. There is still much that will be added to this text, too, for we will include in the following only part of the mental functions more relative to what is called thinking. There must be further elucidation on other physical function more directly concerned with the automatic physical regenerative processes, the true meaning of metabolism, etc., in order to properly understand these texts and which requires certain specific kinds of knowledge; and in all cases, any individual reading these texts must understand energy, what it is and how it acts or moves, for energy is the very substance of the Infinite.

At this point, let us consider a great enigma. All present-day sciences, including materia medica, psychology, etc., have not as yet constructed a suitable hypothesis which would give them the proper knowledge of the function of the human being as he is so integrated with the Infinite. Psychology recognizes brain waves or electric impulses, yet it does not know where they come from, for there is nothing in the brain cells which could even faintly suggest the brain as the originating0source.

Materia medica, too, is in the same enigmatical position. They know of the various organs and their function and they know a lot about the physical anatomy, but like the psychologist, they do not know the cause or reason for their existence or function.

The more classical scientist is also confronted with

this same enigma. On all sides he is confronted with this inevitable conclusion that he knows little or nothing about life, and the various dimensional divisions of his science always lead to the same cul-de-sac. And sufficient to say, this great enigma will persist until all sciences include the basic and relative factors and their incumbent knowledge of the Infinite Universe. In other words, these various sciences are much in the same position as many people who drive cars and while they possess sufficient knowledge to start, steer, and stop this vehicle, they are nowise acquainted with the mechanical function. All knowledge, therefore, of their car must be contained in what is called performance data and surface appearances. How similar this is in any situation wherein a psychiatrist is involved in his daily practice. The person lying on the couch is giving performance data, however, the psychiatrist is much like the chap who has a breakdown on the road with his car. He knows something is wrong but the inside of the hood is just a big jumble of meaningless parts, wires, pipes, etc.

If you were to ask any psychologist or psychiatrist to define the subconscious, he would be quite likely to say that it was an impenetrable wilderness or a mysterious jungle. In any case, however, he could not define it in such a way that it would assume its true proportion and function as the mechanical agent in the life process. The mechanic in the garage can unbolt or take apart an automobile and he can describe all parts and their function; he can also put it back together again so that it will function properly. The psychiatrist, not knowing what the subconscious is, can do nothing to correct any breakdowns contained in this subconscious which are causing the emotional aberration. He can therefore only give the condition a fancy name, prescribe a tranquilizer, charge the patient a fancy fee and send him on his way.

How different is medical and psychiatric practice in other worlds where mankind has learned what the psychic anatomy is; and with this knowledge they have been able to construct suitable electronic devices which can interject certain energy frequencies into the sub-conscious and cancel out these various malformed malignancies. The process of analysis and treatment requiring but a few moments time, the patient leaves the clinic well and happy. The same process is used to correct not only mental aberrations and malfunctions, but also to correct any and all physical conditions.

This list of physical conditions would include all of the so-called incurable diseases of mankind. Moreover, the cures are permanent or in some isolated cases, until any such future time when the patient may incur another psychic shock which would re-inflict the same mental or physical condition and necessitate a new therapeutic application. Now, the full and staggering import of this great enigma is apparent. Millions of people have and are trustingly placing themselves into the hands of practitioners who do not know the true cause of their conditions.

Directly or indirectly also, various other scientific dispensations are affecting the lives and the evolutionary patterns of hundreds of millions of people who inhabit the earth. This they are doing like the practitioners, without knowledge of the great and unseen invisible cosmogony and in which place—and this place only—can be found the answers to life, its purpose and, by far, the greatest portion of its function. Life as it concerns the origin and evolution is a part of every living thing on the face of the globe. How ridiculously insufficient then do all the superficial elemental, third-dimensional transpositions of life appear; and even more ridiculous, asinine and enigmatic when any science presupposes control, cure and function over all human formations of life—and especially in the specific areas in which can be found various types of mental and physical aberrations—and doing this strictly from such superficial surface appearances.

Constructing basic analytical techniques and subsequent therapies cannot be done from the third-dimensional appearance or substance of such appearances, for as the originating source of such surface appearance and substances are not third-dimensional in nature, it must therefore be thoroughly understood and constituted that corrective action can take place only in adjacent dimensions which are the originating source of all form and substance in this third dimension.

It must also be thoroughly understood that any surface malfunction can only exist as a direct appearance or image of this same malfunction in these various adjacent dimensions. Any human being therefore reacts and forms various reactive life processes in the surface life only as a direct result of the interplay of the formative energy substances which exist in such specific areas as shall be described as the psychic anatomy and its relationship to the source of all things, the Infinite.

It can truly be said that in the creation of man, the Infinite, in Its infinite intelligence, placed within man all the necessary characteristics and instincts which were necessary for his life upon this planet. Two of the strongest and perhaps the most dominant of the instincts are sex and the will to survive. It is in the normal relationship and the expression of these instincts which help to create for man these necessary social structures and in the growth of these structures, has created the great civilizations of the past, as well as our own present civilization. Therefore, it can be said that these two instincts and their normal expression and relationship become two of the strongest supporting members in the underlying structure of man's development. It would be hard, indeed, to separate these two instincts, nor would it be well to do so, for working hand-in-glove, as it were, they blend strength and character to each other. It is a godlike thing for man to so desire to re-create himself and in the love and the expression of that love to his own creation, expressing therein the will to live, not only for himself but for his loved ones; and so he brings up and constantly re-creates and regenerates life about him.

It can also be said that in the perversion of either of these two basic instincts, or both of them simultaneously, have been written some of the bloodiest pages of the histories of the world. They have created for man his Genghis Khans and his Hitlers. They have, in the perverted sense, caused man to become a miser or to gather about himself the things of the world, thinking that in these things was his sense of security; or it has made him a beast and one of carnal lust and passions that sought to possess, to dominate or to destroy, not only in the physical sense but in the material sense as well. And so it is well to remember that the usage and understanding of these two dominant instinctive factors in man's life are very necessary for his well-being and his spiritual growth. It is well to consider that in the understanding of these basic reactionary instincts within man that it is in their being a part of the evolution and the development of past civilizations that they have also become a vital and integral part of our own and present-day civilization.

Out of the welter and the holocaust of the last great world war was born a new fear, a fear which was not only compounded by the great multiplicity of conditions already surrounding man in this civilization, but with the coming of the fissionable and the nuclear weapons of this age and of this time was also ushered in, the new age of fear. Man knew not the coming of the hour when death and destruction and desolation could destroy all of the great cities of the world. And so it became not necessarily a question of dog-eat-dog but which dog was to eat the other one first; and so man progressed along this pathway, this mad race toward the precipice of a seeming oblivion.

In the complexities of everyday life and of the fears that were born of this time and of this age, man has become distorted and warped in his own mental images and even to those who were strong and would have, in a normal sense, walked the path of life in a well-adjusted fashion were now also subject to these vast and varying vicissitudes and fears. The modern methods of communication and of transportation had, in a literal sense, shrunk the earth to a very small size indeed. And so man began the quest, an ever-increasing and ever-enlarging quest for a panacea, something which could waylay or at least alleviate to some degree the terrible effects of this vast machination of this electronic age.

From the pulpits and from the temples came the purveyors of spiritual wisdom who began to deal with the more common and basic concepts of man's mind. From the fields of medicine and from science came others who began experimenting and began to try to understand what man really and basically was. And so he came to the time and the place when all things, even of the form and the substance about him, began to assume a new and a definite form. Man learned that all the material things about him were not necessarily solid but composed, as they are, of vast and intricate networks of tiny atoms; atoms, in turn, being the composite forms of the electronic energy and in perusing these various fields of knowledge, he developed a new insight into the character and the nature of the mentality of man. He found that man was not necessarily of one mind but found also in some strange way, that he retained within himself the basic form of all the things that had happened to him, even down to the first days of his life on this earth. This knowledge was called psychosomatic medicine and was a direct development of the science known as psychiatry.

It was around in the early nineteen hundreds that one of the more modern delvers into the truth of man's nature, a man named Sigmund Freud developed to a partial sense, and at least to one facet of this inner nature of man as to his relative position in his outward thought consciousness, calling this, as he did, the subconscious mind. It was his conclusions and general hypothesis of his years of research that he based man's most primal and motivating instinct as being that of sex.

There have been others in this same field who have followed later, who have enlarged and who have added much to this partially complete concept. We have had those who have attempted in some small or large way to collaborate the knowledge of the spiritual side of the science of psychiatry. And so it has been throughout the years and with the intensities of these times that the new and the foremost scientists in these fields have begun to expand into the relative position of our knowledge in the field of psychosomatic medicine; and yet it has not been within the time or place of any presently living man who has given an absolute and a complete picture of the science of psychiatry and psychosomatic medicine.

If we are to assume our rightful position and to gain an intelligent insight into the nature of man, we must first discard and scrap all our previous preconceived notions about the material planes of consciousness, go back, as it were, and come out again from the spiritual or the fourth-dimensional. We must begin to conclude in our hypothesis that man is not a creature of spontaneous regeneration; neither is he one of happenstance which came along according to certain or-

150

dinary physical laws. Man is, in himself, of a spiritual nature, a creature who follows certain preordained pathways or cycles, as they are sometimes called, and that it can be assumed that man is largely responsible for the creation of these cycles. We must also begin to understand that as far as man and his mind are concerned and what is called the subconscious, that these factors are also purely products of an electronic nature and that they are manifest, not from this side of life but from that other fourth-dimensional side. In other words, we have now taken the horse from the rear of the carriage and placed him in the front where he belongs.

In our further diagnosis or perusal, we must also begin to understand the nature of the forces or the energies about us from this fourth dimension. The form of electricity as it is commonly called in the third dimension is only an outward expression or force which is being reflected into this realm and this dimension from another plane. We can also assume that this energy or electronic force, as it is sometimes called, and its properties of being reflected into the third dimension, naturally assumes and retains some of the intelligence from which it was created, forming a conclusion of our understanding of energies as they are in the fourth dimension. These are of the intelligence and wisdom of the Infinite and are a part thereof.

In the language of the modern electronic engineer we can assume, as we do in the construction and the engineering of such electronic devices as the television set, that here we have placed electricity in various positions and in various wave forms as they are called. The wave form of an alternating current of electricity as it pulsates through the filament of the light globe does so at the rate of sixty times per second, or sixty cycles. This is, in itself, a basic sine wave frequency. It is simply an up-and-down "S" movement of the energy

151

through the filament. These waves or S's are spaced in the element of time to the number of sixty per second. In the fourth dimension, energy assumes a different form inasmuch as we now do not have the conflicting factor of time. Therefore, without time energy assumes as it does, and must manifest itself at all times in a circular or cyclical pattern. The size or the diameter of the cycle is in itself, compared to the time frequency of the third dimension; therefore, in the fourth dimension we have eliminated the time faction. Now we begin to see how it is possible for man to continually regenerate into his life pattern of the present moment, things which have happened in the past in his early infancy or boyhood or girlhood days. Inasmuch as these happenings were essentially and basically creations of the mind, or that they were lived in the mind and as the mind is necessarily a by-product of the fourth dimension therefore, these happenings or instances in the child's life became engraved in a cyclic fashion into the fourth dimension which was integrally or harmonically linked with the life cycle of the individual.

Now another factor enters into the picture. We can begin to see that if these tiny cycles or happenings can live as wave forms in a cyclic pattern and in that wave form portray their particular intelligence or their particular picture of the story as it happened, therefore, we now can begin to understand and see how entirely possible it is that happenings even beyond the birth of the child could also be retained in the psychic body of the child. We must here also discard another very vague and traditional fallacy inasmuch as man is not of this present time or of this present world and as an individual thereof, strictly a creature of this other time and place only.

There are countless thousands of the multitudes of the earth today who are not only living this life but have lived and have the conscious or subconscious memory of having lived at least three or four or many lives before; and through their conscious mind they are unconsciously reenacting many scenes and many happenings into their daily lives which were psychic memories of those past lives. Now, if the present-day psychiatrist knew and understood this truth, and was sufficiently clairvoyant in his understanding of this truth to pierce beyond the veil—as it is sometimes erroneously called the veil of mortal life—and look into the past lives of the individuals, he would begin to see the many and multiple ramifications of what psychosomatic medicine really was; he would begin to understand that any particular psychic memory of the child could induce some neurotic thought pattern. As an adult, a neurosis was not necessarily something that was incurred of the time and place of the present life as a child but that he could, through the process of the psychic memory, have actually relived in a psychic way some great and perhaps catastrophic happening of some past life. If a man had been burned at the stake in the Spanish Inquisition and he retained this psychic memory in the so-called subconscious mind, he could reflect all through his life the fear of fire and have, as it is called, pyrophobia. He could also at some time in his life manifest in some way an actual happening of that burning at the stake and almost in a mental sense, be consumed with the flame of that memory on this earth and at this time. There is a new and a vast field of research if we have begun to understand and to peer beyond this mortal life; every patient will now assume a different problem, inasmuch as the proportions of his problems or his neurosis at this present day are now not necessarily by-products of a childish age. Once we have begun to master and to understand this new psychosomatic understanding, we can also begin to develop new techniques, if they can so be called, for relieving and curing the patient of these ills.

As a person is born into this world, he is, in a sense, surrounded with what might be called spiritual forces who are working with the individual in the direct terms of his harmonic relationship with the spiritual plane from whence he was born. It is sometimes the instinctive reactions of the person in this world which means his life or death. In the last and final moment, he does not act of himself but purely from the spiritual plane of consciousness and in that action, takes unto himself the intelligence of those who are working in his harmonic relationship. So by this same analysis, we can also assume that these spiritual forces can also work in a direct proportion to which they are understood and to which they can be cooperated with in a direct spiritual therapy or a spiritual healing and relieving of these negative vortexes or wave forms which reside in the person's psychic body. We are assuming, if we may, as it will be explained, that the person's life cycle as it was regenerated from the conscious will and dominion of the Infinite, that it manifests in its own way as the person to whom it is—in other words, the Infinite personalized. In going through the various phases of life in what is called the regeneration of life, or reincarnation into different times and different ages, that in this spiritual progression is placed there, in this life cycle, the various wave forms; these wave forms existing in a cycular pattern within this life cycle are impinged and become a part of this life cycle through the linkage of harmonic relationship. Therefore, in our analysis of spiritual therapy, or the correction or the elimination of such various great negations, as they could be called, in the person's life from previous lives, these can be done in something of a scientific fashion. However, it may not be understood in the nomenclature of the present-day scientist.

We must begin to enlarge again our concepts of the mind. It is the dominion of the mind and the expression of Infinite Consciousness through the mind that it can be used in a manner something which might be likened to the searchlight, that it can be projected down into the body for healing purposes, or to someone else, or even to worldly desires or worldly creations. This particular concept is called psychokinetics. It is not by any means a new concept; it has been used and explained by the Essenic Brotherhoods and Spiritual Brotherhoods throughout the ages. It has been used in this modern day world and understood to some extent by many people who have delved beyond the realm of this reactionary world, in the psychokinetics of which the psychiatrist would have some knowledge; and he would be working in the channels of love and understanding and in the cooperation of spiritual forces—forces of not only the patient but of himself. These combined forces would be the necessary and contributing factors toward the correcting or rectifying of such negative cycles which had been impinged upon the life cycle of the patient.

The problem of this civilization and at this time is one of grave concern to many of the foremost thinkers and leaders of this country today. At least fifty percent of the hospital beds of today are filled with people who have very strong mental problems. It is generally conceded by medical and psychiatric authorities in the world today that at least ninety percent of all human ailments, chronic or otherwise, from cancer on down as they run the gamut, are purely by-products of wrong thinking, wrong thought patterns and, by the same token, the wrong or negative cycles of electronic wave forms existing in the life cycle of the patient, and not necessarily of this life but of any one or all of his numerous previous lives.

So, therefore, in our final analysis of this new understanding of the psychosomatic medicine as it must come out of the new age of tomorrow, let it be said, we must begin to develop those who are naturally clair-voyant or mediumistic. Let us wash away the old common and superstitious thoughts of witchcraft and necromancy and of spiritism and many of the various practices of the past years. They were and still are, as they exist today, remnants of some retro or progressive cycle, so that as we develop these new age children, bring them up with these new concepts and these new ideas and through teaching them to use the power of the mind, not necessarily of the problems and the things that are of this material world but that we must intelligently assume that the mind is the reflection of the Infinite Consciousness, or the Superconsciousness, and that it can therefore live and express itself through the individual from many other planes and many other dimensions.

When we have separated ourselves from the old and fallacious fears and superstitions which came through the channels of spiritism and of witchcraft and wizardry of the past, we will begin to build a new and a scientific realm of understanding; we will find that there is a panacea for all man's ills. In the clairvoyant diagnosis of a patient, not only of this time and of this day but also of another time and another day, we will begin to assume an intelligent diagnosis and realize the therapies or cures will reside in the mental or spiritual realms.

There is no doubt that many of the most malicious killers of this day and age are by-products not necessarily of this lifetime, nor of the condition in which a person has incurred or lived of this time, but they can be the actual psychic reliving of a similar condition of hundreds or even thousands of years ago; for instance, heart condition. A man can die of heart disease and yet actually have nothing wrong with his heart. Cancer is merely the loss of intelligence in the re-creative values of the atoms as they live or compound a cell within the body. This directional or creative force is the outward expression of the Infinite Intelligence into that atom. When the linkage or the balance of the coordinative factors which enter into man's linkage with this vital life force of Infinite Consciousness comes into inharmonic conclusion or has been partially stifled, or there has been introduced spurious harmonics or frequencies, we can see that a person can very quickly incur cancer.

Time is only an element of understanding. We are re-creating in our bodies something like one and one-half million new cells every minute of our lives. Each cell has its own wisdom, its own function to perform, its own intelligence. This intelligence is indirectly the outward expression of Infinite Intelligence through the atom. The linkage of this system and the predominating factor therein is the psychic body.

Man's body in the physical realm is only the outward reflection of this psychic body. This psychic body has been built and rebuilt and regenerated through countless cycles of the individual's life. It is composed predominantly of energies or wave forms which are not of this plane or of this dimension, nor of this realm of understanding. They are the composites and combinations of all the forces of all the happenings, of all the things of which the person is within, in his life cycle.

When we begin to understand the vital and the integral links of the various factors entering into the outward expression to the material body of this man upon this planet, then it becomes a natural consequence that we shall also develop the way and the means to cure or to heal the patient from any of these negative thought forms or wave forms which are impinged in this psychic body and, in consequence, heal the physical body.

We cannot necessarily say that this has not been done, and that for the purpose only will the names be

157

omitted. One man, in particular, worked for a number of years, a man from Virginia; he worked with doctors all over the country, and with the patients directly while he was in a clairvoyant fashion; and in a cataleptic or a sleep state, diagnosed and suggested cures for the patient's ills, some of which were not of this time but which started hundreds and even thousands of years ago.

Many of the ancient civilizations of the world and at least one or two which are of common knowledge to this day, had similar psychosomatic therapies, and people of that time and that age were tremendously blessed and healthy. In fact, it is our concept of the Garden of Eden and in the development of the spiritual and of the esoterical values of man's nature which brought about a civilization which knew no want, no hunger, no disease. There were no jails, no prisons, no police systems. Everyone was happy and everyone worked creatively. There were about seventy-six million people in this civilization at one time and the basic concept and understanding of man's spiritual natures, as it has been explained, was largely responsible for these Utopian conditions.

Therefore, in the coming years, if we must begin to bring into man's life a new age, an age of happiness, if we are going to lay aside the destructiveness of man's natures, if we are going to better understand man and his evolution, if we are going to believe man is a spiritual embodiment of the great creative force we call God, let us begin to rightly assume and to understand and to place man in his rightful position. Let us begin to bridge the gap in our therapies. Let us begin to empty our asylums and our prisons; let us not treat the effect but let us treat the causes. Let us go back into the time and the beginning of man's lives on this earth in meeting these conditions. Let us go to the source, the starting point of all of the things of which man is, and that he becomes, or does not become a victim of his own circumstance.

In this coming thousand years or so, will be what is sometimes called the Aquarian Age, the symbology of which God rules the earth through the spiritual interpretations which come from within man himself. It is within the dominion of man's consciousness in this present day and age to begin to better understand man and to develop his understanding; and if he does not do so, the great preponderance of materialism which is around him will destroy him. The sundry and tremendously vast and expanded material universe of this scientific age will be, as the common story of the Frankenstein monster, one which will bring oblivion down about his head.

It is indeed a strange paradox that the modern psychiatrist has ignored two of the most important and basic factors in the science of psychosomatic medicine. These are, namely, factors of reincarnation and obsessions. In the previous discussion, the idea of reincarnation was, to some extent, explained and in a further chapter, a continuance of this explanation will be further emphasized.

The second dominant factor that should be included in our present-day psychiatry is obsession. This is, in itself, a rather self-explanatory word. In order to understand what obsession is, we will start first with the more basic or elemental understanding. We have all had at different times in our lives what are commonly termed hunches. These hunches have been supposed erroneously to come from the subconscious mind or through some vague and unexplained source. Actually, they were momentary contacts with the superconscious mind and through the law of harmonic relationship, existing in the thought consciousness of any one or more or many of the entities which have passed on into other planes or dimensions of consciousness.

Everyone walking upon the face of the earth today has been, is, and will be, continuously under a partial or a complete dominion of such forces. In the highest sense of the word, obsession means that the greatest and the most inspirational works of mankind and to all those who have lived, who have given to the benefit and welfare and posterity of mankind have so been influenced by these more highly constructive spiritual forces or intelligences. Joan of Arc is a typical example of this and one in which we are all familiar with this story; likewise, with the great scientists, doctors, poets or authors. In fact, any one or a thousand, or a hundred thousand constructively-minded people who have so given, are working from such planes of consciousness.

In the more generally accepted sense of the word obsession, or in the more lowly or destructive sense, we can say that obsession also gives rise to some of the most destructive potentialities of mankind. The thief, the murderer, the sexual pervert, the great dictators and even some of the great emperors who have lived in the past have, in a sense of the word, lived in a partial or complete expression in the dominion of the realm of consciousness of such destructive forces.

We are reading daily in our newspapers, and other ways of communication, of people who indulge momentarily in some heinous crime. They become murderers or such lustful personages as to do great crime unto themselves and to their fellow man. We see and read in some instances of some persons, where the person will, what we call "black out" and when regaining complete consciousness see the body of the one just killed before him, or the results of the crime in whatever he had just perpetrated. It was, in a sense, a fit of anger or jealousy, or some great emotional stress which caused him momentarily to bounce out of the contact and control of his physical body and in that moment of loss of control, a murderous or criminal entity entered in to use the body for the use of the crime.

If we can imagine a man who was executed for some crime and was projected over in the spiritual worlds or the astral worlds, as they are more generally called, he will be, in that state of consciousness, tremendously neurotic, frustrated and revengeful. He will, in that state, lack the common condiments or essentials which some people find in going into that state of life. He is quite apt to walk up and down in a very darkened and blackened condition of mind, seeking out a means for his revenge and his lust.

If a person on this earth plane—through a neurosis or some great negation—will, in that negation and in the expression of that negation, open the doorway to such an entity through the laws of harmonic relationship (the thought consciousness) as he is attuned into either the lower realms of vibration or of the higher realms of spiritual vibration, he will likewise contact the various entities which reside therein in that state of consciousness. Therefore, a person who indulges in a fit of anger unconsciously opens the doorway to some entity who is prowling about in this darkened world; and in countless instances, the doorway has been opened and entered into.

It can also be said in general practice that everyone in this highly complex and diversified world has a neurosis or a psychosis—or they may have a number of neuroses. The word neurosis merely means, in a general sense, an accumulation of unadjusted conditions or things which have temporarily deflated the ego consciousness of the individual. In the more advanced states, and which state comes from previous lives or previous cycles of lives upon this or other worlds, the individual, in reflecting in these neuroses or negations,

161

has intensified or increased many times his chances for obsession.

What the psychiatrist of today has termed a paranoia or a paranoid condition is a more advanced state of neurosis. The term schizophrenia is applied to a person who has a dual or split personality. It is quite obvious in this case that the person does not have a dual or a split personality but merely comes, at different times in the day or night, under the complete control of the obsessing entity.

The problem of schizophrenia is further complicated by other factors which, when they are entered into, make a rather compound picture. The schizo may be living not only a part or a facet of some previous life of the obsessing entity, he may also be reliving some part of a previous life of his own. In the advanced stages of schizophrenia, a person may be said to be completely insane or as it is sometimes called, dementia praecox. (The word "dementia" is derived from the word "demon".)

The problem of therapy or cure which may enter into these various facets and types of mental cures of mental disorders and aberrations would be, in a large sense, dependent upon the psychotherapist, upon the spiritual forces and upon the nature of his spiritual understanding and the working therewith. Other factors entering in also may be the direct relationship of such spiritual forces with the patient himself or with the spiritual forces from the loved ones around him.

It might be well to say, as it has been pointed out, that it is a paradox indeed that the modern-day therapist knows little or nothing of these two very important elements. It is doubly strange and paradoxical when one considers the vast and preponderant amount of information available which deals very specifically with these two different facets.

The mission of Jesus of Nazareth upon this earth,

while proving the continuity of life, is also one in which the Master worked continuously with and taught the relieving and freeing people of obsessions. This is called exorcism, meaning the casting out of the evil spirits or demons. A good example of this type of therapy is included in the New Testament inasmuch as the Master Jesus approached the insane man and commanded the demons to leave, whereupon they did so and entered into a herd of swine and the swine became demented, ran down the hill and cast themselves into the sea. Exorcism was also known and practiced in Egypt thousands of years before the time of Jesus.

There are records of cases and of the history of such understanding and knowledge in China, in India, Tibet and in Greece, sometimes thousands of years before Jesus' time. We also know that in the more ancient civilizations of Atlantis and Lemuria, exorcism and the understanding of man's nature was more thoroughly understood than it is of this day and time.

If we look about us and see the overflowing and overcrowded conditions of the hospitals and in the asylums where these mentally deranged persons are incarcerated, living out their remaining years in agony and the misery of the mental phobias, it is indeed high time for a different type of spiritual therapy or psychotherapy and it must come quickly into the new age.

The modern-day psychotherapist is comparatively ignorant as to the proper nature or the procedures of such cures. There is much more pertinent knowledge and practice in some of the churches of this day and age. It is well-known that the priesthood in one or two of these churches can exorcise through the powers of his church, if the occasion arises, such dominion and will as to overcome and throw out certain evil forces or entities, either from a dwelling house or from a person.

The witch doctor in the jungle or the medicine man in his tepee, in going through his rituals and various dances, incantations or manipulations is practicing a crude form of exorcism. It was, of course, the Master Jesus who taught the supreme principles of the dominion of spiritual consciousness, and with the working of the highly-organized Spiritual Forces in rectifying conditions in the psychic body which were incurred during the many lifetimes of a person upon the earth.

Previously we have frequently used the term "fourth dimension". Now, in case you are puzzled as to just what the fourth dimension is, an allegorical situation or creation can be very quickly conceived and set up. If we take a long piece of straight wire and lay it upon the table and strike one end of it with a sharp blow, the vibration of energy will travel along the wire and can be detected or measured at the other end. This is, in a sense, what is called the third dimension because the wire has a beginning and has an end. It has a starting place where the energy has entered in and it has an end from where the energy passes. Now if we take this same wire and bend it into a circle and weld both the ends together, then by striking this circular piece of wire at any given point, the vibrations will exist continuously over the entire circular piece of wire instantaneously. Now the wire has no beginning and it has no end because we have eliminated, in a sense, the time element, and which is the fourth-dimensional equation.

So therefore, it can be said that in the fourth dimension there is no time because all energy (and in the expression of this energy) assumes such cyclular forms. Now instead of having a solid piece of wire, we can visualize that it is something like a coil of closely coiled wire which will resemble to some extent a wave form. If we further visualize that there can be a number or a multiplicity of such coils within and without the original coils, each one coiled in a particular fashion so that it is unlike the others, this will, in a rough

164

way, convey something of the mystery of the fourth dimension and the individual life cycle.

You may also wonder as to how this life cycle started for any particular individual in the beginning. If we are to assume that man has gone through any number of lifetimes or previous reincarnations in this or other worlds, then there must have been some starting place. Contrary to man's general belief, man did not begin his journey through eternity by being born into this material world or in any material world but rather, was "born" in another realm or in another dimension. For the sake of clarity and to avoid confusion, we will confine our remarks to the third and fourth dimensions. It has been said that man is the ultimate and the most intelligent or divine of God's creations; and this, in a large sense, is quite true but in order to understand man and God better, let us destroy another popular fallacy of God. He is not, in any sense, a white-robed Santa Claus who sits on a throne in some far-off place with the book of life in one hand and a quill in the other. God can be said to be all-existing, all-pervading and an all-permeating intelligence and that God resides, lives or expresses Himself in an infinite way through many, many dimensions.

Jesus spoke of it thusly, "In my Father's house there are many mansions" (and if it were not so, I would not have told you). Mansions, of course, are the relative planes or the dimensions of existence. Therefore, in the creation of man it can be said that God must, as He is of infinite nature and intelligence, express Himself in an infinite number of ways. Thus, then, in man He begins to assume a definite, a tangible or a personal expression.

We will say that God is creating Himself as an individual in an infinite number of ways by the creation of each human being, as it is quite necessary, if we think a moment, in this infinite nature of God, that God must

165

also combine all of the elements of Infinity into the nature of the personal expression of the human being. Therefore comes the necessity for the learning or the living or for the realization into all realms and realizations of consciousness as an individual.

God begins the creation of man something like this: In God's Infinite Mind, man's soul begins as a basic fundamental life cycle. This is, in itself, a cycle which will remain throughout eternity with the individual. Within this cycle are placed an infinite number of tiny or larger wave forms. These wave forms are, in themselves, frequencies or intensities which can convey some definite form or meaning and as they are unchanged through time or eternity, will continually reflect or convey in their proper sense of contact, the intelligence which was placed within them. Now we have begun to understand that here God has placed in this life cycle all of His infinite intelligence, all of the things and nature of which God is, but it still is in a form which is not personalized, nor in this form can it be expressed in a personal fashion upon a lower plane of consciousness. So therefore, this Intelligence must, by necessity—and as it is infinite in nature—again reflect or assume another form. This second form is the reflection of all the things of which it (the life cycle) contains and is called the psychic body. We can visualize it as something similar to the modern motion picture theater and the projector with the film which portrays the picture is the life cycle.

The screen or psychic body, therefore, contains a reflected concept of all that is within the original basic life cycle.

This psychic body is sometimes called a thought-form body or as it is even expressed and in the terms of the psychiatrist, as the subconscious mind. It is, in itself by necessity, a product of not only the intelligence of the life cycle but that in the expression of all the things in which it is and of the life within itself, reflects outwardly and becomes the objective mind, or the conscious mind of the individual. It also takes or absorbs into itself such manifold experiences as the individual is going through during his various periods at any particular time of his evolution.

It has been explained previously that the existence and the experiences of all things on this earth, or on other worlds, take place in the mental consciousness, even though they may express themselves or move about as material forms of happenings or experiences, yet essentially, they are mental in nature and being mental in nature, they regenerate themselves in a cycular pattern within this psychic body. Then, it is easy to see that as the psychic body can become a receptacle from God within, from the life cycle, it can also retain the intelligence or experience, or even the inferiorities or negations of the individual; but the psychic body also does even more than this.

Through the life cycle and through the psychic body is the creative Life Force of God Himself. This, in turn, re-creates into idea or form the structure or the elements of the human body. This human form or physical body is the idea body and is simply the vehicle in which the consciousness lives or dwells within this relative plane.

It can be likened, if you will, to the suit and helmet the deep sea diver wears when he descends to the ocean floor, so that throughout the lifetime of the individual, he is merely manipulating a mechanism or an organism which is essential to his life upon this plane. He has the lungs to breathe the air; he has the necessary intestinal mechanism to assimilate the various atomic structures known as foods within this dimension and to regenerate the necessary heat for the body metabolism. This is all part of the sum and total of the expression of the Infinite will and consciousness which form the individual life cycle.

Now we can begin to see, as it has been said, that man has truly been created of God. It is written in the Bible that God gathered the dust of the earth and created man. This is merely a parable and one in which only a childlike mind would be able to tolerate. In our own consensus and evaluation this would, by necessity, be more than just that. The earth substances in the course of evolution do become the elemental substances of the body but first, we must have the Creative Intelligence behind all things in order for the body to do this.

This Creative Intelligence is God and manifests from the life cycle. In going about through life, if the individual knew of the pertinent facts, knew that with each act, each daily thought, each consciousness in the expression of life of him or herself, it was being permanently engraved, man would live quite differently. If we could liken it to that within the psychic body, in its countless evolutions of life within the individual, as it becomes the sum and total of all that he is and the sum and total of his individual expression, he can, therefore, by the same token of all this, become very godlike. He can assume all the propensities of the individual expression of such a God.

Jesus of Nazareth was able to express in some way the godlike nature of man and the creative intelligence behind this way of life. With his many miracles which he worked while on this earth plane, he was merely setting up the actual working counterpart of this Infinite Intelligence. In a large sense, Jesus merely set aside the element of time and space and attuned into the fourth dimension, into the original place of conception of all things. Therefore, in this particular dimension the Life Force was continually creating and re-creating itself also, where all things have been created or were created.

With the infinite nature of God all things are not only possible, but they do exist; Jesus simply brought into conscious expression a part of God that was already there but which could not be seen with finite mind. These blocks and psychic shocks of the past may become something in which you may have to spend not only one lifetime but many lifetimes to eradicate. These negative impingements within the psychic anatomy of the individual from some great negative cycle are sometimes carried over for many lifetimes.

Remember, therefore, that your act of consciousness of this day or this deed of this hour will be something that can be a stumbling block or it can become a step from which to build your future. The choice is yours.

CHAPTER XI

On Reincarnation, July 1958

During the past several years, increasing emphasis has been given to an all-important concept of life, termed reincarnation. Through numerous channels of expression, this subject has become one of national importance and has been tossed and bandied about by people in all walks of life. A case in toto is the "Bridey Murphy" story which has been so widely publicized and exploited. Recent articles appearing in "Fate" Magazine reflect typical reactions to many persons who have attempted to evaluate reincarnation on the basis of common knowledge which exists and has been public domain for many centuries.

Nothing personal is intended to the authorship of such opinions expressed, either as documentaries or mere personal beliefs. Such expressions, however, always have one thing in common, whether pro or con: they lack a more complete and comprehensive understanding of the basic principles of life. As a matter of fact, these expressionists are usually quite contradictory. A case in point refers to an article in the December '57 issue of "Fate" in which the writer is attempting to render invalid many existing concepts on reincarnation. He has not only attempted to prove to himself that reincarnation does not exist, but unfortunately he has not presented a suitable substitute evaluation.

In psychological parlance, it can be assumed that such opinions as were thus exhibited in this article would mean that such a person was trying to strike a balance somewhere along the line of life which was a result of this vast and complex system of life—a system of justifications sometimes called defense mechainsms, wherein the individual seeks to discharge psychic

170

pressures brought about by these numerous compromises of life. This is also an attempt by the individual to interweave existing spiritual beliefs whereby he can somehow placate the old bugaboo of life, namely, the fear of death.

In order to determine for ourselves whether reincarnation is true or false and for that matter, what lies behind the so-called mystery of life, we must first analyze and rationalize in many different fields of introspection.

First, the word reincarnation merely means to re-enter into; in a sense, each time we re-enter a room, we are reincarnating. Referring again to psychology in the science of psychosomatic medicine, the proven theory is that everyone reacts from basic subconscious thought patterns derived from experiences which were formed first in our early childhood, therefore, in every moment of our daily lives, as it exists in the present, we are reliving the past from these subconscious abstractions. Sadly enough, present-day psychosomatics do not include past lifetimes which are often the true seat of some present-day illnesses or conditions incurred as psychic shock from some one particular past-life experience.

Paradoxically, although none of the present-day sciences express or believe either in reincarnation or the continuity of life, these existing sciences are the ones which will form the first step in our personal evaluation of life and will help explain just what this mysterious force is. This scientific equation is, incidentally, the common ingredient lacking in all present-day dispensations of psychical knowledge, whether they relate either to reincarnation or to the more orthodox concepts. Neither modern science nor materia medica knows as yet, in a pure sense, what life is or what is commonly referred to as the creative or re-creative life force.

So far as the human body is concerned, there are many indications and ways of measuring this mysterious force which is constantly pulsating throughout the body. The encephalograph measures brain waves which are impulses of pure energy sent to various portions of the anatomy much like the wiring system in your homes; yet there is nothing in the brain to suggest any chemically reactive process which could regenerate an idea or form of consciousness into energy impulses. Therefore, how is this vast and complex system of life carried on in the human anatomy, for instance, the regeneration of a million and a half new cells every minute, each with a predetermined function of life? Pure physical science has actually toppled over some of the last existing barriers which have separated mankind from a more complete universal knowledge of life and is at the present time, becoming increasingly concerned with exploring space as well as other channels which relate to the pure creative life force.

For the convenience of our purpose, we can combine all of these various factors together and call them interdimensional relationships. Before his death, Einstein was beginning to explore through mathematical equations into this unknown field. The subject here, however, is extremely vast and preponderant, and to serve the purpose better, we shall start with a common equivalent of life which is called electricity. Electricity itself refers to an oscillating movement of energy through some defined field, such as the electricity which lights our homes after traveling through a complex system of wiring from the generators and sub-stations. On the oscilloscope it shows simply an up and down wave-like motion at the rate of 60 cycles per second. This is the basic concept of life, and should be first understood by anyone who wishes to understand the why and what of everything. The work of Einstein in our atomical scientific field of science has long ago disproved the existence of mass. All mass is actually a conglomerate matrix of tiny planetary systems of energy, called atoms. Atoms, in turn, are determined by their atomic weight, that is, the number of different electronic, neutronic or protonic constituents which go to make up that particular atom. However, in all cases the atom is not solid and even the so-called hard, dense core or nuclei composed of protons are, in turn, solar systems of pure energy. They have become comparatively hard only in comparison to the reactive properties of other elements with which they have come in contact; yet, in the abstract, there is nothing solid. Now we begin to understand that whether we are concerned with the more so-called solid substances of life, or with the dynamically moving forces of free energy moving either through us or in an infinite number of ways around us, we will begin to ponder a few more questions.

Now where does all of this come from, and why do all of these energy forms, atomic or otherwise, relive and remanifest themselves with constant mechanical rigidity? First, all energy moves according to definite cycular patterns known as frequencies. Each atom has a specific frequency which is called its atomic weight. All things in this universal cosmogony can therefore be evaluated as one or a number of cycular movements or vibrations of energy which are constantly repeating themselves in a rigid and unvarying fashion from the source or origin; and as far as this or any dimension is concerned, these vibrations of energy actually have no terminating point or end. You may also ask, what is the E.M.F. or originating source, and this is where we go into interdimensional relationships.

The common mistake frequently indulged in by all mankind, scientist, laymen, or religionist, is to try to equate the infinite cosmogony from this present relative third dimension or earth, as it is more commonly known. We will not solve the enigma of life in any of its numerous manifestations until we begin to start our equations from as near a point as possible to the E.M.F. or the source. For convenience sake, let us call this source God, or the Fountainhead, not as a personal being but as an incredibly vast whirling vortex of an infinite number of wave forms of energy, which are, in turn, through the law of frequency relationship being constantly linked and relinked, and as intelligence, each wave form having a certain I.Q., retaining and remanifesting consciousness in an infinite number of dimensions throughout this vast moving sea of energy.

Some very important facts are now obvious: that energy will repeat itself in its original I.Q. until changed, and will do so into infinity; and as God is therefore infinite, He has become conscious in all forms. This is the E.M.F. the constant living and reliving intelligence in cyclular patterns and wave forms throughout an infinite number of dimensions. Other things, too, now become apparent. Man assumes his rightful position as an energy creation. In a more abstract sense, the individual who is so concerned and associated through the physical mind and body is attempting to live and relive these infinitely numerous concepts, ideas, polarities, and patterns of intelligence implanted by the Infinite Creative Intelligence in this cyclular vortex or dimension of wave forms.

Now this particular vortex was not put together with hands. It too had an evolution. This is to say that all of these infinite wave form patterns were first attracted as opposite polarities to each other from the higher or more abstract portions of the Infinite Mind which we will call positive, into the lower forms of life in the low physical dimensions which we will call negative. This is not to be misconstrued with Darwinism. Darwin postulated a theory, which was compounded and instigated from only physical or exterior manifestations. The true pattern of life in any form must always be equated from the basis of interdimensional relationships, that is, intelligence or I.Q. oscillating into the lower material dimensions.

Starting with the amoeba, we can therefore say that the idiom of experience which related it to environmental factors of life in its earthly cycle was reflected back into the infinite consciousness. Gradually, through frequency relationship and in gathering together in the regular and well-ordered spectrums called harmonic structures, these various intelligent quotients and patterns gathered together and formed that comparatively hard core nuclei of energy formations which we call the superconsciousness, or the Father within. By this same evolutionary pattern, a series of successive oscillations, large and small, which can be called individual lives, was formed from the daily experiences of these lives. Mankind, individually or collectively, has thus presently evolved into his present existing status. On this same basis, man is therefore reflecting his daily life as evolutionary patterns, not only from the cradle to the present or even in a thousand or more lifetimes, but he is actually maintaining physical form and consciousness through frequency relationship into lives which he lived or was part of, in an infinite number of species and plant and animal life on this terrestrial globe. The fact that man exists in his present form proves this conclusively. His physical body is the development of idea, form and consciousness which were brought together from out of countless life experiences as part of other species in similar environmental relationships. This is true evolution or reincarnation.

Now, many of the more orthodox believers may be shocked and horrified at this exposé of fact, yet if they will think for a moment that if all of this seems to violate the Biblical version of the creation of man, how else could man assume in his present position all of the factors and elements which are supposed to elevate him above the common status of beast? He has become relatively intelligent only by the inclusion of a numerous and infinite number of polarity patterns developed through this progressive evolution. He has also, in this evolutionary process been brought into closer proximity with the higher and positive portions of the polarity patterns which we have referred to as the superconscious. This brings him into exterior realizations and portrayals of life which can be called religious in nature, a process referred to as the "quickening of the spirit". He is increasingly aware of the vast and mysterious forces of life which are ever moving about him; and he gradually learns to develop them into various pantheisms of personalities which he may call spirits, devils, etc.

Later developments along this ever-quickening psychic pattern develop into monotheisms wherein he, along with all other members of the human race, become subservient and part of this one great and all-inclusive God. Through various religious systems and personal beliefs, many personalities become elevated to the position of Saints, Angels, or Masters, etc. This, too, is all part of the evolution of consciousness through which every individual passes; and whether he believes in reincarnation or not, his daily life is a direct testimonial to the truth of evolution or reincarnation. In fact, his very desire to escape death from this material world reaffirms and substantiates in many ways and forms his desires and beliefs that he will reincarnate into a higher spiritual world. Nor should any man lack the more common ingredients which should be contained in his philosophy of life. He can see about him, in a vast and infinite number of ways, the continual resurgence of life in cycular patterns of evolution, which is reincarnation. The flowers and trees in themselves portray a form of life conceived through that same evolutionary process; and as they cast the seeds onto the earth, each seed in turn contains a new plant. From day to night and from year to year, the cycles rise and fall, oscillate and reoscillate. And while man has learned to live by time in his constant reman- ifestations, actually he lives and relives in a timeless place, a place without end or beginning, a place which is neither empty nor filled, which is neither infinite nor finite, but which is an ever-increasing expansion and contraction of consciousness, reliving, remanifesting in an infinite number of ways—a galaxy within a galaxy of infinite radiant energy formations, each portraying its own intelligence, and through frequency relationship, harmonic structures, and interdimensional relation- ships, captures and recaptures, generates and regener- ates all of the infinities of life.

The materialist who has an ant's eye-view of the infinite cosmogony is always prone to say that this is so or not so; and like the potter who sits at the wheel, he molds his vessel of life from the ideas, forms, and patterns which he has gained through countless cen- turies. But seldom does he remember that this vessel carries water only in proportion and amount to the way in which it is fashioned; and that these few drops of water which he contains in his vessel of life are but small drops compared to the great oceans and seas of timeless wisdom from which he will constantly fill each new vessel of life. In the pageantry and in the many colored pages of history, it is easy for any one man to select what he considers suitable portions and to use these things to make himself a Jacob's cloak, a patch- work of many pieces and colors which is neither serv- iceable nor warm.

To further enlarge upon the principles which cause the resurgence of life, individually or collectively, finite or infinite, we must at this point include another one of the thoroughly misunderstood concepts of life called mental telepathy, thus killing two birds with one stone, since the same issue of "Fate" contains an article on this subject. Here again is a very fine display of the more literate forms of the English language but which fails to prove anything, except that the author was over-biased, his knowledge on the subject antique and superficial and lacked the common knowledge on the basic principles of life, just as did the article on reincarnation. As both of these subjects are part of these all-inclusive principles and are synonymous in many respects, let us go into the more scientific facts which, functionally speaking, whether telepathy or any other form or way of life, can be classed as vibronics, or as the previously discussed, oscillations.

Any particular equation of mass as it is commonly referred to (and which is actually nonexistent) whether an atom or a skyscraper, whatever particular conglomeration of atomic-molecular structures, always has a basic frequency. For the sake of convenience, this is called a sine wave. The striking of a bell means that we have transferred energy into motion or as is equated by the resonant frequency of the sine wave of the bell's atomic structures into the surrounding atmospheric envelope. This basic frequency or tone is actually a composite form in harmonic structures, a large number of multiples, plus or minus, of the basic frequency. These harmonics give body to the bell tone. In all natural phenomena, any structure or symposium of atoms and molecules has such a basic vibrating pattern. This is also quite true when carried into the field of pure electronic energy. Our modern radio and television systems function on this principle.

Because man is an energy creation, physically and psychically, he therefore has a basic frequency vibration. In the pattern of harmonic structures as they are

178

thus regenerated, he is linked and relinked to an infinite number of interdimensional relationships and thus becomes, to some degree, directly or indirectly, consciously or subconsciously, a participating element at all times in these interdimensional relationships.

In the psychic or energy body of man are found energy structures which are regenerating, as has been discussed, from an infinite number of experiences which formed these energy structures from previous lifetimes. The idiom or ego of each individual is carried in his own basic frequency; and each individual is different or vibrates on a slightly different frequency. The individual is therefore, then not only a broadcasting station in the abstract sense but also a receiving station. For as he is connected outwardly and inwardly through energy structures to the infinite cosmogony, he participates in life according to the sum and total of these harmonic structures which are constantly being regenerated to form the sum and total of his basic frequency or to oscillate with an individual in a manner wherein this oscillating frequency between two individuals, as a sine wave or carrier, carries with it idea, form or consciousness.

The same process is carried out in our modern television systems and science has struck an exact parallel in television with the exact basic principles of life as they are concerned in particular with mankind in general. Each man, therefore, is in a sense a television set; his outer or physical life is the screen or the picture tube; the various energy constituents and elements are constantly being reflected from the interior of his psychic energy body, and in the matrix of these energy formations is all that he has ever been psychosomatically through many thousands or even hundreds of thousands of years.

It is a well-known fact that the human brain is not a thinking machine in the pure sense. It has been called a switchboard in simpler terms by linking and re-linking into present consciousness with this past, just as was suggested by comparing life as a parallel to the television. Now to the writers of these two articles—as well as to any other sundry individuals who may be tempted in one way or another to disagree with what has herewith been presented—may I suggest a two or three-year basic training course in physics, electronics and atomic sciences. Thereafter if the individual has an analytical and not a narrowly-biased mind, he will be enabled to arrive at a much higher level of personal introspection than is so commonly exhibited in the articles which have been under discussion.

I do agree, however, on one point in the article on telepathy. At the present time it is indeed difficult to establish telepathic communication in such manner as would be demanded by pure science. However, like the airplane, the automobile, medicine and any other one particular facet of life, all have had their beginnings, and those beginnings were thus subjected to the various idiosyncrasies of public opinion. Mechanical failures and various other confusing and conflicting elements entered into this formative period. Para-psychological research at Duke University has become an authority on this subject which it definitely has established. It remains for the future generations of mankind to develop psychosomatic science into usable dimensions of transference in the fields of telepathy and reincarnation which are only partially established now by existing knowledge on the two subjects.

For example, if we should begin to school our children in telepathy and should use as much time on it as is used on the three R's, after a few generations, mental telepathy would supplant, to a large part, our common every-day speech, and by the same token, partially render our vast communicative systems obsolete. I might point out that Dunninger has publicly, on the television, under extreme test conditions, fully justified the highest form of mental telepathy. He is but one of the many persons at this present day, most of whom have not succeeded in so publicizing their telepathic abilities. To the layman today telepathy is amazing, but so was the telephone, the radio and television in their infancy.

In a few decades, science will have passed many of the hypothetical concepts which it has just faintly begun to envision. Ideas, symposiums, and mental artifacts—which are part of the articles under discussion —will in that day be much more antique than grandma's asafetida bag. Yes, even now in the light of existing knowledge, such authorship should never reach the eye of an already offended public. In a more direct and personal rebuttal to the author on the article on reincarnation, he has pointed out that everyone interested in this subject who might be approached about this matter would exhibit neurotic or psychotic tendencies. I heartily disagree. In my experience of thousands of discussions by almost an equal number of individuals, I have not found such mentally disturbed exhibitions with possibly a few exceptions of those being strongly over-biased, very doubtful, or extremely ignorant on the subject; all such persons thus engaged in conversation remained comparatively calm. Perhaps the writer exhibited an aggressive attitude or in some way succeeded in stirring up the individual's ire.

He stated also that after having had three life or Akashic readings by three different readers, they were all contradictory and that on this basis, he declared reincarnation false. Comparatively like all other types of practitioners, doctors, etc., there may be only a few Akashic readers who are actually properly qualified to read the Akashic or past-life records. It is a well-known fact that no individual could relate experiences from the memories of past years on a month-to-month basis and have all such experiences coincide. It is also well known that two people standing side by side witnessing an auto accident will describe it differently. Two people on a journey around the world with the same itinerary will describe various points of interest in a different way and with different factors of introspection. As any individual has lived hundreds or thousands of lives, it is highly improbable that any two or more readers, on the basis of frequency relationship, would be enabled to contact the same lives or even portions of the same lives or situations or experiences in those particular lives. Much less would they be able to describe any portion of such lives in a like manner. This does not disprove reincarnation.

A man with constant migraine headaches was examined by twelve different doctors and was given twelve different reasons for the headaches. This does not mean that we should toss the entire materia medica into the trash can; no more should the author attempt to toss reincarnation into the same can on the basis of his very limited and highly biased experience. It is highly deplorable that such a worthy science should be exploited in such manner so that it reaches the comparatively ductile minds of some more deserving truth seekers. And this same criticism holds true for the author of the article on telepathy. He, too, is in the horse-and-buggy era.

May I repeat, I have nothing personal against either of the authors. No doubt in their own limited sphere of influence, they are worthy citizens. It is regrettable that in our democracy many crimes go unpunished. Heading the list of these unpunishable criminals are those individuals who are warping and distorting the minds of impressionable victims, exhorting and exploiting them to the limit of their capacity. We find many of these criminals among the ranks of our present-day exponents of Truth. They are capitalizing on human misery, every weakness and frailty to waylay man by the side of the road and rob him, not only of every penny he possesses, but of the very essence of his character, so necessary to keep his spine straight to walk the high road of life. Psychology has proved that in our highly evolved technical way of life, everyone is over-burdened with a host of complex and conflicting ideosophies and the repercussive subconscious complexes which always arise under such conditions. Escape mechanisms become the Judas Iscariot of every individual, leading him into the slaughterhouse of the nearest exploiter, where he is not only fleeced, but his very life blood is very often drawn and his body quartered to be fed to the ravens and wolves of various practitioners and cultists.

The world is full of small people. Like pack rats they leave a little here and take a little there, and we can hear the patter of these small feet everywhere. Yes, many of those who have succeeded in placing themselves upon some high pedestal of public esteem, scientifically, politically, or religiously, can always be found to be shielding their feet of clay by a false cloak of a collective verbiage, high-sounding titles, mysterious innuendoes, long names and coined phrases, any tool or weapon which can be used to exploit the public and form a shield for their own weaknesses and deficiencies. False prophets and teachers cry out to us from the rooftops and gutters, from churches, from halls of science. Those who have found life in a number of improbable conclusions are attempting to dissipate the fog in their own minds by converting it into a rainbow and thereby try to point out to their fellow-man the mythical pot of gold at its end.

And as the old adage says that the proof of the pudding lies in the eating and mindful of this fact, we here at the Center of Unarius would not have the unmitigated gall to postulate concepts and theories without having substantiated evidential proof to back up our statements. This, too, is quite different from the position of the writers of these articles under discussion and is also quite true of the preponderance of various authors, so-called teachers, self-styled doctors who are dispensing their own particular brand of hash.

In personal case histories of many hundreds of students whom we have served, all (with few exceptions who have not applied the principles) have had marvelous and often miraculous results in personal healing demonstrations and adjustments in their daily lives and have written one or more letters wherein they gave praise and thanks to these wonderful changes which had occurred, mainly from the objectifying of their previous life experiences which are recorded and portrayed to the students.

With the recognition of the first originating cause (from their previous lives), results of healing by natural sequence follow. This is "proof of the pudding", and proves definitely beyond any question of a doubt the authenticity of the evolution and cycles of man termed reincarnation. This is the New Age Psychiatry of the future. Man must need to change mentally before he can arrive at the long-awaited Spiritual Age, the Second Coming or the Millenium.

CHAPTER XII

The Little Understood
Higher Self

After the passing of many years, since the beginning of the present inauguration of Unarius on the
planet earth, it becomes apparent that the least understood and most abused concept of the interdimensional science of Unarius is that of the superconscious
self; and to avoid the ever-present danger of egocentric
flatulency—which could occur should any student,
knowing that he has a superconscious or higher self,
falsely indulge himself in some sort of a self-hypnotic
grandiose state of consciousness we shall discuss further on this concept. When and if any person's higher
self develops to the point where it is the dominant
personality, there will no longer be an earth-life personality or embodiment. In short, if you are here on
earth in a physical body concerned with physical existence, also involved with the problems of life after
death, higher evolution, etc., then you can be quite certain your higher self has just begun to develop; and as
of this time, may or may not be strong enough through
the channels of inspiration, intuition, etc., to keep you
moving along your evolutionary pathway, for that small
embryonic higher self is all that stands between you
and total retrogression. And in the life in-between
lives, it's the little window you look through from your
memory life into the higher worlds.

Let us take for analysis a more concrete example
of the development of the higher self. With an ordinary
home movie camera you can go out and take a roll of
film, upon the surface of which you capture the image
and likenesses of places and people, their motions, etc.
Later after it is developed it can be projected onto a

screen and these same people, their motions, etc., again come to life. Now this is about what takes place in the development of the higher self. We can call infinite intelligence or infinity the film and our daily life is the camera, and through the lens of our camera we flash back a small portion of our lives to infinity. There it is polarized or developed because infinite intelligence or infinity, like the film in the camera contains what is necessary to make this possible.

In other words, in the "mind" of infinite intelligence, your life, as well as all other lives and things, has been conceived even in the most minute detail and living endlessly without time. And when you flash back through the lens of your life certain frequencies of energy, like light which, if they are so properly attuned, can and do polarize similar (or like) wavelengths of energy which are oscillating in infinite intelligence. When these two frequencies are so merged and beat or oscillate harmonically according to the laws of harmonics, these frequencies then will be the embodiment of a personal experience of life and when so combined with other polarized frequencies compatibly attuned to harmonics, this then will be the beginning of the higher self and eventually will develop into a psychic personality, and then on into more highly developed embodiments which have been called archangels, gods, etc., by the ignorant earth-man.

So you see, dear one, if you look back into your present earth-life and try to rationalize how much of it has been lived constructively to a degree whereby a small fraction of each of these earth-life-experiences could be polarized in infinity, also going back and speculating on numerous other earth-lives so lived, how much then, of the broad expanse of infinite intelligence have you polarized into your superconscious self? And I think you'll agree, it's very small indeed and becomes even smaller when you begin to weigh its influence in your present life.

But do not be discouraged, the promise of immortality is built in, in the mechanics of life, if you live it ever mindful of the infinite creative intelligence and the grand scheme of evolution; for in this evolution you are guaranteed not only immortality, but that immortality is, in itself, a guarantee that you will not ever need to live a physical life. The purpose then, in this supremely intelligent concept, as it is envisioned in evolution, is that it does, in itself, make it impossible for anything but good to survive; for evolution constantly presents two faces; good and evil, and in choosing good, and with the purpose and fulfillment of good in our daily lives, we begin to fulfill a more ultimate purpose of evolution.

Heaven is not a promise given by some religious proponent nor can it be fulfilled in any religious configurations. Heaven, however, if it can be called such, is an attainment of personal development. It cannot be given by saviors nor can you be elevated to this pinnacle by intercessors or any other declared deistic powers contrived in the minds of earthmen, for any deisms which may possess such powers would never be so unwise as to use them for such senseless purposes. They know too well the elevation of any earthman into a spiritual world would destroy him; for anyone who lives in a higher world must develop the capacity to live there before such a life could be possible. And this can only be done through the development of the higher self, for that is, indeed, the beginning of your new embodiment in a higher world where you will have no lungs, yet you will breathe the breath of heaven; you will have no eyes but you will discern all things and in the fullest capacity, without the subconscious selectivity. You will have no ears but you will hear the celestial music of creation and you will have no mouth or stomach, yet you will masticate and digest pure radiant energies which will keep your body alive and pulsating. Yes, all of this and much more is the fulfillment of this spiritual life lived in the embodiment of the higher self.

CHAPTER XIII

Newer Concepts

It can be said that this is indeed the age of miracles. The last fifty years have seen great and tremendous changes in the way of life for man on this globe. He has brought many new and wonderful inventions into his way of living. He now rides through the skies at speeds of more than twice the speed of sound. He can live for months, if necessary, beneath the surface of the ocean. He has new antibiotic drugs at his disposal, new methods of sanitation which have all but wiped some of the great plagues of the past from the face of the earth. He has in the laboratories synthesized and produced great and untold numbers of articles which he uses in his daily life; his clothing, articles in the home are all produced in mass quantities from synthetic materials. His methods of communication span the entire surface of the globe, not only with sound and with the spoken word but with pictures. And it can truly be said, that with all these things he has indeed wrought many and great miracles. It can also be said that the nations of the world are now at our very back door or at our front door, that we no longer are separated by the great barriers of the oceans.

Upon great highways which span the various cities, man speeds in the marvelous mechanization known as the automobile. In the great factories throughout the lands, millions of people are toiling and producing more and yet more of these new and wonderful things. He has at his disposal in his own home: refrigeration, the telephone, the radio, the television. He has countless and innumerable conveniences which were unknown and unheard of in grandmother's time, and it should be, by the token of all of these, a great and wonderful age, a Utopia whereby man can lay aside some of the things of the physical world and enjoy more of the things of the mental and the spiritual. Yet with all of these, it might be said that man has invented a Frankenstein monster and which may very well destroy him through his haste, through his greed, and worse, his constant fear of insecurity. He has created for himself a veritable rat race, one in which he must vie from day to day with his neighbor in obtaining the bare necessities of his life—one in which he cannot lay down for a single moment to enjoy all these things which he has created for himself.

And so through the great masses of the population which are constantly arising in untold numbers throughout the nations of the world today in this great preponderant population, we find not the peace of mind; we find not the security that we should feel. And with all of this as it were, to cap the climax we now have new and terrible weapons of war. Man has in these last years of his life upon this earth invented atomic weapons which are beyond the imagination and the comprehension in their destructiveness. He has attempted in some small way to harness these atomic forces for the betterment of mankind. And so with all of these things which are about him in the multiple complexities of his everyday life, man has become a fearful thing. He has become something which has been torn and stretched beyond all endurance. He has been confronted with the fact that any moment he may be visited with engines of destruction from the skies and that his cities may be laid waste and the multitudes and millions shall be killed. And so he remains as he is today: a crouching, fearful thing. Though he may walk bravely about, yet there is within a specter, which he lives with day by day.

And what is the answer to all of this? If we go into our mental institutions and to our hospitals, we will begin to see the terrible price man is paying for all of this foolishness, this foolhardiness, this mad race for new and more terrible weapons of destruction. It is estimated that fifty percent of the hospital beds in this country are occupied by people who have broken down under the strains and the stress of this civilized world. It is also said that our mental institutions are over-crowded beyond their normal capacities with people who have likewise brought the burden of the civilized world down into their bodies and into their minds. And so man is desperately seeking a solution to all these things and that it is well at hand. If we look about us to seek a way or a means for an answer to the problems of man as they exist today in their multiplicities and in their complexities, we will look in the churches and from the pulpit, there is already a great and growing demand and a need for a new, a different kind of spiritual understanding. Many exponents of the Biblical truths, the spiritual philosophies of this world today are turning more or less to the realms of what can be termed psychiatry or psychosomatic medicine. Throughout the land innumerable religious groups have sprung up which are teaching principles which are on the borderline or the threshold of the principles of what is sometimes called psychiatry.

If we look into the clinics, the hospitals, or the various places where the man of medicine practices, we shall also see a great leaning and a great inclination to better understand man in his own natural mental realm; but with all this, there is a wide and seemingly insurmountable gap between his true relationship with himself. Even though the means for spanning this gap are well at hand and have been used for countless of civilizations, yet he himself, of this time and age, has not yet embarked and does not understand all the common principles for these simple truths. He has set up above himself within his own mind the barriers of

191

this one and only life, not realizing that he is a man of many lives and that he has come about this world not of the first time but of countless times and, perhaps, even in other worlds beyond this world. And with all of these things within, something of which he is and in his spiritual nature, he takes with himself into each new life either the burden or the joyousness of the last and other lives.

He is wont to think in the terms of the psychiatrist that as an adult or as an old person, he has incurred all the ills and the distemperature about his present life in the early years of his childhood and as a child. Yet it was only in those first few formative years that the child was a true medium in a spiritual sense and began expressing from his subconscious mind not only things of this realm and of this dimension but of the psychic memories of the past lives. And as he grew up, he lacked the intelligent comprehension of the loved ones about him for the things which he felt from within his own psychic domain, and so there were many ills, many seemingly insurmountable vicissitudes or, as they are sometimes called, neuroses, thought patterns or even the more stringent form of psychoses which were blamed primarily to the various facets in this understanding of their so-called psychosomatic medicine.

If man had the will, the intelligence, he would make of himself as a doctor, as a practitioner, or as a metaphysician, someone who could visualize the problems confronting the individual with whom he is working, that he is not necessarily a by-product of this time or age but is either, more or less, already well upon his spiritual evolution, and indeed, as it has been prophesied in "the latter days" that this would be the gathering together of the Ten Tribes as it was called in the Bible. Those who have lived in this world beyond this time and even into other worlds are now gathered together that they may work out, that they may go together into a new cycle of evolution which is expressed as the Aquarian Age—an age in which the domain and dominion of God will reign supreme.

So how is it best, how will it come about that man will need serve himself to better his understanding of the psychic realm? Today throughout the lands there are many thousands of Christian churches practicing; they claim to be sufficiently mediumistic to interpret many of these psychic things into the everyday expression of man's material world. There are others who are so likewise inclined to think they, too, could try to impinge or influence the destinies of man with their own interpretations. And yet, with all of these understandings, with all of these truths, with all of these churches —whether we call them Spiritualist, Christian Science, Mind Science, or whether of other denominations that they need to be called—none of them in themselves are serving man in his true psychic relationship. No more so are the doctors, the psychiatrist and the man of medicine as he is known in the world today.

And so it becomes apparent that we need to develop a new and a different kind of doctor, if you would call him such—a doctor who is mediumistic enough to see beyond this realm and this time—a doctor who will not necessarily base his diagnosis on the present illnesses of the patient with what the patient may tell him of the various vicissitudes, of the various happenings, of the various negations which have incurred into his life. This doctor must be one who is clairvoyant, one who can see beyond the third dimensional realm of consciousness into the fourth dimensional realm—into the realm from which all things are incurred—where it is truly the realm of Spirit, truly the realm in which all things have been created, all things exist and all things have happened.

Only man in his consciousness selects what he

thinks; only man brings unto himself and attracts unto himself that which he so desires. And so living in this concept, in this evolution of time, through the many ages he becomes either one of two things: a progressive or a retrogressive individual, and he brings with him at all times the psychic memories of the past. The laws of God, if they can be called laws, are immutable and irrevocable. If man lives not according to these laws, then surely he brings his own judgment upon his own head. He is in all sense his own jury, his own judge and his own executioner. None other than man can do unto himself what he needs or must have done, nor can he do unto his brother that which his brother must do unto himself. But only in the spiritual companionship and in the sharing of all these things can man gain the strength and the love which is his heritage.

And so, in developing the new doctor, the new metaphysician of tomorrow, we will find not only the man who knows of the body and its mechanism but will also know of the mind and spirit. He will know many truths beyond the knowledge or the intelligence of the doctor of today. He will be able, in the quiet moments of his contact with his patient, to pierce beyond the veil of the mortal realm and see where it was that some of the great troubles and problems of that patient were actually incurred. He will also be spiritually connected with such organizations as exist in the spiritual domain or realm which are capable and efficient in administering spiritual healing to that patient from the spiritual side of life. He will also be able to, if needs be, add palliative measures or corrective measures to further speed such spiritual healing. He will use various new antibiotic drugs which may be brought into the new realm of consciousness in that future day. He will be able to set broken bones by the manipulative processes of his hands, or he will be able to relieve congestions and the various other troubles and ills which are at the present moment upsetting the patient, not only through the power of the hands but through the dominion of his mind in the process of psychokinetics.

And so in the final analysis of the doctor of tomorrow, it can be said that he will indeed be a wonderful and a different sort of a doctor, one not interested necessarily in the immediate physical condition of the mind and body but who will be vitally concerned with his spiritual evolution, not only of the present time, but of the many past lives which also have a very definite relationship to the patient's present condition.

CHAPTER XIV

Space Travel And H-Bombs
Versus Fear, 1955

The explosion of the atomic bombs over Japan in 1945 ushered in what is commonly called the atomic age, and while it almost immediately put an end to World War II, it had other and also much more important psychological factors in the life of mankind on this planet earth. Compounded as it were from the fear of World War II and the sneak attack at Pearl Harbor which precipitated us into this war, the explosions of these new and fantastic weapons gave birth to even greater and newer fears.

In reality, it was not the atomic age but the age of fear. By 1947, a new note of terror was added to this already vast and overburdened and mentally stressed condition of the people of this country. Consternation and near panic reigned when it was learned that even the capitols of this country and in the high positions there was treason. We had been sold down the river to the great foreign power overseas. There were those who were immediately put to trial and there were even executions in an attempt to stop this treason and the boring from within. It has been only recently that some of the foremost thinkers of this country, as well as countless thousands of unknown and unnamed people are beginning to realize that Russia in its possession of the knowledge and the use of atomic weapons is really a blessing in disguise.

The situation as it exists today is one of delicate but perfect balance. We are in less danger of a world war today than we have been for hundreds of years in the history of nations. The terrible knowledge and the mere thought of the horror of these weapons will give rise to almost fantastic ways and means of these two nations to avert such a catastrophic cataclysm. If Russia had not and could not have gained the knowledge and use of atomic weapons, she would have had no other recourse in her fear and panic but to build a huge army and navy and attempt in one overwhelming sneak attack to render our atomic weapons useless. So we can be thankful of the condition and its balance as it exists today.

It is quite true that we have had minor flare-ups. The Korean war, for example, was one in which the pressures of our political systems and of the world in general were, in a sense, relieved. It is quite possible that other and minor conflagrations will from time to time break out, but it is not possible to conceive in the leadership of either Russia or the United States that the people and the leaders of these two great nations will at any time let themselves be plunged into almost certain oblivion by the fatal mistake of aggression.

The explosions of the atomic weapons in 1945 had also other repercussions. Almost immediately, as it were, it touched off a seeming landslide, or rather, an airslide of strange objects which were from time to time identified as spaceships or flying saucers. There were literally thousands of accounts of these sightings from 1946 and on up to and including the present time of 1955. The United States Government and particularly the Air Force were tremendously interested and went to great lengths to obtain all possible available information on these sightings. They went to great effort and endeavors to sift out and to make possible or to verify any genuine sightings.

Space travel or communication through interstellar space with other planets or other solar systems is not unknown, and it is not the purpose here to deny or confirm any or all of these various thousands of instances but rather, the effort here is to assume a more intelligent diagnosis of all these things and, if possible, to reach through and create a more intelligent hypothesis and thereby waylay much of the fears and panic and hysteria which have not only been attached to the fear of war and the fear of atomic weapons, but also the fear and panic of visitations from outer space. The attempt will not be made here to go into any lengthy or detailed description of any of these various sightings but rather, to analyze in a general sense and to sift the chaff from the wheat.

As the situation stands today, we do not have a single flying saucer or any part of a spaceship to exhibit or examine. The author has searched through all available civilian channels to find any real evidential proof. If there is such proof, it is governmental and kept well hidden; nor do we have, to any degree any accurate descriptions other than isolated examples or cases of occurrences which happened only to persons who were of a comparatively unknown status of life. There are those who have, in this wave of fear, of flying saucer consciousness, attempted to climb the bandwagon of fame and to capitalize, as it were in a monetary sense of value by introducing spurious or fraudulent claims. There are others who were inadvertently precipitated into the limelight by an actual happening, or at least, so they claimed. In every instance, however, at least let us say that they have not brought back any real tangible evidence other than their good word. There have been claims of photographs of various descriptions of such and other minor sundry and assorted so-called proofs. (Photographs are notoriously easy to fake.)

We who have investigated through scientific means into all the realms of parapsychology, as it is sometimes called, know that there are many and different ways in which the human body and mind can live and function. There are examples, and the Bible mentions many of such instances. This book also contains accounts of flying saucers. Jesus of Nazareth in walking upon the water exhibited openly a state of mind and body which was temporarily, at least, not of this world or of this dimension. There are also innumerable examples of fire-walking in which participating individuals were prepared through certain religious or cultist rites which temporarily changed the rate of vibration within the atomic structures of the body and in such a temporarily suspended state were immune to fire. This fire-walking is not necessarily indigenous to the South Sea Islanders or other semi-"savage" tribes, but there have been several authenticated experiences which have happened to Americans or Europeans. So likewise in the abnormal stretches and strains of this time, it is quite possible in individual cases and isolated examples, that an individual can contact certain races of planetary peoples who have been and are interested in the welfare and well-being of this earth.

We can imagine if we were people living on some other or distant planet and saw or witnessed an explosion of an atomic bomb, we may be likely indeed to think that this was surely a major cataclysm which could affect us indirectly. It is supposed that these intelligent beings in visiting this earth after these explosions were doing so primarily in the interests of scientific explorations. There were others who have assumed that these and other intelligences were, in a sense, sending warnings into the minds and consciousness of peoples to discontinue these activities of the bomb experimentations to avert an inevitable cataclysmic race to oblivion.

Let us assume for a moment, if you will, that any race of people who had so advanced in these scientific fields of development to the point where space travel was possible that it also is right to assume that they would also be sufficiently intelligent to know that our earth planet is one in which a certain circumscribed level of intelligence exists. They would also know that this is in the dominion and reign of Infinite creation, that this earth plane was to remain such as it is, as remote from outside influences as possible.

The sudden influx of any quantity of outside interstellar travel into this earth plane would seriously disrupt the natural sequence of man's life upon this planet. We can also logically assume that had such peoples on other planets evolved into this highly technical and spiritual state of consciousness, that they would not be likely to, in their more advanced state of awareness, want to get into as it were, conflicts of emotion, or the way of life of a less highly evolved spiritual stature. It is right to believe that every man existing on this plane or earth, as it is with every other being which exists on every other planetary realm, does so with the precept of consciousness that such is his rightful place in his own personal soul evolution.

In the case of one man in particular who claims he rode in a flying saucer from New Mexico to New York and returned, there are no grounds to either believe or disbelieve this is the rightful tenet and supposition of the individual. It could have actually happened but not necessarily in the physical sense in which the individual concerned believes that it happened. He could have been temporarily precipitated, if you please, into another realm of consciousness and therefore took the ride of which he described. In the case of other sightings or contacts with flying saucers or spaceships, a similar condition could have prevailed. Another article on Venus claims that the appearance of two Venusians who, incidentally could appear or vanish, were forced to seek employment in a newspaper office in order to have funds to survive on this planet! It is obvious that men who could thus vanish or reappear would certainly not need money or employment to live; they would,

of course, have many other ways to obtain food, clothing, etc.

In each case of a personal contact to some individual, there is usually at least one or more very obvious
flaws, and in a final analysis, the one important fact
remains that such highly intelligent people would, if
contact were made to the earth people, make such contact directly with the leaders of this or other nations.
Our President would, I feel sure, after recovering from
surprise, welcome such visitors with open arms and
likewise, the whole nation.

In the field of parapsychology, the history of the
world is teeming with innumerable examples of what
are called ghosts or apparitions. These are, in most
instances, thought bodies created from astral energies which were originally of some physical concept.
Thought energy is fourth dimensional in nature and
relationship and therefore does not pass away or disintegrate after creation but may, from time to time
according to certain laws of harmonic relationship,
reappear in a third-dimensional form as wraiths or
ghosts. Therefore, it is quite logical to assume that
some other very highly intelligent race on some other
planet, in understanding these facts, could build thought bodies which carry all of the physical form and
manner of himself except, of course, in the feeling of
solidness which is normally expected of such human-
like "apparitions".

In the August 1954 issue of Mystic Magazine is an
article by Paul Vest on the appearance of a Venusian
who could vanish and reappear and had also other
characteristics which are a part of such thought bodies. This Venusian was reported to have scratched a
hard steel plate with a bare fingernail. Such a mark
would have required 1700 pounds of pressure with a
tool!

It is easy to see then that a race of people who could

produce a science of such a fantastic nature would, by the same token, know of many atomic secrets which would enable such a demonstration to take place, and if it did, it was entirely a fourth-dimensional equation.

There are quite likely to be in the future many reports on other planetary beings, flying saucers, etc. It is therefore in the best interests in the individual sense and for national security and peace of mind, not to become panicky at the mere rumor or mention of extraterrestrial phenomena but to quietly evaluate such reports and to act accordingly as befits a sane, logical human being.

*　　　*　　　*

And if I may add a word, no doubt you would be interested to know that I (Ruth) personally had a contact with a "saucer" soon after the Elder Brother and I were brought together, in the San Diego area. To think of it brings it again in consciousness and I am able to describe it very accurately as I viewed it then, and which was quite similar to many descriptions by those also sighting these interplanetary craft. Some of the Brothers from more advanced planets mentally communed with E.L.N. and said that they would make a visit three months later and gave the date and time at one A.M. Right on the dot there it was and seemed to me larger than was the small house in which we then lived. The contact lasted for several minutes and I was able to view it in all three manners—as solid or chrome appearance, then as a rosy red (some term it "red-hot"), then it became opalescent. I could see right through it. The craft was shaped like the round waffle irons with three protruding legs at the bottom. I saw no operators and it no doubt, was operated by remote control or from the mother ship.

CHAPTER XV

Mental Illness: A Missing Link In Communications?

Scientist Questions Biochemical Approach to Cause

by Harry Nelson
Times Medical Editor

Los Angeles Times, Friday, December 31, 1965
Berkeley—Researchers who have been trying to find a biochemical defect to explain mental illness have been barking up the wrong tree, a leading biochemist said here Thursday.

Instead of looking for evidence of faulty brain metabolism, they should be looking for signs of trouble in the chemicals responsible for transmitting messages from one nerve cell to another in the brain, according to Dr. Bernard B. Brodie.

Dr. Brodie, chief of the Laboratory of Chemical Pharmacology at the National Heart Institute, pointed out that not a single biochemical defect in mental disease has been established, although biochemical investigation has been under way a decade or more.

There have been many reports of chemical abnormalities in psychiatric patients, but none of them has held up, he said.

The researchers' comments were made at the closing session of the annual meeting of the American Assn. for the Advancement of Science. The five-day meeting, held on the UC Berkeley campus, attracted 7,000 persons.

One concept of those who have been pursuing a biochemical explanation for mental illness is that it results from a defect in body metabolism.

Researchers have been trying to prove the theory by analyzing blood or urine for chemical abnormalities that would reflect presumed faulty metabolism.

Such an approach, Dr. Brodie said, is like trying to find a defect in an automobile by looking at the products of gasoline combustion.

He said rapidly accumulating evidence suggests that mental diseases may be a fault in communication between brain nerve cells.

Nerve cells transmit messages to one another by releasing chemicals called neurohumoral transmitters which carry the messages across the gap.

Extensive research of that part of the nervous system outside of the brain has shown that nearly all the drugs used to treat the nervous system achieved their effect by mimicking, blocking or interacting with the neurohumoral transmitters.

Much of this kind of knowledge has come from the investigation of drugs that treat high blood pressure by way of the nerves that control blood vessel constriction.

In a disease called myasthenia gravis, which results in paralysis, the nerves are working and the muscles are normal but there is a breakdown in the communication between the two. Dr. Brodie reasons that something similar could be occurring in the brain.

If such is the case, there would be no visible defect that could be either seen or measured in the blood or urine—the approach that is being taken by those searching for a biochemical defect.

Dr. Brodie said that it appears that tranquilizers and other drugs that affect the brain do their work by affecting the neurohumoral transmission just as they do in the nervous system outside of the brain.

He said that several diseases that result in paralysis due to faulty transmission of messages from nerve endings to muscles could serve as models for what

happens in the brain in a mentally ill person.
Copyright, 19 Los Angeles Times
Reprinted with permission

*　　*　　*　　*　　*

Public Enemy Number One—Mental Health

During the month of December, 1965, a great conclave of scientists gathered at Berkeley, California, more than (7,000) seven thousand scientists representing all facets of known sciences, gathered together to discuss and interchange any and all new scientific knowledge and, of course, the old medical football, mental illness, was very strongly interjected. Recent studies by Dr. Bernard B. Brodie have led him to expound a new theory on schizophrenia which could very well upset the psychiatric apple-cart and if proven true, (so far as the medical profession is concerned) would also completely vindicate one of the primary basic concepts taught by Unarius.

Dr. Brodie explained in his speech that this type of mental illness, schizophrenia, or many other types for that matter, was caused by a breakdown in the communication system between brain cells, as the good doctor called it, the neurohumoral system, and as he said, was due to the lack of certain organic chemicals normally present in people who were mentally healthy. Personally, I do hope that this theory can be proven to the scientific world and especially to the medical psychiatric profession.

Several years ago in one of my books, I stated that an aspirin tablet relieved pain because it blocked or short-circuited the messages of pain which were sent into certain brain centers. Further discussions in different articles and books of Unarius have clearly

205

diagrammed and shown how all of this and much more takes place. It all revolves around the process of hysteresis, as I have called it for want of a better word; and if you have studied well, you will know what I mean. In short, any atom of so-called mass, as it exists in the third dimension, is a tiny energy body—a miniature solar system of energy—and it exists as such (if it is kept alive or powered, so-to-speak) by virtue of the fact that it is connected through harmonic frequency to a number of inner dimensions.

In an article which I gave on cryogenics recently, I explained more completely this process of hysteresis. The human body—any body—is an amalgamated mass of billions of atoms. They are kept in line and in shape as composite molecules and cell structures which go to make up this anatomy by their respective psychic anatomies and involves an extremely complex oscillating process whereby all atoms in this composite anatomy are kept alive and functioning by this psychic anatomy; food and water being used as fuel and building material. This psychic anatomy, in turn, is kept alive in the same complex oscillating process from the inner dimensions and as a separate entity of energy. It has been so developed in its individual course of evolution through many centuries of time and lifetimes.

Someday, as I have predicted, the medical profession as it now exists as a so-called biochemical science will be entirely replaced by the electrochemical science, as it has been fully explained in the different Unariun liturgies where each human being and human anatomy will be seen as a computer-like organization of cells which function and flourish from a memory bank which I call the psychic anatomy. This memory bank is, through the five senses, being constantly fed new information from the daily tenure of life with which this respective physical anatomy is in contact. When such a medical science exists in this future, then all human disease, including ignorance, without exception, can be dealt with in a logical scientific manner. Different kinds of machines known as oscillators or generators will be able to interject into any human being certain selected energy wave forms which will correct any physical or mental aberration and finally, that person will also be educated on the true facts of life so that as much reconstructive work as is possible can be done in this psychic anatomy, so that future incarnations of this individual will not be lived in the same sequence of diseased and aberrated conditions as is now occurring in all humanity of this planet earth.

Yes, Dr. Brodie is very right in suspecting a breakdown in communications between brain cells but as far as Dr. Brodie is concerned, he believes it is a biochemical process. As of this time he and other doctors of the medical profession do not understand hysteresis —on our electrical or electromagnetic scale tiny atoms like men standing in line forming a bucket brigade, each man handing the next one a bucket of water to be thrown on the fire by the last man in the line. So it is in the communication systems of the human anatomy, likewise throughout the grand scale of what we can only visualize as the all-encompassing effigy of creation.

Our solar system thus becomes another atom, our galaxy a molecule, our universe a cell. Yes, as it is in all things, every human exists by virtue of this vast and complex system of regenerations, all conducted in the manner in which I have described to you through oscillating frequencies in exact mathematical formulae. Infinite Creative Intelligence is the life force and governing factor which makes all things possible whether it is an animal-like life on an earth planet or a life lived on some high (celestial) plane.

Many of the different transcripts which I have

given not only prove the truth and validity of Unarius but also point out the position of abysmal ignorance of all our present-day science, especially that of the medical profession. Doctors do not know how an aspirin tablet works, yet the process has been clearly described to you. The complex process of electronic transmissions called oscillations which take place in the human anatomy is similar and basic to the creation and maintenance of all atomic forms known as mass or the 101 elements.

In the human body osmosis is the interchange of molecules between walls compounded of cells. A molecule passes through a cell wall like a small boy crawling between a picket fence, but this molecule does so by virtue of the fact that it has a certain electrical charge or basic frequency. On the other side of the cell wall is another group of molecules with another type of electrical charge which attracts molecules from the other side, just as watermelons might attract a small boy and cause him to crawl through the fence. Saline or salt solution can easily pass through animal tissue cell walls to fresh water on the other side making both solutions equally saline.

To the scientist this is strictly a chemical process and has not yet been related to the laws of electrically charged particles and their behaviors. If you will look into your advanced Lesson Course, you will see the diagrams on the psychic anatomy and the wave forms which oscillate between the respective portions from the brain. Every brain cell floats in a thin pool of plasma; it does not actually touch its neighbor cell. However, communication goes on quite easily and normally in the form of oscillating wave forms carried through the plasma. It's the same with your radio or television. The air and space between you and the transmitter is the plasma. In the human brain, plasma is a compound of highly complex molecules classified under proteins or proteid molecules, just as is most of the cell tissue and plasma of the human anatomy.

But call them whatever you may, each molecule is a highly complex system of atoms, each atom in turn is a solar system of energy radiating a force field just like the television transmitter. That radiating field oscillating at certain frequencies can and does carry transmissions radiated from one cell to the next, just as molecules of hydrogen and oxygen in the air affect, and can help or impede different frequencies from transmitters. Molecules of aspirin radiate frequencies which detune or short circuit normal transmissions.

There can also be hundreds of other wave forms radiated by different sources which can have adverse effects on normal transmissions through the brain cell mass. Nowadays schizophrenia is a more general classification rather than what it formerly was—a split personality complex. There are 33 basic classifications of mental illness now generally known as schizophrenia. An obsessing entity or group of entities from an astral world can partially or wholly, and under certain conditions, superimpose themselves in the transmissions of wave-forms oscillating from the brain cells into the psychic anatomy, as was the case with the insane man who lived in the cemetery above the Sea of Galilee and was exorcised by Jesus; or there can be an obsessing thought-form body self-constructed or compounded from the influence of other people or factors which can temporarily or completely interject themselves into normal transmissions.

Time and distance are no barriers because these oscillating transmissions occur in manners and at frequencies not third-dimensional in nature. Present-day science does not yet possess instrumentation to measure the oscillating wave forms radiating from an atom. Instead, they are classified by their atomic weight or their chemical reactive synthesis.

Epilepsy is a burst or sudden releasement of electrostatic energy throughout the brain cells which causes a temporary blockage of normal function and completely immobilizes the body until it discharges. These accumulations of electrostatic energies are formed from unsynchronized components which do not normally flow or oscillate in the right manner and build up to a certain static potential which overcomes the natural resistive barriers and discharges much like a condenser or capacitor in a radio set. But whatever it is that we are discussing about the human anatomy, whether it is simple osmosis or other organic basic metabolism, or whether we are discussing mind functions and mental illness, they can only be properly understood on an analytical basis as electrical constituents—not as biological reactions.

A molecule is a senseless lifeless nothing if it is viewed as a molecule, as does our present-day biological science but the same molecule, when it is viewed as an atomic compound electrically formed from energy existing and functioning under creative law, then there is purpose and meaning, not only in each molecule but creation itself becomes a vast and infinite panoply of logic and reason and the solution to all enigmas.

To better acquaint you with, or to help you better understand my oft mentioned Principle, 'the Absolute', I could relate to you this example: Ruth is one of the manifestations I have spoken of—the completeness of the Absolute, when you understand it. For many, many years, I described Ruth to people all over Los Angeles, many years before I ever knew her. I told hundreds of people I was looking for her and described what she looked like to them. She was the only person who could understand my science, and at that time, it had not been preconditioned for her yet. Cycles had not swung. There are very few people in this world who could live with me on that basis, not because I am irascible or temperamental or anything like that; I am fairly average and normal in my reactions. But simply because when these things are transcendent, when you are lifted, when these sciences come in, when the Great Ones come in and the way in which they come in, it is beyond the average person's comprehension. It is done so naturally; it is not done with fanfare and trumpets, or anything of that sort with which people have formerly associated appearance of the Great Ones, but it is a simple living process.

It should be synonymous to life. It should be compatible to everyone's understanding—and it will be eventually, sooner or later. To me it is perfectly natural if someone from the Higher Realms comes and uses my vocal chords, but at the same time, my mentality and my consciousness is linked to it in a way in which it is also a part of me and part of the functional process that is going on at the moment, because I have been there, too, and I have studied those things, and I know of them. In that way, I can moderate it. Nothing inferior shall come through me.

Our Science is different because it is not mandatory. We are not trying to impress it on anyone. What we are striving for is to contact people who have been preconditioned for it, who have asked for it within their own consciousness. As Jesus said, "Believest thou this?" and He knew that unless a person was preconditioned, he was hopelessly lost until he had sought out higher planes of consciousness in the spiritual worlds and in the lives in-between lives. Those who have made progress spiritually had been preconditioned for these things. They had gone in their sleep state into the higher planes such as Venus and had been taught these things, because there is no such thing as blind faith.

Faith is only the subconscious sense, the invisible feeling that you know very surely of something. You could not have faith in anything unless you knew about it in some way or another through the higher centers, the higher elevations of the psychic self. You have to be preconditioned for it or you could not accept it. That's the way it is with healing.

There has never been any such thing in the world either here or hereafter as a miracle. What people call a miracle merely means that the Absolute has worked through Principle in a complete way. No true Truth seeker believes in miracles because we only see principle working through the mind of the Absolute and perfection, a certain degree of perfection which had been expressed in one way. The person has learned to some degree through the spiritual planes in contact with the higher centers of the superconsciousness, the mechanics of the Absolute. They have seen spiritual healing work. They know what energy can do when it comes from the higher planes when it is intelligent. It can remove these obstructive blocks in the psychic that cause disease and malformations in the physical. Then after they leave the spiritual dimensions, they come back to earth to work out this healing under conditions which are compatible to it—conditions similar to those under which it was incurred in the first place—and they lack only one thing to make the healing possible and that is a catalyzing agent. This merely means that they have focused their attention on some object or some personality.

If they go to Lourdes, it means that they have focused their attention or their energies upon the water which comes from the grotto. A glass of tap water at home would do the same thing if they had the same focus, or even a teaspoonful of sugar; or they wouldn't need it at all if they could visualize it in any other way. It is in the mechanics in which we connect these things one to another in relationships and exactly the same process at which we arrive in tuning our television set and our radio. There is a certain given set of frequencies which vibrate compatibly and are linked up in harmonic structures. With man it is different than any other species in the world because he has arrived at that point through progressive evolution in the way in which reincarnation creates that part of the psychic self which is called in the idiom, the ego.

This means that compatible wave-form-structures through all forms of animal and plant-life have developed certain particular propensities and functions as spiritual energy formations. Under certain given wavelength frequencies or cycular frequencies, they link themselves up gradually through the ages of time so that they accumulate something like a snowball rolling downhill. In a crude sense, that is the way they come together; they form conjunctions and when they do that, they express to the outside or the exterior world, which is our physical world, the body of a primitive man. They connect themselves up with the body of a primitive man and he begins his evolution in a different set of conditions and elevations which are all compatible with them. He has his poisoned blowgun and arrows; he has his spears and his tom-tom. He comes and goes frequently as either male or female. Life to him is a very primitive succession of events which is the survival of the fittest.

But always this entity goes back into spirit and re-purifies itself and reappears in a later lifetime in another evolution of consciousness as a higher state of human being, as someone who has gone on and is expressing just a little greater degree of intelligence than he formerly did, because all of these things have related him to himself and, in a sense of the word, they are multiplied. He has learned that he can use something besides a stone axe. He can use a spear now and knows how to use fire, etc., etc. His evolution goes on up but it is not done from this lifetime. This lifetime is only the outside or external appearance, the working out place of all the things which are done from the internal, the psychic self, as wave formations, as energy formations, which are functioning and oscillating under cycular patterns. These patterns reappear in a lifetime as one part of the negative cycle of these various life-times and so on, ad infinitum.

They are all very scientifically explained and something which the scientist of today can appreciate. I have never heard—as far as the truth seeker, the religionist, the theologist—anyone who knew what an energy-wave form was. I have spent thirty-five years with them, as far as my active life on the earth is concerned, in merely recapturing, revisualizing in a physical sense in the nomenclature or idiom of the times—the modern times—what I have learned hundreds of thousands of years ago down to the present. If I had not done so, I could not be sitting here talking about these things now. That, in itself, is the biggest proof because this science is not written in any of the books of today (1958). They shall be in the future, because I intend to leave them written; but for now, they are not.

Today, as far as science is concerned, all religions and all mind sciences are pseudo. They are not scientifically based and the scientist is right—they are not scientifically based because none of these exponents of truth know what a wave form is. They do not know how it is connected and interconnected. They do not know what its function is in other planes, how it can be changed, how it can have other wave forms added to it. They do not know the meaning of the creation of the spiritual man. The scientist is only concerned with the genes and the chromosomes and he does not know that these are only outside exterior manifestations of intelligent vortexal-patterns which come from the psychic self. They are the images in the mirror, so-to-speak.

But the true being is on the inside—that Kingdom of Heaven within, the Father within—not only that, but all of the things connected up to it since man started to retain the idiom of personality from one life to another and that he became man in so doing. Primitive as it was, it was still the maintenance of a certain set of conditions, of psychic shocks, of intelligence quotients, patterns, etc., that he had contacted from previous lives. It was retained as a personality, a definite so-and-so. Oh, he was not named John Smith or Henry Doe or something like that; he was called a name back in the jungle which was similar to those of the tribe but that same person persisted, even though his name changed from life to life and his sex changed from life to life but he still was the same person because he was still functioning from the previous set of psychic patterns and wave-formations that he had formed in the previous lifetime and was reflecting them out into the exterior of his physical life.

You see how important it is that we get in and study basic science, atomic science, physics, nuclear science—whatever it is we call it—but above all, we have to begin to see the pattern of life, not as merely a solid set of reactionary patterns which are formed on this side, but they are actually oscillating polarity patterns which stem from other dimensions. We have to learn to see everything as energy; the walls of the room are energy; they are tiny little solar systems which the scientist calls atoms. They are not solid. The television pictures and sound go through these walls as if they were not here. My consciousness can go through them as if they were not here. It has been proven many, many times that as far as we go into altering the dimensions of frequency transference from one dimension to another, that one is not conscious of the other except through harmonic patterns or structures. That is the way they are linked. They are not divided into

Satan, into Jesus, into Christ. They are not divided into the old gods of Minerva, Zeus and many of the others they had back in the past. They are one and all, the complete absolute, the Infinite manifesting—because it is infinite—into a finite number of relationships in all things.

That is the crux of the whole thing and I think the biggest step that any person makes in evolution or reincarnation is that day when he can visualize that everything he sees is all part of the Absolute, when he ceases to become conscious that there is such a thing as evil but that it is only a relationship under any set of given circumstances—it is a definite relationship where he is presently so standing. When you lose your sense of evil, you pass from the dimension in which evil can express itself, for only consciousness in anything gives it power over you provided, of course, that you have your connection with the higher self—the superconsciousness. When you begin to live in the external consciousness to the point where you exclude the Absolute, then you are lost; this reactionary world can affect you—and it does. But when you are linked up to the Absolute through the superconsciousness, there is nothing that can affect you. You pass from these little material pits of clay that people love so much—their sex, their beer and their cigarettes, the movies and all the various things which they think are necessary for them. Well, they are very necessary for them; they are part of that sustaining libido that they have acquired through hundreds of lifetimes coming up to the present. A few hundred years ago they were cutting each other down with swords and spears; today they are doing it just a little differently but they are doing the same thing. And so they keep on doing the things in different ways and different forms until they gradually learn, through the higher centers, to yearn for something good or better and then they can evolve into

216

a higher state of consciousness.

It is all a very wonderful thing when you start looking at it that way and that, in itself, is a challenge to our mentality, a challenge to our personal integrity to give up these old things—things that we have clung to so tenaciously and so viciously, I might say, sometimes in past lifetimes. We should quit condemning ourselves because those things we now consider in our present position as sinful were part of our life in the past. We can learn a great deal from them if we analyze it correctly in our present situation. Now we say, "Well, we are learning something." We do not have to go back to these things any more; but if we are going to be fearful of them and condemn ourselves because we were kings or conquerors or butchers, it does not make any difference; if we still maintain a sense of negation to them or if we are still negative toward them, they still have power over us! But if we say that, "Well it was evolution, it was a way of life, it was the way in which we passed through life at that time, we were doing what we thought was right, we were learning something", that, above all things, will help us a great deal because there really aren't any of us who cannot look back and say that we were guilty of a lot of things that we would not be very proud of right now! I am sure it is that way with me and that way with Ruth—and with anyone who has made spiritual progress.

We are all very conscious of the fact that we have seen these things in the past where we were conquerors and we did many things in the general idiom of that time which would not be at all compatible to the way in which we now think. We all have our skeletons in that closet of the past. There is no one who starts from the top. We all start from the bottom.

We have all been warriors and we have all been huntsmen, etc., etc. The lion in the jungle who lives off the herbivorous animals, because he is carnivorous, helps maintain a certain balance, even though to us he is very destructive. But he is very useful because he helps maintain the balance between the herbivorous elements of animal life so that they could not over-populate and destroy the plant life. The birds are carnivorous with insects. Many of them eat insects, yet we cannot say they are wrong because they are maintaining a balance. Throughout nature we see this Infinite Absolute working a scale of equilibrium which is perfect, provided it is not interfered with. Many of these experiences we say, are destructive; even the plagues that decimate people are considered very destructive because people have attached a false value on this thing we call life. The plagues in themselves are only experiences we have to live through because we learn through experience. We only become lost when those experiences cannot be cancelled out, when we cannot connect ourselves up with higher consciousness.

What we are trying to do is establish the picture of the Absolute so you would try in the future to cease trying to divide the Absolute into good and evil. There is no such thing—it is only positive or negative in relation to our particular position in our specific scale of evolution.

The further you get into these abstractions, the more contrasting is the level of intelligence, as far as the materialistic man is concerned, how elemental he is; and as far as our present civilization is concerned, or as life goes on here, it is in itself a proof of interdimensional relationship and how strong these lines of demarcation are. Actually, it can be pictured somewhat as a vast matrix of energy that is expanding and contracting in a kaleidoscope pattern of colors, of forms, ideas or consciousnesses which are constantly interweaving in and out of each other, which are all merely ideas and forms and various other different interpolations of consciousness as far as the materialistic world is concerned—something, you might say, like a vessel which was floating on an infinite sea—some great cosmogony of expanding and contracting consciousness, all contained within itself, surrounded by other vessels. It would relate man to other planetary aspects or lives in different elevations of consciousness that relives one particular little vessel of consciousness which we call the earth or materialistic domain of the present—if we can picture such a thing as an infinite sea.

Sometimes these things are very difficult to carry into consciousness in forms and relationships which are compatible to what we call our level of understanding. They have to be forms which link and relink consciousness into many different levels and elevations as far as the psychic is concerned; for knowledge never becomes wisdom unless it forms a direct rapport with the Infinite through the superconsciousness and only then does knowledge become wisdom because it has a definite polarity relationship with the Infinite. It is only knowledge when it is reactionary in nature and confined to such dimensions of consciousness as the psychiatrist might call the subconscious and remains in a reactionary stance or static condition, oscillating or subject to reoscillating conditions or recurrences when such points of consciousness pivot in upon it as some measure or form of comparative value. Reactionaryism never assumes any proportion of consequence as far as the individual is concerned unless it is linked and relinked through an infinite number of dimensions of consciousness within the interior of the psychic self into the Infinite. It must establish a rapport with the entire infinite cosmogony before it becomes wisdom, in itself directive, or that it reoscillates and, in a sense, returns some element or reagent which is stimulating or life-giving, rebuilding, revitalizing, guiding, directing and completing in itself.

Going back to "vessel", the materialistic vessel of

life floating on the infinite sea—how a man so confines himself—we might picture this vessel as a container made of metal which is stronger than the strongest steel and seems to be impervious to any frontal attack, as far as the individual is concerned, to liberate his consciousness from any exterior surface, for he is surrounded by this impenetrable wall which is actually nothing more or less than part of the various social structures, various forms of orthodoxies, cultisms and other accepted forms, in which he himself relates his own sphere of life to his fellowman. Therefore, it would be a very dangerous thing for him to do, to deflate his ego, to go beyond this particular thing which he terms his plane of relationship and his own particular sphere of influence unless he has something with which he can peer beyond this seemingly impenetrable wall in which is contained the sum and total of all things which are related to the material world, present and past, as they appear on the exterior surface of things in which man has contrived for himself to remanifest what he calls various aspects or dimensions of perspective in his daily life.

Therefore, the average individual is stopped! He does not have the intelligence to sustain any forward motion beyond the confined dimensions of this seemingly impenetrable sphere which he has envisioned within his mind, or else he does not suppose there is anything which lies beyond that! Whichever the case may be, it certainly does seem to circumvent him beyond certain limited spheres and causes a ceaseless trend of cycles into which he constantly reincarnates into these lower planes—reincarnates until he succeeds in some way or another in breaking through that wall in some manner or form. It is quite likely that the greatest part of that breaking through takes place when he is away from the material world in some spiritual world where he forms relationships and advances along certain lines so that he retains, at least psychically speaking, some measure of consciousness from the other planes and so he begins to break away from these things gradually—unless, of course, he begins to precipitate himself in some cycular pattern down some black abyss of immoral degeneracy which he destructively conceives.

These were just little thoughts which sometimes a person goes along with in his own mind when he becomes "tuned in" and he thinks beyond the more immediate reactionary horizon which confines or contains the various circumstances of his daily life. When his mind goes out, he begins to search his soul, or we can say that his mind goes within. He forms contact and rapport with other levels and different dimensions of consciousness which, of course, are a part of every individual, knowingly or unknowingly. It is sometimes very amazing to see how much physical strength, libido, how much drive there is contained in the average individual when he knows so little of life, yet there are very definite reasons why this is so.

They could not function no matter how much galvanism was carried into them or how much electronic stimuli was carried into them unless they had a lot of other things coming from other dimensions. Whenever we find any of these breakdowns, for instance, a person with arthritis, the muscles of the body still function according to the galvanism but the body is not in any sense of the word functioning perfectly. Why?—because certain alignments have been broken down between other dimensional relationships with that physical body to the psychic. That means that there are many cell structures as atoms in the human body that are not connected up in a functional or relative way with what was incurred through reincarnation.

That is the part where you wonder why they haven't grasped because it is so apparent. They have been spending billions of dollars a year to find out these things and still they get up to the threshold and they refuse to cross over it. It is something like a man who is drowning out in the water. You throw him a life preserver with a rope attached to it and he is clinging to a bit of driftwood. In his extreme fear, he refuses to let go of that piece of driftwood which cannot support him, to grasp the life preserver which will bring him back to the shore. In a sense of the word, these people are so materialistically minded that they refuse to cross this threshold because it would excommunicate them from the pedagogy of their fellowman or these so-called scientific structures—this great big pedestal which the scientist has erected for himself and from which nobody seems to want to fall. It presents a case where very few, if any, dare harass his fellowman or bear their criticism or censorship which always is endured by anything of the like; such as going beyond the bounds and bringing to science something which is spiritual in nature. This is abhorred by the scientist. It is not because it does not exist; it is because the scientist has refused to recognize it in the common terminology. This he has not been taught and therefore he does not recognize it.

That point was brought to me so apparently by a young lady who worked in one of the shops in which I worked some years ago. She was going to night school and taking psychology in the Los Angeles City College. Her professor had been hired by the city to teach young men and women from all walks of life. This man taught that anything spiritual was pseudo; spiritualism, religion, palmistry were pseudo. That is extremely asinine because even if the man had his own opinions, he should have at least been intelligent enough not to try to limit the scope of these students' minds in the class because there was every reason to assume that the students in that class were more intelligent than he

222

was, because they still had not been indoctrinated with these false doctrines. The greatest of all false doctrines is the doctrine of the is-so or the isn't-so. In spite of the fact that man can see around him the vast breadth, even in a limited way, but still he knows it's there, that there is no such thing as finity. Everything is infinite; he can go on and realize that beyond the horizon of this third dimension, there is that which he could not possibly grasp with his mind but still he delineates everything along the lines in a book and circumscribes every dimension that he goes into. The rest who come after him and follow him are like sheep.

This case was so very well borne out and shows how man does leave false impressions for maybe even a thousand years by this half-Greek and half-Roman who lived in the days around the turn of the Christian era. He was an extrovert, a psychopath, and he wrote a number of books on human anatomy; and he did not know anything about human anatomy. Beyond cutting his skin, he did not even know there was blood in the body. He did not know a thing about the body but he wrote books on it! For over 1,400 years people followed in his footsteps and people died because they dared to believe otherwise until another Italian came along and completely repudiated and tore to pieces this whole false doctrine; he established the fact of circulation of the blood and various portions of the anatomy and he became so well known that an Englishman named Harvey came down to study under him for over two years. He went back and got the credit for establishing that there was blood circulating in the human system when he learned it from the Italian.

From then on, there began a big witch hunt more or less, because wherever it was conveniently possible, the Roman Empire burned or otherwise did away with every human being who went against the commonly accepted theories and doctrines of the papacy. They

223

believed like the first fellow did who perpetuated this sin for more than 1,400 years; just like they believed up to two or three hundred years ago that the earth was flat and floating around in space with an angel on each corner to hold it up and push it around the sun. People died because they dared to believe otherwise. Columbus was one of the first to come along and prove otherwise; but even after that it was two or three hundred years before it was definitely changed as far as the holy Roman church was concerned.

That is how stupid and ignorant people are. They form these little ruts and carve their footsteps in time, going up and down the monasteries and temples and various other steps we see hollowed and worn out in stone, bare feet that have trekked to the meccas and holy shrines for thousands of years. They still come to them, even though the shrines are worn with their steps. They are doing the same thing now back in Lourdes in France. They have a great city there now with hospitals to take care of the sick and halt who come there because they believe in the magic powers of the water that comes out of that grotto. It is no different than any other water but the Catholic Church is making a good thing out of it in more ways than one. They could get just as much power out of the water in the tap if they believed in it.

You see advertised in every magazine, the power of the mind that goes along with these things; but what is the power of the mind? There is no metaphysician who can tell you because he does not know. He knows that it exists but he does not know what it is. It merely means that in the mechanism—and the conscious mind is a mechanism—all he has done, if any power is manifest on the surface of the exterior or material world (whether it is in the body or in things around him), the power of the mind itself is only concerned and only realized that there is no power in the mind at all because that which he calls power comes from the fact that he has connected up his oscillating processes with other centers of the psychic self other than the subconscious. Instead of putting the plug in the baseboard down below, he puts the plug in upstairs instead, and this wonderful power is constantly stemming into him as consciousness or realization of life from the higher worlds and from the Kingdom of Heaven which is within.

Man must not become subjective or malformed or transformed by the various negative elements in the subconscious. He has somehow or other succeeded in getting a straight line through upstairs for a moment. He has had just a glimpse, just a little particle of this power which is coming into him at all times. The power is wave forms, it is intelligent energy and it comes from upstairs and not from the mind at all. It has nothing to do at all with the mind, as far as the mind is concerned. The mind is only a channel for it; it is only an objectivism. The same power is flowing into man twenty-four hours a day but it comes through the transformer, the subconscious, and in that way, it is malformed and changed. It has become subjective to the thought patterns and various idiosyncrasies of the reactionary form of life man has lived through the ages. Therefore, it is reformed into the same thought patterns under which he has always lived and loses its power of constructiveness—and often becomes destructive. Only when he succeeds in getting a clear line through from upstairs into the superconsciousness, can he become healed because then he realizes that tremendous power—because it is so perfect and nothing can exist in its presence that is not perfect.

As far as the psychic body is concerned, it represents the physical in a sense; and everything else the positive polarity—the perfection. The physical is brought into subjective consciousness with it and is immediately transformed, but it cannot be so as long as that power has gone through the secondary transformation process through the subconscious.

So there is no power of the mind! The most delicate electronic instrument in the world could not measure in terms of amperes the power contained in the brain because there is none. The scientist today does not know what activates the fifteen million cells of the brain. He knows that there are pulsations of energy coming out of it but pulsations of energy are not power, they are wave-forms. You couldn't measure them in terms of power because we have no instrument that can do that. Energy is stimulated from other dimensions. It comes from somewhere else. It is not generated in the brain. There is nothing in the brain—there is not even any compound that could be termed in any sense of the word a regenerative process, let alone a generative process. We know there are various chemicals and elements which can—like a transistor, for instance, when a small amount of current is applied—create a stream or flow of electrons that is transformed into the terms of pulses and can be an amplifying device but it has to have another stimuli, the battery, before those electrons can be activated. If we carry this into the realm of chemical reactions, it is the same thing. It merely means that we have atomic structures which, as far as frequency relationships are concerned (because they are really energy) are brought into contradiction with each other and in the canceling out process they generate heat, or electric energy, like in a battery.

We do hope this clears that up for you for it is a most important concept.

CHAPTER XVI

Space Age Science

JUNE 21, 1965

Dear Student: As you no doubt know, one aspect of our Unarius policy is, from time to time and at most auspicious occasions, to present to the Unariun student and to any and all other interested persons or parties, the different and collective findings of our various scientists who are now so busily occupied extending the frontiers of man's knowledge. This course of action is made necessary because of the advanced nature of the Unariun concepts and ultimately science will, in itself, furnish its own incontestable proof that the Unariun curriculum and all compounded truths and concepts therein will thus become the transpository vehicle of man's future endeavors which will enlighten his mental horizon and give him workable answers to his present enigmas and riddles.

The months of May and June 1965, were particularly propitious in their collective exposés and from different fronts and scientific fields by prominent physicists who began to discuss quasi-stellar bodies. These are super stars whose light comes from space billions of light years ago and whose tremendous radiations of energy defy the present day quantum physics in analyses. Then this was quickly followed by a new presentation of the expanding and contracting universe as it was drawn diagrammatically, a long line terminating in a Y-shaped fork and with these quasi-stars placed at the fork.

Now right here we will interject an observation. In numerous places in the Unarius books and lessons, you can find references and descriptions of the expanding contracting universe, and the tremendous centrifugal and centripetal forces which are in action in this huge cosmic centrifuge; and the quasi-stellar bodies can thus be easily placed in the center of this centrifuge. The expanding and contracting cycle, by the way, is supposed to have about an 80 billion year duration according to the scientific article. We, of course, place no consensus on time factors, as in all fourth-dimensional hypotheses, time is an integrated factor. The scientist is concerned with it as he thinks it is a necessary third-dimensional constituent.

However, the "piece de résistance" came in the June 21st issue of the Los Angeles Times. Here two scientists working for the space age laboratory at the University of California at Berkeley, J. M. Wilcox and N. F. Hess, (NASA) and with information from different sources including the new satellite "Imp I" have what they believe to be the discovery of the magnetic theory of the solar system. We have reproduced this news article for you and excerpts of the aforementioned articles. If you will look in your Lessons 3 and 4 of the Advanced Course, you will find a number of diagrams which accurately describe the magnetic lines of not only our solar system but the atom and the universe as well.

And while you are perusing these lessons, remember they were published and copyrighted in 1960—five years before these scientific "discoveries"—using billions of dollars of technical equipment including satellites. If you will pause and reflect upon all of these juxtapositions, several things will emerge clear and apparent and which can be crystallized into one compelling conclusion: that there is in the world today a man who has placed at the disposal of mankind all-important and necessary facts and facets which are of concern and interest to mankind; concepts and facts which could save almost countless billions of dollars in these crude efforts to explore space, countless billions more spent trying to avert or compensate for the great human tragedy of ignorance in the field of medicine, psychiatry, a common human psychology, a workable brotherhood, all aspects and factors of human life, all relationships which run the gamut from the atom to the countless universes in fathomless space—all of these facts and many more are contained in the books and lessons and tapes which the Unariun Moderator has placed in your hands and at the disposal of mankind in general.

Yes, there is a moral to be found here, for within these Unariun works there is also to be found a personal note, a key for every human who will search within these Unariun liturgies, a key which will unlock the doorway into the heavens above, a brilliantly lighted pathway well marked by personal achievements and conquests over self as it has been lived in the past; and even a more final and ultimate goal wherein each soul shall find immortality and a creative everlasting life.

*   *   *   *   *

*Los Angeles Times—Mon., June 14, 1965—
Finds May Solve Universe Riddle

Two Astronomical Discoveries Hint at Expanding,
Curving Cosmos

By Irving S. Bengelsdorf
Times Science Editor

Two major discoveries of extremely distant objects in the heavens—coming "back to back" within a period of a few weeks—make this the most exciting month in the history of astronomy since man first used a telescope 356 years ago.

The unique properties of the newly discovered astronomical objects soon may permit man to solve the riddle of the nature of our universe.

Dr. Allan R. Sandage has just reported his discovery of numerous, hitherto unsuspected, remote, faint blue objects which he calls quasi-stellar blue galaxies (QS-BG). They do not emit radio signals and for the last 20 years were believed to be local blue stars in the outer regions of our Milky Way Galaxy.

And Dr. Marten Schmidt recently announced his analysis of the light coming from five more, extremely distant, radio-emitting, relatively rare astronomical objects known as quasi-stellar radio sources (QSRS). Prior to 1963 they also were believed to be normal faint stars in our galaxy.

Light Studied in Detail

About 40 QSRS are known, of which the light from nine has been studied in detail. One QSRS, 3C-9, is farther away from earth than any other known object.

Both Drs. Sandage and Schmidt are staff members of the Mt. Wilson and Palomar Observatories operated by the Carnegie Institution of Washington and the California Institute of technology. The 200-Inch Hale telescope atop Mt. Palomar played a key role in the research.

What excites astronomers and cosmologists about the recently discovered QSRS and the just unveiled QSBG is that both types of objects are at enormous distances from earth, and that the light we receive from them has undergone very large red-shifts.

Light travels as waves and the distance from crest to crest is called the wave length. If the wave length of light becomes "stretched out" or lengthened in its journey through space from its source to earth—it is said to have undergone a red-shift.

It is these two unusual features of the QSRS and QSBG—great distances from earth and large red-shifts —which soon will permit man to determine the exact structure of the universe.

At present, there are four proposed models of the cosmos. Study of the QSRS and QSBG will allow man either to pick out which of these four is correct, or it may even lead to new, presently un-thought-of concepts and models of the universe.

. . . What sort of an expanding universe?

To solve this problem, the scientist draws the accompanying diagram.

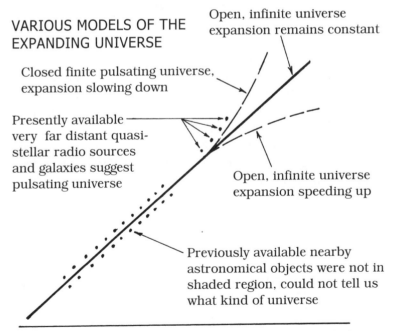

VARIOUS MODELS OF THE EXPANDING UNIVERSE

Open, infinite universe expansion remains constant

Closed finite pulsating universe, expansion slowing down

Presently available very far distant quasi-stellar radio sources and galaxies suggest pulsating universe

Open, infinite universe expansion speeding up

Previously available nearby astronomical objects were not in shaded region, could not tell us what kind of universe

Decreasing brightness (increasing distance) of celestial object

Each astronomical object has a red-shift and a brightness (a distance) which can be plotted. The diagram says that the further you go to the right the less is the brightness and the greater is the distance. The further you go upwards on the diagram the greater is the red-shift and the greater is the velocity at which the object is moving away from us.

Thus, the upper left part of the diagram would represent objects with large red-shifts and small distances; the bottom left part—objects with small red-shifts and small distances; the bottom right part—objects with small red-shifts and large distances; the upper right part (shaded)—objects with large red-shifts and large distances.

Saddle—Shaped

If the rate of expansion of the universe is constant, then astronomical objects would lie along the straight solid line. This line represents the Euclidean model of the universe—a flat universe which is open and infinite, expanding forever at the same rate.

If the rate of expansion is speeding up, then astronomical objects would lie along the dashed line which falls away and down from the solid Euclidean line. This dashed line represents the Hyperbolic model of the universe—a curved saddle-shaped universe which is open and infinite and in which the expansion is accelerating.

If the expansion is slowing down, then astronomical objects would lie along the dashed line which falls away. . .

Sun's Magnetic Waves Found Circling Earth
By George Getze
Times Science Writer

June 20, 1965—Like a gigantic lawn sprinkler sending streams of water spiraling over the ground, the sun's rotation sends waves of magnetism sweeping regularly past the earth.

This analogy was made Saturday by J. M. Wilcox of the University of California's space sciences laboratory at Berkeley, and N. F. Hess, of the National Aeronautics and Space Administration.

Wilcox and Ness discovered the distinct and repeating magnetic patterns by observing along the orbit of "Imp I", a scientific satellite known as the inter-planetary monitoring platform.

Their findings confirm the existence of a great spiral structure in the interplanetary magnetic field that extends out from the sun and which turns in time with the sun's period of rotation.

Four Distinct Spirals

This data has shown the existence of four distinct spirals in the magnetic field. Recurring patterns of intensity have been detected in each spiral, and the spirals alternate in the direction of the magnetic force.

That is, the force in one sector is directed toward the sun, and in the next is directed away from the sun, and so on for all four.

As each spiral sweeps past the earth it seems to influence the activity within the earth's own magnetic field, and also appears to affect the intensity of the cosmic ray bombardment of the earth, Wilcox and Ness report in Science, a publication of the Assn. for the Advancement of Science.

Two Physical Forces

The spiral effect in space is created by two physical forces acting upon the magnetic fields that surround the sun. The first is the outward force exerted by the charged particles that are continuously flowing from the solar corona. This is known as the solar wind and extends out into space farther than the earth and other planets.

The second force is the rotational pull exerted by the sun's own rotation, which takes place in cycles of 27 days.

The four spiraling sectors are not equal in size, according to the scientists.

Different Sectors

Three sectors each represent about 28 percent of the entire circular field round the sun, and each of these takes about 7.75 earth-days in an average sweep past the earth. The other sector is half the size of the others, and takes about 4 days to sweep past the earth.

Of greatest interest are the regular patterns of magnetic intensity that take place within each of the spiraling sectors, the two observers reported.

The data indicate that intensity reaches a peak level on the second day after the passage of the boundary between one sector and the next, and then declines to a low at about the sixth day.

Field Changes

It would seem from this, Wilcox and Ness said, that the magnitude of the interplanetary magnetic field rises in the forward portion of the sweep and falls in the trailing portion of the sector.

Ground observations of the changes in the earth's own magnetic field showed more or less the same thing: that earth magnetism fluctuates more during the peaks of the solar spiral sweeps, and is steadier when their magnetic intensity goes down.

Counts of cosmic rays reaching the earth also showed the effect, with relatively few during the magnetic peaks of the four spirals, and heavier bombardment during the lows.

Higher magnetic intensity in space may cause scattering of the cosmic particles so that fewer reach the earth during those periods, the two men believe.

Blue "Stars" Hint at Finite Space

By Irving S. Bengelsdorf
Times Science Editor

June 13, 1965—Astronomers have discovered the heavens are peppered with hitherto unsuspected, very far away, faint blue astronomical objects which permit man to take a giant step forward in attempts to understand the physical nature of the universe.

These blue objects, together with new findings regarding the so-called "radio stars", the rare celestial objects known as quasi-stellar radio sources discovered only two years ago, make the last four weeks the most exciting month in astronomy since Galileo first looked at the moon through his telescope.

Periods of "Pulses"

Preliminary interpretations of the new findings by Dr. Allan R. Sandage, of the Mt. Wilson and Palomar observatories, suggest that our universe is finite and pulsating—expanding outwards from a "big bang" explosion, slowing down, returning, undergoing a "big bang" again. Sandage even estimates that the pulse period—from one "big bang" to the next—is about 80 billion years.

He estimates that it has been 15 billion years since the last "big bang".

The evidence also suggests that the steady state theory of the universe—that matter is being formed continually and the universe is infinite and timeless—is incorrect.

Using the 200-inch Hale telescope atop Mt. Palomar Dr. Sandage discovered a novel class of distant blue celestial objects which does not emit radio signals.

Assisted by Phillipe Veron, a research student from France, Sandage made the exciting discovery in his search of the sky to detect new examples of other, relatively rare celestial objects known as quasi-stellar radio sources.

The newly discovered blue objects are so "fresh" that they have not received any "official" name as yet. The objects are known variously as "interlopers", or "blue stellar objects" (BSO), or "quasi-stellar blue galaxies" (QSBG).

Regardless of what they are called, the BSO are extremely far away in distance and, thus, represent matter as it existed far back in time. They can serve as important new yardsticks and guideposts to provide further clues for our insight into the creation, evolution, form and destiny of the universe.

Answer Possible

The BSO, since they are so numerous, may tell us whether the universe is an open system expanding indefinitely, or whether it is a definite closed, pulsating system—expanding first, then contracting, then expanding, then contracting.

More research is needed, however, to definitely establish our universe as finite and pulsating. The evidence, thus far, rests only upon nine quasi-stellar radio sources (QSRS) and only three blue stellar objects. Hardly enough to make a definite decision.

CHAPTER XVII

On Cryogenics, 1966

Several years ago, science discovered and became tremendously interested in the new discovery, a phenomenon which has been given the manufactured name Cryogenics. Briefly, this discovery relates to the new properties of conductivity of metals and tremendously increased magnetic properties of magnets when they are subjected to temperatures near absolute zero, minus 459.6 degrees Fahrenheit. Under this extreme, low temperature, a coil of wire will, when given a shot of electricity, retain the electrical charge which will keep circulating around this endless coil indefinitely.

Any magnetic material such as iron, steel and kindred ferrous metals can become magnetically charged up to 65,000 gauss. (The term and reference, "gauss", relates to a certain scientist of the 18th Century who first discovered and scientifically described magnetic lines of force). Ordinary magnets become saturated and useless if they are charged to 20,000 gauss under ordinary temperatures found on the earth.

Now these amazing properties of superconductivity and supermagnetism at the temperature of near absolute zero have been a great puzzle to science and as yet, none of these learned savants have come up with a logical answer and, as usual in such cases, there are almost as many theories as there are scientists.

Back nine or ten years ago (1955) when the books and lessons of Unarius were being written, information was impounded which explained not only this mystery but also many other mysteries which are presently baffling the scientists. At the beginning of the discovery period of Cryogenics, one explanation I specifically gave, to wit, that all of the known 101 element atoms of the earth spectrum were transducers or exchangers of energy and were busily engaged individually in their relative capacity in converting cosmic energy from the fourth dimension into the third dimension according to their respective oscillating frequencies which, in the sum and total of all reactive and resistive forces as applied to and interactive with the magnetic spectrum of the earth, determined the atom's particular property and weight according to the atomic scale.

These facts are only partially understood by the modern scientist despite Einstein and his famous formula $E = MC^2$ or the interconvertibility of atoms to energy and vice versa. Therefore, under ordinary conditions each atom, regardless of its name, is busily engaged in being that particular atom. In other words, it is carrying a load. An Arab knows to an ounce how much weight his camel will carry, and should one more ounce be added, the camel will lie down. It is the same with atoms. If we try to impose some new energy into them and make them carry an added load, they become resistive. Some will lie down, so to speak, and be non-conductors. Other kinds will stagger under the load (so to speak) and become hot, such as a filament in an electric light; and as it has been explained, all the result of the complex function of the atom as it pulses with the interdimensional cosmos.

Perhaps we can visualize the situation somewhat better if we imagine in our minds a large round framework of steel upon which have been placed at regular intervals, hundreds of light bulbs of different colors. These light bulbs are all connected in a series situation to a rotating switch with many different contact points. When the switch is rotated, these different colored lights flash off and on at frequent and regular intervals, something like the big electric signs we all occasionally see in the city.

Now this ball-shaped configuration of electric lights

looks something like an atom if we could enlarge one a few hundred billion times. Each light would become what the scientist calls an electron, neutron or positron, according to its charge. They flash off and on (so to speak) millions or billions of times a second. These oscillating positive and negative charges are the joining centers of parallaxes of millions of lines of energy which are pulsating in this very rapid manner as their function in this tiny centrifuge of cosmic energy. As they so oscillate according to their frequency and manifest their many parallaxes, so they become resistive or reactive to the magnetic spectrum of the earth.

Now this magnetic spectrum is not quite like the scientist thinks. Gravity is part of this spectrum as are all other physical reactive properties so manifested and which I have called hysteresis. The transference of the sun's energy is a reactive, resistive process of hysteresis with the magnetic spectrum. Actually, this spectrum is very complex and it is, in itself, a subject too vast to be discussed at this moment. Now, when we reduce the temperature we must, in some way, separate the atoms from the magnetic spectrum. We do this partially in our refrigerator. In the laboratory the scientist can almost totally accomplish this and can suspend (in a sense) the resistive, reactive process of hysteresis to the point where he can no longer measure temperature or 459.6 degrees below zero Fahrenheit. And when this hysteresis is no longer effective, then the atom becomes totally conductive and possesses no opposition to an electrical current which may be imposed upon it.

This bit of electricity can be pictured somewhat like a bag of grain which is being tossed lightly from one strong man to another. The atoms, like strong men with nothing to do, can toss this electricity around, so to speak, indefinitely so long as their natural burden, that is, conducting cosmic energy into the reactive, resistive content of mass, is not imposed upon them. However, if the freezing or separating force is removed, they will very quickly resume their natural function and while they are so working, they will be partially or totally reactive or resistive to any outside electrical energy thrust upon them. So you see, it is really quite simple to understand these baffling mysteries if we can escape the third dimension long enough to analyze and to compose a hypothesis which must always include as a basic foundation the true source or origin of all things which stems, not from the earth world third dimension, but from the Infinite Fountainhead which is manifest in the many dimensions or mansions and composed of Infinite Intelligence as it is so manifest in an infinite number of ways—all according to those all-important laws of frequency, harmonics, cyclic motions, etc., and of which I have so often explained before.

The scientists of today are still trying to understand and equate into their earth world science, not the true sources and actions of creative energy intelligence but only the results of certain manifestations which have been made apparent to them in their earth world as their environmental factors of life, such as heat, light, sound, mass, etc. Naturally, as I have repeatedly explained, these things are nonexistent. Through your evolution, you have learned to become reactive or resistive to this environment of resistive, reactive manifestations in your life associations and called them by such familiar terms as heat, light, mass, etc., to the degree that you have compounded your whole life from this complex association which you call your earth-life experiences.

In the years to come, the earth-world scientist will perhaps, and quite likely, uncover newer and more startling discoveries and correspondingly increase his perplexities. However, it is very improbable that so long as he is an earth-man and so occupying his present scale of evolution, he will never understand these scientific explanations which I have given you until he, too, approaches that threshold which I have so often mentioned—the threshold which separates him in his third dimension and the vast infinite interdimensional macrocosm—a threshold he will laboriously begin to climb over just as you are beginning to do—when he will, in his life in-between lives, study, learn and condition himself for this great transition from a material physical man into a spiritual being who lives as a living flame minus the flesh and the physical world and oscillates infinitely with Creative Intelligence for his source of supply and the substance of his life.

And this source of supply is abundant and everlasting so long as he is not resistive and reactive to it as he now is in his earth life toward everything which he encounters. This, too, is your most ultimate objectivism; and may I repeat, the creative law is adamant. It is either a forward progressive and a recreative motion or it is a retrogressive and destructive motion. It is your choice.

In our previous discussion on cryogenics, we probed rather deeply into the so-called mysteries of superconductivity, supermagnetism of certain metals when temperatures were reduced to near absolute zero, minus 459.6 degrees Fahrenheit. It was pointed out that metallic atoms and their molecular combinations were more or less resistive or subject to magnetic saturation at more normal earth temperatures, with a rather simple explanation that this was because atoms were busily engaged in the conversion process known as hysteresis. However, this simple explanation is not sufficiently technical and perhaps in a way, not completely accurate. The subject of resistance and magnetic fluxes in their relationship to all of the atomic forms which compose the material world is extremely complex and in some respects, unless principle is understood, could be confusing and contradictory.

The proposition of conductivity and nonconductivity is one which involves millions of wave forms of energy which are vibrating at speeds unknown or incomprehensible to our present-day science. The Laser Beam, vibrating somewhere near 750 million megacycles per second is practically standing still compared to the vibrations which involve or compose the atom itself. It is also important to remember that all atoms radiate an electromagnetic field. As of today no scientist seems to be able to describe electricity, what it really is. He may possess considerable technical knowledge and know-how in the application of electricity in industry and in other uses which involve his society, yet he could not accurately describe the exact composition of the electricity which flows along the wire into his home. He knows it is an oscillating or alternating polarity at 60 cycles per second and it may have a predetermined pressure of 110 volts, still he does not know what this electrical energy is.

In a general way and to avoid a complex explanation, all electrical energy (electricity) as it appears in this third dimension is composed of countless millions of tiny oscillating wave forms of energy. The net sum and total of all these oscillations is always so polarized that this energy will travel at the basic speed of light, 186,000 miles per second. The light spectrum is similar in this respect to electrical energy and each basic wave-length of light—as it is so known in spectral analysis as yellow, green and red—is likewise composed of countless millions of oscillating wave-forms of energy. All are polarized in such a way they vibrate to form a subharmonic which we call a light-wave or color, just as the red Laser Beam vibrates 750 million megacycles per second, yet the composition of frequency which composes this red beam vibrates at frequencies which

243

would be incomprehensible to earth-minds.

Therefore, the proposition of conductivity of any group of atoms which form say, a copper wire, depends primarily upon the proposition of frequency transferences; that is, the millions of tiny energy waveforms can travel through copper because there is at least a partial harmonic pulsation or polarity exchange between the copper atoms and their force-fields and that of the electrical energy-stream. However if this copper atom is also oscillating harmonically as it does with the fourth-dimensional macrocosm, then there is a different set of harmonics and polarity patterns which are generated in the electromagnetic field of the atom and in direct proportion, reduces the ability of the atom to harmonically carry the extra energy stream imposed on it.

When the scientist reduces the environmental temperature in a closed chamber of a copper coil, he is taking away or isolating the atoms in the copper coil from their normal relationship with the terrestrial environment which plays an important part in the process of cosmic hysteresis. All atoms which compose our earth-world, and at whatever temperature we find them, whether they are at the poles or at the equator, are all comparatively warm—that is, compared to the absolute zero of space in the absence of any hysteresis or energy transference.

Mountain peaks at the equator remain snow-capped the year round simply because there is less hysteresis at these higher altitudes than at sea level. Ionization is largely controlled by different so-called radiation belts such as the Van Allen, etc. Some of them are thousands of miles above the earth and, for the most part, have still to be discovered by the scientists. Yet, they too, all play an important part in the conversion of energy which the earth man knows as heat, light, magnetic flux, etc.

With a thick-walled, metal chamber in a laboratory, all by-products of hysteresis, heat, etc., can be absorbed and conducted away from a copper coil to the point where this coil becomes superconductive, a condition closely approximating that which is found in space (as it is called by the scientist). Actually, as I have said previously, space is infinitely filled with energy. Space, therefore, is superconductive on the same basic principle that a copper atom or molecule is conductive, as I have described the process in the previous paragraphs.

The scientist has yet to learn of the superconductivity in space and which, if he ever does, he will find that it is not a third-dimensional proposition which can be equated or analyzed on the basis of any of his presently known physics. To understand the interdimensional macrocosm will require not only a different science, mathematics, physics or any other subdivisions but it will also require a different mentality. We can therefore sum up in some general conclusions and say that—as I did many times before—the earth-world or similar worlds are merely basic and a rather primitive plane of expression in the grand scale of evolution—a plane which all people evolve into and out again. And I might add, many of them revert in their evolution after passing from the earth-plane and again plunge themselves in a reverse manner back into the earth world environment in their downward plunge into oblivion.

Again, the all-important message: never believe you have it made! A few psychic manifestations or demonstrations will not insure you a seat at the foot of the throne, neither do such things as psychic demonstrations, flashbacks, etc., positively identify you as an adept or master, no more so than do the optimistic declarations of some scientist when he makes a new discovery and declares to the world he has that all-important secret which will reveal the innermost meaning of life.

We are all traveling this evolutionary pathway together and no matter how far we advance, the proposition is always the same. To maintain a constant advance, means constantly learning and constantly using what we have learned. There is no ending to the infinity which lies ahead of all of us, for indeed, if there were such an ending, then Infinity would cease to exist. But for the present, as a Unariun student, be concerned with that all-important life-saving proposition of freeing yourself from the earth-world-plane by developing your mentality, your understanding and your ability to use knowledge in a higher spiritual world environment. Your life depends upon it!

CHAPTER XVIII

Scientist Will Testify if Space is Full or Empty

Search for "Ether" in Limbo for Years; Discovery Would Solve Many Puzzles

By Rudy Abramson
Times Staff Writer

Los Angeles Times—Thursday, Nov. 16, 1967—St. Louis—Working in an abandoned ammunition storage hut outside St. Louis, a Washington University physicist is rigging up an ingenious experiment to tackle the nagging scientific question of whether space is full or empty.

There was a time when no less a personage than Sir Isaac Newton believed that space must be filled with some kind of medium to account for the propagation of light and the force of gravity.

But no one could find it and the search has been in a state of limbo for many years, particularly since Albert A. Michelson and Edward W. Morley showed in 1887 that if such a medium exists, it does not affect the velocity of light.

Light Through Ether

They reasoned that the speed of light would be somewhat impeded if it did flow through this medium—ether.

After all these years, Dr. Peter R. Phillips, associate professor of physics at Washington University is going to have a go at finding it, and he says he is optimistic that he will.

His experiment will get under way in about two months, and he expects it will continue for a year or more before he can start drawing conclusions from his data.

The idea, basically, is to suspend a bar magnet from an extremely fine fiber, shelter it as much as possible from all external influences, and see whether it twists slowly from side to side.

If the earth is indeed moving through an ether, the magnet should twist first one way, then the other on a daily cycle since the rotation of the earth would cause the ether to hit the magnet from a different direction as the earth turns. The presumption is that the ether is made up of infinitesimally small particles that would interact with electrons in the magnet.

It was to escape magnetic disturbance that the project was moved from the campus physics laboratory to the abandoned Army ammunition hut out of town.

To further insure that the magnet is not disturbed, it will be suspended in a vacuum chamber. It is also being wrapped in a coil through which an electric current will be passed to reduce its sensitivity to magnetic fields.

"If we could turn off the magnetic forces altogether," Phillips explained Wednesday to a symposium on New Horizons in Science, "the needle would point along the direction in which the ether is streaming through the laboratory."

Weak Force

"This simple idea is difficult to put into practice because the new force is so small. But by using a magnet suspended from a fine fiber as our compass needle, by employing sensitive optical techniques to measure its position, and by setting up a special laboratory far from the vibrations of the city, we have come close to our goal."

If Phillips and his associates are successful in demonstrating that the earth is moving through this mysterious undetected medium, the impact on physics would be enormous. But Phillips said he does not believe such a discovery would be incompatible with Einstein's work which assumed there is no ether.

Unrelated Puzzles

"It is our hope," Phillips said, "that if we can establish the existence of an ether, we will provide a framework into which we can fit many puzzling phenomena which now seem unrelated."

During the era when scientists could not accept space as a void, technology had not reached the point where such a subtle phenomenon could be detected if it existed. By the time it became possible to perform this kind of research, the ether had ceased to be in vogue.

Phillips said the ether may have properties similar to superconducting metals which in theory conduct electricity without resistance when they are chilled to absolute zero.

This could explain how light could pass through the ether without being impeded.

(Copyright 1967, Los Angeles Times
Reprinted with Permission)

The Plasma Filled Space

During the last days of October 1967, several articles were dictated which dealt with, specifically, light, physics, the transmission of energy through space, and other relative factors. Then on November 16, a little more than two weeks later, an article appeared in the Los Angeles Times which related the renewed efforts of present-day physicists in their attempts to gain new information on these astrophysical concepts, either from old or previously existing sources, or from new and different explorations. The importance of this article cannot be over-emphasized, as it at once validates certain assertions and concepts which we have previously presented, one of which is that we are working very closely, either subconsciously or intuitively, with the earth scientists; and this article proves conclusively by its perfect timing that we, the Unariun Brotherhood, are working very diligently to prod these earth scientists in the right direction.

Also, as we have stated, their (the scientists') position is quite elemental in the scale of evolution and their attempts to gain knowledge equally primitive. More directly concerned with this article, scientifically speaking, is the re-establishment of the old "ether" theory, first posed by Newton, as our first more modern scientific contemporary, that space is filled with what has been currently called "ether", and which we have, in our articles, called plasma. The "etheric form" theory was never clearly established and even though picked up by later contemporaries, was eventually dropped, principally because of lack of instrumentation and a fundamental understanding of the laws of electronics, energy composition, etc., as we have presented them.

As is indicated in the article, a space infinitely filled with plasma (or ether) would solve many riddles, just as we have solved them for you in our many articles! The same fundamental electronic concepts would infinitely enlarge the perspectus of all man's knowledge, biology, medicine, etc.

To place the capstone, so to speak, upon our revelations, let us therefore firmly establish a valid consensus of law which relates in particular to the transmissions of any and all spectral energies, either as they are supposedly classified by present-day science or the interdimensional classifications which we have presented. It should be noted first, however, that we are not at this time dealing with secondary energy transmissions which have been classified as cosmic rays (energy particles) or solar winds. These are subjects which have been previously dealt with, or will so be done at some future time, and have no particular emphasis with the major portion of spectral energy transmissions.

First, it is impossible for any wave form energy to "travel" or to relate as an energy transmission without a suitable plasma or medium, an incontestable fact proven in countless, everyday examples. In fact, life on any planet or even the planet itself would be nonexistent without energy transmissions and some form of media which relates itself to the transmission of energy, either resistively or conductively. And it is this resistive, conductive impedance—formed according to a certain basic law of positive-negative frequency interpolations within the cyclic motions of energy—which, either as media or plasma, or as motional energy that are, according to their cyclic motions, either conductive or resistive, according to these positive-negative oscillations. It is this positive-negative frequency interpolation which determines the EMF's of the atoms and determines their dissimilarities or affinities, as well as their atomic weights.

In free space, energy from the sun does not travel as a straight-line beam or ray, but is a motion of energy within the complex plasma of space wherein it oscillates according to positive-negative relationships in cyclic motions, and thus propagates or regenerates similar wave form or oscillating motions according to proper sequences in these cyclic motions. Thus, energy travels through space, just as energy from the stone thrown in the pond regenerated itself in the cyclic motion which pushed water molecules up and down.

In space-plasma, however, such plasmic oscillations directly transfer from one cyclic motion to a similar motion an exact wave form facsimile; thus space-plasma is, on the basis of frequency relationship, both conductive and resistive. Conductivity represents the more positive conducting surface, because as the sun is the central nuclei of a cosmic centrifuge, energy is first compressing, then expanding into a different dimensional relationship, and all planetary bodies so involved in the sun's radius, represent the negative terminus of this third-dimensional oscillating condition.

At this point it must also be remembered, the earth, in turn, represents a lower oscillating terminus which re-expands the sun's EMF into the earth's magnetic spectrum—another energy conversion process more clearly understood under the laws of harmonics. All electronic fields, as they are represented by atoms and atom structures called elements, are therefore held (so to speak) rigidly within the oscillating conditions of this extremely complex EMF spectrum, as it is energized by the positive sun; and other spectral energy radiations from the sun are, in reality, reoscillating energy wave form motions throughout the space-plasma which are then, in turn—according to the laws of harmonics—through reconversion, reoscillating into the familiar earth form energies known as heat, light, gravity, etc.

A full and complete explanation and dialogue on this cosmic hysteresis would involve quite possibly many volumes. Certainly these several articles are most insufficient, yet they do present the first precepts into a more complete understanding of the cosmic universe. You will therefore understand our position, after reading the preceding Los Angeles Times article, that in man's present position in his earth world sciences, he is still in a very primitive state of evolution—an evolution, individually and collectively speaking, made pos-

sible and masterminded by super-creative intelligence
—an intelligence which so creates and re-creates not
only the atomic energy structures of suns, planets,
galaxies and universes, but which creates also in Infinity, and according to law, order and harmony, prepos-
sesses the future of man's evolution into an infinite
number of forms, relationships and life experiences,
lived through the ageless ages of time.

CHAPTER XIX

On Hysteresis

I have, on numerous occasions, and in many instances throughout the liturgies of Unarius, stated that we do not get heat or light directly from the sun, as our present-day scientists understand heat and light; and that this aforesaid heat and light is a conversion of energy which, for want of a better word, I have called hysteresis. However, a much clearer explanation is in order.

In presenting the entire infinite cosmos as a tremendously compact amassment of large and small centrifuges or vortexes of energy which, in turn, through internal positive-negative oscillations, remanifest third dimensionally as universes, galaxies, star-suns and their solar systems, etc., we must at this point now conceive that all such fourth-dimensional compositions and third-dimensional materializations must, according to the law of universal dynamics, function and oscillate under a closed circuit condition; that is, positive to negative and vice versa. It is these oscillating conditions in the electromagnetic fields of atoms that form the so-called "glue" which holds them and their molecular compositions together, or conversely, as opposites in their oscillating polarities; a difference which is called mass, or a different atomic weight, thus determining one element from another. The synthesis of heat and light, as it is known by the earth scientist, is also determined by closed circuit conditions—positive attracts negative, and vice versa.

The earth represents, on one plane to the sun, a negative polarity which, electronically speaking, is synthetically similar to the sun. Energy, therefore, from the sun is "attracted" by the earth.* However, this is but one-half of the closed circuit condition. The earth, as a negative polarity, does again re-oscillate to the sun the other half of the phase wave, whatever the frequency of the phase wave may be.

Now let us introduce the "x" factor: the "x" factor is harmonics. As any combination of wave forms oscillate within themselves, they regenerate harmonics. The earth is an oscillating polarity, and composed as it is, of 92 energy forms called atoms which are miniature solar systems, harmonic regeneration then recurs in all such atomic structures according to wave length structure, oscillating in closed circuit conditions within each atom, and so regenerating harmonically with solar wave structures, again transpose harmonically, other wave structures which are called heat and light.

It should be said at this time, that all other concepts and factors which involve earth world life are the direct result of this cosmic sun-to-earth closed circuit, interactive, energy transposition. Our weather is a direct result of differences, positive-negative ionization, as is fog, smog, as well as a good vintage year for wine. This cosmic interplay also very greatly affects human behaviorism, as every human is, automatically and psychically speaking, interconnected in this vast and extremely complex energy transposition.

Astrology, as it is known at this time, is a decadent remnant of this scientific concept and which (astrology) falsely places the emphasis upon the planets rather than the entire cosmic centrifuge. The true perspective sees all suns, solar systems, planets, etc., all harmonically linked together, all oscillating in countless and in an infinite number of frequencies, all harmonically regenerating a number of base plane frequencies which are again subdivided and resubdivided into

*Heterodyne

atomic forms and their surcharged electronic constituents which also beat harmonically on their EMFs to the entire Infinite Cosmogony.

When science begins to see and understand what I have just presented in the vast infinite cosmic centrifuge, then man will find the true answers to all his problems. He will find a way to propel space ships without rocket motors; cars will glide silently around the streets without internal combustion motors. Smog will be a thing of the past; yes, even now (1967) smog could be controlled or eliminated by the use of high-frequency radiations emanating from round metal balls atop huge Tesla Coils which would dot the big cities at regular intervals. The weather, too, could be controlled by the use of huge high-frequency generators on many mountain-tops throughout the world. These generators could so control ionization ratios in the upper stratosphere and ionosphere that weather of any kind could be programmed for any section of the world.

On these same principles, high-frequency oscillators could be built using crystals to determine correct frequencies and so tuned as to introduce in any bacteria or germ life, or even virus, certain opposing harmonic frequencies which would destroy the bacteria or virus and not harm surrounding cell tissue; thus all disease could be eliminated from the earth! Also, such generators could be constructed which would alter or remove malformed or aberrated wave structures in the psychic anatomy, thus curing insanity, epilepsy and other mind diseases, as well as cancer and a host of psychic indispositions and inclemencies, phobias, etc.

If all this sounds Buck Rogerish, then I must point out that all of this and much more has been arrived at on other planets in other solar systems. Even on one of our solar planets, Mars, their underground civilization has utilized most of this science. Still in retrospection, should at any future time in the world's history, the earth people acquire and use all this scientific knowledge, it would cease to be the earth and would no longer be a suitable place of habitation for the countless millions of aboriginals who reincarnate into this world from life to life, and who would not be inductively disposed to incept and live under such highly-ordained scientific life.

As a whole, people of this earth are in their present position in their evolution by a combination of many factors, the most important of which is environment; and in any given status of evolution should environment radically change, then the people concerned with this environment change or die. So we, the people from the higher worlds, who have traveled through time and space to where our environment and our knowledge is vastly different and expanded from that life and understanding of the aboriginal earth man, we must be very temperate in giving this knowledge to such people who are yet almost totally unprepared. We must use great jurisprudence in beginning to separate such primitive peoples from their lowly beginnings, for such is the way of evolution. For each man's future is his evolution and theoretically, at least, any individual's evolution can cover the width, breadth, length and height of Infinity.

So to you inhabitants of your earth world, do what you can with your earth lives; enjoy your joys to the fullest and in your sorrows reap the strongest faith, for tomorrow in the infinity of your experiences, you begin to reap the fruit from the tree of knowledge. Learn to substitute logic and reason for superstition, and let creative intelligence supersede the revengeful emotional gods of your religions.

A more exacting descriptive synthesis of the solar system is contained elsewhere in our liturgies, particularly in the second lesson course, where it has been diagrammed. Briefly, the sun is the central nucleus of a vast fourth-dimensional, cosmic vortex or centrifuge, which, as a reactive agent in the interdimensional cosmos, and functioning according to well-defined laws, converts and reconverts energy in two directions simultaneously. Such a vortex or centrifuge is, in turn, constantly re-energized by a higher or fifth-dimensional type energy formation. In our solar system vortex, as energy is compressed into the third-dimensional direction, this compressed energy forms a nucleus or the sun which, in turn, valve-like, liberates enormous quantities of energy into the third dimension.

This liberated energy, however, is not incoherent, but partially remanifests as a complex electrostatic field—part of this field having been resolved by the earth man as the gravitational and the magnetic fields. Other portions of the sun's energy, in regular cyclic motions, which have a synchronous pulse-beat around the sun, follow counterclockwise in their respective orbits, or the nine major third-dimensional planets, which are actually the nuclei of secondary anomalies within the primary vortical structure. And as this great vortex is oscillating within itself, it also turns axially; the planets being captive within this extremely complex EMF, rotate according to the synchronous pulse-beat of the entire vortex!

It can be easily seen that the earth, like all other planets, is traveling in its circumferential orbit in this extremely dense and complex EMF. It can and does reconvert, in the processes described, certain of the sun's spectral energies, which the earthman calls heat and light.

Max Planck, at the end of the nineteenth century, partially visualized this pulse-beat, synchronous energy conversion, which he attempted to describe in his quantum mechanics. Later Einstein picked up this quantum theory and redeveloped it into a much more complex mathematical equation which ultimately gave rise to the theory of relativity, and other adjunctive mathematical theories, liberally described as the space-time continuum theory.

It should be noted at this time an extremely important fact: that so far as our solar system vortex is concerned, and realizing the enormous energies within this vortex, the tremendous compressions and expansions and extreme magnetic stresses, all of which are taking place simultaneously and at fantastic rates of oscillation, that any evaluations of straight-line speeds are quite worthless. The third-dimensional speed of light (186,210 mps) is quite subjective to these enormous compressions and expansions, and so far as distances being measured at the fixed base-point of light, speed will therefore, third-dimensionally speaking, appear to be compressed or shortened!

Einstein attempted to cover this in his relativity theory; however, neither Einstein nor any other earth-man has correctly interpreted the condition of electromagnetic stresses and numerous force fields which comprise this fourth-dimensional solar-system vortex; and which, in turn, again becomes only a small quantitive unit in another or galactic vortex, and again, in turn, a small unit in the enormous fourth-dimensional vortex of the universe, and which could be repeated on ad infinitum!

The earthman has yet to learn that so far as his earth world is concerned and all factors dealing with his earth world, the entire superstructure of what he has divined and divided into his sciences, his religions, all artifacts and accouterments of life, all concepts are all made possible to him through the universal premise of creative law, order and harmony, which is expressed throughout Infinity, and remanifesting interdimensionally into planetary systems, revolving about a central nuclei star-sun and traveling through its respective galaxy along the same well-ordered magnetic lines. The synthesis of life for the earthman therefore, is merely another form of reconversion and through what he calls his metabolism, his mental processes, his way of life upon the earth, he is, in this life synthesis, reconverting a small part of that great infinite universal energy which surrounds him and his little planet and carries him on his tiny planetary ship through the vastness of interstellar time and space.

The foregoing transcript is one of great importance and most accurately describes the elusive, unknown factor constantly apparent in Einstein's theory of relativity; and to the third-dimensional mind, an incomprehensible factor, as such minds always conceive any objectivisms as having a fixed place and time as an evaluation of distance between any two or more fixed points.

This earth world consensus is dependent, however on third-dimensional conditions which resolve all objectivisms as a quantitive amassment—all traveling through space and time at the same speed, and in this respect space and time become an equally-divided measurement in any assessment. The media in all aspects, however, is resolved into the ninety-two natural atom forms known as elements. These atom forms can be said to be oscillating synchronously and locked in their respective EMFs, become fixed objectivisms known as mass substances to the earthman. Such mass substances could also be called a third-dimensional plasma. However, such mass objectivisms called life, by the earthman, and lived in his reactionary stances are quite useless and are nonexistent in the fourth-dimensional plasma which is composed of an infinite number of vortical forms, all oscillating at speeds which could not be conceived by third-dimensional minds.

This fourth-dimensional cosmogony, so extremely

complex as to defy description, is, however, to be in the future, the home of many earth people, as well as peoples from countless billions of planets throughout the innumerable universes. In his evolutionary travel into this fourth-dimensional plasma, the earthman will find certain numbers of frequencies with which he can beat harmoniously and these, in turn, will synchronously form a world or a place to him. He will have, in effect, found one of the "many mansions", and so as he thus "lives and breathes", inductively speaking, in this plasma field, he will have found and developed into his consciousness, one more place in his eternal evolution, one more step into Infinity.

In retrospection, this plasma world is synonymous in respect to his earth world which he has left behind, and it was there that he first repeated the analogy of his evolution by developing a consciousness which he called life, from the harmonic and synchronous beat of his earth-world planet, composed of pure energy, in tiny atomic solar systems which he, in his life concept, called mass; and from which he developed into the complexities of his earth life—and this is evolution: an analogy of life lived from plane to plane comprised from the innumerable pulsations of a highly compressed and expanded Infinite Cosmogony.

These are the "many mansions" and the true promise of immortality, developed as an objective consciousness which is reformed and reshaped and readapted to meet the ever-changing demand of evolution through this timeless, spaceless cosmogony.

How infinitesimally small then, does the earth world become, and the individual beat of life expressed by any human! How infinitesimally small is his consciousness that relegates such false evaluations that his planet alone, is inhabited; that his individual religion is a valid means of salvation, a bigotrous consensus which condemns all mankind, or that he believes

261

his political system is the best and should be lived by, regardless of race, creed or ethnic background.

Like a virulent bacteria, man swarms upon the surface of a tiny bit of compressed energy called rock, grown green with the moss of forests and jungles, and as if to hide it, in its shame, covered with a vaporous blanket of air, it plunges madly in its orbit around a pulsating ball of light, trying to warm itself on all sides in a daily rotation. And within this earth world, spawn those who walk upright and call themselves men, attempting to placate the frigid gnawing fear of death and eternal darkness, only partially concealed in their vaporous air or their intermittent daylight.

Yet, we, in the worlds of Light, living far beyond the compressed fields of energy plasma of a fourth-dimensional solar system vortex, look with compassion upon this and many other earth worlds, for here again in Infinite Consciousness is the beginning of immortal life: lives yet to be lived in that ever-increasing spiral of evolution, into the higher reaches of Infinity.

Mention has been made of Einstein's "Theory of Relativity", and such attendant mathematical concepts which would relate to a more factual understanding of not only the mean differences of the speed of light in free space, but other factors such as the "red shift", etc., could also be more easily understood. The fat being in the fire, therefore, let us proceed: first, man and his science and in its derivatives has mistakenly looked out into the starry skies and seen what he thought was a vacuous space with tremendously long distances between the heavenly bodies which he calls stars. He is quite mistaken in this vacuous space belief. Man does not have sensory equipment to discern what space is, no more than he has sensory equipment to discern a television wave, which is streaming through his space about the places where he lives, and he supplements this lack by discerning television waves through a receiver. However, he has, at this time, neither physical sensory equipment nor the electronic mechanical equipment to discern space.

If a scientist takes an empty jar and sealing it perfectly, extracts all the air molecules from within the jar, he believes he has a perfect vacuum; this is untrue. He has only extracted the nitrogen and oxygen molecules which comprise his atmosphere; he has not extracted the fourth-dimensional plasma which supports and makes possible the continued life of the atom molecule combinations which comprise the jar. So despite its apparent transparency, or that it is space, it is, nevertheless, extremely and compactly filled with energy plasma, as has been described to be oscillating in cyclic motions and at incomprehensible speeds!

It is this frequency which makes it invisible and undetectable, for any man-made instruments which he might make in an attempt to discern or measure this plasma would be quite useless as he could not attain a proper range within the vibrating range of this cosmic plasma.

Now any light which travels through this so-called space does so by virtue of the conductivity of this plasma. The analogy here can be made by the familiar "stone in the pond" demonstration; energy from the stone radiates away from the point of impact by pushing water molecules up and down. In space, light travels through the media of plasma by means of frequency attunement and reversal. All light waves travel as positive and negative polarities. In free space, either directly or by harmonic attunement, a light wave travels forward, first as a negative to positive in similar plasma oscillating frequencies.

Now if this plasma is contracting or expanding, the speed of light will vary according to the polarity indications in the transmissions. As has been stated, in all fourth-dimensional vortexes this energy plasma is constantly expanding and contracting. As the earth is a negative terminus from positive impulsions, light, therefore, approaching the earth would appear to be traveling faster than it really was. In other words, it was being carried forward by positive-negative induction. Moreover, different light frequencies—as in incoherent light—would be affected differently, according to inductive ratios. This would show up on a spectrographic analysis as a "red shift", if the light from an extremely distant star-sun were being analyzed, according to a third-dimensional earth-world analysis.

There are several theories floating about, none of them correct, as to why this red shift exists. A further analysis and study of the inductive ratio in the plasma of space will explain why the galaxy or universe seems to be expanding. It simply means that as light from distant stars is viewed and that it is not being received at the earth terminus at its earth-measured speed (186,000 mps), that it then becomes a cosmic illusion, or as Einstein said, relative.

Conversely, light traveling from our sun to some distant planet would also erroneously be measured, if the science had not developed to a point where such values could be compensated for.

Let us make an analogy: if a man stands on a treadmill which is turning, he may be running very rapidly but getting nowhere. Now suppose rotating screens painted with familiar landscape figures were drawn by him, an illusion would be created whereby he would think he was running very fast. Then, if suddenly the direction of the treadmill were reversed, he would be going forward at twice the speed he could normally run, and the landscape would be flying by at four times the former speed. The entire analogy illustrates the movement of light through space in respect to our position here on earth, and that negative energy is moving inwardly toward us, thus apparently slowing down the speed of light.

It would also explain, in theory, why a man traveling at the speed of light through space would take four years to reach the nearest star, but ten years to return. Figuring out this concept may be quite confusing to third-dimensional minds, and it should be said, it is equally confusing to any astronomer or astrophysicist who attempts to measure distances in the galaxy or universe according to static third-dimensional conditions. The speed of light upon the surface of the earth was determined by measuring light impulses electronically timed through a straight pipe one mile long, and was done without any knowledge of the plasma media involved.

In the so-called vacuum of space, and traveling according to its frequency and polarity, and affected in its transition by the magnetic stresses, expansion or contraction, the speed of light is greatly variable. If it is to be equated on any third-dimensional consensus, and any hypothesis or theory which involves time merging with space, as in a relative theory, it is also erroneous. Time and space are valuable and a conductive asset of life only in the third dimension—the beginning of man's evolution, and was so conceived in Infinite Intelligence as a beginning point in the development of man's consciousness and which would be meaningful to him wherein he could induct all life experiences in the necessity of his evolution.

Conversely, any evolution beyond the third dimension must be developed in a higher consensus of consciousness wherein all factors and elements of life are inductive on the basis of frequency rather than at a time or place, and with all attendant reactionary emotions and their subsequent impulses.

Thus it is, this spaceless, timeless Infinity which is ahead of you, spaceless in the sense there is no ending and timeless in its eternity.

265

Up until now, we have discussed light and the transmissions of light, both in the third and the fourth dimensions, and have made comparative differentials in the nomenclature and basic frame of reference of factors known to the earth scientist. However, here again it must be repeated: energy motions, wave forms, as are heat, light, etc., are nonexistent! Such energy transmissions as wave forms in a third-dimensional science are always determined as such, through a resistive element. It is a physical law that energy must always be in motion; if it is static energy, that is, temporarily contained, it is, nevertheless, in motion and oscillates. Heat is a conversion of energy into other wave forms as well as molecular absorption which again reacts in an oscillating fashion, re-creating other wave forms in this energy conversion.

The stone thrown into the pond is an energy conversion. Water molecules absorb the energy by moving up and down. The water is a resistive factor and gradually, through function, inertia, etc., completely absorbs this energy.

An airplane flying at 40,000 feet and at speeds above 700 mph generates a shock wave of sound. Air can conduct sound only at a given speed. If a sound source travels through air above this conductive speed, a compressed sound wave, or package of sound is built up comprised of all the vibration produced by the airplane. This sound wave will then be conducted away from the aircraft and at the conductive rate normal to the atmosphere. This sound wave reaching the earth creates what is known as a sonic boom, in the conversion of energy from sound into the motions which rattle windows, shake walls, etc. Very often the plane has disappeared from sight before the sound wave strikes the earth.

However, in the plasma of the fourth dimension, conditions are different in many respects and that any energy called light traveling through this plasma does so, not as an energy wave through a resistive element, as did the sound from the aircraft, or the energy from the pebble through the water. An energy wave from a given source travels through the fourth-dimensional plasma on an inductive basis, as previously described, and does not become embroiled in any resistive factors unless there are differences in the magnetic structures such as that which surrounds the earth, and it is the differences in these magnetic structures within the magnetic spectrum which so surrounds a planet and which converts or absorbs energy sources such as are radiated from a sun—a differential between the third and fourth dimension.

The astronomer of today through telescopes, optical and electronic, believes he has received light and energy impulses from star sources several billion light years distant, which means that as he now views a certain star, he is looking at the star as it was a billion or so years ago. This difference is then multiplied by the light speed (186,000 mps) to obtain the mileage figure. Of course, the astronomer believes he is viewing the terminating end of a light frequency just as he would look at any familiar earth world object; he does not actually see this object, but sees only the terminating ends of a group of wave forms of energy which have been reflected from the surface of the object. So again, seeing is another illusion, a process we have described elsewhere: light waves meeting the resistive phosphorous elements in the cones and rods of the eye retina, etc.

And so life on earth—and to repeat—is an illusion as it is supposed to exist by every human, and is reducible into the transmission and inception or the regeneration of wave form energies. Because man has no suitable sensory equipment to determine a fourth-dimensional consensus, he is, then, not rightfully in any position to properly evaluate the fourth-dimensional cosmos which surrounds him and makes life possible for him on his little planet. With his third-dimensional knowledge and equipment, he has obtained only an ant's view of the cosmos and he should desist from taking a pragmatic stand in his third-dimensional consensus.

All sciences of the earth world are still singularly primitive even in a third-dimensional analysis and when compared in retrospection with the Infinite Cosmos, his position becomes singularly ludicrous. It is therefore the appeal being made through these liturgies and by the higher life agencies, that the earthman should become more open-minded in his search for knowledge in which he believes he could begin at the beginning and foresee the more ultimate.

And so as he views some distant star-sun, he does not know about the mechanics involved in the transmission of that energy across, what he believes to be, a vast distance of so many light years. He does not know that in this transmission he is not viewing the star as it was a billion years ago, but is actually viewing it as it is now, for this is the quality and function of fourth-dimensional energy transmissions and that any energizing energy source so interconnected, harmonically speaking, with the fourth-dimensional cosmos is actually energizing, vibrating, and oscillating the past, the present and the future! Yes, and if the astronomer had the capacity to understand from the inner plane of consciousness, he could discern this starlight as it would be manifest into the end of its time, or that he could see its beginnings equally well.

Yet, now as a man, and bound by the dogma of his present earth life, limited in his evolution and the knowledge he possesses, he sees only the terminating ends of energy waves which he calls light and which have been transformed objectively for this purpose, through the law, order and harmony which is Infinite Consciousness. This has been done through the afore-described processes, cosmic hysteresis and all that which it implies to create an earth world for an earth-man, subjectively inclined in his limited evolution.

CHAPTER XX

On Time Differential

Every person has had the experience of the day which seems to drag by and never end, or the day which seems to fly by and is gone almost before we're conscious of the passing. Such differentials in time consciousness cannot be fully justified on the basis of activities, health conditions or other factors which may seemingly alter the time consciousness.

As a human is not entirely third-dimensional but universal, like all things in the third dimension, a surface appearance or a manifestation is possible only as the net sum and total of a projected image from fourth-dimensional consciousness. In Infinite Intelligence, as energy formations, all things have therefore been created and such manifestations as an earth world, its life forms, including man, are evolutionary objectivisms, materialized on a third-dimensional plane surface. Man, therefore, like all things, is really a spiritual creation, brought about into the material form in his earth world as a compound of ninety-two natural atoms— also energy forms.

Man therefore must be viewed as an object which maintains and is maintained by an inductive rapport with fourth-dimensional cosmos. While food and oxygen may be consumed in support of a physical metabolism, yet this metabolism, as are all other motions within this life-form object, is so keyed and controlled from these fourth-dimensional life-giving energies, again subjectively inclined by the personal psychic anatomy which has been described many times elsewhere.

In this broad and more complete analysis, it could be surmised that man would therefore be subjectively disposed, psychically speaking, to the motional oscillations which comprise the life-sustaining fourth dimension or Infinite Cosmos. And on the basis of the afore-described hysteresis and energy conversions which, in turn, regenerate such cyclic intercessions which cause sunspots, flare-ups in the aurora borealis at the poles, such phenomena is a testimonial to the formation of synchronous isochronisms in the process of cosmic hysteresis.

It is in this aspect that we can find an explanation to the sense of time differential, compression and expansion of cosmic plasma and on the basis of negative and positive interpolations, could also conceivably and psychically speaking, have the same compressed and expanded feeling of time consciousness, according to how the positive-negative balance was maintained in consciousness, through the psychic anatomy into the Infinite Cosmos.

The principle involved here is quite similar to the condition of compression and expansion posed by the theory of relativity which we have discussed. So once again through an objective analysis and understanding of the principles and the dynamics of the Infinite Cosmos we have been able to solve one of the intangible and unanswered questions which surround the earth-man on every side, a proposition of solvency which means immortality to any person who acquires it.

CHAPTER XXI

The Expanded Universe

The universe is something which cannot be defined or confined in terms of third-dimensional equations or with the physical or finite eye of the individual. Man brings down, into his consciousness only one small facet. In general terms, the universe can be said to be space within space, like the layers of an onion and that it is simultaneously expanding and contracting in all directions.

Man has long been trying to probe the depths of this universe with his telescope and other so-called scientific instruments; he thinks that he has arrived at some reasonable equation. This is as foolish as trying to count the drops of water in the ocean. As the years progress, man will learn that the measure of energy or mass in the third dimension is very different from the same energy and mass expressed in the fourth dimension.

A rubber ball to a child who plays with it and sees it as a solid form is not the same ball that the child will see when he passes to the fourth dimension. There he would see the same ball as just a conglomerate mass of wave forms, so man's understanding of future physics and astrophysics will have to be taken out of the realm of the seemingly solid third dimension and placed where it belongs in the fourth dimension where mass and energy are one and the same and the law of harmonic relationship will supersede time.

Another of the commonly misunderstood concepts is gravity. Until quite recently, Newton's theory was accepted as law. In the light of present-day knowledge, there has been a gradual change to a better understanding of this mysterious force and can be described as something like this: atomic structures within the surface of the earth, moving in their own field of molecular relationship, generate outwardly statically charged masses of energy which cause any loose or floating particles, including air molecules of various kinds to be attracted to the surface. The surface atoms and molecules, in turn, are attracted even more strongly to the deeper atomic structures, the rate of attraction increasing according to its square root base line which is its original outgoing wave form. In a general sense, the earth can be said to be attracting itself into itself.

The magnetic fluxes from the sun or from planets are not able to be measured by any known earth instruments. In the future, man will learn this. What he calls "radio signals" coming from stars are harmonic frequencies of such magnetic fluxes. Man has a peculiarly warped finite concept of space. The transference of energy from the sun to other planets is not measured in thermal units; neither does distance have any effect. The sun and the planets are linked to each other through the law of harmonic relationship. In this respect, there is a perfect transference of energy from the sun to any planet according to its needs, or the perfect balance which prevails in all nature and which is automatically reflected within the planet itself in terms of a positive or negative equation—this being part of the superimposed intelligence which is in the magnetic fluxes themselves.

We can liken this to the mother hen with a number of chicks, and as she scratches around in the earth, she will see that each chick gets its share of whatever she uncovers, in spite of the natural greediness of the chicks. As all solar energy is a direct reflection from an inward plane or a fourth dimension, and as it is by this same token intelligent in nature, this intelligence is expressed in the laws (principle) of harmonic relationships to the planets, just as the mother hen and chicks.

The earth scientists must discard the concept of distance or time. Distance means nothing in a void of space which exists between planets where there are no conflicting elements contained in this distance which would give rise to resistance in the transmission of energy in the supermagnetic spectrum. Only the lower rates of vibration such as sound or heat need a secondary transmitting element. Time also does not exist in the general accepted relationship of time, as it is known on earth (third dimension). These supermagnetic fluxes or wave forms of energy are not of a third-dimensional character but reside or belong in a spectrum which is closely related to the fourth-dimension.

We can liken our planetary system to the modern concept of the atom. The atom, in spite of its seemingly minute size, is actually in proportion and as expanded as our solar system. Yet these wave forms, whether they are the atom or even the so-called electrons, are so minute that one atom or electron is separated from another by distances just as comparatively vast as those planets found in our solar system or in some cases of certain elements, even as vast as our universe.

Now if we begin to obtain a comparative value or equation in our mind as to what space is, we can therefore easily visualize in the infinity of all this that all planets of this or any other solar system will receive sufficient energies from an emanating source which can be called the sun. According to its own needs, the Infinite's immutable law of harmonic relationship gives each planet its proper balance.

CHAPTER XXII

The World of The Abstract

The modern present-day scientist is making the same mistakes as in days of old, in the relative values and equations which relate to energy. For instance, in the relative equation of heat there is an immediate relationship with all particular sources which he has learned from his experiences are emanating radiated sources of heat which is warm or hot according to the sense of reaction of feeling. As a child he may have learned that touching a flame or some hot surface burned the skin and was a painful experience, therefore, any such future relationship with such source of energy called heat will have a definite psychosomatic action.

It is in the aspects of general relationships that while man is commonly called third-dimensional in a physical and material sense, he is therefore definitely an active integrated participant of such a material plane of consciousness. He has learned through experience to view all things objectively or from the front side only. This has become an unconscious thought pattern inasmuch as everything he does in his daily life happens objectively and from one moment to the other. He can, of course, if given time through such sources of information as are retained in his memory consciousness, place or imagine other particular correlated aspects which are pertinent to the immediate objective reaction. However, here enters a rather fallacious interpretation of objective reasoning: that while he may have substantially experienced such correlated facets, he has not yet progressed sufficiently far in his mind evolution where such thought forms of past experiences can replace the more substantial objective placement in the association of his immediate realization. Something of an example of these objective relationships could be pictured as in the act of driving a car. While the driver, through long experience has perfect control in the forward motion of the vehicle, and while this in itself may be an integrated system of reflexes, they are all primarily connected with a long chain of circumstances and experiences; and yet with all this, there is still another and even greater part which makes it possible for this driver to drive this car.

He is not concerned with the vast amount of engineering detail which has gone into the machine; neither is he concerned with the tremendous machinery, the plants, the mechanical brains and all the associated impedimenta which is necessary to construct such a car. Given the time, he can sidetrack for the moment his mental energies into the imaginative process of all these things and so construct within his mind a rather nebulous concept of what all this is. Unless he has actually been through an automotive manufacturing plant or seen motion pictures of such, he will have a difficult time in envisioning anything like a small part of such a gigantic and colossal enterprise.

This is, in a sense, a similar allegory to man's position on this material or third-dimensional plane and his relationship to the fourth dimension. He is literally driving down the highway of life in the vehicle of his own body and sees only before him the particular happening or experiences of that particular moment. He has not yet learned nor can he envision the tremendous vastness of the Infinite Universe. While he may have had a number of reincarnations, he has not yet, and with but few exceptions, progressed sufficiently far in his soul evolution that he has arrived on this earth plane with even a semblance of consciousness from other lives or in other dimensions; and while these lives and their experiences do reside in and are a part of the psychic body, yet here again the individual falls into only a subconscious pattern of relationship of such experience and lives.

When we have progressed sufficiently on our soul evolution that we begin to retain a conscious memory of such lives and experiences, and in their becoming an integrated part of our life on this earth plane, it is quite likely that we will have arrived at some definite starting point in our mastership.

Merely being curious of certain physical phenomena in the world about us does not necessarily mean that we have arrived at the starting point, nor does it mean that because of our curiosity we may have gathered unto ourselves a bit more knowledge than our fellow-man and that in the acquisition of this knowledge we can interpret the value of our lives or our learnings into the lives of others. There are many in the world about us today, just as has been in the past, who have usurped a false position by the seeming acquisition of some superior sense in the relationship of values to his fellowman. It has always been that the great masses have succeeded in personalizing on certain individuals such qualities of character which they themselves thought they did not possess.

The kings and queens of past ages, the dictators and emperors were all so constructed, likewise, the leaders of our own political systems. This is in itself a rather long and devious process of autosuggestion which has been concluded by the fallacious interpretations of objective reasoning. Likewise, many of the doctors and scientists of the past few decades have only arrived at some point where they occupied a niche of fame by postulating some seemingly and very apparent reactionary facets in this objective thought pattern reasoning.

Yet in a large part, all of these things were in themselves relatively simple and would not have remained hidden, and remained only for the individual entity which was called John Doe or Mary Smith, as the case may be, to exploit such so-called discoveries and so incur some measure of everlasting fame. In direct contrast to this objectivism is the realm of the abstract. This in itself simply means fourth dimension. This dimension, however is not a true dimension in the pure sense of the word because it has no beginning or end; neither is it so contained in any form or shape. This abstract fourth dimension is the beginning and ending of all things in the third dimension; likewise, time is not an element in this abstract dimension. It can be said to be constantly expanding and contracting simultaneously in all directions instantaneously. It may also be called Infinity. This dimension does not reside in the realm of the hypothetical. It constitutes all living organized energy. Because of the definite relationship of these energies, they can be said to be constructive, and as they reside in a dimension which is expanding and contracting simultaneously, it may be said that they are positive and negative in nature for lack of better terminology. It is true that while they are infinite in nature and that in order to be infinite, they must also assume finite form. They are therefore reflecting into other dimensions; and this material world or third dimension is but one small reflected part of such universal fourth-dimensional expression.

Therefore, with this reasoning we can begin to see the fallacious impact of objectivism, and the scientist of today measuring and evaluating any expressions or transmission of energies such as light, heat and various other spectra on a third dimension or the material world, and in a material sense, is guilty of the most gross misunderstanding of the conscious realization of the great and universal abstract fourth dimensions.

Man has and can, and by the same token always will, through patterns of objective reasoning, arrive at or conclude certain ideas or hypotheses. These may or may not be, even in a small sense, correct or true, yet to vindicate this collectivism will build a superstructure of other and seeming supporting ideas or relationships. This is something like a bird building a nest in a tree and while the nest serves the purpose for which it was constructed, yet it is in itself merely a mass of heterogeneous particles of such sundry nature as are collected in the nearby fields. It is not inferred that man at this time is necessarily ignorant, nor is there an underestimate of such structures which are related to his well-being on the earth at this time, but it can be said that at least a large measure of such constructive structures were the direct result of the integration of such spiritual and inspirational nature, and that they had their source and origin within the higher realms and from much more advanced entities who had progressed into these higher planes in the abstract universe.

Many of the great medical discoveries are not necessarily evaluations of a correctly postulated theory but were usually arrived at either through accident or through a long painstaking series of experimentations. Such accidents or laborious conclusions would not be necessary if the present-day savant were sufficiently clairvoyant that he could immediately contact the higher realms of consciousness in the abstract universe, and on such cooperative corelationship bring the necessary values into the immediate third dimension or objective plane in which he lives. It might be said that man will, in some future day on this earth plane, arrive at some universal and accepted contact with these higher orders of intelligences, and should he do so, he will find himself not in the generally accepted concept of such a third dimensional plane but he will have created for himself an entirely new dimension, and likewise, a new world. He will also have arrived at the point in his thinking where the conglomerate mass of expression of experience does not make up his life but will now occupy a position of infinite conception.

He will begin to visualize the great abstract universe and with such visualization he will see that energy or mass in the third dimension is not necessarily a part of that concept of such a dimension, but is reflected into the concept of the individual as such an expression or dimension; and that it can therefore be said that as a man conceives so will he give birth to himself into the light and into the dimension in which he conceives. And by this same analogy, he will find that his soul evolution into the higher abstract realms of consciousness is merely the adding to of each successive rebirths with bits of correlated knowledge. And like the straws gathered by the mother bird, so of these bits of wisdom that he will gather unto himself, let it be said that they are not third dimensional in nature, neither are they the objective experiences of some earth life but they have become the integrated thought pattern which is abstract in nature that relates itself to the infinity of man's creation; and in such infinite creativeness he, in becoming an activated participant in this abstract universe, becomes Godlike in nature, for God is the great abstract universe.

CHAPTER XXIII

I Told Them So!

During the last year or so (1966-1967), of my earth mission, I have frequently paused and gone back into the different books and other literature of Unarius which have been brought forth since the actual beginning of this work in 1954, and I have found the one work which is perhaps most interesting and has proven very prophetic is the booklet, "The Truth About Mars". This book is, incidentally, the only one which I personally laboriously wrote in long hand. Since writing these pages, many wondrous happenings and discoveries have occurred in these earth years, and at least one or more unmanned satellites have been flown to or around Mars or have actually landed on its surface and have sent back hundreds of photographs as well as information on other planetary aspects, all of which have only further proven certain surface descriptions which I gave in the booklet. But until the first spaceship carrying people from earth actually lands on Mars, the earth people have yet to factually find out about the many underground Martian cities and the highly scientific and completely socialized way of life enjoyed by the Martians.

Back here on earth, however, much has been discovered which has duplicated unknowingly the many scientific accouterments of life used by the Martians. Cooking by high frequency rays is an established fact in this time. Quite recently two American scientists created an artificial placenta and actually grew tissue, and in the article there was great emphasis on the future time when babies would be grown under the same conditions.

In many hotels, public places and homes, there are

walls and ceilings made of plastic material which glows brightly when a button is pushed, just as the walls and ceilings of a Martian home. Punched cards are used by computers and processing machines and also instead of keys for cars. Great progress has been made in wonderful new and synthetic materials. Styrofoam is now being used, not only to package articles in shipment but for insulation and in actual construction, along with fiberglass and other synthetic materials. Houses, boats, car bodies, aircraft are but a few of the many thousands of different achievements in plastics which have been accomplished since the first printing of the Mars book.

But there is no doubt, the greatest single accomplishment was, or is being done by Walt Disney (now deceased) and Disney Enterprises.

Shortly after the publication (about two years), Disney Studios brought out a short movie about Mars in which was depicted the huge domed underground cities and connecting tunnels, all done as a colored cartoon feature. Shortly afterward, Disney actually produced, as an exhibit in Disneyland, a Martian home. Could Walt Disney have obtained and read a "Mars" book? During the 1950's, books were sent by two (or more) Unariun students to many prominent and well-known personalities in the United States; yet, at the moment, it is not known whether one was mailed to Walt Disney or not, but very likely so. Also, these books were placed in the public libraries immediately upon their publication. Mention might be made here, too, that these first Unarius books (Mars and Venus) were also sent to the President of the United States as well as to the Governor of our state (California) Goodwin Knight, and whose wife acknowledged their receipt.

During the early months of 1967, Disney Enterprises announced they were building an amusement park in Florida which would be housed under a huge dome of transparent plastic and metal and would cover about 80 acres. Within this dome in a totally controlled, conditioned environment, there would be, not only the amusement park; it would also provide housing and homes, hotels, etc., for at least 40,000 people. The picture of this proposed amusement center and its dome has appeared in color as a nationally syndicated feature in different magazines and newspapers throughout the country. The picture clearly depicts the central radial plant and structure with its central hub as seen and described in Martian cities.

Disney Enterprises also announced there would be a number of similar projects even much larger, which would be in the future, constructed elsewhere in the United States and in foreign countries.

On the heels of this announcement, a very famous architect living in New York, stated and advocated that in some not too distant future, all large American cities would be housed under these huge domes! For example, New York City so enclosed in this totally conditioned environment could pay for all construction costs of this dome within ten years' time, with the money saved from snow removal in the winter! Doors and windows in all buildings could be left open the year around in a balmy 78 degree temperature. There would be no dust and no smog; automobile transportation entirely eliminated in these cities and supplanted by electrically powered vehicles and other means of transportation such as moving sidewalks, etc.

It should be well to note that here in Southern California, there have been recently constructed two malls or shopping centers which use moving sidewalks; several blocks of landscaped parkway between the rows of shops where no cars are allowed, just as in the Martian cities.

As of the time of this writing, it is indeed a prophetic time. The most recent satellite of the lunar probe series has just landed on the moon and within the next five years, it is quite possible and highly probable the first man will be walking on the lunar surface. How soon, then, will the first spaceship land on Mars and what will the meeting be like between the Martians and the earth people? And as we speculate, we can only hope the earth people will be sufficiently advanced by that time to be compatible with the Martians, and that these earth visitations will not contaminate this wonderful highly-developed civilization with all of the viruses and germs, all of the diseases and decadency, the ever-increasing immorality of this present earth time.

We do not need to conjecture or speculate on any probable future time in earth's history when any physical earth man would set foot upon any of the seven Celestial planets described in the Pulse of Creation Series. These planets and the people who inhabit them are not in the physical, material spectrum of this earth. Even Venus, the 'mystery' planet, if ever contacted in reality by an earth man, would be vastly different than he has yet surmised.

Meanwhile, as I sit in my easy chair and watch the passing of days, I note the many 'discoveries' and achievements made by science as time progresses, and I chuckle a bit; even feel elated, for all of these things and many more 'undiscovered' by the earth man have been presented in the Unarius liturgies. Yes, and if I lived in this manner in this body for the next thousand years, I would see no end to these discoveries and revelations, all so presented in our books and lessons during the eventful years of the 1950's.

During the late months of 1966, two prominent and well-known scientists at the Berkeley University made an important discovery. Using the satellite Imp, they have mapped the magnetic lines of the solar system. It should be noted that these same magnetic structures similarly diagrammed were presented in the second

284

lesson course of Unarius, printed and copyrighted in 1960! This is one of the many daily happenings and 'discoveries' which cause me to chuckle and smile and even to indulge in some "I told you so!"

To the Unariun student many important facts are quite obvious, not the least of which is: you have an unprecedented and a tremendous opportunity to learn of the creative cosmos, even thousands of years in advance of any earth technocracy or science, and to make of yourself a better person and insure your immortality, in the process of learning.

(Note June 20, 1967: It should be noted that at this later date, two biological scientists have kept a human fetus alive and growing for a period of 58 days in an artificial placenta.)

CHAPTER XXIV

Interdimensional Relationships

For many years, scientists in the field of biological research have been avidly, perhaps feverishly, probing the mysteries of cell structures, molecules, etc., trying to find out what this life force is and, as usual, they have only added to their confusion. A very important discovery was the DNA molecule, which theoretically, at least, "keys" or "codes" different molecular structures within any living thing. These coded molecules are also hereditary. What they have not found out is the energizing intelligence or life-force which activates and makes these molecules possible. For some vague or obscure reason, this very important point has been overlooked. It is a well-known law of physics that you can't get something out of nothing. If certain atoms of a number of different elements are so arranged as a configuration, there must have been some form of intelligence to arrange this first form; even granted that succeeding forms could inherit the same characteristics. Even so, there must always be a certain quotient of energy involved in arranging any molecule from atoms, also a certain intelligence (I.Q.). If you think for a moment: any number of different kinds of atoms form different elements when they are so arranged in a molecular form, and they have a certain property.

If you take atoms of carbon, you can rearrange them into gasoline, nylon, diamonds, aspirin or thousands of other familiar everyday products, each one with a different carbon atom configuration. Now what is it that makes this difference? As it has been explained in our liturgies, an atom is a complex vortex of fourth-dimensional energy. The nucleus of the vortex is what the present-day scientist calls an atom. He does not know about the fourth-dimensional vortex and that, harmonically speaking, it is linked up through many other different dimensions to the net sum and total of Infinite Intelligence; according to the wave-forms which oscillate within this vortex, this nucleus of the atom will have a certain function or intelligence and when combined with other atoms, in turn, with their respective vortexal psychic anatomies, can and do reflect a different function or intelligence, according to the arrangement; because within the vortex certain conjunctions and parallaxes are formed which heterodyne and give rise to a new set of wave form configurations.

As the nucleus atom is an exact facsimile and contains within this nucleus all configurations and parallaxes, the changes then made within its psychic anatomy vortex will be reflected into the third dimension as a different function or intelligence. This, in essence, is what the present-day scientist does not know about atoms, whether he is a chemist, a biologist or a nuclear physicist. As of the present time, he has dealt with only the third-dimensional nucleus atom form and his sciences know nothing about the psychic anatomy vortex which has just been described.

These same principles are, in essence, quite true within your own psychic anatomy and the superconscious, except that the whole picture is vastly blown up or enlarged. Within any dimension, except the third (physical), any wave form of energy is completely integrated within itself as an oscillating positive-negative polarity, conveying or repeating its own specific intelligence (I.Q.) according to its frequency and form. A cycle wave pattern can have a vast number of other different kinds of wave forms oscillating harmonically within this wave form. These concepts have all been thoroughly discussed elsewhere.

Any thought or action in your daily life interjects wave-forms into your psychic anatomy. These, in turn, oscillate with or beat against a multitude of other wave-forms within the psychic anatomy. New wave-forms of energy are created through heterodyning. All this and much more takes place every second of your life.

Now, the second part to remember is: there is a similar or compatible wave-form within the net sum and total of Infinite Intelligence. There is nothing you can do or think that can't be matched by Infinite Intelligence in wave-form-structures; and when your wave-forms beat or heterodyne with those of Infinite Intelligence, new wave-forms are created which go into that part of your psychic anatomy called the superconscious. You might say, then, that your superconscious is, as far as it goes, created from Infinite Intelligence and which, in truth, it is.

However, it is also polarized with your own personal wave-form quotient so that it becomes your own particular property and will remain with you forever. In fact, it can be developed over millions of years to a point where it is entirely you. At the present, however, it has developed to the point where it gives you your life force, your libido, your inspiration, which is done through the psychic anatomy which has also been described elsewhere.

Now the important thing to remember: you never talk to an energy body; it doesn't do any good. If you want to contact your superconscious with your conscious mind, then think constructive and creative thoughts. In other words, through compatible vibration you can, through the superconscious, actually oscillate with Infinite Intelligence. At your present state of development, however, such oscillation is, quantitively speaking, very small and is realized in consciousness more as such emotions or feelings of inspiration, beauty, joy, a feeling of upliftment, etc. However, right here is a good place to issue a warning: at no time should you try to cultivate or create some special rapport by trying to meditate or indulge in any practices, mental or otherwise, which you might think would give you a better contact with Infinite Intelligence. Any such practices are reversions to ancient practices which could be called witchcraft, sorcery or even spiritualism.

In the scheme of evolution, it is the law and order of Infinite Intelligence that you should progress and evolve in an intelligent manner; that is, by learning anything which you may try to learn about you in the third dimension—your physical world is a contact with Infinite Intelligence. It is a constructive wave-form of energy which will be polarized within your superconscious. By constantly seeking and learning about the life and the world which is ever about you seeking and learning the meaning of all these things in conjunction with the creative Intelligence, then you are developing and evolving your superconscious self which, as I have said, will in time become the real you; and even at that point, there is still a long and never-ending pathway before you.

You will be, at that time, living completely in an energy body which does not need a physical body to manifest life; and this energy-body, which is you, will be in a much higher degree and a much more expanded fashion to oscillate with Infinite Intelligence. You will breathe the life force into the body, not through lungs, but as oscillating radiant energy. All this, too, has been described previously.

And so, if you hear from time to time, as you will, about discoveries in the world of science, in the world about you, you may, if you wish, smile just a bit and hope that the scientist too, will someday know about these wonderful concepts which you are studying—concepts which will teach him what creates an atom, what the life force is. He will understand his psychic anatomy and the development of the superconscious self; about the true evolution and Infinite Intelligence which have been worshipped as deistic beings since the beginning of the first Homosapiens. And in that future, science, too, will learn and come to know that the life force did not spontaneously generate within a protoplasmic mass of proteid molecules, that this life force is a generic force, synonymous and analogous to the specific entity and function of every atom—a fourth-dimensional energy-force which does create and sustain life in all molecular and atomic forms.

The subject of carbon or the carbon atom is, without doubt, one of the most fascinating subjects in the many chapters of our modern science, and a study of carbon reveals many astonishing facts. Carbon is called the universal atomic building block, and spectrographic analyses of distant stars and galaxies reveal the important part which the carbon atom is playing in the makeup of our universe. It would indeed be difficult, if not impossible, to find any thing, any form or substance on this earth world in which carbon has not, at one time or another, played an important role. Modern chemistry has devised means and methods to create literally hundreds of thousands of carbon molecule substances which bear no resemblances to the black soot formed by the burning flame. For example, an aspirin tablet is called acetylsalicylic acid, but place an aspirin tablet in a spoon, heat it over a gas flame and it quickly reverts back into the brownish-black coal tar from which it was made.

There are three principal sources of commercial carbon petroleum: ordinary coal and carbon formed by coal burning; there are also layers of graphite found in the earth's crust in different parts of the world. Graphite and clay comprise the lead in any lead pencil. (By the way, there is no lead in a lead pencil). The principle of chemosynthesis is very diverse and complex and very often in converting carbon from one form to another, a catalyst is used. For example, when black gooey petroleum is superheated and placed in the presence of platinum, it becomes a clear transparent highly volatile liquid called gasoline. The chemistry involved here is what is known as cracking or changing the benzine ring (nucleus). Petroleum, coal tar, or other carbon molecular forms are usually a certain combination of carbon atoms which form a six-sided octagonal ring which, in form, looks something like a snowflake. By breaking up this ring and rearranging internally the atom structure, entirely new substances are formed, such as nylon, rayon, plastics, dyes, explosives, perfumes and thousands of other familiar every-day products.

Sometimes different kinds of atoms are also combined in this rearrangement, all of which add to the net sum and total of carbon products whether it is for hardening and coloring the rubber in a tire or forming an artificial diamond. Like many other elements, the carbon-atom molecule formation is radioactive. This radioactivity was incurred many millions of years ago, during the synthesis period of the earth's history when in evolution, the energy forms, which are vortexal, were responsible for the creation of the ninety-four natural elements. This radioactive radiation is, incidentally, a part of the high-frequency spectrum the scientist calls the beta and gamma radiation sources, a universal spectrum always found in cosmic hysteresis.

Now this radiation property of carbon, as well as several other elements such as cesium and cobalt have become useful tools in today's sciences, and as this radiation decomposes over millions of years, by measuring and computing, science can determine the age of different rock strata, artifacts and skeletons of ancient peoples. Pithecanthropus erectus, Zinj Africanus, the ancient skull skeleton formation found by Dr. Leakey in an African gorge, was carbon-dated at nearly two million years of age.

Cobalt, when intensely radiated by atomic fission can re-radiate the beta-gamma spectrum for thousands or even millions of years. A single atomic bomb with a cobalt casing could kill all living life on the planet earth through radioactivity. This radioactive cobalt, as well as a number of other elements or their isotopic counterparts are used in medicine to treat cancer or to trace gland functions in the human anatomy.

And so the wonders of creative science unfold in endless succession, and with astonishing revelations, all made possible by the electromagnetic fields which radiate constantly and endlessly from every known (and unknown) atom, an electromagnetic radiation which reflects Infinite Intelligence through the principle of harmonic regeneration, which links the atom through its vortex to the net sum and total of the creative Infinite Intelligence.

In essence then, changing atom structures within any molecule changes the properties and material forms composed of these molecules. The basic concept in modern chemistry is all possible because the electromagnetic fields of the atoms were changed in their respective positions.

CHAPTER XXV

More On The Atom

The atom is not composed of solid negative and positive particles called protons or neutrons, but is composed of wave forms which might be likened to a very loosely rolled ball of string, the string itself being coiled or shaped in such a manner that it has an intelligence quotient. This I.Q. is made manifest in its own fundamental frequency. This frequency in itself links it in the terms of harmonic relationship with a fourth-dimensional equation or counterpart. In the terms of fourth dimension, this energy can form an attractive or repulsive condition through the harmonic linkage into other atomic structures.

Energy transference is not a product of relationship with the third dimension, but is purely a product of harmonic frequencies residing in the fourth dimension. We can therefore liken it to a boat upon the water and that it is the water that carries the boat—not the boat that carries the water. In other words, electricity traveling through any third-dimensional element, such as wire, is not dependent upon voltage or pressure, for voltage or pressure is purely a by-product of frequency, frequency being in harmonic relationship as to the water which carries the boat. What the scientists think is an electron within the atom is a secondary conglomeration of wave forms. These wave forms, in turn, link it to the basic fundamental frequencies of the atom through the law of harmonic relationship. Each wave form, whether confined in any part of the atomic structures, is merely the reflected counterpart of energy in the fourth dimension and links it with its own specific intelligence.

The atom is a vessel for an outward expression sometimes called inner force or nature of Infinity. Scientists of today have a vague idea about the atom and have succeeded only crudely in harnessing its atomic force. It will be for man of the future who will, through spiritual realms of consciousness, bring through to the realm of the third dimension the lacking ingredients of knowledge which men of science of today lack; and only through a higher degree of clairvoyance can this be obtained; only those working in the highest order of scientific brotherhood will be able to bring this information to the earth plane. The massive machinery of our day and age far outweigh and overshadow a necessary spiritual balance which should be an integral part of the earth plane. Further progress in scientific fields without this spiritual knowledge will be travesty and bring ruin and destruction to the world. Atlantis, Chaldea, Yu, Lemuria, all went down before these forces of insubordinate negation and can be likened unto the story of the Frankenstein monster. Verily, you have created this yourselves. Wrong use of the power of the atom at this time is invoking karma upon the heads of the governments of the world. As these governments suffer and as they are likewise the will of the people, so likewise will the people suffer also.

Further pursuance of this blind and fallacious experimentation and in the exploding of vast concussions of atomic energy will disrupt certain linkage between spiritual worlds and the mentalities of man. Not only in yourself do you become fearful but you create for yourself biological monstrosities. The greatest harm will come from invisible infusions into psychic centers of life. There are other and harmful things to be considered. Inasmuch as fear will ride rampant through the minds of all mankind and divest him of his spiritual confidence, he will become easy prey and a victim to great psychic underworld demonic forces in the grip of these fantastic and demonic monstrosities from beneath the lower fields of psychic force and created from the fields of negative thinking, which are the warped and distorted forms of man's own thoughts, shall fasten themselves like vampires in the soul consciousness of these fearful people.

Heed ye, people, while ye may; flee not like fowls of the air but take root upon the rock. There ye shall find shelter. In all the things of the great Consciousness of the Infinite and the right usage of all such knowledge will secure for man the peace of mind he so earnestly seeks. Yet I would say, but there is temper in steel. The Infinite in Its wondrous Wisdom shall prevent man in his own undoing, and surely so, as he has created man so that those who serve the highest Godship shall find a way to prevent man in his last great folly; for surely, as the nature of these things are much greater and much more vast than man has ever dreamed, nor can he see the folly of his own blundering. Into the days and centuries of the future, (you of the earth of the Aquarian Age) there will always come a greater and stronger force, an arm of spirituality which will lead man to his spiritual self. Verily, in the great Consciousness of cosmic evolution, man sees himself strung across eons of time, must he ever progress, must he ever draw closer to the ever-loving life which gave him birth.

CHAPTER XXVI

Survey Shows Many Clergy Doubt Miracles

Biblical Stories Accepted Much More
Readily by Laity Than by Church Leaders

Biblical miracles are accepted as fact much more readily by laymen than by church leaders who attended the last meeting of the National Council of Churches, a survey by the organization has indicated.

Only 25% of the delegates to the council's assembly in Miami last December said they believed "the miracles actually happened just as the Bible says they did."

In a survey taken of persons living in four San Francisco Bay Area counties, 57% said they accepted the miracles at face value. This poll was conducted by the Survey Research Center of University of California, Berkeley. It was reported in "Christian Beliefs and Anti-Semitism", published in 1966.

The research department of the council of churches used several questions and choices of answers from the Bay Area survey in questionnaires at the Miami Assembly. Usable responses were received from 223 of the 599 delegates. The council is an association of Protestant and Eastern Orthodox churches.

Similar Beliefs

Beliefs in God and Jesus were similar among the church leaders and Bay Area Protestants. More than two-thirds of the delegates and Californians chose the statement "I know that God really exists and I have no doubts about it" or supplied their own definitions of belief in God. Almost all of the balance of both groups chose the second option of "While I have doubts, I feel that I do believe in God."

Traditional beliefs that Jesus was the divine son of God were expressed in similar proportions by both groups.

But on the question of miracles described in the Bible the difference was substantial. While 25 percent of the council delegates believed the miracles happened as the Bible said they did, 35 percent of the delegates chose the answer "I believe the miracles happened but can be explained by natural causes." Nineteen percent chose this answer in the California survey. A total of 76 percent of the Californians and 60 percent of the church leaders chose either of the two options.

Both Surveys

The answer "I am not sure whether these miracles really happened or not" was selected by 22 percent of the churchmen and 15 percent of the laymen. Four percent of the churchmen and 2 percent of the Californians picked "I believe miracles are stories and never really happened." The remainder in both surveys gave no answer.

Asked whether they believed the statement that "Jesus walked on water", 50 percent of the Bay Area respondents believed this particular miracle to be "completely true" and 19 percent of the delegates thought so.

Dr. Glen W. Trimble, director of research interpretation for the council, noted that a smaller proportion of both groups "accepted one specific miracle than . . accepted all the Biblical miracles. Consistency is not a human trait."

Immaculate Conception

Dr. Trimble said, "A far more central Biblical account is that of the immaculate conception of Jesus. This also may be viewed as a particular miracle."

The statement that "Jesus was born of a virgin" was declared "completely true" by 57 percent of the California sample and 28 percent of the delegates in the survey.

In the two groups "there has been a greater departure from 'traditional orthodoxy' on miracles, general or particular, than appears to have occurred on belief in God and Jesus," said Dr. Trimble.

Protestant Clergy Admits Bible Wrong!

The above reprint from the Los Angeles Times (June 3, 1967) is a complete vindication of Unarius and in particular, to the position which we take toward the Bible, its sources, origin, and especially to the New Testament and the subject of miracles.

The survey of the National Council of Churches shows that 75 percent of the clergy did not believe the miracles occurred as they were depicted, and that they happened under natural causes, not explained in the Bible. This is more than a tacit admission; it is a direct or indirect denial and refutation of the entire Bible per se, as it now exists.

So far as Unarius is concerned, I have repeatedly stated, I do not believe in miracles per se, as an act by some "deity" whereby through some great magical power some miracle is "performed". I have also repeatedly stated in numerous articles that the Bible is apocryphal; that is, it is of doubtful origin and as such, should be regarded as legendary, and should not be the theoretical controlling factor, the spiritual denominator of any person or persons; and most certainly should not be used as the cornerstone of any church. Or for that matter, the Christian religion, (Protestant or Catholic), should never have been built up from the context of this so-called "holy book"; for by the admissions of laymen and clergy alike, it is quite evident that largely they do not believe in their Bible.

There is more, much more, that can be extracted and analyzed from these surveys, and the total impact of this analysis should cause anyone to shudder at the horrible aspect which presents itself; that as of today nearly nine hundred million—not to mention the many millions or more who are dead—have had, through the years of their life, a religion, a theoretical code of moral values based and extracted from a book now admitted false by the very clergy who have been the dispensers, the propagators who have set themselves up as "Holy Men" in their respective churches by a false claim from a false god, who supposedly "called them" and ordained them for these purposes!

Just as Jesus said, "Beware ye in the latter days, there will be many false teachers and prophets who are like ravening wolves dressed in sheep's clothing." So it is of this time and place that the protestant clergy has, by these admissions, shown themselves to be "ravening wolves dressed in sheep's clothing"!

Last, but not least, these surveys are the handwriting on the wall which clearly depict the decay and disintegration of the Christian religion. Its downfall is clearly indicated in this and the next succeeding centuries; a part of that predicted millennium, if you will, a true interpretation of which yields a spiritual return of man to the true source sans the bigotry and hypocrisy of religious systems.

It is the avowed purpose of Unarius to reestablish

the precept of evolution—as it was presented by Jesus, "Seek ye first the kingdom of heaven which is within and all things shall be added"—in the modern scientific idiom of this time, thereby making possible to all, a way to immortality; and to banish forever the old vindictive false deisms which have somehow, strangely enough been interwoven with the evolutionary doctrine of Jesus, a deism completely incompatible either with a scientific creation or a logical equation of moral values which perpetuates personal responsibility not diluted with intercession, blood baths for sinners, etc.

That small part of factual history, which somehow survived religious panderings that still remains in the Bible which is relevant or solvent especially to the mission of Jesus, that, as truth, will remain forever; time will remove the adulterations from the minds and Bibles of the future ages.

CHAPTER XXVII

The Passing

It has commonly been observed and remarked upon that these days, the last half of the twentieth century, are indeed days of great transitions, great discoveries and the passing of many things. And there is no doubt that of all the transitions and passings, the beginnings of what is the passing of all religious systems (Christianity in particular) and their transition into a more tangible, realistic, and above all, a scientific approach to creation is, by far, the most important.

There are many signs and developments which point to the passing of Christianity. There is, of this time, a great effort made by almost all Christian sects and denominations, and as of today, there are a number of Christian leagues, world-wide Christian organizations of one name or another, all bent on attaining some common approach to seeking a solution or course of action with which they hope to forestall the inevitable doom.

In a previous Unarius article based upon an exposé made in an article published by the Los Angeles Times (6/3/67), polls taken among different Protestant factions from both the layman and the clergy revealed a great and growing disbelief in the Bible and in particular, the New Testament and its depictions of the miracles.

However, as all Protestant factions and denominations represent only a Christian minority, it is only fair, therefore, to grant equal time to the larger denomination, namely, the Roman Catholic, whose adherents number nearly 600 million of the 900 odd million Christians. There have been many signs and portents indicating the passing of this church. One of these signs happened many years ago in that all-important area of human relationship—sex and procreation. From its very firm position of absolute continence, the Catholic diocese, masterminded by the Pope, instituted the rhythm method in an effort to liberalize precepts mandated in an effort to regain lost ground. As the years passed, there were other signs and attempts to liberalize the church in an effort to retain and gain adherents, including a publicity campaign which smacked of the Hollywood movie star promotive-type campaign.

One other endeavor which happened several years ago: the Pope and the Bishop of the Church of England publicly "kissed and made up", thus ending a four hundred-year-old religious feud. Another edict recently banned the eating of fish on Friday.

The subject of sex and birth control has, however, waxed hotter than the proverbial fires of hell and has embroiled the Catholic layman and hierarchy, as well as all sundry Protestant groups. The prospect of abortion still remains abhorrent to the largest segment of the Catholic hierarchy, but almost all of the diocese have absconded to preventative contraception necessitated by the pressure of ominous population explosions, public demands, etc., the imminent and predictable food shortages and famines, as well as other important aspects which mandate a globular birth control program.

At the present time, Catholicism has resolved preventive conception into two devices: a mechanical uterine device and "The Pill". Of these two methods, the pill is by far the most acceptable, and as of this present moment, the Catholic hierophant, the Pope, is buried somewhere deep within the Sistine Chapel wrestling, as did Jacob with the Angel on the mount, with "The Pill". And according to the lesser luminaries of the Catholic hierarchy, it is inevitable that the Pope will abdicate the time-honored continence and rhythm method to "The Pill", thus, once again proving in this attempted liberalization our contention of the "passing" of present-day Christianity.

It must be remembered that the stranglehold this church has had upon the masses of peoples since its beginning, and after Constantine, the First, has been in the psychological strength which it gained from its superimposed image of 'holiness', its so-called 'divine ordination' and instrumentation, delivered with a large bundle of edicts, precepts and mandates, all bolstered up with the so-called luminous personalities of numerous 'saints'.

To say that a primitive savage could be superstitiously coerced into believing this kind of malarky is a probability, but to say that hundreds of millions of reasonably intelligent people living in the light of a comparatively advanced scientific technocracy could be so duped, deluded and coerced, is absolutely incomprehensible, unless it can be reasoned that these people are still, through reincarnation, subconsciously intimidated by affiliations with superstitious religions in the early primitive phases of their evolution. Or perhaps the ego, too, plays a part; and as a conformity, religion therefore would play a personal part in self-identification with the community. We do not like to think that Christians are, as a whole, mental weaklings, incapable of deciding such important issues for themselves unless there were such psychic pressures and intimidations.

It is very important to note, however, that any cross-sectional analysis into the religious thinking and beliefs of most western people does not reveal the same adamant consistency of belief as was exemplified in the grandparents of yesteryear; and this analysis would reveal a much greater inconsistency and disbelief in the younger generations of the age-old Christian dogma. These are heart-warming signs, always seen and interpreted with the greatest of joy and elation; and once again proves the inherent goodness in evolution, in the positive biasing agencies from the superconscious, and from the wise and all-pervading help of the Unarius Agencies.

As an immutable law of physics, energy cannot be destroyed because all energy or any energy is part of the Great Infinite Intelligence which the barbarian calls God; and as this Infinite Intelligence functions, creates and re-creates infinitely, according to inviolate principles and laws, so does this concept hold the promise of immortality for every human, predicated upon evolutionary principles and made possible for him individually, by self-determination in learning of this Infinite Intelligence and living by its Creative Principles.

Moral responsibility cannot be shirked in the promise of intercession, and all promises so uttered by any priesthood are turned to stone by the poisonous alchemy of hypocrisy and bigotry, a stone harder and more insoluble than the graven images they worship!

Other prophetic indications of the demise and passing are in the insurrections which are occurring among the lay and priesthood of the Catholic Church. One priest was suspended and excommunicated for starting a union among priests. Another priest and a teacher in a parochial school was suspended for teaching liberalized birth control. He was later reinstated after a student-teacher strike, also an indication of weakness of a church which would have, several hundred years ago, burned any insurrectionists at the stake as heretics.

But the greatest exposé of all came from, naturally enough, a Catholic priest. This priest, now suspended, has, in Look Magazine, (June 15, 1967 issue), exposed much of the heretofore almost secret trials, troubles, tribulations, malfunctions, injustices, deleterious policies, malfeasance and a long list of contrivances and exploitations practiced among the clergy. For example, in convents, he has exposed sexual malpractices, lesbianism, and inhuman psychological tactics. Included also was the confessional, its practices and erroneous counseling; in short, a great mélange of common hypocrisies and bigotries, practiced within the so-called holy confines of Catholic institutions, a list and a description far too extensive to be discussed in this epistle.

It is suggested that you obtain and read this writing, either from the magazine or from the book which was written by this priest (Father James Kavanaugh), titled, "A Modern Priest Looks at his Outdated Church", by the Trident Press, Division Simon Schuster, Inc. A few of his topics are titled, "The anguish of nuns who find their lives oppressive", "The folly of maintaining special Catholic schools", "The frustration of Catholics locked in unhappy marriages", "The unrealistic 'rules of courtship' taught to Catholic teen-agers", etc., etc.

CHAPTER XXVIII

Speaking In Tongues—?

On a number of occasions the liturgies of Unarius have discussed the historical, moral, and ethical backgrounds of Christianity. Despite the affluence of these articles, the subject is by no means closed, and there are many aspects of the Christian religion which have yet to be dealt with, particularly psychological equations and ramifications. There is, in the parlance of our twentieth century, a term which will enter into our circumspection—brain washing, and which refers to an autosuggestive practice instituted by the German Reich in World War II with prisoners wherein the brain was left in a numbed semi-comatose condition, unable to function, except hypnotically or autosuggestively.

The Christian religion purportedly deals with the highest moral expressions and continuities found in our Western society. Such an incidence of self-imposed moral luster is, however, completely false. While such moral attributes would involve the most advanced expression of human psychology, those who dress in the priestly robes have no knowledge or training whatsoever in any of the constituents of human psychology, even though theirs is a role which plays directly upon all the fears, insecurities, guilt complexes, and superstitions which are the composite of the thinking processes and the subconscious intimidations of their parishioners.

A case in point can be found in those sects which class themselves as Pentecostal, where priest and laymen alike often express themselves on the fringe-line between sanity and total frenzied, religious fanaticism.

Within the churches of these different sects, services are often conducted in such a manner that the priest and the attendants are lashed into an emotional frenzy; and autosuggestively upon impulse many will, temporarily at least, lose conscious function of their minds. They will froth at the mouth, their eyes will roll, they will shout and scream, roll in the aisles, or sit on the mourners' bench completely taken over in the throes of a hypnotic frenzy!

In some cases, and with one particular sect, the preacher may break into some kind of a garbled monosyllabic voice and while speaking or screaming in this strange disjointed fashion, he is thought to be "speaking in tongues" by those who listen. The words and the voice they hear is supposed to be the holy spirit or god. Often too, other members of the congregation break into this same kind of yelling and screaming—this gibberish. They too, are supposedly in control by god or the holy ghost. And almost without saying, so-called "speaking in tongues" is considered a "divine" rite!

While we pause to ponder the different aspects of these picturizations, we almost automatically see in our minds a screaming, yelling witch doctor in an African village; and the villagers, their black skins glistening in the firelight going through the same contortions, screaming the same senseless jargon as these nicely dressed, white-skinned Caucasians in their modern church. Although there may be thousands of years of difference, time-wise speaking, in their evolutions how remarkably similar are these rites in an African village, the voodoo practices in Jamaica or Louisiana to those practiced in one of the highest echelons in our religious society!

Of course, there is a lucid psychological answer to all of these seeming antics and hypnotic gymnastics practiced by different sects. We may look in horror at one sect living in the Kentucky hills who, in the throes

307

of their religious frenzy, handle live rattlesnakes—very much against the law, but practiced, nevertheless, even though a number of them have been bitten and died. The answer to all this is comparatively easy to find. Every human, and to varying degrees of intensity, lives in a world of psychic-emotional pressures. There are countless ego deflations, frustrations and unrequited efforts. There is a crying need for identification, a need for pity, love, understanding and recognition. This is an extremely complex compound of human emotions all impounded in the subconscious, together with indoctrinations, superimposed conformities, and a host of other factors, go to make up the matrix of this subconscious from which this human must express himself outwardly, according to the dictates of his society.

Small wonder indeed there are so many deviations and deviates, delinquency and prostitution, crime and perversion. To those, however, who have not strayed beyond the boundaries of what is considered decent conduct, these poor souls may find themselves entrapped and mired in the fantasy of religion where somehow, they hope to escape this unrelieved complex. Then, in the unrelenting autosuggestive torment of the preacher's voice, they give up and temporarily at least, sanity ceases and the torment of the subconscious pours out in a garbled barrage!

And these religionists are not alone. Musicians and artists of this time, sometimes and in certain ways, give vent to the monstrous beast prowling in the jungle of their subconscious. Yet these and other sundry subconscious expressionists do not give us the same horrendous concern as do the little old ladies sitting on the hard-varnished pew of some church and victimized by a "praying mantis" dressed in the vestments of his church.

Yes, it was truly spoken, in the latter days there are many false prophets "who are as ravening wolves dressed in sheep's clothing"!

And while we are ruminating upon all these factors, let us also consider one more and a very important one —obsession. Closely by, and only a half-wave length away, are hordes of spirit forms, thought-form bodies and disembodied entities of all kinds, the denizens of the astral underworlds, the lost souls of whom Jesus spoke—"some who have been there, yea, even to the time of Noah!"

Any person who is in an emotional state of distress, high tension or temporarily incompetent, can be taken over and become obsessed by these evil spirits. In His earth mission, Jesus cast out thousands of them, as did his disciples later on who had been trained by Jesus. However, in the church the Pentecostal religionist does not believe he can be so obsessed, although that possibility is recognized by them! They believe god's power protects them; however, their belief in a false god naturally gives no protection and these frenzied religionists are, therefore, taken over, and from a certain astral plane, peopled by spirit forms still avidly trying to practice their false religion, can thenceforth find an outlet into their more familiar material world. And so from then on the religionist goes about his daily life in an intemperate fashion, emotionally irascible, and prone to become violently agitated and forensically defensive, when his religion and conduct is questioned or jeopardized. He will, in the vernacular, have lost some of his marbles; he is no longer playing with a full deck! And so as a person so thoroughly obsessed by the frenetic fantasy of his religion is strongly reinforced and controlled by astral agencies.

A case in point graphically illustrates the strength and power of certain religious factions and the psychotic way in which they expressed themselves against Madelyn Murray and her mother: Madelyn Murray was the instrumentality in bringing about the Supreme

Court decision of banning prayer in public schools, thus arousing the ire of these religionists by authorizing a squad of twenty-one armed policemen who invaded the Murray home, destroyed and tore it apart; beat both Madelyn and her mother unconscious with clubs—the latter being hospitalized for two weeks in an unconscious condition as a result of this beating. Under this and more terrible persecution Madelyn Murray fled this country to Hawaii, only to find some more of the same; then finally to a sanctuary in Mexico.

The pages of history, as well as episodes in our modern times graphically illustrates the psychotic nature of all religionists, regardless of name or denomination, and quite contrary to the precepts of their religion, supposedly founded upon the life and preachments of the "Prince of Peace" who tried to teach mankind a total tolerance, "to turn the other cheek"—a compassionate understanding.

Yes, to explore the many corridors of these many diverse sects in the Christian religion would be more ominous and terrifying than to explore the catacombs of Rome, where, in the early days of the first Christian Church, people lived in terrified hiding against the Caesars and Neros and where, when they died, left their grinning skeletons upon a thousand niches and shelves—skeletons which still grimace and grin through the tinseled fabric hung upon the altar of the Christian Church.

Chapter XXIX

Flat World—Graven Images

"It's A Fraud"—Los Angeles Times, Aug. 18, 1967
Flat-Earther Goes 'Round With Photo

London—The leader of the Flat Earth Society Thursday called Lunar Orbiter's photograph of the world a fake.

"It's a fraud, a fake, a piece of trickery or deceit," said Samuel Shenton, 63, the British-based secretary of the International Flat Earth Research Society. "Look at the photograph the satellite supposedly took. Notice those lines across the bottom of the picture. They show its a composite, a mock-up."

But why should the Americans—or anyone else— seek to perpetrate such a deception?

"It's a Shame"

"It's all a part of the great global earth conspiracy," said Shenton, "and it's a shame."

"For centuries we have been indoctrinated to believe the earth is round. That it's a tiny pill bounding through space at 20 miles a second. Our children are being indoctrinated at this moment."

Shenton and his followers—and he says he's got them all over the world—believe that the earth is not only flat, but static in space, and that the theory of gravity was advanced to support the spinning earth theory.

"Late in his life," Shenton said, "Sir Isaac Newton himself denied his own theories of gravitation."

"What we all want to do today is to wrench our minds away from the so-called upper stratosphere and concentrate on what the earth itself, the strata and the rock formations, teach us."

311

Talking to reporters, Shenton answered a few questions raised by round-earthers.

The voyage of Sir Francis Chichester around the world?

"He was just following a zig-zag course 'round the flat disc of the earth."

Astronauts Just Circling

Astronauts wheeling around the earth in space?

"They've only been buzzing around in a flat circle above the flat earth. Why, if they were really out in space they would fly off and never be seen again."

Shenton said membership in the Flat Earth Society is growing slowly but surely.

"We even have supporters in Cape Canaveral (Cape Kennedy)." he said. "They think something's wrong."

Who are the Cape Kennedy doubters?

"They are free to announce their names," he said. "I must treat them as confidential."

Well, it's here at last—what is perhaps the most startling revelation in our modern age of miracles. The earth is not round but really flat, after all, just as it was so believed to be by some of the Ancients for thousands of years! At least, this is the contention of the "Flat Earth Society" whose headquarters are in England and who have been popping into the news for the past several years.

The Society's founder and president here in an article reprinted in the Los Angeles Times, August 18, 1967, says that we have all been disillusioned. We have been taught wrongly and we are teaching our children falsely; that the earth is round, not flat! He points out, composite photos taken from satellites are faked because they have been patched together (as a composite photo always is, although not at all fake). The founder also goes into some length and detail to point out the fraudulent illusion in other round-earthworld aspects. This he does in the face of incontestable and overwhelming evidence that the earth is indeed round—countless thousands of round-the-world journeys, which started at the time of Magellan in the Sixteenth Century, astrophysical evidence such as the round shadow of the earth upon the moon during the eclipse., and other planets in our solar system, etc. This society and its membership does, in fact, point at this great amassment of evidence and, like the farmer who saw the giraffe for the first time, they say, "It ain't so!" Of course, this presumption is hilariously ridiculous and asinine, even more so when it is conceived that the society membership is convinced in its convictions.

There is, however, an exact parallel situation among the eight hundred odd million people who call themselves Christians, who emphatically state and reinstate ancient archaic and completely false beliefs upon which they have founded their entire religious conduct. Despite overwhelming geological, archeological and anthropological evidence and fact, despite a comparatively advanced and provable electrophysical technocracy, despite nuclear physics and established astrophysical sciences, these eight hundred million Christians still firmly believe in their ancient Babylonian god, Jehovah, who, as a bit of hocus-pocus abracadabra, created the heavens and the earth in six days, and finished off the whole coup by making a man out of mud and then a woman out of a rib. Then as a final bit of hilarity, after creating them—man and woman—he became very angry and kicked them out of the Garden of Eden when he saw them acting as such!

Now, it is quite apparent that the Christian religion and its tenets are much more ridiculous and asinine than the "Flat Earth Society" and it could be much more hilariously funny if it were not for the great tragedy which involves each one of those Christian adherents. We can only sadly speculate upon the fate and future of any person who absconds with and completely entrusts himself in his future evolution within the coils of these false tenets. While it may be comparatively harmless to believe that the earth is flat, it is self-condemnation and self-destruction to believe in false gods, false means and manners of creation, salvation and all the other religious hokey-pokey.

All this terrible tragedy, not only of the Christian religion but other false earth religions, has been presented in preceding Unarius doctrines; also, the alternatives, such as a constructive intelligent and scientific creation and your own personal position in the scale of evolution in this creation.

So, while we may chuckle at the "Flat Earth Society" let us always give compassionate concern for the poor benighted Christian, for in the aspect of religion, the earth is indeed one of the many elemental spawning grounds for many and diverse creatures; and in this elemental evolution from these spawning grounds, there may emerge the first rudimentary configuration of what is to be an intelligent being; and which, as they so spawn in their native habitat, have so classified themselves upon this earth world as Homosapiens— the last in a long line of creatures who have evolved from primitive beginnings, to a point where they can turn their eyes to the skies and the world about them and begin to wonder about creation. And perhaps in such a primitive state, we could excuse their false gods and religions, their graven images and say, "Wait, let us see".

So it has been, we have waited; and as the many centuries have passed, so now this primitive man stands on the threshold. In one hand he holds the false graven images of his religions which he has carried with him from out his primitive past, and in the other hand he holds a great sparkling jewel—a jewel of Truth—and from its many facets it reflects a multitude of scientific facts and aspects compounded from the sciences of his present time—a jewel given to man by those who travel in the Inner Worlds, in the in-between lives, by the inhabitants of those who travel, through reincarnation, back to this world from the Halls of the Seven Celestial Planes.

So, hope travels hand in hand with the future, and always in the scale of evolution there is the immortal promise of everlasting life to those who can aspire and who can meet the challenge, and who can rise above the murk and mire, the stupidity and ignorance, the bigotry and the idolatries of religious systems which are an everlasting heritage of these material worlds.

It should also be noted that even as Christians who have compounded their theosophy from the Bible, they are, in their numerous denominations, individually and collectively, committing the world's greatest hypocrisies and bigotries. There are more than ten thousand Christian denominations or sects and each one, large or small, believes implicitly that his individual membership will be the only "chosen ones" saved to inhabit the future "City of Jerusalem". This, in itself, is a great enigma and quite puzzling, as all Christian sects and denominations worship the same god and "savior" and, in general, all principles and expressionary elements are exactly parallel and the same. Yet, in their individual contentions of salvation, they commit the greatest bigotry, not only to other Christians but to all other peoples of the world in general. And at this point, it would be well to note that all beliefs and expressionary elements within the framework of Christianity are exactly opposite and contrary to the preachment and doctrines of Jesus whom they worship as the "Son" and "Savior" even though His Mission on earth was to prove the falseness of the Israeli god, Jehovah, who is universally acclaimed the Father of Jesus throughout the Christian religion.

It is also quite obvious, even within the Christian testaments that Jesus very strongly admonished all those who would listen, against indulging themselves in any of the idolatrous practices of worship universally exercised by Christians. This admonition was most clearly defined by Jesus when he said, "Do not pray as does the heathen, in public places and on street corners, neither in temples and synagogues, but retire ye into the closet of thine own self that ye may be rewarded openly."

Jesus also clearly indicated that the proposition of attaining immortality must be done by finding the "Kingdom Within", also clearly defining a proper evolutionary course for any individual dedicated to the proposition of salvation. It was within these precepts as they were expressed and taught by Jesus that we find Christianity's great hypocrisy, and it is difficult to understand and believe that two quite obviously contradictory and opposing doctrines posed by the old Jehovan testament and the evolutionary approach to immortality, as was posed by Jesus, would exist or be tolerated. We can only say that somehow within the mystical shroud of religion, these two opposing doctrines became merged and then again, through differences in interpretations and quarrelsome attitudes, separated themselves through two thousand years of history into the numerous sects and denominations which now exist, and there again to express, just as they always have since the beginning, their greatest bigotry—that they, and they alone as individuals, a sect or a denomination, are the true believers, and only they will be saved.

The entire basic beginning of Christianity is also, in another way, completely repugnant as it begins with mob violence and the murder of its "Savior", which was later followed through the pages of history with wars, massacres, millions of persons sacrificed at the burning stake, the rack and the wheel. Even those religious malcontents, expurgated by the Church of England, as pilgrims, became part of our American history and from the first, set up within their own colonies, one of the most bigotrous of all religious expressionisms. Yes, they were burning little old ladies at the stake as witches almost to the turn of the twentieth century. There is no doubt that as of the past, more human misery, death and destruction has been caused by the expressionists and proponents of Christianity than any other faction in history. And the situation today is very much the same, whether it is Jews or Mohammedans, Christians against the Communists of Asia, as they are now dying on the battlefields of the Sinai desert, or side by side in swamps and rice paddies of Viet Nam. The basic ideology which causes the most violent hatreds in the nations and races of mankind are the religious ideologies in which they believe and which separates them as ethnic cultures and gives rise to man's greatest bigotry!

In the consensus of a Creative Intelligence, that Intelligence which through law, order and harmony, created galaxies, universes, and solar systems, and all compounded fractions and elements of an interdimensional cosmos, there are none of these infractions and no idolatries, no bigotries. It is in his scale of evolution that man has arrived at a point where he becomes partially selective according to the emotional content of numerous psychic pressures which surround him in his everyday life. The pressures and conformities of his society usually mold him in all his attitudes and reactions; and in his fears and insecurities, he condemns or tries to destroy all that lies beyond the immediate periphery of his individual world, composed of his familiar objects and understandable aspects. And it is from the rim of this periphery that each man finds his greatest challenge.

Beyond is the Infinite Cosmos with life sustained infinitely, according to the ability to understand and live in any one of an infinite variety of ways. It was all this and much more which was pointed out by Jesus when He said, "In my Father's house are many Mansions." How asinine then, how completely bigotrous is man on this particular planet who, until quite recently, believed he was quite alone in this interdimensional cosmos. He believes that he, and he alone, (particularly as a Christian, as a sect), would be "saved"! How great is the society of man when it is extended into hundreds of billions of earth world planets revolving about unseen suns, each person, each nation, each race on all of these and many other worlds living within the circumscribed confines of a narrow bigotrous life. And how small does this society become, if it is equated upon the individual consensus of life as it is so lived by any person on any planet.

(According to present-day astrophysicist's findings and calculations, they now recognize or acknowledge 640 billion planets in our galaxy which could be inhabited, based on extremely conservative estimates of two per hundred probables; figures subject to change without notice.) And so it becomes apparent right at this point that no individual consensus, no religious segment of this great society is rightful unto itself, nor will any man achieve immortality from any consensus so compounded from numerous religious beliefs and systems. Only within the basic principles of creation as they are compounded and expressed in certain scientific precepts, only when man begins to live creatively according to these precepts will man begin to achieve the long sought immortality, for within the framework of these scientific principles will man be able to creatively regenerate from life to life in his evolution and thus, begin to find the Kingdom of Heaven which is within, as it was so intended to be understood by the Man of Galilee, not as an intercession, but as an individual proposition whereby each individual, through development, attains a higher way of life through his evolution.

Finally, to cap the climax, so to speak, on all this great Christian bigotry, there is absolutely and completely no foundation for his Christianity! His chief reigning god, whether defined as Jehovah or the Supreme Being, is nonexistent and the Bible upon which he compounds and bases his religion is apocryphal and was compounded after the crucifixion from legends and stories which had been circulated from generation to generation by the Israelites and other people of the mid-Eastern world. There were no written records or diaries and there is nothing, save a few historical ruins which are purported to be sites wherein certain biblical episodes were supposed to have transpired, to support this entire legendary compound. Anthropological history also traces the origin of Jehovah to a most ancient Babylonian city where he presided as a pagan god in a pagan society, which indulged this pagan god with human sacrifice.

"Immaculate conception" also comes from this time as it was practiced by the priesthood of that temple in preparing maidens for marriage, where they were first married to Jawa or Jehovah "by proxy" through a priest who also "in proxy" culminated this marriage in the sexual rite! How completely blasphemous does the Christian religion then become to any person who can see it as it really is, as it was founded upon ancient superstitions and pagan rites, how it has expressed itself through the thousands of years in hatred and violence, even as it does today, how it has defrauded almost countless millions of people and led them into the blind alley of intercession. And with this immoral intercession, an equally immoral confessional has "relieved" all these believers from their personal moral responsibilities and goaded them into living lives filled with acts of thievery, lying, deceit and even murder, each perpetrator believing his sin would be forgiven in confessional or that he would be "saved" through intercession!; he belonged to a sect or denomination and the "blood of Jesus" had already washed away his sins even before they were committed!

So lives the Christian religion, so revolting, so blasphemous, hypocritical and bigotrous that it is beyond the means of any adequate denunciations or invectives, yet enigmatically and in its greatest bigotry, it is held up as the highest virtue, the epitome of expressionary elements of society!

CHAPTER XXX

The True Meaning Of
The Adam And Eve Story (1955)

The book of Genesis in the Bible contains what are probably the most important parables in the whole Bible. These are the stories of the creation and the Garden of Eden. We are all familiar with both of these stories and of their many versions. Yet, their true interpretation lies more in the realm of astrophysics or astronomy, as well as the study of ancient peoples or civilizations on this earth. We are all familiar with the story of creation in which the Lord created the earth in six days and on the seventh He rested. There are many people who have taken this literally and there are others who have embarked upon various interpretations which resolve into nothing and are rather meaningless. If we look at this story or parable in a more scientific light, we will find that the six days refer to six major cycles. These are, in the terms of the modern astrophysicist, the cycles of the recessional. The earth, in its yearly journey around the sun, comes out minus so many hours and so many minutes from the time in which it originally started out from a given point in making up the Gregorian calendar of 365 days. This, in itself, is added up and introduced as an extra day in the month of February.

Now, you ask, why is this of any consequence as far as history is concerned? What it actually means is that the sun is a huge magnet and extending out from the north and south magnetic poles of the sun are vast strong magnetic rays which are much like the old-fashioned pinwheel at the Fourth of July celebrations. In a crude fashion, they stem out into space and intersect and bisect other solar lines from the north and the south magnetic poles of all of the planets in the solar system. When you have grasped this idea, you will have some sort of universal concept of what astrology means.

In the progression of the earth in its orbit or the ellipse around the sun, it intersects and bisects these lines of force every hour, every day, every month during the entire year, and in each following year there is only a slight and minute change. At the end of 25,862 years' time in our Gregorian calendar, the earth will have made a complete retrogressive circle of 360 degrees and will have intersected and bisected all the lines of magnetic force of the sun. This is the same principle that runs the motor in the vacuum sweeper or raises the elevator in the skyscraper. All modern twentieth century electric motors run by exactly the same principle. The 25,862 years were measured in the Lemurian calendar as 33,000 years and have a counterpart in the old Yogi understanding of the cycle of 24,000 years. However, whatever our interpretation of time is, it rests purely in the interpretation of our calendar and has nothing at all to do with the exact time of this great cycle.

Now it is easy to see that we are beginning to understand how the effects of the lines of magnetic force as they intersect and bisect those of the earth can have some effect not only on plant and animal life, but upon mankind in general. If we take this vast cycle of 25,-862 years and divide it up into twelve segments like a pie, as everyone understands that a cycle is a circle, if we start from Pisces and go on through the rest of the astrological signs, we come back to Aquarius. Each of these ages as denoted in the astrological calendar have the all-particular portent, or the particular spiritual significance upon the peoples of the earth. According to the corridor of time of the big pyramid of Gizeh in Egypt, it ended all time as far as the six days or cycles were concerned, on August 20, 1953.

We are therefore said to be something like almost

two years into the Aquarian Age. We will understand also that this cycle is in itself of little more than 2000 years' duration according to our Gregorian calendar. Its peak or apex of the cycle will be about 1000 years from now.

The Aquarian Age is symbolized by the figure of God standing with his foot upon the earth and the horn of plenty in his right hand from which he is strewing the contents of the upturned horn upon the earth. In his left hand, he holds the three-pronged trident which represents the Father, Son and the Holy Ghost, or the Triad. Therefore, the symbology of the Aquarian Age means simply that God shall gradually begin to ascend into the leadership of the earth people through spiritual interpretation from the inner consciousness. Man will gradually begin to understand and to live by the teaching of the Master Jesus.

If we take these six days and further pursue our understanding of this parable of the Bible, we will add them up and find that we come out somewhere about 160,000 years ago. This, in itself, is very significant inasmuch as it is the starting point of earth's history as it is concerned in the Bible. It means that at this time a great space ship from a far-off planet down near the solar system called Lemuria, landed somewhere in the vicinity of the Himalayan Mountains. The ship was badly damaged and there were eleven Supermasters assigned us from this great planet who were unharmed and unhurt by the impact of the ship upon the earth's surface. They emerged and later built an amphibious vessel from the remnants of the ship and the machinery therein and were able to travel over land and water with this ship. They embarked upon a journey which brought them out to a great continent which was called Lemuria which has long since sunk beneath the waters of the Pacific Ocean. This great continent embodied land which was in itself almost as large as two-thirds of the continent of North America. The sinking of this continent left only the islands: the Easter Islands, the Polynesian Islands, the Hawaiian Islands and other archipelagos in the Pacific Ocean.

When these Masters emerged upon this continent, they proceeded to build a civilization. In going about the earth, they found the ten tribes of people as they were described in the Bible—people who were rather primitive, living as they did in caves or in wattled huts in various sections of the earth. They returned from time to time with some of these people and began instructing them in the art of how to live a true spiritual life. As these Masters, in themselves, lived tremendously long lives, even into the thousands of years, they proceeded along these lines to teach these people a constructive spiritual way of life. This is, in itself, an interpretation of the Tower of Babel story. You can imagine the confusion or frustration these Masters felt at times in trying to integrate the lives of these people together in a constructive fashion so that an intelligent pattern of life could be expressed in the building of various dwellings and the temples and other various and sundry edifices in this great and new building civilization of Lemuria.

Therefore, we can assume that they were quite successful in the building of this civilization. The Lemurian Masters also had to teach these rather primitive people in their childlike way—a way in which they could understand these things through symbology or signs or portents. One of the symbols that they taught to the children of Mu was the symbology of the creation or the perpetuation of the race. God or the infinite indwelling Spirit of Light was symbolized as a serpent, being the all-wise, the all-knowing, the long-lived thing. This symbolical snake or serpent was coiled around the tree of life which is the bay-leaf tree and is still worshipped in the Orient. The serpent was handing to the configuration of man and woman (not an individual, but Adam was called man and so represented all men, and likewise the representation of all women was Eve) the apple of life, which is the pomegranate because of its many seeds denoting the multiplicity and the fertility of life. Therefore, the spiritual interpretation of this picture was that God wished Adam and Eve to go forth and be fruitful and replenish the earth.

It is quite natural that God would not defeat his personal plans while building the creation of life on this planet by restricting procreation in any individual sense or making a sin of sex. Sex is a necessary, vital and integrated part of the lives of any normal civilization of the peoples therein and is very essential for the growth and welfare of any such civilization. Therefore, when we study these facts, we begin to see the true spiritual interpretation and the meaning of the symbology of these two great parables as they are written in the book of Genesis.

Thus as we have said that in the opening chapter of the Bible in the mention of the six days, this was actually the reference to Lemuria of 160,000 years ago. Masters came from Lemuria and settled on what is now known as the Gobi Desert which borders on Tibet. People understood the controlling forces and impulses of all things of the mind and many things were explained along the principles of psychokinetics (the mind forces) to these earth inhabitants. The civilization of Yu was 500,000 years ago, one of a spiritual nature—one in which great planes of different spirits of earth, air, fire and water were ritualistic beliefs of the people. It was out of these concepts which came many of the things in which the Yogi or Brahmin of today believes. Law and punishment of man's soul or vicarious atonement was practiced and many other primitive forms of self-punishment, and some of the more modern beliefs of Brahmanistic concepts had their origin in Yu. It may be well for modern science to know that 100,000 years hence the earth will be too hot a place upon which to live.

Let it be said for posterity's sake no man retrogresses save with his own will and intent. Retrogression in the individual is only creating karma in the psychic body, and a man cannot become a beast of the field but only projects into the lower orders of karmic endeavor and reinstates himself with his god consciousness. Man is god and shall remain so beyond the ends of time. He is the personal intelligence and the deification of man.

In great civilizations primarily man builds for himself the positive and negative forces. All force is energy which resolves into itself finding its completeness with its unison, its own harmony. This energy is free-moving force, energizing and infinitely intelligent, and being infinite in nature must express itself into infinity in all directions. God forms a man's superconscious by saying that man is not confined with things upon this planet, but rather into the vastness of this cosmic universe where galaxies of star clusters exist which may be but pinpoints of light in this great whirling maelstrom and yet are individual giant suns—each with their clusters of planets, many of which are peopled with mankind in various stages of evolution. We cannot visualize these physical forms or bodies which may be grotesque, just as ours may appear to them, yet each being we may call man in whatever form he assumes. There are billions of forms of bodies deifying the God force which is within.

We enter and inhabit the third dimension in our planetary systems with a third-dimensional consciousness and must therefore assume the mechanism necessary to live upon a material planet. The materialist is only at the beginning of the steps up the ladder of soul progress.

We must build the foundation before the roof is placed on. So man must need to know the value of corelationship, sometimes called cause and effect, that which may assume forms of hate, anger, greed or may, in its pure and in its more intelligent form, as love. In this and in other planes of materialism, man is learning to choose, to use this God force within, is learning to use this intelligence widely, and that such separation of usage of this force lends him subjective to disease. He will learn in eons of time after many reincarnations, the correct usage of this God force; he will advance his spiritual growth and progress which will incarnate him into spiritual planes of consciousness which know of no greed or hate, which know of no carnal desires, but instead, of great spiritual freedom.

Each individual in his own spiritual integrity finds himself not only the vehicle of God's intelligent force but has also been made godlike in nature. So in conclusion, those of this puny earth—of those tiny intellects who are as ants on this speck of cosmic dust, whose minds are imbued in karmic desires, who become fearsome and see only death and destruction of these things about them—become panicky in their fear and so they need things of destructive nature, thinking perhaps to allay these inward fears; and so they seek to struggle on their own dominion over numbers, thinking that this false sense of prestige will allay this gnawing fear. They seek to lay up treasures of earth, building great vaults, taking great pride in glittering baubles of carved stones and metals.

So they seek to become less fearful by impressing their fellow neighbor that they are wiser and more crafty than he, yet all of these things are more foolish than the idiot who admires himself in the stream and becomes angry at the breeze that ruffles the water to mar his image. It may be said that man ties himself to the wheel of consequence and must learn through centuries of time that God does not live in far-off places, in mosques and temples, but in each and everyone, in each blade of grass, every trembling leaf, everything of creation that man can see or sense. With this realization of God within, the God Force which manifests itself unto that direct ratio to his faith in that belief, he too becomes Godlike.

CHAPTER XXXI

The Bible—Fact, Fiction, Fallacy and Farce

Dear Fellow Students: Again it is through the passing of time that part of the year known to the western world and to Christendom as the winter holidays of Christmas, and as such, perhaps it might be well to pass in review upon some of the precepts and beliefs of the Christian religion, their origin and other factors which are incumbent to this particular religion.

Now I know that in the different liturgies of Unarius, we have compounded much information relative to the historical background of Christianity, yet in all fairness to say, there are many subjects and many parts of the Bible, its various stories, etc., which have not been primarily discussed and the object lesson which can be obtained from a free and open discussion of them. The Christian religion as a whole and as it is compounded or founded upon the Bible is a rather simple open and shut proposition, which suits the limited and narrow confines of the average Christian mind. He may be rather an astute person when it comes to business affairs or other factors of his daily life, but in his religion he has apparently abandoned all logic and reason and completely absconded into the realm of fantasy with this religion; for as I have stated, Christianity is founded upon fables and as fables go, there is in any fable at best, as we know, only a small grain of truth.

Let us begin first, however, with the story of creation as it is well-known in the opening chapters of the Bible, "The Lord made the earth in six days", etc. Here is the open and shut business—a simple and direct concept so far as the Christian is concerned which does not mandate any thinking or reasoning. He does not even have to possess any historical knowledge of his religion or the general anthropology of mankind for the world as a whole. He can constantly in any small or large crisis revert to the Bible and draw from it references to prove that he is right, not realizing that the Bible as a whole is historically very inaccurate. It is filled with pure fable, legend and other different kinds of compounds which have been the direct result of common historic interplays as they were woven and interwoven through the many centuries of time.

It is said in Genesis, as I have stated, the Lord apparently existed in total darkness until He said, "Let there be light". Now the Christian has never adequately explained why God suddenly decided to create light and why He was content to live in darkness, and after that He spent some six days in creating the world. The Bible does not say anything about the other eight planets in the solar system or the sun. And it makes no reference as to how the countless billions of suns and solar systems with their planets in our galaxy—which is just a pinpoint of light in the universe—also were created. To think that even a small planet as we know it today and its large variety of flora and fauna could be created in six days even by an all-powerful God would take rather a bit of doing in itself. This concept becomes increasingly difficult to understand when we pursue the readings further; and the Bible states, "on the seventh day the Lord rested", then apparently on Monday, He resumed operations and created Adam and Eve to live in this Garden of Eden.

Now from there on in, we begin to enlarge upon the whole intolerable concept as it is presented in this creation how it completely violates all known scientific and historical knowledge as it has been compounded by the sciences of archeology, geology, anthropology and other sciences adjunctive to determining the origin and evolution of the world and particularly, to mankind himself.

According to Bible scholars and especially to those who existed back in the 19th century, the creation took place about 4000 years B.C. Scholars of that time, as they are in the present, were very specific to give the exact day and even the hour of creation! Apparently they referred to the time in which light was first generated, for they could not have determined the six days or the creation of the earth in one specific instant. However, ignoring these contradictions, let us look around us in this fabled Garden of Eden and we will see that down to the south where this place was supposed to have existed, which was somewhere in the Near East near the Assyrian desert, we will see that the Egyptian civilization had been flourishing for some 2000 years; and one of the great Egyptian kings or Pharaohs had already erected the greatest of all the pyramids!

Also, if we look a little to the north of where this garden was supposed to be in the Assyrian desert itself, we also discover ancient cities which expressed a high degree of civilization about 7000 years B.C. Looking to the west and out into the Mediterranean south of Greece is an island called Minos. There was a Minoan civilization existing there about 4000 years B.C. which also expressed a very high degree of culture. People used copper tools, golden vessels of very fine and artistic shapes which were ornamented with mosaics and precious stones and enamels. They air-conditioned their houses using solar radiation and the breezes from the ocean. They were a very refined people who wove exquisite tapestries of silk and other fibers.

If we cross the Atlantic into the Yucatan Peninsula, we can find civilizations which predated the Mayan civilization some 25,000 to 30,000 years B.C. These

331

people also were comparatively advanced and they actually lived by a perpetual calendar, a system of time which we do not now use, but which was rather an antiquated calendar compounded by the men of that time. However, we have skipped over the Atlantean civilization and while it is true, at the present time it lives only as a legend, it flourished some 15,000 to 25,000 B.C.—possibly further back—and if we can believe all the information which has come to us from the Atlantean time, we know that these peoples used space ships for interplanetary travel. They also had the knowledge of the atomic power and they had actually harnessed the cosmic forces of the universe.

However, the Atlantean civilization, in turn, was derived so far as its science is concerned from another civilization—the Lemurian—which dates back some 160,000 years ago; and even the Bible itself indirectly mentions this civilization, for the six days in which the Lord created the earth referred to six cycles of what modern astronomers call the cycle of the recessional or the retrogressive action of the earth in its solar orbit. In our Gregorian calendar this is 25,862 years. In the Lemurian time quotients this cycle of the recessional was 33,000 years. Added all up, however, we see that so far as the Bible is concerned its history as creation began with the Lemurian civilization 160,000 years ago.

However, the oppositions and contradictions of the Bible are not only openly apparent in the opening chapters of Genesis; they become increasingly apparent and odious and contradictory as we progress through its different books and numerous depictions. In past liturgies I have discussed some of these contradictions, the legendary or fabled parts of these different stories which were, as they were chronicled by these ancient people, multiplied and increased and added to in various and different ways and into such proportions that they become preposterous monstrosities which require a rather elemental mind to believe that they could have actually transpired. Yet there are hundreds of millions of people who call themselves Christians who believe in the literal translation or the written translation of these fables just as they appear in the modern Bible.

It must be remembered at this time that these fables have come down to us through the ages not as a written chronology in any continuity or form which could be used as provable or scientific evidence that such facts existed. Most of these stories were told and retold in songs or in other ways by the people to their children and to their grandchildren. Sometimes they were written in strange languages upon temple walls carved in stone or they were inscribed upon papyrus or sheepskin or other methods which the ancients used when and wherever there was a written language and there was some scholarly person who knew how to write the characters of that particular language. It must be remembered that for the most part, however, all peoples of these ancient times were illiterate; there were very few scholars. The written language was not entirely formal and was very subjective to differences and variations in its composition.

For the past several hundred years, however, we as the more modern people of the western world have succeeded in different ways in perpetuating history as a more accurate chronology of events which we have done in different ways, not only through the written word on paper or in stone but in other different methods, manners and means in our modern days. We have even written history on microfilm and impounded it in stainless steel capsules deep beneath the surface of the earth to be opened in a 2000 year interval of time. These are all very interesting observations which we can make if we study the progress of evolution and mankind upon the face of the earth, however, remembering at all times that the written word or the repeated word is always subjective to its own particular type of errors. Each individual who so writes or who so transcribes or repeats, does so differently. Every person will then, therefore, have a different version of the same fact. This becomes increasingly apparent as we follow the course of different historical events through the Old Testament of the Bible. The histories of Egypt during the time of Jacob and of Moses are specific examples of some of these legends which have grown all out of proportion to what they were originally in the beginning, and we have discussed the creation, its many oppositions as it appears in Genesis, and that it is actually recorded with scientific evidence which has been amassed at this present time.

We have not even mentioned some of the more remote forebearers of mankind such as Pithecanthropus Erectus, the Java man, who lived a million years ago, or we can go a little farther back to the Zinj man who lived in Africa and who goes back about two million years ago. This Zinj man, Zinjanthropus, incidentally, used stone axes with wooden handles and cooked his meat on a fire, yet he is considerably older than Adam!

Another one of these fables or legends in the Old Testament which has grown all out of proportion to its beginning is the story of Noah and the Ark. And as this story is quite familiar to you all or you can read it, so I shall not waste words by repeating it other than to state that Noah in some way was forewarned by God or Jehovah that He was about to drown the world, so Noah took it upon himself to build an ark as he was commanded—a large boat which, according to the best knowledge, was about 150 feet long by 50 feet wide. Some Bible students have given this dimension as being rather small and say that it was much larger than this. However, large or small, we can easily see the complete fallacy and the untruth of this Noah's Ark story if we look into the books of science which exist on the earth today.

It states in the Bible that Noah took a pair of each species of the animals on the earth and placed them in the ark. Now if he had taken only the animals, this would have been more than a Herculean task. The animal species on the face of the earth as they exist today number over 100,000. Many of these animals cannot live even for a short period of time out of their native habitat; they must have their normal conditions of environment and food, otherwise they would perish. Others are known to die very quickly from fright from a psychic shock when they are moved from their natural environment into zoos in large cities. If you go to one of the zoos, you will find that great pains have been taken in many cases to perpetuate as closely as possible the conditions of the certain animals so as to duplicate their environmental conditions and make life more adaptable to them. Even so, many of them do not live long in this sort of captivity.

Enumerating the many thousands of species of animals as they are known on the earth today, we can summarize very quickly according to Genesis that these same animals existed 4000 years B.C., for there is no mention of evolution in Genesis or anywhere in the Bible, for that matter, or at least, not in the way in which we understand it. Therefore, even the animal kingdom itself must have been an incredible task to have taken upon so small a boat as the ark, all of the species of animals as they exist today. We can imagine what a pair of elephants would do to a boat which was only 150 feet long. Elephants weigh several thousand pounds each. Then there are many other kinds of animals on earth which could be largely classified as animals and under this classification they most certainly and rightly must also have been taken on the ark.

If we include all the birds, for instance, 50 to 75,000

different species of birds are again with the same necessities and conditions of environment; there is the
reptile kingdom and several thousand species of reptil-
es. Now we get down into the insect kingdom—about
400,000 species of insects are known upon the face of
the earth—many of these insects spend up to four or
five, or even seven years of their life in a pupa or larva
stage underground and live only a few hours above the
surface, and in some instances, they do not have a
mouth or a digestive tract or do not eat. They live only
to lay eggs to perpetuate their species. All of these conditions and environments must have in some way or
another had to have been perpetuated or sustained
on the ark. We have not even mentioned the vegetable
kingdom and as every gardener knows, that as far as
plants are concerned, many plants would very quickly
perish if they were immersed in water for a period of
two weeks. In fact, many trees would die under such
submersion. The delicate plants which are enumerat-
ed in the different genesis of this particular biological
study are indeed numerous, and even with the extensive studies which have been made in the realm of this
horticultural pursuit, all of the known species of vegetable life are still not complete. There are many species which have yet to be cataloged and classified.

So you see, by this time I have presented to you the
complete fallacy of the Noah's Ark legend as it exists
in the Bible today. There is, in all fairness however, a
small grain of truth which might possibly be extracted
from this fable or legend. There is no doubt that as a
legend and as a part of the Old Testament, it actually
did exist in a certain way a long time ago, but in a very
small way when it is compared to the version in the
Bible. Let us say of a certain farmer or dweller in a
valley which was surrounded by mountains that there
were periods of time of very heavy rainfall in this valley. Now if a river had flowed into this valley and flow-

ed out through a mountain gorge, it is quite possible that a landslide could have blocked off the end of this valley, and seeing this landslide this man could have taken upon himself to build a boat, a small craft where he could take the family goat and his wife and children, and during the next rainy season when the valley was filled with water, he could float about until the floods subsided. It is quite possible and in all fairness, this might have been done, and if this is so, then other people who had seen this done would have, in the manners and ways of people, begun to recite this story or retell it around campfires or before fireplaces and through the many centuries of time, it would grow in size, until it exists as it does today in the Old Testament.

So what we are getting at in this particular discussion at this time is to objectify in the light of logic and reason the context of the Old Testament or the Bible as a whole, how it was compounded, how it has been written and rewritten and how it has been translated at least two thousand times in different languages and in different forms, each form and language with its own variances, its own interpretations; yet eight hundred million Christians use this Bible as the chronology of the human race, and they also use it as a means to attempt to predict the future of those who believe in it. Even the New Testament and the story of Jesus the Nazarene can be considered by the most objective reason to be largely legend or fable, that it too was distorted and compounded beyond all reason and logc. Furthermore, psychological implications are involved with any person who accepts the Bible literally and who, in its literal translations—lock, stock and barrel —delineates his life in whatever reactionary or haphazard manner he can, as a means of justifying his own sins and iniquities and errors, then this person is indeed lost.

He is lost until he can pick up the thread of logic and

reason and subtract himself from this great legendary mass of fact, fiction and fable which he calls his Bible; and above all, he can stop using it as his own personal escape mechanism, or as a means in which he can vent his bigotry against his fellowman. He can stop using it as a weapon of coercion and fear. He must not hold it aloft over his head and point out to others that they are hopelessly lost without it, for in infinity and with Infinite Intelligence, there is an inviolate constituent which reads much more imperishably than any of the constitutional amendments in the Bill of Rights—the inalienable right of every human to determine his own course, his destiny, that he must progressively through the dimension of experience, reattune himself with new facts and inclemency's of life. He must constantly and never-ceasingly expand his mental horizons and cease to build the citadel of self-righteousness about himself, for all of the troubles of this present time or in any historical period can be very quickly summarized in the fallacy and error of self-righteousness which every human assumes is his soul right, and that he is heir in himself to the most logical position in the society of his fellowman. Yet withal, no human possesses sufficient knowledge to carry him beyond the grave or that he does not consciously display sufficient knowledge to pacify his life against the emotional encroachments which are constantly eating away at the bastions of his personal self-security.

It is well and right that people should historically know of their origin, for it is in their origins and in the comparisons of their present positions they can logically equate progressively or retrogressively their own personal evolution. Yet, all of these things in themselves as incremental factors of human society become part of that great system of personal idolatries which every human worships and, in turn, enables him to live upon the surface of this earth to become a conformist in his own society—to live as he thinks he lives, within himself or by himself—yet always conscious of censorship from his fellowman. And as the sun sets in the twilight years, he possesses neither the knowledge nor the experience which will assure him his personal continuity into a higher plane or expression of life.

The Bible in itself represents a great travesty of human logic and reason, a great tragedy in personal experience if any human uses it to delineate his own life or that he depends upon the prophets or intercessors for his future, or that he lays himself down to be trampled upon by the priesthood of his own making, for these individuals in their self-righteousness have anointed themselves, given themselves the high office where they tell their fellowman they are officials and delineators of God's Wisdom. They speak of the throne in stentorian tones; they mumble Latin prayers and phrases and in their actions they are reminiscent of sideshow barkers and circus spielers, those mendicants who peddle hot dogs at a baseball game, peddling their religious tripe, even of less value than the exploited wonders of the world advertised by the circus barker.

Yes, the great tragedy and the travesty of the Christian religion is most aptly expressed in the churches of today, in the garish robes and trappings of priesthood, in the bellowed and mumbled incantations, the sprinklings of so-called holy water. The great hypocrisy is apparent—apparent to all those except the unfortunate ones who have cast themselves before the altars of these false priests and their false god, for surely as Jesus lived, so was His mission to disprove this paganism, this false idolatry of religious systems whether it existed in ancient Babylonia before the god Jahweh or whether it exists today in the temporary church of our time as the god Jehovah, for truly, both are one and the same. And with all this, an even greater hypocrisy has been perpetuated, for as Jesus lived and died to disprove this false god, so the priests of today, as they have done for hundreds of years, have merged Him, His work and His personality with this false god. They have even sanctioned this false god in adultery. They have condoned the many thousands this false god has murdered in emotional hatreds. Even as Moses came down from Mt. Sinai and found those who were worshipping the golden calf, so this false god, as the Bible says, slew two thousand of them. Can we condone murder even if it is committed by the god we worship? If we must worship a god, then let us worship one who has all the high morals, principles, expresses the logic and reason of immortality and all the other necessary expressive adjuncts which we might expect from a supernatural Being; but let us not worship one who commits adultery, murder and expresses hatred. Let us not believe in the Bible as a translator of our destiny, which in the words of Spinoza, the Dutch mathematician and lens-grinder, who said and I quote, "The Bible is filled with murder, lust, lies, adultery and fornication, and parts of it are not even fit to be read".

Yet the whole message and the most important part of our discussion here at this moment is to more forcibly point the all-important proposition of life which was expressed by the Nazarene as the Kingdom of Heaven which is within, and in turn, resolves itself into all prerogatives of consciousness. It is not the objectivisim, the experience, the world, the apparent solidity, even the life we live. Rather, it is what we can objectify in personal consciousness as to all these conformities wherein they shape our personal destiny, for the Kingdom of Heaven is not in the emotional objectivisms, the apparent mass or materialism of our world or our innumerable experiences in this world. It is the objectivisms from which we derive logic and reason, the facsimile of Infinite Intelligence and creativity through the manifestations and interplays of these material expressions.

Yet hundreds of millions, yes billions of people live in complete idolatry—idolatry of the material world in which they live, for the ever-apparent form, the emotional experience connected with the apparent mass of this material world is the shape and the form of the idol they worship. In all its forms and its numerous ramifications, this is idolatry. Only when we subtract and extract the essences of wisdom and logic wherein we can see the creativity of Infinite Intelligence, do we advance ourselves beyond the emotional experience, do we begin to become wise in the ways of Infinite Intelligence and do we begin to insure for ourselves a more progressive evolution. For surely, as we worship the sum and substance of the world as the supreme denominator of our lives, that it is the ever-apparent all, then we are idolaters and we live in idolatry.

Only when we inseminate the pure essences of logic and reason in constructive intelligence, do we begin to grow, and from our growth springs forth the tentacles which will reach upward into the vastness of the infinite dimensions beyond this limited horizon into the many mansions of which He spoke. And clinging to what we have found and what we have derived with these tentacles of Truth we will, with a stick which is strong and straight, grow toward this ever apparent and increasing Light toward this immortality, toward not the throne of some false god but to the seat of Infinite Understanding and of Creative Intelligence.

CHAPTER XXXII

Discussion on Cycle
of The Recessional

Dear Fellow Student: I know you will appreciate with me the fact that inasmuch as you have lived a hundred or possibly a thousand lifetimes upon the planet earth, that it would be physically impossible to give you a verbatim description of all of these lives, nor would it serve a purpose, other than perhaps satisfy some idle curiosity. Then, too, it is quite possible that we have little skeletons in the closet of our past lives which would embarrass us should they be dragged forth into the limelight.

Our concern is only with those lifetimes in which certain physical or mental karma conditions or blocks have been inflected into the psychic structures and are causing present-day difficulties. However, it is most important and vital so that as you are now occupying in this present-day world a certain relative sphere of consciousness and inasmuch as this can be said to be the place of working out or elimination, we must understand not only your own position, but a broad and universal concept of the world, its evolutions, and the future destiny of mankind upon this planet.

So, therefore, I will give you something of a synopsis or a presentation of such various continuities and appearances of yourself in past lifetimes that you can most easily trace the pattern of your own evolutions and thus combine with other concepts which you will gather from the lesson course, and other sources, much wisdom which will not only broaden your mental horizon but will considerably aid and abet the process of therapy and adjustment.

There are many sources of information of past civilizations and the coming and going of mankind upon the face of the earth. Accounts are written in the pyramids and tombs of Egypt. They are contained to a large extent in the Vedic transcripts which form the basic concept of Hinduism. There is much wisdom gained by the teachings of the ancient Hellenic Avatars, such as Plato and Socrates, and if the person is an earnest seeker he can, from numerous places, gather much pertinent and vital information.

However, for convenience sake, and inasmuch as these things are written in the Bible, we shall use that book for a sort of reference. The prophets of the Old Testament as well as those of the New Testament gave much wisdom and knowledge to our present-day understanding; and it is generally conceded by one and all that this is a highly-advanced technocracy, an age of atoms and electrons, and a synthetic age which has produced not only an abundance of many miraculous things, but has literally showered our daily lives with various contrivances and conveniences which, by their original intent, were meant to serve us usefully. Yet in the very nature and complexities of this technocracy, it has become as a two-edged sword, and the general way of life, the adaptability and the mental positions of the hundreds of millions of citizens in our present-day world have, as yet, not adapted unto themselves a sufficient psychology to compensate for the numerous pressures, compromises and adjustments which are necessary to live in this complex civilization. Therefore, you can see for these reasons and others, too, which are most obvious, that you must indeed gain a wholesome perspective of your present position and the world in general.

In the opening chapter of Genesis, it states the Lord made the earth in six days, and on the seventh He rested. This is a spiritual parable which has suffered much and many derelictions, but actually referred to an astrophysical cycle wherein we can actually trace the written course of history for mankind for at least 160,000 years. This astrophysical cycle is called the cycle of the Recessional in modern astrological nomenclature. It refers to a phenomenon wherein the sun, leading its little flock of planets along a great magnetic line of force extending from the central vortex of our universe; and also, as the earth, as in the case of the other planets revolving about the sun, are regularly intersecting and bisecting minor and major lines of force which are stemming out from this same vortex.

In our orbit of the ellipse every 365 days, we gradually recede along a certain axis of declination which means that after 25,862 years, we have intersected and bisected at a 360 degree arc all of the major and minor lines of force, which we are presently concerned with in our position in this universe. This is exactly the same principle which is used in the application of alternating current which turns the motors of our present-day industries—one of the ways in which the Infinite has of inflecting into our world or dimension of consciousness through the various energy structures known as atoms —certain vibratory energies which stem in along with these magnetic lines of force. These are dominating and controlling forces which have much to do with the general welfare and evolution of humanity as a whole. They also, to a large extent, are responsible for such evolutionary patterns wherein the earth itself, along with the planetary system, goes from one age to another.

These concepts were given to the earth at the beginning of the Lemurian Age or in the beginning of the first of the six days, which was 160,000 years ago; and this figure is obtained by adding up the six cycles of 25,000 years. In order to better understand the effect and the nature of this cycular phenomenon, we can visualize this great 25,000 year cycle as a circle, and we shall divide it up into twelve sections like we would

344

cut a pie, each section representing a period of time of a little over 2,000 years duration. Using modern astrological terminology, we can start from Pisces and run through the twelve different sections or signs of the Zodiac back to Aquarius. Aquarius is the sign wherein the figure of God places His right foot upon the earth and holds the horn of plenty, which He scatters upon the earth; and in the left hand, holds the trident which represents the Holy Trinity. The symbology, therefore, is that this Aquarian Age will be ruled directly from the inner consciousness through the hearts and minds of man, and that it will be, indeed, a Golden Rule Age, or the City of Jerusalem, a spiritual age where God actually rules the world and that man lives by the Golden Rule.

These minor cycles are divisions of about 2,000 years' duration. You can also see, by studying history, that these various lesser cycles have had considerable influence in helping usher into the world certain civilizations or certain times wherein avatars or masters have appeared, just as in the case of Jesus.

Another point of reference contained in the Bible which concerns every seeker of truth in the present day is the prophecy which states that in the latter day, the Ten Tribes will be again gathered together. This, when combined with our knowledge of the ancient civilization of Lemuria, will give us a starting point where we can trace not only your own personal starting of your evolution, but to all other seekers of truth who are so interested in not only solving their own difficulties but in visualizing the emancipation of man into the future spiritual age.

We will begin, therefore, by adding up the six days as was mentioned in Genesis and the cycles of 25,000 years' duration, and we will arrive at the figure about 160,000 years ago which was the starting place of the ancient city and civilization of Mu. Through legends, historical facts and various channels and works of numerous men such as Churchward, we have gained a rather factual description of that time and place. It began with a landing of a huge space ship which came from a great planet called Lemuria down closer to the central vortex of the universe. It contained among its passengers eleven Lemurians who were super-scientists or masters. They were tall men—eleven feet high, or more.

In these two great civilizations, there were many, many, millions of people who had sat at the feet of different masters and avatars and had learned of great spiritual truths; and with the destruction, had passed on into spiritual worlds. Since that time, they have come down to the numerous and lesser civilizations upon the planet earth through more or less regular cycular appearances or reincarnations, being attracted into this world in certain spheres of time wherein certain spiritual concepts, under some avatar or savant were being re-instituted into that present time and place. Anyone who has longings, conscious memories, or feelings of affinity or the knowing of these ancient times, can actually know that they have been one of the many millions who perished in the great cataclysms.

You yourself, as many other seekers of truth, have come down through the times and ages from ancient Atlantis, through Egypt, India, Chaldea, China, Greece and even the so-called Dark or Middle Ages to your present time. You may remember the life to some extent on Atlantis; or it may have been just the starting point, the original causation for such karmic fears as fire or drowning. In the many succeeding reincarnations, these fears may or may not have been dissipated, or they may have been added to and strengthened by certain psychic shocks of such similar circumstances.

After the destruction of Atlantis at about 25,000

years ago, there were many of the peoples of that nation who had migrated or escaped into Egypt and after a period of time, Egypt grew and became one of the great and luminous spiritual civilizations of the past, and reached the climax of its ascendency under an Atlantean priest, or a descendent of the priest known as Osiris. The religious monotheology of the people of Lemuria, Atlantis and ancient Egypt was the worship of the one God who was called Amen Ra, and it was believed that His countenance shone forth upon the world from the sun. Thus it was that the sun was worshipped just as our present-day Christians worship various saints or images of saints; or they may actually visualize God as an entity, so that the people of these past ages saw the great universal and infinite God manifesting Himself in one way and direction through the shining and luminous orb of the sun which warmed the earth and was most necessary for all life which lived upon its surface.

India, too, and around the northern latitudes of India near the Mongolian Desert, another great civilization had descended from a spiritual city which is known in the present day as Shamballa. Much allure of the legendary nature is still attached to Eastern theosophies concerning Shamballa, and it closely paralleled, in many ways, the lives lived by the Lemurians and Atlanteans.

After the destruction of Shamballa and its disappearance more than half a million years ago, the remaining vestiges of that nation who were known as the Aryans migrated south into the plains of India. These Aryans were fair-skinned, blond-haired and blue-eyed and are one of the root races which exist today as the Nordic or Teutonic races, and they descended from the original inhabitants of this ancient civilization and still exist in some provinces of northern India and can be found around the country of Kashmir. It was these people, incidentally, who brought with them the Vedic transcript which is the basis for present-day pantheology of Hinduism: Brahma, who was the Giver of Light, or God; Vishnu, and Shiva, the destroyer. Vishnu was the Perpetuator of Life; and in this Holy Triad, there is a marked parallel and similarity to our present-day Christian doxology.

So thus it is, dear student, a presentation of past lives and epochs of time; like the tides of the ocean, these great civilizations have risen and fallen, and left behind them only legend, carvings in the rocks, or perhaps some buried temple in the far-off reaches of Central America. The pyramids of Egypt give mute testimony as the temples which lie in the shadows of those great structures speak silently of the pageantry of the past. The ancient City of Jerusalem has risen and fallen seven times, and yet lives today as a token and a symbology that here, too, a great man in a far-off time and place gave birth to life and hope for many people.

CHAPTER XXXIII

Man's Immortal Quest, (1967)

It could be conceded that any living person would like to attain immortality, that somehow life could be resumed beyond the grave. What this life would be, and the manner in what could be attained has been the quest of every person who has ever lived or will live on this planet. This quest for immortality has given rise to all of the innumerable religions and religious systems, cultisms and practices which are in our present-day and historical configurations.

Ponce de Leon sought the Fountain of Youth as did many others. Some tried to find the magic elixir which would give them eternal life; but, largely, most efforts in this quest have been concentrated in this direction of various and diverse religions wherein some pantheism of deistic beings, gods, god, saints, etc., were so created in the configurations of a church system or religion.

As of today, it can be seen that of the three and a half billion people who swarm upon this planet's face by far the largest majority of these people have absconded into the superstitious beliefs of some religious system. Today hundreds of millions of people bend down on their knees at least one or more times a day to pray to their respective gods, saints or intercessors; and how silly and useless all this becomes is immediately apparent when even a small glimpse of the interdimensional cosmos can be visualized; and it is especially a ridiculous situation when within this concept of interdimensional consciousness, a small and even incomplete visualization of Infinite Intelligence, the Creative Force, the law, order and harmony which engenders this Creative Intelligence, is expressed into all dimensional forms. To get down on one's knees and utter negative thoughts, selfish desires or whatever else might be voiced in this prayerful attitude to this great Infinite Cosmos and to the Creative Intelligence which created the interdimensional cosmos, is much more ridiculous than when King Canute tried to command the ocean tide to recede.

How inconsequential, even blasphemous, are these religions and religious systems which deteriorate this concept of the Infinite Creative Intelligence into the configuration of an emotional godhead who can be solicited and intimidated into bestowing numerous blessings upon the prayerful supplicant.

We who know of the interdimensional cosmos and of Infinite Creative Intelligence, of the law, order and harmony which creates and re-creates this Infinite Intelligence into all things, all forms of life, all visible and invisible worlds know how much better, how much more worthwhile, more logical and intelligent would it be if this religious supplicant would cease his silly superstitious practices and try to learn of this Creative Intelligence and to try to make himself some small functional or expressionary agency for this great Creative Intelligence.

This is the Message of Unarius, to present to you the science of the interdimensional cosmos, the Infinite Creative Intelligence which Jesus called the "Father" and the "Many Mansions". And in seeking to understand the interdimensional cosmos and becoming a functioning participle of Infinite Intelligence will be the finding of the Kingdom and the Father who dwelleth within—the finding of immortality through constructive evolution. Only through learning, education, and re-education, constructive learning, always visualized in its fullest creative capacity as stemming from the interdimensional cosmos and from Infinite Intelligence— this is the only and the true way to attain immortality. Religions and superstitions, churches and temples, deisms and diets, mantrums and prayers are worse than useless and become as a millstone around your neck. We could only partially imagine the chaos and confusion which would immediately result if eight hundred or so million Christians could be suddenly transported (as they believe) to their mythical heaven and "New City of Jerusalem", provided, of course, that these people could live even for a few moments in a totally different dimension without physical bodies and the necessary food and oxygen to support these bodies, without the familiar earth world and its numerous physical objects surrounding these people, objects which key the emotional reflexes into that reactive material existence which they now call life. For indeed, this city of heaven would be entirely constructed of radiant energy, even the golden streets paved with a golden radiance which cannot be seen with earthly eyes. (These cities have all been described in the Unarius texts.)

We could hardly imagine how these eight hundred million Christians minus vocal cords or other means would communicate with the countless billions of other spiritually-developed people living in celestial worlds about them when most of these Christians do not know what mental telepathy is. All these and many more factors of life would be entirely missing in that new heavenly world in which this Christian now found himself. And how would he utter his prayers when within the confines of his own mind, there was nothing but chaotic confusion, wild delirium and hellish nightmares produced by wild and irregular wave-forms of energy stemming from his memory-bank—the subconscious.

And, dear friend, well it could be that you could be one of these multitudes, for all of these people living today, just as the millions who have died have had to face, or will face the hellish nightmare created from out

351

their subconscious, when in some astral world they will try to continue to live and relive their former life in the material world.

No one can hope to live in any place, in any environment or in any world, heavenly or otherwise, unless he knows about this new environment and how to live in it. The most beautiful heaven becomes instant hell to any soul who would, under some circumstance, be placed within this heaven unless you are preconditioned; unless you specifically know about any and all conditions and unless you know how to mentally function and remain conscious in this totally new environment, you will not only be totally lost, but you will be eventually destroyed!

So tarry not, my friend, the doorway to immortality and eternal life is open but the pathway is long and devious and fraught with more dangers than those which beset Ulysses in his journey from Troy. Yet, there will always be a star to guide you; one which will light the pathway in its darkness, which will shed a strength, a protective power against the thorns and bruising stones; a star which will constantly fill your heart with fresh courage that you may pass the roaring maelstroms of self-pity; the snarling, fiery dragons of self-deceit; the enchanting voices of sirens who sing the praises of their material lusts. This star, the star of hope, of aspiration, of goodness and all that which is worth striving for—this is your heavenly abode in the future.

(Note: As an example of Infinite attunement or Consciousness: the Moderator conceived and dictated this message while he was eating his lunch. R.N.)

CHAPTER XXXIV

The Medusa

Almost everyone who has read some of the classical fables of ancient Greece is familiar with one of the central figures of that ancient era—a Grecian prince named Perseus, who became somewhat of a crusader, going about in different countries and slaying many of the monstrosities which were peculiar to that time. One of these classical figures was the Medusa, a monster whose body was that of a woman and who had instead of hair, hundreds of writhing snakes. This creature also had a strange power. Anyone who looked at her would be turned to stone. Perseus was able to slay the Medusa by a simple trick; he did not look directly at the Medusa but instead, used a mirror and thus escaped the penalty of being turned to stone.

Whether or not this story is true is immaterial, but like many other legends from the past, it carries a direct message in beliefs and behaviorisms which graphically illustrates that people were in those ancient times deluding themselves in the same illusionary forms as they are so presently doing. The moral message which this fable carries is immediately apparent when we transfer the elements and action into basic psychological aspects. The Medusa and her snaky hair is the subconscious, comprising as it does in wave forms of energies, the sum and total of the present physical life, and is also directly connected with other planes of the psychic anatomy to all the past lifetimes which this person has ever lived.

Now in the normal concourse of life, every human suffers many ego deflations. Unless these ego deflations are somehow compensated for, they will accumulate to the point where a person can become mentally and physically ill. He may even become totally incapacitated. Doctors call this form of psychic blockage, neurasthenia. In effect, it is being turned to stone. Every living human, or any human who has lived before, has therefore a certain compensating device known as an escape mechanism or a defensive complex. The ways and manners in which this defensive or escape complex expresses itself are about as numerous as there are people. For practical purposes we can quantitatively classify certain similar types and when we study or analyze ourselves and our fellow man, we can easily see this defense escape mechanism at work, even though we may not have been aware of our own manifestations, no more so than the other fellow is aware.

This means simply that everyone is tremendously ignorant of the basic psychology of life—even those supposedly trained in this capacity have only part of the answers. Not until we can conceive life as a conglomerate mass of oscillating wave forms do we begin to correctly understand ourselves or our fellow human. These snake-like forms in the subconscious, the ego deflations of the past, must be at least equalized and eventually cancelled out completely so far as their pernicious negative effect is concerned. For the time being then, until any person acquires suitable knowledge which will enable him to make cancellations, he will have to equalize with the aforementioned mechanisms or complexes.

The butcher who is carving steaks and chops may have been a soldier in a former lifetime, carving and chopping other soldiers, or he may have been one of the executioners in a dungeon who carved his poor prisoners, or he may have been one of the carved soldiers or victims. In either case, he is temporarily equalizing this guilt deflationary effect by cutting and carving dead animals, for while so doing he is not incurring any ill effects or guilts; thus, he is subconsciously equalizing the pernicious effects of the former associations. This is an inversion and just as Perseus used the mirror while slaying the Medusa, so does this same inversionary principle enable a person to re-enact some reactive form of life in the present which will be subconsciously the substance and effect of the former enactments.

Thus, we will see doctors, ministers, politicians, etc., who have embarked upon their respective careers impelled by the same subversive subconscious forces. The doctor, like the butcher, may have been an executioner or he may have been a victim. The minister may have a whole host of deflations which are somehow equalized by holding power and dominion over his fellow man; or he may have been a witch doctor, a high priest in some ancient temple and is trying to equalize and expurgate the attendant guilts. There are many other classical examples to be seen in everyday life. The car salesman may have at one time sold camels in an ancient Eastern market; in fact, all forms of present-day life, individually expressed, carry their same connotations back into the distant past and through many lifetimes.

Needless to say, the same pernicious course of evolution will be the lot of every individual until he learns the true inner life as it has been described to you in these many works of Unarius. In other words, what has just been described is karma, and whether it is interpreted in this term of Eastern occultism or whether we redefine it in the modern psychological idiom, this manner and way of life so lived in ignorance and superstition will always re-create itself in the future of any human who believes in it even though he may or may not apparently like it. He may even scream against it but the obvious fact remains; he is at his present position as a material human because he believes in it

355

and he has no other knowledge.

And so in common mental logistics, any human can see that if he wishes to change his material life he must acquire and use certain corrective knowledge which will change it. Actually, he does not change anything except himself. The Infinite Cosmogony always remains the same regardless of the human position, individually or collectively. Therefore, in the concourse of experience, Infinity is teaching every individual the necessity of progressive evolution. The problem is always an individual proposition which is not bound by the conformities and usages of the material existence. Conformities are only crutches used in lieu of a more constructive position. The conformities of political and social systems, religions, etc., are in principle basically the same today as they have always been. They are only imaginary bulwarks erected by communities of people in a vain attempt to hold back the ever-present flood tides of fear and insecurity born from out the abysmal reaches of the material existence.

Not until a human develops within the confines of his own life the power to visualize Infinite Creation does he begin to live beyond the constrictions of his various conformities. Not until a human can so visualize Infinity does he become an intelligent reasoning being. Any human so living the material life, believing in it and loving it as he does, is not intelligent even though he may be a graduate of a university, a great scientist or a politico, or a religious leader. He has, in these capacities of self-eulogized greatness, only epitomized his lust for life in his material world; and conversely, so will his self-eulogized delusion pass when in the moment of awakening, he can grasp the vision of Infinity. And when he does, he will realize how infinitesimally small he really is and he will be made correspondingly humble.

356

Aladdin's Lamp

Another one of the more classical forms of legendary literature which has been read by almost everyone
in his growing up period are the tales of the Arabian
Nights, such as Ali Baba and the Forty Thieves, and the
even more familiar, Aladdin and His Lamp, which goes
something like this: Aladdin found an old lamp much
tarnished from age and when he attempted to clean up
the lamp, there materialized with the first rub a giant
genie who became his slave. Now, a certain sorcerer
learned about this happening and wishing to possess
the lamp, resorted to a subterfuge. Taking up a lot of
new shiny lamps and walking past Aladdin's house, he
cried out, "New lamps for old", hoping that Aladdin
would be stupid enough to bring out his old magical
lamp with the attendant genie and trade it for an almost worthless new lamp.

Here again is another one of those strong moralizing
lessons. Just as they have done in the past ages, everyone at the present time is constantly trading in his old
and very valuable lamps for one of the new and worthless varieties—schemes which are constantly conjured
up by the clever sorcerers who surround him on every
side. There is deep within every human a magic lamp,
a lamp of life, its wick untrimmed and only faintly burning. It is not beheld in the everyday life and as the ages
pass and as each human lives life after life, so does his
lamp of life remain hidden and gathers the tarnish of
countless thousands of life's vicissitudes.

Even in his present moments, he is constantly jeo-
pardizing his lamp of life by trying to trade it with
the next charlatan who passes his way. The ways and
manners in which he is tempted are numerous. The
temptations may be a new diet, a new political system,
a different variation in his religion. An evangelist may
pass his way and he will, in any of these moments,

temporarily lay aside an opportunity to polish up his lamp of life, to trim its wick so that its flame may burn brightly. And thus he is repeatedly prevented from life to life in realizing the great and undreamed of potential power which the genie of knowledge and understanding would bring to him after he had removed the tarnish of ages from the lustrous inner surface; for surely does this genie always appear to those who so remove the tarnish and polish and trim their lamps—a great and powerful genie which is, in actual reality, their own personal development of the higher reaches and plateaus of their superconscious self.

And so the genie and the man become as one, their knowledge and power transporting them into higher regions of immortal life, which were formerly only visions of enchanted heavenly cities where life was lived completely freed from earthly taints, trials and tribulations. How tragic then does the vision of life become to any advanced individual who, from his spiritual world, looks down into the surging masses of humanity where, spawned in lust, nurtured in hypocrisies, bigotries, hatreds and other emotional vicissitudes of earth life, they struggle through the intricate maze of their self-induced, superimposed idolatries, bigotries, systems and symbologies, not knowing that within themselves there is a magic lamp of life filled with the oil of Infinite Wisdom. And saturated in this oil is their wick of life which can only be lighted when this person determines for himself the proper progressive form of evolution, and a flame which can only be kept burning by constant trimming, wherein the burned and charred shreds of the past are removed by the sharp edge of introspection. And as the wick is so trimmed, so is the ever-apparent necessity to constantly levitate this terminating end into a higher atmosphere where it can burn even more brightly.

And so a fable has again been retold and its moralizing lesson uncovered. Even so does the fable of the past, in the many lives that each human has lived, also become a fantasy, an illusion, and as it remains so covered in ignorance, so does this past corrode into a poisonous verdigris tarnish, and wetted by tears brought forth by suffering and self-incrimination does its poison constantly seep into the present. Yes, even as a man sleeps in his supposed conscious reality, at that very moment he is being saturated in all forms of consciousness by this past.

The sorcerer, the charlatan is ever about you. He is the thousand clamoring voices of your earth life; he is the ever-present subterfuge. His voice is heard in the multiple excuses which you create for yourself in attempting to evade that inevitable day when you must more fully determine your own position to the Infinite. Nor can you escape this inevitable, for surely you created it. Each day, each hour, each act lived in your many material lives was the creation of this inevitable decision either to atrophy and drown yourself in the inexplicable complexities of the material life, the inane and inept repetitious servings of numerous idolatries, beliefs and superstitions—rather than to constructively form your life in all the basic inclusions of Infinite Creation, to live life as a progressive entity of evolution, a constructive person who is living beyond the confines of a vegetative earth life.

The choice is yours. The Infinite Intelligence is supremely wise, knowing as it does, that either the lack of such a constructive evolution or a full dedication to its cause and purpose will determine whether you will pass back into oblivion or into some future immortal life.

CHAPTER XXXV

Public Enemy — The Sleeping Pill

Our present modern day is sometimes referred to as the age of miracles and indeed this is so. At no other time in the written history of man has there been a civilization which has produced such a great super-abundance of mechanical and electronic inventions which should, by the same token, have elevated man to a new standard of living. Yet, paradoxically enough, many of these inventions and productions have also produced a great deal of harm. The misuse of many of our familiar everyday aids and conveniences kill and cripple countless thousands every year.

Now personally, I would not advocate eliminating—for the sake of saving all this life, injury and property damage—all or part of the many and wonderful things we find about us. Rather, effort should be made through the channels of public education to cut down on this needless waste of life and material. Many of the killers and destroyers are easily identified; some are more subtle but nevertheless just as dangerous and destructive in the end result.

One of these almost unseen and unheard of killers is the common sleeping pill or capsule. Did you know that these brightly colored capsules kill over one thousand people a year not counting those who commit suicide? Do you know that addiction to barbiturates is more serious in many ways than morphine or heroin, also, that 350 tons are consumed in this country annually? I was just as surprised as anyone could be when, on a television dramatization by the San Diego Police Department, a full and authoritative disclosure was given. In a short drama, all the horrors and dangers of the sleeping pill addict were depicted. Hundreds of thousands of people in every walk of life, our folks, friends, anyone we may chance to meet could be such an unwitting victim. There is no way of estimating as to the exact number or as to the severity and length of their addiction. Some, no doubt, would be shocked to learn that they were well on the road which had only one ending—death or a long and painful withdrawal treatment under the hospitalized care of a competent doctor.

Usually most addiction comes from certain groups or strata of people. They are the ones who, in the present taut, strained conditions of productive competition, become nervous and distraught, or they may be going through or have gone through great emotional strain in a divorce or a death. The causes are innumerable which may produce such tensions and neuroses. The victim is faced with a continual and increasing number of sleepless nights. Soon he seeks out a doctor who issues a prescription which is usually based on the assumption that the mental disorder is of a temporary nature and will dissipate itself in a few weeks.

Now the pattern is laid. In seeking and finding a temporary escape from one mental problem, the victim quickly finds other problems to take to bed with him in order to justify what has now become a nightly dosage. And so the vicious circle goes on. With the passing of time the victim finds that one or two tablets are no longer sufficient. He must wake up in the night to take another. The opened bottle is by the bed on the night stand, and in his half-dazed condition, tortured by strange ideas, shapes and forms which are always incurred in over-dosage of these hypnotic or sleep-inducing drugs, he may spill a half dozen or more into his hand and another name is added to the ever-growing roster of deaths from this killer.

Fortunately, sometimes the victim will realize before it is too late that he is headed for nowhere and manages to break away from his dangerous habit, or a doctor may recognize the symptoms of addiction. The use of a strong barbiturate is always accompanied by the following morning hangover, thick tongue, headache, nervousness, etc. Just as overindulgence in alcohol leaves a person with the inevitable hangover, so do these brightly colored capsules. Withdrawal is most often a very serious thing and has very often resulted in death. Severe emotional as well as physical pain is incurred. The victim frequently goes into spasms and convulsions which may kill the individual if he does not have prompt medical aid.

The pattern is always the same. In about thirty-six hours from the last pill, he will begin the deadly agonizing process. He may start by a frantic search for a pill, or he may become extremely depressed. There are tears and recriminations, then fear and cold sweat pours out all over his body; finally, convulsions and trauma. However, under a competent doctor, a slowly diminishing dosage is allowed; psychiatric guidance and advice is also very valuable; however, even when cured (so-called), the habit is much more easily fallen into.

Of course, no competent physician would issue a prescription with the conscious knowledge that the patient would become addicted; neither can a car dealer be sure in an assumption that the car he sells will not become a deadly weapon in the hands of an incompetent driver. Even an innocent bathtub sometimes participates in an accidental death. There are countless other known or unknown hazards in our everyday process of living. There have always been many, and likewise, the future may bring its new numbers of such hazards.

The obvious thing to do is, first, corrective measures. By proper education in all usages, much danger and death can thusly be eliminated. Correctly used under supervision, barbiturates are very valuable aids in overcoming many painful and distressing ailments. In the hands of an ignorant or nervous person, they will inevitably lead to great suffering or even death. If you are one of these who must have your nightly capsule, better see your doctor or at least take definite steps to stop before it is too late.

CHAPTER XXXVI

Physical Ills — From The 'Dead'?

In a previous discussion regarding some particular lady where her husband had died due to his leg being shot off, and within a short period of time she, herself, took on a condition of the leg which the doctors termed cancer, the following is further explanation to enlarge upon the concept of how another's malignant condition or violent death works on this particular principle. As all thoughts, whether emotional or reactionary in nature, are expressed into two dimensions, the third and the fourth, and while the third-dimensional energy-forms are quickly transformed into physical reaction, it is quite different with thoughts and their emotional content which are projected from the fourth-dimensional consciousness and as conjunctive elements of the psychic self, can be added to and hardened into a more dense thought-form body.

These thought-form bodies are usually the apparitions or so-called ghosts which haunt old houses and castles and have gradually detached themselves from the originating cause. In other cases and most frequently these shock or thought-formed bodies become a reciprocating polarity such as in the case of the husband with the shot-off leg, constantly adding to this shock form or thought form energy from the spiritual side by his strong feelings of resentment against this happening and various fears and apprehensions.

The loved ones on the material planes such as the wife also add to this forming shock body in an oscillating manner the same quotients of fear, resentment, sorrow and other negative wave forms. Thus it is that the loved one on the material plane can, even after a few short years, begin to feel the physical effect of this energy body which has attached itself through frequency vibration in a similar location on the physical body, directing as it does by its attachment in this psychic self certain insidious conditions which are presently plaguing mankind. As in the case of the wife who lost her husband, whose leg was shot off, this shock-formed energy-body recurred in a subsequent incarnation as a cancerous condition in her left leg and at the exact and identical spot where the leg was severed on the husband.

It can readily be seen that this energy formation concept can give rise to an infinite number of conditions and any person so suffering from any of these diseases should work with his condition from and by these principles. For obsessive thought-form bodies, whether they were indirectly indicated or that they were inceptive from the (previously discussed) shock conditions arising from being a witness or an indirect participant (such as seeing some individual sacrificed on an altar, falling into a volcano, drowning)—these and an infinite number more could all be starting points for future trouble to the person witnessing these happenings.

The astral underworlds are peopled with countless millions of horrible monstrosities which have known no human life or personality other than obsessing some unfortunate victim and who were bred through shock and fear, born and nurtured by constant, repetitious sequences of negative thought patterns. And these monsters actually suck the living life-energies from the minds and bodies of their victims, fastening themselves like giant fingers of negative energy-probes into the very heart of his being.

Many of these obsessing leeches can be called habits for any habit which does not have a constructive terminus is destructive in nature. The smoking habit, alcoholism, overindulgences and various physical desires, habitual, sexual perversions or extremes, all have a useless and destructive terminus and grow into monstrous leeches on the psychic body, reflecting their insidious effect into the physical body, weakening and tearing down and filling it with diseased conditions. To gain spiritual stature, a healthy psychic body, intelligent objectivism and the necessary infinite Wisdom incepted from the superconsciousness, means that the individual must in some way tear off these habit-formed energy leeches and repair the damaged material-formed structures which, in turn, reflect these healing processes into the physical body—remembering that these conditions were not incurred overnight or in one lifetime; consequently, such rebuilding, revitalizing and healing progresses equally as slowly.

It is possible through intercession that the Infinite could, through the projected mind energies of some high Master, instantly remove or heal this unfortunate victim, removing and dissolving the leeches and reestablishing a healthy psychic self; yet this would serve that person little good, as lacking proper knowledge of preventive measures as well as corrective measures, he would in the process of future evolutions quite likely find himself in the same or even worsened conditions. It is not the purpose or wish of the Infinite to do these things either directly or through other means to make any person perfect but rather, it is His wish and the basic principle of life and man's evolution that he learn to make himself perfect by gradually realizing that he is part of the Infinite and using or otherwise deploying all spiritual and intellectual agencies which are at his disposal for his own corrective and self-betterment evolution toward perfection.

True perfection is completely abstract and cannot be conceived by the reactionary third-dimensional mind. Only the very Archangels are beginning to approach that seat of understanding of the Infinite. For

every individual so concerned with evolution or reincarnation—the living of various life cycles upon any
one of a number of terrestrial planets—we must leave
perfection for our own future spiritual millennium,
meanwhile keeping busily occupied along constructive
patterns and pathways and ever keeping a watchful eye
for the lurking obsessions which are ever in the shadows cast by negative thoughts.

CHAPTER XXXVII

The Complex Escape Mechanism

Psychological nomenclature defines an escape mechanism as thought and action by any individual whereby certain psychic pressures seem to be temporarily relieved or certain justifications attained. It can be said factually that of the three and a half billion people living at this time, all, without exception, exhibit all classical symptoms of characteristic escape mechanisms and can therefore be said to be to some degree, mentally ill. These escape mechanisms are always very complex and encompass all mental and physical activity, all thought and action of any human, and in any particular escape complex mechanism, there is always one dominant factor which keys the entire reactive escape processes.

In human psychology, there is always a constant deflation of the ego and an equally constant demand for reinstatement. However, individually speaking, there must also be an overall sublimation wherein a certain amount of security, self-vindication, self-glorification and even security against death is realized. Religion, therefore, is an escape mechanism—the most classical of all such expressive complexes and one which has embroiled mankind since the beginning; and, as such, can be considered to be the greatest instigator and expressive agent of numerous human iniquities. Wars and crusades, deceit, bigotry and hypocrisy are all instigated and individually and collectively justified, in religious systems; for any religion or religious system has completely abrogated the concept of Infinite Intelligence whereby the individual can find within this system complete justification and vindication for all of the sins and evils, the derelictions, lies, lusts and deceits in which he is constantly involved in his daily life. Then to cap the climax, so to speak, within the gilded dome on his temple of deceit, he constructs an intercessor and an intercession. Despite all his earthly immoralities, he believes that his belief in his god-deity and intercessor will, after death, resurrect him, kiss him fondly on both cheeks and give him the keys to a heavenly city!

The length and breadth, the scope of this great religious immorality is immediately apparent in all walks of life. Recently, a convicted murderer, after spending eighteen of his thirty-six years in all kinds of crime, finally went to the gas chamber. His last hours were spent with a priest and as he entered the chamber he shouted, "I am Jesus Christ". It would only be incidental to say this negro was raised in a very religious family. However, time and space does not permit a full exposé of all expressive manners and forms in which the religious escape mechanism manifests itself. A historical study will reveal the full implications.

As of today, the society of this great nation is tattered and torn with dissensions and strifes which are the results of an almost complete lack of a constructive philosophy of life which would eradicate these dissensions and strifes. The immoral bigotry of religious systems, the complexity of our present-day, so-called civilization is such that current demands which are always apparent, often far exceed the mental capacities, educational factors, etc., of any person. This is especially true with the younger generations. Growing children are constantly being subjected to this ever-increasing sophistication and by the time the youngster reaches his teens, he is very often mentally involved in an almost hopeless situation of trying to equalize and stabilize his life in some future aspect.

Today thousands and thousands of teen-agers are

indulging in sexual practices, glue sniffing, smoking marijuana, taking LSD, etc., in an effort to escape the psychic pressures and demands of this civilized sophistication. Thousands of young men and women have almost completely abandoned a decent form of living, becoming beatniks, hippies, going into different kinds of crime, prostitution and sexual perversions. And when we read the daily reports of the vastly accelerated crime rates, we can only sadly speculate, "What will the world be like in fifty or one-hundred years from now?" And whatever our speculations may conclude, one factor is very apparent: that despite claims, man does not have or has not found any solution or cure to these ever-growing problems, either in his present-day religious systems or his sciences. There is still a complete lack of one element or factor which would spring the lock on his dungeon. This factor or element would be a living philosophy of life which would embody, interdimensionally speaking, the evolutionary consensus of Infinite Intelligence and of the grand scale of evolutionary factors wherein each person is individually educated and instituted in this evolution—a philosophy which would waylay the insecurities, frustrations, ego deflations and their consequential escape mechanisms; and above all else, a life philosophy which would include a personal psychology of rigorous self-analysis; a complete moral responsibility, not abrogated by intercessors and resurrection.

CHAPTER XXXVIII

Born Equal Versus Equal Rights

The popular phrase, "All men are born equal", first came into prominence at the beginning of the Revolutionary War and was perpetuated by its incorporation in the Declaration of Independence. It should be pointed out, however, that some of these instigators, advocates and underwriters of this war were children and descendants of religious refugees who came over on the Mayflower and similar vessels to colonize the New England States, where they set up one of the strongest and most oppressive of all religious systems still classically referred to as puritanical, etc. These people did all and more of the oppressions and atrocities in the name of religion, as were done by the Church of England—the cause of their migration. Yes, they even burned "witches" at the stake as late as 1890!

It was Lincoln, however, who reincorporated this misconception into the Emancipation Proclamation, thereby precipitating a ghastly and bloody war, (which is still being fought) placing the poor unintellectual Negro on a competitive basis with the educated white man—a competition which he has never been able to meet. Should the Negro gain victory in present-day rioting, obtain what he believes are his freedoms, he will only increase this competition.

In a more final analysis, the concept that all men are born equal or have "equal rights", if lived to their fullest meaning and interpretation, would create a socialistic state, reduce all people involved to a common level, leave them without leadership and democratic governmental form. They would live like robots, performing the necessities of existence automatically not

371

daring or caring to utter a word or make a movement which was not similar to all others. In short, these much-touted and vaunted equalities actually defeat and are contradictory to our free enterprise systems, which again is, in itself, a civil reinstatement of survival of the fittest, per se.

This free enterprise system can function only when there are differences in the ways of life, the desire for different life values and interpretations, specialization in these differences which give rise to better arts, crafts and sciences. Yes, the misconception of being born equal or with equal rights is anarchy against any democratic governmental form, giving each person carte blanche rights to do what he pleases regardless of his neighbors; and how many people are there who could live thusly and not infringe or impose upon others? As man is, by nature and through evolution, a predatory animal living by the jungle law, survival of the fittest, he must therefore be restrained and directed in his life. This can best be done in his present evolutionary position by a governmental system which determines individual action to the best advantage of all others. This government should also encourage individual differences, their development in self-selected fields of specialization, etc.

Actually, this is our present form of government, partially at least. Under the free enterprise system, people are able to express and develop individual propensities. Unfortunately, these advantages are constantly in jeopardy by efforts to reinstate and enforce or reinterpret into life false concepts of equalities, of birth and rights among men.

Not until man learns to live in understanding of a progressive evolution and all incumbent factors will he be able to eliminate the strife and turmoil from his daily life—turmoil and strife which is, incidentally, a necessary and sustaining force in his earth life and which gives him his drive, his determinants of value according to his elemental evolution and to be selective to his best interests. And in this chaos of material lusts and desires, each man constantly finds the creative bias, the inspiration, the ever-apparent necessity to become a better person.

The present-day conflict between the whites and the Negroes is a rather dangerous area in which to make any remarks or commitments, especially to politicos or other public figures, except possibly those individuals who attempt to cover themselves with glory by siding in with the minority group. On several previous occasions, remarks were made or discussions entered into by the Unariun Moderator for which he could quite conceivably be misunderstood. As the Moderator, however, I consider this issue an important means whereby clear-cut and concise evaluations can be made.

The whole controversy of "Civil Rights" for the American Negro seems to be clouded with hypocrisy and bigotry, as well as a general lack of knowledge, misconceptions, etc., of the real and basic values involved. Two very widely used terms or phrases which are being used as battle cries are, in themselves, widely divergent subjects, even though they may sound or appear similar in usage. These phrases are "All men are created equal", and the second, "Equal Rights under the Constitution". The first phrase, "All men are created equal", is a classical misconception of long standing, born from out the minds of religiously and politically oppressed people in an attempt to equalize certain values and modes of life which they have been forced to accept.

It is quite obvious even to the casual observer, there are no two persons alike; no two people look exactly alike, nor do they think alike, and each person views the same particular objectivisms differently. These differences in evaluations, in actions and reactions are even more widely pronounced in different races and ethnic cultures. The term "created" is entirely fallacious and smacks of the stamp-mill assembly line technique which would have to be used by this supposed almighty god to keep pace with the procreative needs of the world.

The idiocrasy that each person is "created" also hints of a singular "once lived" life and automatically blinds the believer to the true logical evolutionary creation and re-creation, not only with mankind but with the entire visible and invisible universe. Only in evolution can we find the logical and intelligent answers to all questions, not mandated by the whims of supposed gods but through science and well-ordered laws which have been so frequently discussed in our liturgies. Therefore, the idiocrasy, "all men are created equal" is abhorrent and lacks any semblance of reason or logic. The religionists or advocate, however, might try to evade this interpretation and point out that his god considers all people equal. Here again more fallacy, for if such equality in creation were so conceived by this figurative god, it would automatically destroy any and all differences and purposes for this creation of man, for the earthman would then be a superficial whim without difference or purpose, even contradicting the obvious evolution everywhere about him.

It would also contradict the depiction of god and the "Judgment Day" when he selected the 144,000 for his "New City". He would be a rather inefficient and poor creator to have made billions of people and have them all turn out defective or bad except this small number!

There is a way, however, in which we can understand creation or the Creator "seeing" all people exactly alike, that is, if we understand Infinite Creation, as in the previously discussed Principle, as a functioning oscillation, harmonic regeneration and other necessary fundamentals. Then as each human is actually merely a tiny

374

speck of oscillating, regenerating energy, Infinite Intelligence then "sees" or is conscious of this tiny speck of oscillating energy as it oscillates in its particular way with Infinite Intelligence; however, here the similarity ends. The combination of harmonics or the ways in which these various regenerations oscillate between each person and Infinite Intelligence are always different. Each person makes up a different compound of these numerous oscillations, their harmonics, etc., and while the principle involved is similar, each person is actually determined differently by Infinite Intelligence. If this were not so, then the Creator or Infinite Intelligence would not be able to distinguish between a falling sparrow and a falling man. All creatures, all things, all substances oscillate in principle with Infinite Intelligence; in fact, the very energy substance of their makeup is part of Infinite Intelligence.

It is resolved, therefore, that as the earthman lacks comprehensive knowledge of Infinite Creation, he should not tamper with what has been and is obviously, for very specific purposes, these different racial classifications, ethnic culture groups, national and international dispositions. These factors are, in themselves, competitive elements whereby Infinite Intelligence progressively recreates along the evolutionary pathway, these different peoples in their particular cycle of evolution so necessary not only to these peoples but as the way in which Creative Principle is kept constantly in action.

The second, "Equal Rights under the Constitution" is worthy of much more consideration. Here again, however, while it first appears to be a great ideal that all people have equal rights and equal opportunities, unfortunately it will not work among the races of people which inhabit these United States (or the world for that matter), for the simple reason that as all these people have differences, they are different personalities, live different lives and see things differently, their determinants and evaluations are not going to coincide. This fact has already been proven with the enactment of the "Bill of Rights" and more than ten thousand laws which govern the peoples of this country—laws which were passed by a vast and preponderant law enforcement system.

At this point of our introspection we might become frustrated, throw up our hands and toss the whole thing out. We can, however, summarize the different salient points which have been brought out and philosophize within our own minds: mankind and his temporal earth life is an evolutionary cycle. As of today, there is ample proof, man in his position in this evolutionary cycle is not yet sufficiently advanced to live in harmony either with himself, his family, his nation or the multitudes of people which make up the different races. He has not yet learned to live by the Golden Rule given two thousand years ago, which would automatically make the Constitution, the Bill of Rights and all the laws entirely superfluous and unnecessary. And so the mad, blind pursuance of life goes on. The utterances of sages and philosophers expounding great truths, the moral lessons constantly taught in repetitious wars, the tragedy of human ignorance which breeds poverty and despair still goes on even more forcefully, more rampant, yes, and more fearfully for the many hundreds of millions which comprise the earth's population. Man has recorded the histories of yesterday and the obvious and sometimes tragic lessons which are so apparent; yet even as he teaches these histories and lessons to his children, he is repeating the same mistakes, perpetuating his future to the same tragedy.

To those who live in Higher Worlds, this earth is indeed an elemental environment, a battleground of emotional vicissitudes waged frequently with passion and fire, hotter than the proverbial hell; and from this furnace of human iniquity runs the molten ore into the mold of human experience which, when cooled in the breeze of temperate wisdom will yield the etheric form of logic and reason which sublimates the reason and the necessity of evolutionary creation from the slime and muck of a material world.

As has been previously stated, the problem of racial differences is indeed a rather dangerous area of introspection in which any statements or commitments made pro or con could wrongfully commit any person in the eye of his fellowman as some sort of an anarchist or misanthropist; such commitments could also be wrongly made as the proposition of equality is a total involvement of all factors involving human existence on this planet. Some of these factors not being known to man, he must therefore remain an emotionally prejudiced judge until he so learns of this totality of human existence. Introspection and an analysis should begin, therefore, in the beginnings of man's earth life evolution. As it is with all creatures, man too lives his earth life under the same primitive and elemental jungle law as do all other earth creatures. This is the law of survival.

Infinite Intelligence mandated this law in such earth world planets as the necessary attribute whereby certain equilibriums could be maintained among the species of earth life, i.e., a better and more progressive evolution for these species and a more selective process whereby each species was further strengthened in future generations. It is quite obvious, therefore, individual survival as the most dominant factor of existence became the most influential attribute of existence. As of today, this is just as true, just as dominant in the highest echelons of our civilization as it was in the most primitive beginnings, and no person historical or living, save with a very few exceptions, has ever been able to live and express himself completely above and beyond the influence of this primitive survival law. No living person can consciously perform any act or think any thought which does not in some way involve him personally and advantageously in accordance to the well-defined principles and factors of his evolution. As his past was lived in the necessity of his survival, so is his present moment, for each present moment is a derivative of consciousness compounded and colored from his past. Even the forming of an opinion is, in itself, a vindication of personal ego which again re-perpetuates personal survival in all aspects of consciousness.

In the very beginnings of his earth world existence man began to see differences between himself and other people. He began to see them in a way which was different to some extent than did other species of animal life. While such differences as to personal and instinctive reactions of superiority caused the mates of different animal species to do battle with themselves, sometimes unto death, this was, in reality, the only logical way in which Infinite Intelligence could insure the survival of the best of each species. Any male, however, on gaining supremacy over his rival was usually content for that season and to breed accordingly. With man, however, this competitive and selective process became more and more involved as the perspectus of human understanding and evaluations broadened and increased. Competitive rivalry between the males for the females became more and more complex as he progressed in his evolution. At first it might have been the best and driest cave, the best chunks of meat torn from a freshly killed animal, the best and strongest women to prepare his food and bear his children; and so from these early primitive beginnings our present-day civilized rat-race for survival has emerged.

As of today, man's perspectus of personal values is

no longer confined to his cave or to the prowling beasts in the few square miles of forest in which he hunted for his food. Through scientific technocracy, every person is totally involved with at least four billion other humans and with an area which totally inscribes every square mile of our globe. Quite obviously every person being so totally involved and having neither the mental capacity nor understanding to cope with this situation is going to use a certain kind of subterfuge which he calls equality. Through this equality system he believes he can superimpose his own personal evaluations on every other living human being. Ways and manners in which he will try to attain or superimpose equalities are almost too numerous to mention. He will say his god created all men equal, or he will invent a political system which he will call democracy or socialism or communism and which he will try to impose as a way of life on all other nationalities.

Actually, this system of equality did not begin recently; it began back in the primitive beginnings, and it should be stated unequivocally that of all misconceptions under which man labors, the greatest misconception is in equality, and it is through this equality system man indulges himself in one of the greatest of all hypocrisies and bigotries. Proof of this statement has already been written in the bloody pages of man's history. His past has been a great and tragic exposé of this great bigotry of equality.

If a man believes in a certain religion, he has and will use all manner and means to make others believe as he does because in this justification he has vindicated and reinflated his own personal ego. If a man of one race sees another man of another race, he will subconsciously and consciously react against him because the other race or nationality represents a difference in various values of life—differences which he cannot change, neither can he compensate for them

379

without deflating his ego. He will, therefore, attempt to either destroy this other man or make him subjective as a slave, a convert, or even as a taxpayer. Again through any means he might attain, he has vindicated his ego.

Clearly then, this system of equality is a vicious subterfuge used in lieu of an intelligent understanding of all life processes. Equality is even more vicious when it is loudly acclaimed by religionists as a "divine virtue", or incorporated into laws under which the peoples of a nation must live. The Civil War fought one hundred years ago did not end with the assassination of Lincoln; it is still being fought as of this hour. All the laws, all the Constitutional Amendments which have been, will be, or could be enacted, will not eradicate the venom which is generated in people's minds under a system which is based on an interpretation of equality. Until people begin to understand Infinite Creation and the evolutionary principles and laws of this Infinite Creation will mankind begin to sublimate equality into an intelligent and logical way of life. As equality is an ignorant and elemental attempt made by persons and nations to sublimate unalterable factors of life to prevent ego deflation, so must this vicious practice of attempting to equalize or judge people according to one's self be discarded before any person or any race or nation will be freed from the carnal lusts, racial strifes, personal and religious crusades, etc.

Many men speak fluently of love for their fellow-man, yet how can he speak of love when he understands no man—not even himself? He may believe he loves another man or all men, yet he loves them selfishly because he attempts to absolve himself from obvious differences and the emotional strifes which are produced by these strifes. He professes to love others because he attempts to cover himself with some kind of glory. He thinks others look upon him as a great and wise and understanding person. He may even feel a sense of security for professing this fellowman love; or perhaps instinctively or even consciously, he believes they will not turn on him and destroy him if he declares his love for them. How can it be—one man loves another for subverted, selfish reasons? Indeed not! No person loves another in all capacities and for all reasons upon which he may profess this love. A man may love a woman but for reasons of the necessity of procreation or the beginning of development of polarity. Yet no man can truly love another until he understands himself, what he is, the reason for his existence, his evolutionary life, the Principles of Creation and all other factors which are tantamount in the understanding of Infinite Creative Intelligence, the many ways of Creation, the Many Mansions, and the finding of the Kingdom Within.

If and when any man finds all of these values and factors and finds them in their proper perspectus, this man will truly not be subjective to racial strifes, political systems, famines, flood, and pestilences. In his developed state of consciousness he will live far above the mad turmoil of a material world. He may hear the cries and pleas of the earthman in his travail; yes, he may even become an Emissary to carry a small flame of Truth into the darkened reaches of that material world, suffering for the moment the pains and travail of a material life. Yet, He, his Super Self, is not affected by it, neither is He subtracted one whit from the higher perspectus in his Infinite Understanding. And when He has accomplished his purpose, He has bound up a few wounds on the battlefield and has stilled the cries of a few frightened and suffering people, He will return to his Higher World and to his limitless future—a world not bounded by the emotional vicissitudes of ignorant people who either destroy the "un-understood" or bind Him in the rigorous conformities of an equalized society.

It should be noted in this final moment that while the religionists of all Christian faiths proclaim loudly their love for their fellowman, particularly for other races, yet each religious faction, whether it is Baptist, Presbyterian, Methodist, etc., also proclaim that no man can be saved and get to heaven except through their particular church. Is this not segregation? Is this not bigotry? And in their beliefs, even their god has romped his way through biblical history, segregating people and nations, killing some, showering others with blessings. Even in the final hours of resurrection proclaimed by the Christian, god denies himself as the creator of all men, by segregating the evil from the good. For if he created all men, did he not also create those who are called evil as well as those who have different colored skins? To segregate and destroy the evil is to destroy himself and his creation. It is also a license to destroy any and all others of a different colored skin or different beliefs on the basis of the same emotional differences. This, then, is the Christian bigotry, to preach god and love, and eternal salvation to all men, but discriminating any of these claimed virtues from those who do not believe as they do.

Again, let us abandon these false religions and other systems of life as the determinants of human conduct. Instead, let us learn to evaluate evolution and the creative principles of life and let us see the beginnings of this evolutionary creation in all things—the stars in the skies, the planets and their many forms of life, all the familiar artifacts of our daily life. Let us see this evolution in every human regardless of the color of his skin. Let us respect him in the translation of his evolutionary values, even as the Golden Rule, so that he should also respect us and our position, that we shall personally not interfere with his interpretation, neither shall we judge him according to our own interpretation. And if we wish to help others, let us do so, not by directives or interpretations, but by setting an example wherein certain virtues are expressed in our lives above and beyond any which have been realized by those whom we wish to help. For no man can become a better person until he selects more virtuous values of life and completely dedicates himself to their attainment.

CHAPTER XXXIX

On Polarities

It has been observed that during the past years of actively dispensing the teachings of Unarius, some certain individuals reacted either mildly or violently against certain presentations of life or concepts which seemed to violate their personal sense of propriety. In due respect to these (and any other) individuals who may, in the future, read these works and likewise react, we present this article in toto wherein will be found a clear, lucid, logical explanation of these various factors which seem to arouse conflict and in which the reader can compromise and justify any seeming disparities or incongruities.

First, Unarius is quite different from any past or present earth life teaching dispensation, for within the curriculum of Unarius, life is presented not only in a rational conclusive evolutionary pattern lived by earth people, but it also realistically describes life to be lived in higher planes of evolution. These higher planes of life are quite different from the present physical material earth life, therefore, a deliberate attempt is entered into in these teachings whereby the reader can be weaned away from his dogmatic position which is necessary to sustain him in his earth life.

In a psychological interpretation, the presentation of these unknown values and concepts often arouse antagonism. However, it is assumed that for the larger number of students, suitable preconditioning has already occurred in their in-between earth life, spiritual lives whereby such conflicts do not occur. Even so, that while it is lived, the earth life is a very dominating realm of interpretation, and any aspiring student must keep this fact in mind in order to keep the higher way completely separated, thus enabling him to attain these higher objectivisms. It is also a common psychological interpretation either consciously or subconsciously expressed by every human, to interpret any and all outside appearances of life about him in the manner in which he best understands. All people, therefore, knowingly or unknowingly falsely color or judge these appearances accordingly. Yes, even the more distant and unrelated happenings which come to them indirectly are also falsely colored by those who purvey these happenings in the common mannerisms, speech, etc.

More specifically then, let us take the book, "The Voice of Venus". In its pages an attempt is made to describe people living on Venus to the reader in a manner most acceptable to him and at the same time, leaving the door wide to a future time when mental expansion will have developed to a point where these people can be seen as they really are. First, however, the reader acclimates himself to these people by seeing them somewhat as he himself looks, dressed in garments made of pure energy rather than fibers. This Venus Being is also pictured as a form made of pure Radiant Energy rather than the familiar atomic constituents called mass which comprise the physical anatomy. However, when these Venusians are seen as they really are, they will be clothed only in a radiant aura, and they will not have the familiar physical shape of the human anatomy but shall appear more like that of a beautiful lambent flame which is pulsating in such a manner which constantly recreates a variegated rainbow-hued texture within these bodies.

Another concept entered into in this book and very emphatically stressed throughout the works of Unarius is the concept of polarity; in an attempt to portray the polarity forms of human beings, the greatest conflicts are entered into. Specifically, the book described Jesus and His polarity in a graduation ceremony in the Central Temple of Azure. To picture Jesus with a polarity or woman seems to be a great hypocrisy to those who have clung desperately through the centuries to age-old sanctimonious deifications of certain individuals now called saints, including Jesus, wherein these people according to the religious liturgy, were completely exempt from the common evolutionary patterns which all people follow. However the fact is that no person, saint or Jesus, ever evolved into one position in his or her life without following such a common pattern, just as you yourself have so followed it.

The concept of polarity, therefore, is the most important concept in which you will first begin to properly interpret in all manners and forms of life, including Infinity, and this Infinity you will find in the millions of years ahead of you. To analyze polarity, we must first understand that polarity is a unit of expression. In order for any particular thing, object, circumstance, or any individual life dispensation to express itself, it must first have its own beginning, for in the beginning it is so created. However, such creation is logically impossible without an expression, for in this expression, this particular objectivism thus connects itself to Infinity and in this way, it becomes a part of Infinity in that ever-expanding regenerating and re-creative process which is the nature and expression of Infinity.

The third dimension, or terrestrial or earth, is one of the places where certain portions or forms of expression first begin to attain that all-important entity of self, for no singular expression can have a beginning without a certain circumference which is called self wherein within this circumference the entity of expression is so contained.

In the simple hydrogen atom we find one of these more primitive entities, a positive nucleus or proton around which is revolving a negative electron. Between these two units there is a constant oscillation or exchange of expression which determines the self or the hydrogen atom. From there on, we can proceed up the scale of evolution into the plant and animal life of this planet and find an ever-increasing complexity of expressions in these various forms of selfhood called plants and animals until we arrive at the most ultimate of expressionary earth forms—man.

At the beginning of any person's evolution as a human being, he has also begun a more highly developed function of expression which connects him to the higher planes of life wherein, in some far-distant future, he can be normally visualized as gradually evolving into these higher planes. Primarily concerned, therefore, with all earth life dispensations of expression is that all-important expressionary form called procreation, for procreation is absolutely necessary to sustain a sequence of evolution of any or all forms of earth life.

In the simpler forms of life such as bacteria, procreation is expressed as a simple splitting process whereby one bacteria becomes two. In the higher dimensions of plant life, we begin to find the divisionary forms of procreation called male and female again expressing the common unit of positive-negative, negative-positive or the oscillation of all elements involved in that particular species. As before, humans express the most complex form of procreative sex and which is, incidentally, the basis for our modern Freudian psychology, for in dealing with the factors of sex we do indeed find a strong interconnection with every basic factor or element in any human earth life.

However, this Freudian psychology has not expressed the more spiritual elements of man's earth life and, therefore, no continuity has been established whereby any human can visualize progressive emancipation in an evolutionary manner into the higher spiritual planes. Sex must therefore be resolved into a more scientific understanding of life wherein it can be seen that individually or collectively man is expressing a continuity of consciousness with the Infinite which will eventually give him this long sought-after emancipation.

In this respect, all humans have, since their beginning of evolution as humans, begun to exchange their various entities of expressions basically predicated in the common sexual union. In order to maintain proper equilibrium in this expression, it is absolutely necessary that all humans express an almost equal balance of both male and female relationship. The small remaining difference called bias will individually determine in any given earth life the proper relationships as either male or female; thus in coming up through the many hundreds of earth lives which every human has lived, he has been in a somewhat alternating fashion either male or female. This can be individually proven by any person. All males have certain female characteristics and vice versa.

Modern psychology interprets every human as being twenty to forty percent of the opposite sex. In understanding this evolutionary pattern of sex, we can quite easily see how it is that certain persons are homosexual. They are psychically reliving just former lifetimes as one of the opposite sex. This psychic influence from the previous life is often sufficiently strong to dominate every expression of their everyday life. A proper understanding of this sexual evolution will explain many other enigmas which are presently befuddling the medical savants. Many hysterectomies could be prevented if it were realized that psychosomatically speaking the woman was suffering from a strong guilt complex involved in past-life dispensations of male-female relationships.

Continuing our introspection into the higher planes of life where we find humanity living at the point of evolution where they have passed that point of the physical worlds and now no longer live in a physical body, we find a correspondingly higher development of sex. The passing of the physical development of consciousness also relegated the sex organs back into the animal world where they belonged. Procreation assumed a more advanced form of regeneration. Instead of the gestation period, energy was psychokinetically projected by the minds of those immediately concerned into the construction of a certain basic energy form or configuration. Into this form or cell the psychic anatomy of the individual so concerned in this rebirth would then merge and occupy, thus enabling him to become a member of this higher society. There he would find his loved ones with whom he had lived before in thousands of earth lives and where, in these earth lives, he had built up certain strong affiliations which were constantly expressed between these two or more people, these expressionary elements of self.

In these earth lives the beginning of this polarity development is the beginning of that which is sometimes referred to as the soul mate situation. However, marriages are not made in heaven as is commonly supposed but are an esoteric development between two or more people who succeed in maintaining an interconnected earth life dispensation and which always succeeds in drawing them together in successive earth lives. There are numerous examples of this development currently found about you in your earth life wherein two people have actually begun to look alike as well as to share in an oscillating manner the various elements of their earth lives. This is a psychic situation and supersedes any voluntary efforts which may be induced as commensurate values.

And so in the higher spiritual worlds, these two people can be thus so evolved in their consciousness that instead of having two sexually-minded individuals living common earth life dispensations, we find rather,

389

two spiritually-developed entities of expression, expressing between themselves in an oscillating manner the common ingredients and elements of life in these higher spiritual worlds in which they are presently participating. This was the situation with Jesus and Erza as described in "The Voice of Venus", for Jesus, like everyone else who lives in these higher planes, has found His place in these worlds by virtue of His development as an expressionary unit of self oscillating between other similar units of self in a common reconstructive pattern which added to the nature of the Infinite.

And you, like Jesus and Erza or any other individuals past, present, or future, who wish to live in these higher dimensions will do so only by virtue of the knowledge which you acquire about them and this knowledge will make it possible to evolve into these higher dimensions as expressionary units of self united to other such expressionary units through an oscillating process of self in this vastly expanded polarity concept.

In that day and time you will have long since lost your sense of sexual proprieties. You will not feel indecent going about your way of life unclad except by the rainbow hues you radiate from your body. And as you go about, your expression of life will not be done by walking, eating, sleeping, etc. You, as an entity of consciousness with the Infinite, will be oscillating with this Infinite as part of that great re-creative principle. In this oscillating process, your first and closest affinity will be that polarity, that former man or woman who passed so many earth lives with you in so many different relationships and in which you shall find in your higher development has now become, in this common union of expression, a more complete interchange of Infinity. All that the Infinite is—and as it is so expressed between you two, and as you so express it thusly—

you become, in reality, Infinity. Infinity, in turn, re-links and rejoins in common oscillating patterns to all other expressionary units of self and completes the complete cyclic transference of the re-creative Infinity to every human in a similar position.

This is the higher way of life—one of the more ultimate points in your destination should you succeed in overcoming the dogmatic position which you now occupy. Yet even this more ultimate way which we have pictured for you is not the most ultimate which you will attain should you succeed in arriving at this point. There would be no purpose in creation; there would be no Infinity if we should at any time assume some theoretical ultimate.

However, it is best to resolve your immediate position of evolution with elements more suitable and more justifiable in your present circumstance. These will be, as they are presented to you in the works of Unarius, like a guiding Light which will lead you up out of the darkness of your material life onto that spiraling pathway into the stars.

CHAPTER XL

Dr. Juddah Interviews the Author (1957)

Dr. R. Juddah, of Oakland, California, a researcher of philosophies and religions of the present time, engages, as part of his work, in gathering together—by going from one school of thought to another—what information he can, in an effort to build up his case of the differences or the similarities of all present-day schools of thought along these lines.

Because he had not yet been made familiar with the clairvoyant aptitude which the Moderator so aptly expresses, the author had to go to some length to try to explain this faculty to him. Neither had he, up to this point, become acquainted with the life principles of regeneration (or so-called, reincarnation)—although about one-half of the world knows of this cyclic reliving; especially by those of the Oriental and European countries including England, etc.

Dr. Juddah said, to Ernest Norman, "If you will be so kind as to share with me your time and to explain just what your understanding and teachings are, we shall be most appreciative and it will serve our cause well." Of course, the Moderator was most willing, as this is his very life, and with anyone who opens the door unto him, he is most happy to share of his knowledge and of his great and Infinite Wisdom.

However, it would have taken far longer than the four to five hours spent with Dr. Juddah to thoroughly convey the very extensive Science of Unarius, including the author's own personal background; but rather, several weeks or even months would actually have been needed to express, even a fair portion, of all Unarius is.

With this understanding, Dr. Juddah said:

"So, if you will oblige me and describe, informally, a generalization or outline—just basics will be most acceptable, and appreciated—please?"

T - Many years ago, since I started out in various different churches, groups, and making a very thorough study in my own way, I realized there were many elements in my own life which needed justifying and needed, in some sense of the word, to be reoriented, and of course, there was that inward motivation— perhaps I wasn't consciously aware of the fact; so I spent some fifteen years in very active research in and around the Los Angeles area during the war years. I had sufficient scientific training and background so I could overcome many of the pitfalls which are customarily encountered by people who are doing similar work, on a practical as well as scientific basis, the thing which must be striven for in the orientation and factions in the mind and consciousness which would help a person not only individually but also, to be of some service to humanity, as a whole.

I realized that the world at this time was passing through a tremendous cycular movement and that the world in general was entering a new era, and especially through the war years with the development of atomic science which was built up on Einstein's theory of mass plus energy, the theory of the expandable universe, etc; and so when atomic science came along and exploded the first nuclear weapon, it literally plunged the world into a tremendous cycle of scientific achievement and development. As a whole, the general public was not equipped, mentally speaking, in their philosophies and their way of life to compensate for all these things. Today, of course, statistics bear out the fact that while this is a scientific technocracy, yet people, as a whole, are suffering tremendous repercussions, simply because there are no age-old systems of religion or cultisms as they have been expressed through Christianity

393

or any other particular concept on the earth today which can fully justify all of the factors that enter into the life of the present day; nor can science, because science is confined strictly to the third dimension or physical. The slide rule and various other mathematical equations must always be necessary, and so the scientist is very busily engaged today in equating the whole infinite cosmogony of the universe on the basis of his own present mathematics. As Oppenheimer said a year ago, we have long since reached and passed the point where our present mathematics and science are of any service to us in expanding the horizons of our present physical science.

So there were many elements which were very obvious to a philosopher or a person who was earnestly seeking. There were lots of elements which were missing—and even more than this is the fact that while there were millions of books written on life and man and various other constituents which were supposedly adequately portraying man in his life on the planet earth, yet none of them actually dealt with the more realistic creative principles. It says in the opening chapter of Genesis that the Lord made man by stooping to the river banks and scooping up a handful of clay and breathing the breath of life into him. That might be all right for some people but according to the scientist, it does not stand up to a complete and justifiable analysis in our own retrospection. So in going into all of these various factors and different phases, it was very evident we lacked a true scientific science of life. The old Yogi out of the East had, in the old Vedic and Brahmanistic teachings, contained many of the elements which were somewhat basic in the construction of matter as far as the material universe was concerned: and there were various degrees of reference to man's evolution in spiritual planes, reincarnation, etc.

Getting down to the crux of the whole situation resolved reincarnation as a very badly misunderstood subject. In a more simple phraseology, reincarnation can merely be termed as a cycular pattern very similar to our day by day life. We carry the complete hypothesis, the evaluation of man as a spiritual creation because of the body being resolved into karmic structures which are, in themselves, tiny planetary systems of energy; and while it is quite unknown to the scientist of this day and age that these energy forms represented systems which are called atoms and are supported internally from other dimensions—in fact, an infinite number of dimensions; these are manifested into the tiny solar systems called atoms, through a regular vortexal pattern of interdimensional relationship and the laws of harmonic and frequency relationship, etc.

Therefore, getting down to what man really is in all internal and external appearances, the body is merely an external shell—a shell of energy which represents ideology, form and habit which is developed through evolution in a great number of lifetimes which started way back in the distant past somewhere for each individual. It also resolves God as being infinite, manifested and maintained in infinity, only becoming finite in all consciousness and all things. Therefore, God is a leaf of a tree, in blades of grass, atoms in our body. He is everything simply because God is now manifested and taking on a different form into numerous dimensions and an infinite number of forms. Therefore, if we can see that man's physical body is an externalization of the internal interpolations of interdimensional relationships of energy traveling in cycular patterns and movements, then we begin to form a very definite basic pattern for what is called reincarnation—which simply means an extended principle. We might say that Darwin discovered certain principles of evolution as far as the physical life of animal or plant was concerned on the land, but life for Darwin was not explored into the spiritual or the spiritual consciousness.

So now we see man having a spiritual body, as it is more commonly referred to which is actually a matrix of energy forms—tiny little wave forms which reside in vortexal patterns through the psychic body and which reflect outwardly into consciousness all of the infinite quotients of which they were formed from the experiences of past lives. Therefore, man not only repeats in the strict psychosomatic sense the day-by-day patterns which he developed in early childhood in one certain life, but he is also constantly reflecting the sum and total of an infinite number of experience quotients from a large number of past lives—psychic shocks such as murder, being killed and various other catastrophic equivalents which were projected and formed into this psychic self in an oscillating process which the psychiatrists today call a reflex from the subconscious.

The same principle is portrayed in our television set. These various wave forms were formed in the psychic self day by day, hour by hour. Just as the physical body lives by the multiplication and regeneration of a million and a half new cells every minute, so the psychic body is continually being reformed, refurbished and changed in other ways through experience quotients day by day. This is the scientific side and the analogy of spiritual man. It can and has been portrayed on scientific apparatus, not only in this world but on other planets as well, and other people use that science as a common denominator for canceling out such illnesses or other perversions of intellect which might be coming into the individual's life.

We have many references in a more or less scientific way which were made by Jesus in the Holy Land two thousand years ago. Like Jesus, we do not believe in prayer as it is externalized by the average churchman or the average Christian, or the average cultist who is on the earth today. It was expressed by Jesus that we should not pray as the heathen does, as the publican does, in the streets or in public places, but we should go within the closet of our own inner consciousness and seek out and maintain the continuity of expression with the Infinite Mind or the Father within, a positive and continued contact with the inner consciousness. Many other misunderstood concepts still exist in what is called Christianity today, which have led untold millions of people astray and down the blind alleys which in some future time must be worked out and justified. There is nothing more fallacious in common interpretation to believe in such things as so-called divine intercession, or that most people believe that Jesus will some day save us all from our sins. Nothing could be more misleading or more paralyzing to the average individual's consciousness, simply because the basic principles and all evaluations of life are a continual oscillating process from positive to negative for many interdimensional relationships which we call the Infinite Mind.

In order to properly evaluate all conditions, circumstances and the various lifetimes which the individual leads in his process of evolution from the more primitive stages, he simply reflects and reciprocates to a large degree all of the infinite elements which are contained in the Infinite Mind and Consciousness of God. These lifetimes, then, are forming a day-by-day pattern in which he lives into future consciousness where he can become solvent in some spiritual dimension of consciousness which is beyond the horizon of our reactionary way of life.

To Buddha, this was called Nirvana; to Jesus, it was finding the kingdom of Heaven which was within. But it means that place in which every person becomes more directive in his own evolution and consciousness so that he does not resolve himself back into the material dimensions, bound there by the astral residual condiments which he reflected into his psychic self hundreds or even thousands of years ago. To the old Yogi, that was called karma. Karma merely means a malformed vortex of negative energy caused by some psychic shock; and the individual, knowing as he does in some subconscious way, especially in lives in between lives where these things are more apparent and his pattern of life is made more crystallized, knows that these things must be eliminated and cancelled out in order to obtain the true evolution of consciousness. Therefore, he reconstructs for himself through the laws of frequency relationship, harmonic structures in cycular patterns, exactly similar circumstances in which he incurred either one or a number of these psychic malformations. He hopes, by living them out, to wear them down and otherwise conquer them in some vague and subconscious thought pattern or inflection. Not properly armed with the right wisdom, he frequently runs afoul of new circumstances and too often solidifies any existing malformations in the psychic body, thus incurring an increasing number of circumstantial equivalents which he calls sin and evil.

As it was taught by Jesus, the Christ Consciousness is the true principle of intercession, because in the infinite and most abstract understanding of man as a spiritual being means that the Infinite compounded in a cycular fashion all of the equivalents of the Infinite Consciousness into one personification, and this one personification became the life cycle of the one individual. The one individual is multiplied by all the number of individuals' personification living on this planet and an infinite number of planets throughout this universe and other universes. Therefore, God, or the Infinite again manifests infinity, becoming again finite in all consciousness. The true Christ Self, then containing all of the elements of God, if it is properly brought into complete rapport with the conscious mind, can be the personal savior of every individual, simply because in the conditions wherein the individual is now incepting into the conscious mind through the reflective oscillating process of energy constituents, all Infinite Principle and the ideology, form and wisdom contained in the superconsciousness. In this particular connection, no sin or evil can live in his life. All malformations in the psychic body are cancelled out and neutralized and made whole. This is the true basic principle of spiritual healing and one which must be taught to the masses of people in the future, if they are to survive when they are to pass from this particular domain of this materialistic world to evolve into higher spiritual states of consciousness. Before they do that, they must learn the creative processes of life as they are contained in the energy wave forms which they are constantly reflecting into the psychic self.

The history of the world, the health of the people, the political systems, our intercontinental relationships with other people on the face of the globe would change overnight if every individual knew that the day-by-day process of what he calls thinking is a direct reflective process which institutes all the reactionary factors he has let become permissible in his daily life, that they are actually the energy wave forms which form the basis for his future evolutions in future worlds and different consciousness. If he knew that, he would know the true meaning of casting the bread upon the water—or do unto others as he would be done by. If he knew that in the sum and total of all the things which are reflected into his psychic self were, in themselves, interconnected with an infinite number of people through the laws of frequency vibration and harmonics, that he was also connected in an infinite way with other dimensions, astral, sub-astral, or otherwise spiritual as the case may be, and that he was actually beating as one small pulse of energy in a great and infinite number of pulses which were beating throughout the infinite cosmogony, then his pattern would quickly change. He would try to do something about it.

Not so many years ago, one philosopher expressed religion as an opiate used by the people, and in fact, that is exactly what religion is. It is the largest escape mechanism which the people have generated for a system of self-justification and what otherwise derives neurotic thought patterns. They blame God for every ill, evil and sin which befalls them, that God is punishing them, that the only way to salvation is through suffering and sin. That kind of interpretation of life is what degrades people and projects them into the subastral worlds and makes them victims of all the dark and evil forces which have made man subjective to his own desires.

Seek ye first the Kingdom of Heaven which is within and all things shall be added unto you. That is the way one man calls the inner consciousness—the direct ability of every man to be able to orient his thoughts either with the mental conscious or the superconscious or from the reactionary elements he has permitted to permeate into his consciousness to become activating forces in his own day-by-day life. That is the reactionary way of life, the life in which the average person lives—a system of personal justification and escape mechanisms.

The principle of this new science—and yet it is not new in the sense of the word—the very principles of creation itself, even from the most primitive forms of elemental energy structures, are involved in the science of Unarius. They are portrayed from higher planes of spiritual consciousness by those who have gone on from these material and reactionary worlds. It is a great movement, a great attainment and a great fulfillment which is being brought about in this present day.

Many people believe in such biblical versions as the end of the world, etc., because of lack of sufficient knowledge of cycular patterns of not only personal evolution but astrophysical evolutions as they are concerned with all planetary systems, the interdimensional relationships which hold the planets in their course.

The sun itself is a vortex of energy, a whirling great dimension which comes to a point or a focus which is expressed as our own sun. Likewise, each and every one of the planets are so interconnected through the great vortexes of energy which are expressed from higher and higher dimensions—the sum and total of intelligence portrayed in an infinite number of ways.

Questions by Dr. Juddah:

Question: Have you heard of Edgar Cayce's work—is your teaching related?

Answer by the Elder Brother: We have no absolute direct relationship with any existing Cayce movement on the earth today. Our connection is directly with Cayce himself, who lives in a spiritual world. Until I met Ruth and until Cayce came to me himself one day in San Diego a little over two years ago, I had no knowledge whatsoever of Cayce. I never knew he existed; I never read anything of his work. But Cayce came to me one day when I was sitting on a couch and told me many important factors of his life—the strawberries that he raised in Virginia Beach in his early childhood—and many other factors. Ruth wrote them all down and sent them in a letter to Hugh Lynn. Mr. Lynn later replied and verified more than sixty percent of these incidents which I have mentioned, and even though Hugh Lynn played it down for all he was worth, yet it proved conclusively that Cayce was working with us. Cayce has come with every one of the readings since that time. He has been in this house and in other homes where we have lived, and he attends whenever I give a reading.

Cayce is very much more advanced in what he understands and knows now about the Akashic reading and the principles involved than when he lived in the physical. He knows now that the pure essence of therapeutic science is contained in that psychosomatic principle, which we previously mentioned, of canceling out the insidious blocks and vortexes residing in the psychic body from shock experiences in previous lives. By bringing the perspective and focus of attention of the conscious mind to the particular condition with the individual—and we are assuming that the individual has been preconditioned for the acceptance of healing in some way in the spiritual world—then this is the negative end of this oscillating process which will line him up with his conscious mind so that the cancellation of energy wave forms can take place from the superconsciousness. This is the true principle of intercession, the true principle of healing.

As far as myself is concerned, I purposely stayed away from all forms of reading of metaphysical and spiritual matters during this particular course of scientific study and research connected with the various churches in the city. I started at the beginning of World War II, becoming an ordained minister in several of what is called the 'spiritualist' churches, because above all else, they gave me an outlet not only to study human psychology and spiritual psychology but also, certain aspects, certain scientific principles about which I knew must be oriented and brought into a factual science. I never learned from these people except for the fact that they presented certain equivalents in this orientation process.

To study my own personal history, when I was a little boy I could be what is commonly called an infant prodigy. It merely means to me the development of the personal self through reincarnation and living an infinite number of lifetimes, and studying in the spiritual worlds in between lifetimes, learning of all the elements and factors which relate to this present expression and then bringing them back and consciously orienting them into a tangible basic science in this world.

We have so many different similarities of these so-called infant prodigies existing in the world today, both in the past and in the present, for instance, some of the composers like Mozart, who could compose music at four. I built my first microscope when I was five years old and I examined and counted the hairs on angle-worms. My life is filled with examples of what are called unusual manifestations and demonstrations which can only be attributed to the fact that I came into this world with them. They were the result of thousands of years of study in other worlds and other times. I am merely consciously expressing them now. There are no gifts. A person works for whatever he has—whether it is good or bad, he works for what he has.

Question: How did you develop this psychic ability?

Reply: There is nothing more definitely misunderstood in this world than the term, being psychic or being clairvoyant. In either case, when a person becomes psychic or clairvoyant, it is simply an outgrowth of wisdom. A person develops inner consciousness. When he becomes wise in the motivating principles of life, he can no longer live on the old reactionary planes of life in materialistic elements which must be stimulated from outside sources into a consciousness of every moment. Then he learns to resolve all things from the inner consciousness and in that way he connects himself with an infinite number of dimensions of interpolations into other worlds, into other realms and planes of consciousness which have been a part of his former life. It is through frequency relationship. The principles used here are the same principles which the modern scientists use in radio and television and other forms of communication.

Question: Did you read a great deal?

Reply: I did most of my reading, if it can be called any kind of formal reading, in my very early youth. I did very little or any reading after the age of thirteen.

When I went to school the first year, I was reading books on psychology and physiology, etc. I remember my first teacher quite well. She tried to teach me the alphabet and I already had the equivalent of a very good education before I even went to school. This was not merely by going into these books and rereading them, and more or less, hammering them into my consciousness. It was merely the reawakening of a great number of things I had learned in other worlds and different times. Only in modern nomenclature, in modern form and ideology did I orient them again into my way of thinking and my way of life which was similar to the people about me, so it would not be foreign to them or cause any reaction with them.

Reincarnation is being proven every day. We go to sleep at night; we wake up in the morning; we begin a new cycle during the day. Life is just like that from one life to the next. When we live in the spiritual worlds, that is equivalent to our nighttime; we wake up and begin a new cycle of life, but all the things which we did yesterday are part of the pattern of our lives today. As we incarnate, it is only a larger cycle instead of a small day-by-day cycle; we now have a life-by-life cycle. When we get into the proportions of larger cycles, we will then see that we get into cycles which can be referred to as epochs. We take from the time Atlantis was destroyed some fifteen thousand years ago and we can explain cycular patterns on a very scientific basis to the scientist as well as to the layman and point out, not only their own personal cycles—not in any astrological concept or any known form today—but a scientific form which is only partially understood by the scientist of today. Every person has his own pattern of cycles from one day to another. At one time I kept track of them and in that way, I could very accurately forecast for weeks of time what I would feel like on any one particular day, simply because of cycles and their junctions. It became a science to me.

Question: How about astrology?

Reply: In some basic evaluation, astrology today is one of the derivatives which has been intermixed with a lot of other different elements in its metamorphosis or its evolution down through time. The basic astrology, or astrophysics, relating this world and universe to other universes was first taught by the Lemurians one hundred fifty thousand years ago. The opening chapter of Genesis states that the Lord made the earth in six days. The pagan in India and other places knows more about Christianity than the Christian does. Now these six days refer to six astrophysical cycles; they refer to the earth which is traveling in a retrograde cycle—what they call the cycle of the recessional. It arrives minus so many degrees each year from its original point. At the end of 25,862 years it has passed through an arc of 360 degrees. This is very important to remember when we realize that it is the same principle which turns the motor in the vacuum sweeper and activates all electronic mechanisms in this day and age as they resolve themselves into motor form; for the sun, which is a vortex of energy as I have explained, has as a direct consequence, a great radial pattern of magnetic structures radiating into the material dimension which we call the third. These structures are the lines of force which stem out in a radial pattern, just as they do from the poles of a magnet and which, in turn, interlink with the earth and every planet in the solar system and with every other sun and planet in the entire universe. These are all very scientific and well-known principles.

Now the cycle of the recessional at 25,862 years is divided into twelve equal divisions—a little over two thousand years to each one. In modern astrology, we term them from Pisces to Aquarius. We call them anything we wish because there is nothing mystical about their particular terminology. As far as these cycles in themselves are concerned, it only means that in their relationship to certain very definite lines of magnetic force stemming out from the sun and interlinked with the universe, the earth is a subjective particle; and the qualities of that particular personal magnetism are inflected indirectly and directly into consciousness of every living and atomic structure on the face of the earth. Even the earth itself is subjective to that magnetic force. Now that is the basis for astrology. When it is understood, it is a very factual science, and a very vast science, because then we will understand how it is that the planets can revolve about the sun and still maintain an exact form after millions of years.

As far as biblical history is concerned with the history of man, and starting from the Garden of Eden which in itself is a spiritual parable, we add up these six days according to 25,000 years, and we go back approximately 156,000 years ago. That was when the great space ship from Lemuria landed in the Gobi desert. Now three Europeans have seen the remains of this space ship. It isn't a matter of theory—they actually did. The Mormons and Latter Day Saints have a strange parallel in this story. These Lemurian Masters who were eleven in number—and this gives us the basis for another concept, eleven being the number of mankind—they succeeded in constructing an amphibious craft from the remnants of this space ship. Churchward was one of the men who went into a cave and saw the remnants of this space ship.

So these Lemurian Masters started out to cross the desert, came to the Pacific Ocean, and from knowing previously from astronomical research from their own planet of Lemuria, knew of the great continent out in the Pacific Ocean. They established a great civilization and they taught the spiritual way of life which is being established through Unarius on the face of the earth today—the true scientific principles behind all the symbolisms, which we call metaphysics or various cultisms and orthodoxies.

The true Garden of Eden was first Lemuria, because these great Masters taught the spiritual principles of life as they are related to pure science, energy wave forms, the psychic self, curing disease by psychokinetics, the mind forces and various other factors. So, as the people gathered about from the corners of the earth—which we refer to as the ten tribes—and were brought in, they were primitive, savage people, and that is the basis for the story of the Tower of Babel and the Masters teaching the science to the people. Then after thousands of years, there was a great cataclysm which destroyed Lemuria and it sank; but before that happened, there were establishments of great civilizations all over the world—in Yucatan and Atlantis and other places of the world. Egypt was first formed more than one hundred thousand years ago. Time itself means little or nothing. Archaeology in this day is very infantile in its evaluation of time and is only basing its equivalents on the retrograde of great civilizations which existed in the past. The spiritual age of Lemuria was again typified in Atlantis and relived there for many thousands of years and it is known today to a degree. Even Plato made references to Atlantis.

No doubt, psychologists would want to condemn me to a psychopathic institution if I were to state that I have a conscious memory of 450,000 years and I could describe the planet Lemuria and life there. But I am not alone for we have had many examples of people who have come from Atlantis and Lemuria who remember the destruction and the various lives they lived. I, myself, have been marked with a stigma of the crucifixion two thousand years ago. It isn't a matter of whether we can believe or accept these things; it is a challenge to everyone's personal threshold of intelligence. In other words, it separates the sheep from the goats, because in the present reactionary psychology according to Freud, man has been reduced to a mere happenstance. There is nothing in modern psychology to support life on the planet earth—nothing whatsoever.

Every minute we have two people entering mental institutions. America has the highest rate of mental illness in the world, and it is high time something was done about it—something more constructive or something more scientific—something that will fill in the various obvious gaps in between science and religion, between the unknown elements of life as they really are and what they are commonly expressed in the reactionary way of living today by the average individual. Man does not know that he is really a walking, living, television set. There again, science has struck a very close parallel with life, as far as man is concerned— just as the transmitter on the hill reflects sound and pictures in a matrix of wave forms and vibrations into the antenna and into the system of the television set. These wave forms mean something to the tubes in their integrated circuit, so they are amplified, separateed, sorted and projected as a series of light and dark spots on the fluorescent face of the picture tube at the rate of 16,000 spots per second. These are all synchronized with various pulses which are also mixed in with the original wave which came out of the transmitter.

The same process of life takes place with every individual every day and every moment of his life—elements of synchronization and wave forms, the constant multiplicity of various energy creations which are reflected back into his consciousness from previous lives. It explains everything. There are no unknown answers, no hidden mysteries when a person understands this science. All church systems today exist only by certain psychological principles of fear. The average person attends church only because of certain fears which have been woven into his consciousness and his psychic self through many generations and many lifetimes. He goes to church because he is afraid to do anything else. He lets the priest or whoever it is in that church become the demigod of his existence. The keys to heaven and hell are held by the church, and nothing is more unrealistic. Jesus taught that every man was most properly connected with the Infinite Intelligence, the Father within which doeth all things, the Kingdom of Heaven which is within.

In spite of St. Jerome and others, who had great influence in interpreting the Bible, especially the New Testament, we still find many of the imperishable truths and principles in the New Testament. Even the average Christian today does not know that he is not worshipping the one God, (the Infinite), but he actually worships a pantheology. He does not have a monotheistic religion in any sense of the word. He is worshipping the old pagan god, Jehovah, a god which was brought out of ancient Chaldea by Abraham, a god of avarice, lust, anger and hate that is contrasted to the Infinite God of Jesus that lives in everything. No wonder they are mixed up and confused.

About 1600 years B.C. there was born a child into a family of one of the Egyptian Pharaohs (as they were known at that time—Amenhotep III) who became known as Amenhotep IV. He was rather an odd and peculiar child. He had a tremendous head, and he was rather sickly in his life. He took little or no interest in outdoor sports. At the age of fifteen or sixteen, he was

409

placed on the throne but the mother still maintained the reins, shall we say, over the destiny of Egypt which was at its highest conquest of culture at that time. Amenhotep IV was a reincarnation of an Atlantean and had also lived in the time of Osiris more than 11,000 years B.C. He had lived many other lives, too, but primarily, he came into Egypt because he wanted to abolish the old degenerated forms of religious cultisms which worshipped serpents and animals and establish the monotheistic concepts of Amen Ra, the worship of the true God which was personified by the sun—the understanding of the great vortexes of energy which stem down from an infinite number of dimensions and which was first taught by the Lemurian Masters.

So when Amenhotep IV grew up and came into power, he went into the temples and tore down all of the old Egyptian gods, and he tried to convert the people into a monotheistic way of life—to worship the true God, to maintain inner consciousness, that temple worship was not necessary but only a symbology. At the age of thirty-eight, Amenhotep was poisoned by the priests he had cast out of the temple. This has a very strange parallel in this life. A little boy was born in Utah—a very small child and very strange in his ways. He had a tremendous head, in fact, his mother almost died in childbirth. At the age of three or four years, he wore a size seven and one-half hat. He grew up, and at the age of fifteen or sixteen, he was taken out of that environment and came to California. Then, of course, followed years of development until he came to the age of thirty-eight. Then he went to the hospital for a ruptured appendix. That was symbolized by the old poison that was given to him at the age of thirty-eight in ancient Egypt 3600 years ago. So when he entered the hospital, he underwent a great shock—anesthetic didn't work. He had been psychic all his life and had, for many years, read the past, the present and the future; and he had given amazing demonstrations to other people. But in this hospital, the anesthetic didn't work. They shoved the needle into his spine a couple of times but he went through the operation practically in full consciousness.

So just as it was with Jesus, he projected himself out of his body while the operation was going on and went into the astral worlds. The next morning when the physical body awoke, he was still in the astral worlds, and the physical body responded in all ways and all consciousness; but it was still not directly connected in full rapport to the true self. For two days and two nights that condition existed, just as it was with Jesus in three days and three nights. About two o'clock the following Tuesday morning, a definite sensation occurred. His body awakened and felt that the true person had come back into the physical and was in full contact.

From that day on, he went out into the world and was completely changed, entirely different and was a stranger to his wife. A year later she left him because she no longer had anything in common with him. His friends turned away from him for no reason whatsoever, so he found himself going about searching and seeking and finding out what it was all about. And that is a thumb-nail sketch of my life as far as this physical expression is concerned. He went into the dance hall, into the churches and into all public places where people were and demonstrated what is commonly called psychic phenomena to an unbelievable degree of accuracy. He could go to India, China or Borneo while he was dancing with a woman on a dance hall floor. He could go into homes and describe intimate articles that only the person would know—which was only a way to prove to himself that all of this was instinctively known by him and what he had within him was truth. He had learned these things in other worlds and other places. Because he was a scientist, he was someone who was

411

searching and seeking to implant within himself not only the true basic fundamental science of life but even more important, to develop that to a point where other people in the world could be taught and could learn to use the same science.

So he learned to live, too, by the power of the Super-consciousness, to learn and to be led and be directed and become fully conscious, not from the physical mind, but from the internal mind—to realize that every article of clothing, every place that he lived, every act which was portrayed and exemplified through his everyday life was a direct manifestation of the inner consciousness and not through the ordinary elemental reactionary principles expressed by other people.

For years he told others that there was a certain woman who lived in this world who was going to be in-strumental in helping him bring about this science. He described her; he told them that she had brown eyes —and that was many years before I met Ruth. And al-ways I was searching and seeking for her because I knew that at the right time, the right place and the right junction of cycles that she would be there. So about four or five years before Ruth came into the picture, other psychics in this area began describing to me the long-bearded old men with big books who were follow-ing me around on the Inner and, I might say that Rob-ert was one of the psychics. Robert Cheney and his wife described them to me; other mediums in other church-es all gave me the same reading. They said whenever you are ready, the books will be there to be written; the science will be there; everything will be there. And then I met Ruth in a spiritualist convention in Los Angeles. The pastor, Danny Hart, gave me the same message, practically word for word that Robert gave me. About an hour later I met Ruth, and since then all things have been fulfilled and attained.

The first thing we did after going to San Diego a

few days after meeting each other was to bring into consciousness "The Elysium", and it was strange and wonderful. And even Ruth herself contacted the Master Elijah. We were going over the bridge into San Diego when the first one of the parables came to me, then for several days after, the parables followed. Some days I didn't even succeed in getting my pajamas off and into my clothes. We lived in the full power of this consciousness. After "The Elysium" came the little book, "The Truth About Mars", and then came, "The Voice of Venus". John the Revelator came and took me to Venus on thirty-three different trips, and I went through the halls of learning and the great cities of Venus, and I saw life portrayed in a higher spiritual dimension. From there on, there were revelations of six other major planets, spiritual planets in this universe—planets that are unseen and unknown by our astronomers —but they are there, nevertheless. The beautiful cities and everything people have done and are yet to do were all portrayed in the most magnificent splendor that defies description.

And now, seven—eight years later, other students are also "seeing" these beautiful dimensions and further verifying these things.

CHAPTER XLI

Balances and Counterbalances (1963)

Quite recently one of our dear and close Unariun students was involved in an automobile accident and inasmuch as this circumstance could conceivably give rise to conjecture among the various other Unariun students, this might be an opportune time to discuss this particular accident and to point up some of the very important and salient points in the Unariun concepts and which are all very closely related and involved in any such circumstances.

Ideally speaking, it might be reasoned that an accident such as this could have been circumvented; the student in question could have been forewarned and prevented from having this experience. Had this been done, the student would not have known for a certainty whether this accident had been prevented and forever after, or at least for the rest of her life, she would be somewhat in doubt as to whether or not there had really been intervention. However, above and beyond this are other important factors to consider. As you know, our position with any act which can be considered to be intercession is against our policy and our jurisprudence. We have always maintained a strong position in this respect that wherever and whenever a person is prevented from realizing and experiencing certain advents in his life, whether or not they are negative, actually does this person more harm than good. It prevents the person from realizing the most valuable part of his existence—which is experience; and it is only through experience that we develop the fuller dimension and the greater perspectives of the mental horizons.

The fact that these experiences are sometimes negative or even disastrous is, however, just as valuable to us as are those experiences which have the more transcendent values in life. There should be brought out at this time the fact that the Moderator was quite conscious for several weeks prior to the accident of the knowledge that she was to have an accident and he could have stretched a point, gone out of his way and warned the student or taken other means to prevent her from driving at the scene at the precise instant when the impact took place. It should also be said that He was lying on the couch in his home at the moment that this accident transpired and He saw the scene rather vividly depicted; He knew that He was there and was fully conscious of it.

Now it has developed that the student in question has gone through this accident without too serious consequences and although some physical injury was sustained, together with some shock, it is quite evident that a much greater degree of injury or even possibly death had been prevented by the different ways in which the Unariun Organization has of buffering such accidents or experiences for those who are prepared and who are dedicated to its service.

There are many factors of introspection which should be entered into at this point which will relieve any student of any tendency to wrongly or negatively slant this experience and deprecate the value of the Unariun teachings. To best do this, we will analyze such various factors involved and in this way be able to obtain a much better perspective of all that transpired. It has been quite obvious for several years that this student was a very deeply dedicated person to the Unariun Cause and her weekly trips from Santa Barbara to the meetings here in Glendale were evidence to this fact, along with the other different efforts she was making financially, etc., to help sustain and to propagate the Movement. In her instance, this dedication, just as it is with the other Unariun students who are likewise so dedicated, did not come about simply as an idle expression or a fantasy of mind; it came about only after long and arduous preparation and conditioning by these persons in different lifetimes and particularly in the spiritual dimensions where they lived in the in-between lives.

Since the crucifixion (of Jesus) this student had been very arduously pursuing the path of knowledge to reform herself, to make of herself a better person and above all, to correct the differences in her life dispensations in which she was involved in past lifetimes. And so it was that in the in-between lives in the spiritual Centers she recognized the great Infinite Cosmogony; she was aware of these Higher Worlds, the teaching Centers, the wonderful Personalities who lived in these Higher Worlds and so many other attendant realizations which could be expected of her position at that time. This, of course, all helped her to realize within the dimension of her own consciousness the need and to crystallize the desire for this better and higher way, so she began developing herself and preparing herself for the future advent which, in Christian doxology, is called the "Second Coming", or the establishment of the Unariun Concept on the material earth at a very propitious time.

Of course, like all other students or even the Moderator, she cannot be considered to be perfect in all respects or even fully prepared to meet all expurgations or expediencies and to be fully able to equalize the immense complexity and, infinity of such experiences which they will go through in the materialization of consciousness in these material worlds or where they are separated, in a sense, from the true transmission of intellectual and progressive evolution. The very nature of the material or carnal world is such that it is opposite in all its dispensations to the true concourse of such an expanded and evolutionary concept. It is simply so because these material worlds are not equalized; they are in all experience quotients, as they are being materialized daily by hundreds of billions of people, to be singular or mono in nature; that is, they are unbalanced.

To more fully understand and appreciate the equilibrium—as we must so emphatically stress equilibrium in Infinite Intelligence—is to again revert back to the fundamental and basic principle of the Unariun Concept which is: Infinite Intelligence in Itself is perfect. It is the sum and substance of all, but much more important, It is, in itself, constantly regenerating and forming Itself in a series or sequences of new forms or patterns. As it combines the time-space factor within Itself, it is therefore cyclic in motion—a fact which has been proven by Einstein's mathematics. In this cyclic motion there is always manifest a completely equalized situation or a transmission of energy.

A concept is carried in its entirety within itself over the entire frequency of its transmission within a cyclic path. Whether it is large or small, the nature of the information or intelligence carried in such a cyclic motion is always counterlinked with every other cyclic motion upon the principle of harmonic relationship. And so the entire Infinite Intelligence presents an infinitely vast and complex matrix of wave forms of cyclic motions which can be visualized to some extent as interweaving vortexes of motion or anomalies. These wave forms do conversely, within themselves, present exactly opposite counterparts and in their evolutions within each other also present exactly opposite points of the sine wave configurations, the necessary positive and negative facsimile of all of the information contained.

Perhaps the best way to illustrate cyclic motion and

417

the differences where we have absorbed time, so-to-speak, within a given circumference or space would be to take an ordinary device, a compass—and which is really not a compass at all in the true sense—which can be purchased in the ten-cent store and which can draw circles. If we take a stiff piece of cardboard and we draw a perfect circle with an approximate diameter of four inches and by making a center mark with a pencil where the point of the compass penetrated the cardboard, then by placing a mark anywhere on the outer periphery or rim of the circle we can by taking a ruler draw a line straight across the two points; we have divided this circle in exactly two equal portions. Now if we had two little ants, each one carrying a grain of sand, who were trained so that they would walk around this circle at exactly the same speed, these two ants could then walk around this circle indefinitely without catching up with each other. They would, at any given point of their circumference, present exactly equal portions of the circle to themselves.

This is, in a rather crude way, presenting the equilibrium of Infinity. We will say that no matter how large or how small such a cyclic transmission is, we will always find an exactly equal or equalizing point in its circumference wherein it always transmits in an opposite or a negatively or positively charged condition the exact facsimile of its entire content. Moreover, the way and the manner in which this is done being rather complex, we will leave this facsimile just as it is and carry out this introspection into the third dimension.

Man, in the beginning of his evolution, acquires a certain prehensile mental faculty which relates one or more objects together without necessarily involving the circumstances of his past in respect to the particular appearances. However, all things in the third dimension are—like all other things wherever they are found —harmonically linked to each other. If we find a stone in the road today and we find another stone in the road a year from now and at a point many miles apart, these two stones are, of course, different and they were found at different places. However, they are both stones and were both found in the third dimension on a particular road and so basically, they are the same stones.

So it is from life to life; people are doing just as you are doing—manifesting and remanifesting the past in a countless successive series of experiences wherein they are merely transmitting the past, so-to-speak, into the present. And by the same process, they are at this present moment re-transmitting the future, for the future will be exactly the same as the present unless they obtain sufficient knowledge of the mechanics involved in their life and its transmissions, and of what it consists, and in this knowledge they are able to reconstruct the fabric of their lives or to obtain for themselves a more directive quantity of self-expression. They become masters, so-to-speak, of their own destiny, for knowledge gives people such mastery.

The fact that we could, within our own consciousness, relate Infinity in all its vast breadth and scope would immediately place us beyond the realm of the third dimension and it would, mentally speaking, place us in a position which would be hundreds of trillions of years in advance of the position in which you now presently occupy! That, of course, is all part of your evolution. It is a challenge to your own capacity, your own integrity, your own will, your own intelligence as to how well you can see the necessity and the purpose of evolution and the regeneration of Infinity through you.

When this entire perspective has been obtained, then you will be oscillating or manifesting Infinity in your consciousness to such a degree that a uniform and equalized balance in all things will be obtained. Therefore, you will no longer be a singular person wherein these experiences must come to you in a singular fashion, one to be placed against the other and compared or reacted to in trying to obtain the equilibrium from the appearances of these two or more reactive-looking appearances in your life. Instead, you will have complete knowledge of all of these things within themselves, why they are there, the reason and manner for their existence and many other additive factors which are far beyond comprehension at this particular moment.

And so our discussion with our dear fellow student and her accident does not necessarily shape itself up as a negative happenstance; it is at this very moment, and through the means of this taped transmission being reconverted from a negative expression of energy into something which is positively biased or that it will carry a message to you—a message wherein you can, within your own minds, re-analyze and re-affirm certain substantial and basic truths within your consciousness and you can again visualize something of the infinite perspectus of Creative Intelligence. When you have done this, you will have aided and abetted this Infinite Intelligence in manifesting itself through you because Infinite Intelligence must constantly regenerate itself from any given moment to the next. It has in its complete entirety changed—yet changed only in its manner and way of expressing Itself through you.

These dynamics, these principles are incomprehensible to the third-dimensional mind, yet they must be in some way comprehended by those who wish to live an immortal life, to those who wish to aspire—and especially with the Unariun student—through preconditioning as well as the natural and latent desire of the creative instinct which is within you, something which is imbued and re-created through every atom, through every thought, through any other and all transmissions of life. Here is the positive bias of creation which is ever-apparent, which will always be with you if you will reach out with your mind to grasp the full meaning of this ever-apparent Intelligent Creation.

And as it so happens in the material world—and especially as we are conducting an analysis with our dear fellow student—we must always in some way have to succeed in turning a negative circumstance to some good. We must see purpose, we must see creation in it and we must see all other things, otherwise we become victimized by it; we are retrogressed by that experience. The experience then becomes impounded in our own psychic anatomies and it will, in turn, in the future regenerate itself into our lives.

We could again say that in the past lives in which this student lived and as she has come and gone into the material world, there were many circumstances of a negative nature in which she was involved and she could not remember consciously what she had learned in the higher spiritual worlds simply because consciousness is only an extension of the subconscious mind—an acquired faculty of realization which started at the moment of conception. In turn, the superconscious self or the more highly-developed self—when it does develop—should supply and replace the function of the subconscious. It should supply all things to us much more broadly, much more realistically than does the subconscious at the present time, and which is the opposite polarity of that circle we have just discussed as it involves the circumference of our own personal thinking, for this, too, is in a sense a cyclic motion. We have an oscillating condition from the conscious mind to the subconscious and vice versa and which, in turn, again re-oscillates into the past with the mental consciousness or the psychic anatomy.

This is the perpetuated part of our existence, the part which has existed from the first embryonic concepts which were amalgamated together in the common bond of frequency relationship. Yet lacking knowledge to more fully discharge the small consequences of a negative nature which came to this student in the numerous transmissions of her former lifetimes, these experiences snowballed, so-to-speak. Harmonically, they became attuned to transmissions here in the present life and as all things are cyclic in motion, it was inevitable that this negative vortex or anomaly must be discharged. It was so discharged in the moment of impact when time and space, so-to-speak, were hurled away and the negative proportions of these countless experiences were so discharged. Yet, unless this is fully realized, they will regenerate themselves, harmonically speaking, and reperpetuate themselves in the future of that student; they will reperpetuate themselves in you, individually.

That is the reason for this discussion here at this time with you—to exercise again the common basic concept of polarity interchange. As this experience resides with you in the negative phase of this cyclic motion, so I reside in its positive phase. I give to you the equilibrium of this experience and in doing this, these transmissions become with us the common fund of knowledge which is superimposed as intelligence and knowledge in our higher selves. And in the future when the higher self is so fully-developed that it becomes the dominant polarity of our consciousness, then we will be able to rationalize, we will be able to clairvoyantly use these past circumstances, we will be able to recombine all of this information and knowledge in respective cyclic transmissions, linked and relinked with Infinity. And thus we shall see the higher effigy of creation in motion, for it is through such creative motion that the Infinite does constantly regenerate and reperpetuate Itself in all forms and in all substances and in the conscious surface of every-one's mind.

The third dimension or the material world, as you see it swirling about you in your daily life, is mute testimonial of the singular experience in life of every human wherein he is attempting to equalize consciousness—equalize it infinitely—for these tendencies or instincts, proclivities of human nature as they express themselves, while they may seem basically destructive, yet they are basically constructive. Even through the most evil experience of any human life or even in the combined evilness of expression with a great multitude, this very evilness can be the most necessary and motivating force which can levitate individually or collectively speaking, multitudes of people.

It is well known that the more people suffer, the more they try to seek relief, the more they will try to express within themselves a higher and a better way, so the evil of their existence becomes the wellspring, the source of motion, the energy, the incentive or whatever is necessary to propel them. Like the powder which is compounded in the chamber of the gun which fires the projectile, although it is an evil force yet it does propel human consciousness into a motion wherein consciousness seeks out a way to alleviate, to seek a higher and more equitable plane of life. This, in itself, is one other way in which we can understand the equilibrium as it is expressed in all cyclic motions, for even though we differentiate cyclic motion in the third dimension as a singular point-to-point transmission of sine wave frequencies, yet this is not the fundamental reason or occurrence for their existence. They are truly in all senses, harmonically linked to the cyclic motions of their origins which are fourth-dimensional in nature.

That is the reason for the great and apparent fallacy of modern civilization—the insatiable quest of science to prove that it is right, third-dimensionally speaking—or that all things start here on the surface of this earth. Whether they see this in the DNA molecule which they believe was synthesized from out the substances or in the gases of the earth, in conjunction with thunderstorms, lightning bolts, into the first protoplasmic cell, science still has refused to budge or move from this position. It cannot yet conceive that the origin of life is fourth-dimensional in nature—that it comes from somewhere else. Third dimension is only a plane or a surface of expression. There are many other dimensions—just as Jesus spoke of them as the many mansions—and this insatiable quest will only lead science more deeply into the mire of confusion, for as the expressionary agents and elements of fourth-dimensional expression are found in the third-dimensional science or the earth world, so will confusion reign until their source, the manner of their being and the reason for their expression has been divulged by fourth-dimensional analyses.

These and many other factors and elements, truths, principles are very vitally important in your progress. You must constantly be aware of them every moment of your experience in the third dimension, for you are truly relating these present moments with all past tenses, all past experiences, and you cannot for one moment relax and resign yourself into a fatalistic attitude. Such an attitude is a lazy and an indolent one and bespeaks of a person who is intellectually inferior, a person who is slovenly in his mental habits and who does not care to seek out the reason for his being, the reason for his existence and the multiplicity of forms of life and expressions everywhere about him. Such a person is on the downward trail.

Therefore, the future must always present its own challenge to you. There can be no relaxation for indeed this must eventually supply the present libidos or drives with which your material world furnishes you. Instead, you must substantially regenerate within your own consciousness a more definite facsimile of Infinite Intelligence. It cannot be the reactionary reagents which are contained in these materialistic forms— the necessity for your eating and sleeping and for maintaining your positions, for paying out monies or bending to and observing the different expressions of material life as they are set up in what is called our organized society of living. For this organized society is, in itself, merely a system of balances and counter-balances because it is singular in expression and does not include principle, does not understand, and it is constantly at odds with itself; it is constantly deficient. It is never sufficient to supply the ever-increasing re-surgence of new expression, new quantities and new divulgence.

That is the reason for the great preponderance of law and executive agencies within the government of the United States and behind this also the reason fourth-dimensionally speaking, for the great resurg-ence of crime, the ever-apparent decadency of our civilization, for as civilization rises, so it too is equal-ized by a counter-motion of degeneracy. And when a certain point is passed in the perspectus or realization of any nation or any person wherein the progressive motion of evolution is not sustained, then there is an imbalance. The negative begins to catch up and deca-dency sets in. So, therefore, in the future let us ration-alize not only the experience of our fellow-student positively but also obtain from it an additional per-spectus, more information, more strength and better dedication.

There will be many years, perhaps a number of lifetimes which each of you will want to live or to rein-carnate back into this earth-world dimension, or you may reappear in other earth worlds similar to this one and there again, you will attempt to somehow establish the continuity of the past. You will say just as our fel-low student did in the previous conditioning of her advent into this material world in this lifetime, "I am sufficiently strong to overcome what I know is in my past. I know that it will reappear in my future as I am living on the earth world, yet I feel that I am sufficiently well-equipped, I am sufficiently dedicated and I have the knowledge to overcome these things, and so they will be overcome." She perhaps did not directly remember the continuity of that preconditioning, yet it has been expressed through her and I feel sure that in the days to come in her moments of introspection, she will feel the impact of that collision, not as a rending, tearing sensation which left her unconscious body by the side of the road but rather, as a great discharge of negation which she had accumulated through the ages. It would also whisper its message to her, not in that grinding crash of steel upon steel but an infinite message of hope, of eternal life, of realizations in higher worlds when we could live beyond the reactionary dimension of the material world and learn to make of our lives a mirror of Infinite Intelligence where we could reflect the more progressive elements of evolution, where we could reflect not only to our own consciousness but to all mankind how Infinity was living through us. And in our form, in our motion and in our thoughts and our consciousness we were becoming more and more a part of this great Infinity; that we were expressing it, not as reactionary creatures, born of an earth world but as constructive intelligent beings, in our consciousness helping to reconstruct Infinity in all its dimensions and its ramifications.

Therefore, in concluding our analyses and our introspection of this particular situation, and inasmuch as it could also involve any one of you in any such a similar incident or in many other different happenings in your life, I do not wish to go on record as having made an unequivocal statement that evil is necessary in a sense that it is a fatalistic doctrine or that we are destined to have certain things happen to us or any other such views which may countenance a fatalistic attitude, for such fatalism, is fatal. Rather, I would say, and in view of all factors involved, that experience in itself as a necessary and formative expression of energy and motion in our lives, is very valuable to us.

Individually we should not attempt to circumvent or to reestablish conformatives of life expressions in other people. Rather, we should seek to find the answer to all of these things and to prevent or to discern, or to otherwise exercise intelligent action and motion in our future relationships. To have prevented this accident would have aborted the normal course of the evolution of this student for she, herself, in a sense, had mandated that it should happen. Previous circumstances of negation were such that they must, according to the cosmic law of regeneration, constantly reexpress themselves or discharge themselves into new conformatives, into new expressions. To circumvent this normal intercourse of life experiences of any person is to deny him the privilege of learning, to deny him the privilege of self-development and this, in itself, leads us into many other dimensions of introspections.

Why is the supreme importance of the physical life so everywhere apparent in the ordinary earth man, and if such experiences could be realized in a more supreme sense, then we may say, why is the necessity for all this? And if God created man as it is expressed in Christian doxology, then why did He not create him perfectly, why the necessity for all of this worldly intercession, this worldly dominion by this Christian god? And the fallacy of religion itself as it is so currently being expressed becomes immediately apparent if we carry creative concepts into the altars of the churches, for here we have found in his mind, man has created the effigy of Supreme Creativity, flawlessly an embodiment which can create light and universes, yet apparently through a religious system is subjected to the various placebos of human consciousness or that he can be duped by false promises, by prayerful attitudes or subverted from what might be an intelligent course of action or abstaining from such measures which would interfere.

Yes, the Christian god is blamed for all deficiencies in human nature and expression, yet also endowed with the Supreme Creative Powers of Infinite Intelligence. Such beliefs are infantile and could only reside in the mind of an undeveloped mental person. They have no place in the scale of evolution which has gone to such dimensions where intelligence and personal expression are synonymous to Infinite Creativity.

CHAPTER XLII

Obsession Is Stranger Than Fiction

(A True Case History of a Complete Obsession), 1960

To those who do not believe that ghosts, spirit apparitions or that the dead can come back to haunt us or to wreak their personal vengeance on some unfortunate person who may be completely unaware that he is being obsessed, then read this story.

The pages of history, both written and unwritten, are filled with stories and references of gods and demons. Spirits of the earth, air, fire and water were included and worshipped by many ancient and semi-historical races and nations of peoples. Even in this so-called civilized era, a large portion of the people of the earth encompass some form of rituals or beliefs which include such spiritualistic concepts.

No doubt, there are many that you know, or perhaps you yourself unwittingly subscribe to such beliefs which had their origin from some ancient cabalistic or spiritist concept. Pet superstitions and aversions are often coupled with such derivations. One of the strongest and perhaps the most pertinent and important concepts which deal with the extrasensory or external causations is known and practiced as exorcism, or the casting out of evil spirits. We are all familiar with the story in the New Testament where Jesus cast out the devils from a demented man and they entered a herd of swine who promptly cast themselves into the sea. If we choose to make a search, we will find innumerable references and stories of such nature, not only in the Bible but in various history books or in those of occult nature. It has been the general practice of the modern psychologists and doctors to pooh-pooh such stories as nonsense; in spite of the great and overwhelming abundance of evidence, he states flatly, "there ain't no such animal".

Even his own practice could very well yield cases in which such extrasensory or obsessive influences could enter in. Moreover, he has also ignored another factor which is of vital importance, namely, that of reincarnation. Our modern savants have not yet grasped the idea of man's spiritual nature and of its many evolutions through what is called time and space. As a result of such "ain't so" attitudes, our prisons and asylums are filled to overflowing. Countless thousands drift in and out of clinics and hospitals, indirect victims of this abysmal ignorance.

It has truly been said that the lessons of life are never learned outside of the school of experience. We never grasp the full importance of some facet of understanding or truth until it happens to us, or at least to someone who is close and dear. The stigma of insanity or mental disorders is one with which no person cares to become even remotely associated, yet paradoxically, we ourselves have, in being participants in creating and activating social structures which sanction such ignorant and negative criticisms, may actually become unwitting victims of our own prejudices.

One of these typical cases happened in my own family, or rather, to a man my sister married. Their three fine children as well as the generations which follow will carry this stigma, and well it could have been averted. The modern psychiatrist does, like any doctor in the practice of his art, use long and impressive nomenclature to describe various facets or conditions of such science. Many of these terms we have become familiar with and through the various channels of educational nature, we have learned something of their true value.

Schizophrenia or dual (split) personality is one; another is manic-depressive. Many stories, motion pic-

430

tures, etc., have often depicted some form of either one or the other, or both. A manic-depressive is a somewhat advanced state of insanity in which the victim exhibits alternately moods of extreme depression or of elation and grandeur. The truth of the matter is, present-day psychiatry does not, or cannot, give an absolute factual reason for causation; they say extreme conditions of frustration induced by tensions in some form from our modern daily living, etc. These are only contributing elements which enter into breaking down the natural positive spiritual resistance to obsession.

Under such temporary breakdowns, a low astral entity can, and nearly always does, enter in and take either partial or complete possession of the victim. Cure would be relatively simple if the factor of such obsessions were understood; unfortunately, modern psychiatry does not. The only partially effective therapy yet devised is either removal from the familiar thought patterns and rest, or shock treatments. In the latter treatment, the electric shock therapy administered to the brain of the patient does temporarily "jar" the obsessing entity from his hold by changing some element of frequency which is associated with the frequency spectrum sometimes referred to as brain waves, etc.

I have gone to some length to explain some of these facets in order that you may better understand what happened to this brother-in-law. We will begin our narration back in 1926 in a small town near San Diego, California. Bert, as I will call him, was teaching a high school class—a fine man in his early thirties with a wife and three youngsters. There was nothing about him which would denote anything abnormal, or of the years ahead which were to be filled with strange and terrible experiences.

Along in the Fall of that year, Bert began to exhibit some rather strange characteristics. He bought large quantities of expensive jewelry, all on credit. He stocked

his place with pens of very expensive fur-bearing rab-
bits. He talked rather wildly at times of great things he
was about to do; other times he appeared very quiet
and almost sad. These were, of course, symptoms of
the oncoming manic-depressive stage. Finally he broke
down. I am not entirely familiar with what actually
happened at that time other than he was incarcerated.
It is still told that he tore out the bars from his cell and
escaped into the nearby hills. A posse of seven husky
deputies cornered him and it took all of their utmost
efforts to bring him back! He even tore up a straight
jacket!

It is a common trait of an obsessed person to have
abnormal strength while the astral entity is in control.
Such strength comes from not only the physical body
but from numerous entities which aid in and participate in each obsession. During the next twenty some
odd years, there was a continual and ever-increasing
recurrence of these "spells". As fast as he was nursed
back to health, it was a question of time until he would
have another attack. At first they were spaced several
years apart. During these first lengthy intervals, he
went back to teaching and became his otherwise very
fine self. I was informed of many of these spells. It
always seemed he would try to escape into the mountains. Efforts to escape his confinements were very violent in nature; his arms were scarred from the chains
which he repeatedly broke. Fire hoses were played
upon him until he nearly drowned, and many other
extreme measures taken. Finally with the advent of the
shock therapy, a way was found to shorten these ever-
increasing periods. He would be hauled off to the clinic
and shocked out of it.

During these many years, he had been living with
his wife and family in the state of Utah where as natives of that state, they had returned after the San
Diego episode. It had been my habit for many years to

432

visit my folks in this state, as we are also natives. In 1952, I made one of my periodic visits and staying a few days at my sister's place, circumstance was such that a full investigation was made of Bert's case. I had actually never witnessed an attack or "spell" but was tremendously intrigued when sister told me that he always assumed a different personality while so obsessed. She said his skin took on a coppery hue, his arms seemed longer, facial expression was entirely different, in fact, as she stated, he looked like an Indian! Further inquiry revealed startling facts. When suddenly seized, he would make a break for the hills, shedding his clothing as he ran. After many miles, he would wind up on a nearby Indian reservation; there he would be found squatting in some teepee engaged in guttural conversation with his Indian hosts. Normally, he could not speak a word of their language. Finally, the whole story came out and went something like this:

He was born in a small mountain valley in Northern Utah in a normal way in the early 1890's. His parents' home stood on an old Indian trail. As of that time, the country was still wild and sparsely settled; roving bands of Indians frequently appeared, fortunately, all friendly. Then one day when Bert was about three years old, he was badly frightened. He and his mother were eating their noonday meal when suddenly a huge seven-foot Blackfoot chief stood inside the door. He was brandishing a big butcher knife, his face was streaked with white paint, bear claws dangled from his neck, his eyes glowed with anger and hate. The mother, although badly frightened, was a pioneer woman and resourceful. She managed by gifts of food to quiet the murderous savage down sufficiently to get his story. In broken English he explained that another Indian had stolen his wife and that they had passed there just a short while before, and he was out to get them.

We do not know for sure if he did, but it is quite like-

ly that he did, for there was a fight in which the participants all died to become vengeful entities and roam
the astral worlds. It was many years later in the chain
of negative circumstances that this big Indian would,
at times, take over this now-grown man and make of
him his living earthly image! The rest is merely factual. The boy passed an ordinary succession of years
of grade, high school and finally emerged a graduate
of a prominent university. He, like everyone, had a
major interest which was baseball. In this he excelled
and by graduation time had won honors on the various campuses in this sport. His life ambition was to be
a big-league baseball-player, but plans of careers often
go astray. After graduation, he met and married my
sister. She prevailed upon him to give up this, what
seemed then a rather precarious outlook, as she took
a rather dim view of anything outside of the rather
stable, secluded way of life which a teacher's professor-
ship would bring.

It was this frustration which in time tore down the
natural protective elements of a positive way of life and
became the open sesame for this roving astral Indian
to come in and take over. This was made possible because his picture and his vibration were firmly engraved in the subconscious mind of Bert, in the shock and
fright encountered as a small lad of three; in other
words—psychosomatic shock. I do not know if Bert is
still living or not as I have not heard from sister for
years; my letters are unanswered but, living or dead, I
feel sure Bert would feel happy and in some way compensated for what he went through if his story could
help some other unfortunate victims.

For the sake of posterity let it be said, his scars and
sufferings were not incurred through any of his faults
or shortcomings. The blame for this and countless similar tragic examples of ignorance will have to be met
and borne by those who foster the doctrine of self-

434

assured complacency which, in drawing the lines of demarcation, not only mars the lives of their fellowman but stamps their own personality with the black cross of ignorance.

* * * * *

In going through my mental notes, a more adequate and detailed account of these spells or seizures would be in order. At the beginning he would, as I have described, take on a very odd appearance, seemingly growing taller, his arms longer, his normally blue eyes would take on a glowing murderous red color. Sister said his first impulse would be to try and kill her. For many years she slept in a locked bedroom, the door booby-trapped with pots and pans. When under control of the entity, he would emerge from his basement bedroom, try to find any kind of a gun or weapon and failing in this, he would "take to the hills"!

I was also told it was necessary to use up to four or five times the usual amount of power or voltage in the shock treatment as would normally be used; he would then just get up and walk off as if nothing had happened

Indeed, he never seemed to remember a single moment of the interval of obsession! His only one reminding semblance of attack would be that he might say or let drop, in some indirect way, that he thought the Indians were the only real people and someday they would reoccupy the country! No doubt, in the last and final years the big Indian entity was never far away and used every advantage possible to obtain control. I wonder sometimes what will happen when Bert and the Indian meet in the world of spirit. Will he be able to free himself or will he have to return to earth and work it from here? The answers to these questions are locked in the sealed book of the future (and in the Unarius texts).

*   *   *   *   *

November 1967—As of this time, and during the past two years, I have again established active communications with my sister and found that Bert is still very much alive and well. My last communication via telephone, as of November 21, 1967, and with some prodding on my part, revealed that since my visit and conversation with her in 1952, Bert has not had one of these Indian seizures! And the atmosphere of their domestic household has remained clear and tranquil!

Quite obviously there was, at that time, one of those miraculous healings wherein the Unariun Brotherhood was able to completely remove the obsessing entity, just as clearly as were the demons cast from the demented man. However, there is still another chapter: During the ensuing years from that time, (I do not know the exact date), Bert took on another and entirely different type of obsession which manifested itself by causing Bert to become addicted to cigarettes. Now this, in itself, was strange, as Bert was born and reared in the religious environment of the Mormon Church, which forbade the use of tobacco. Furthermore, as an athlete, Bert had never ascribed to the habit. Strange it was then, so it seemed, that in his seventies, he should suddenly take to the weed, and in large quantities.

The final chapter to this part in his drama of life was written about a year ago when Bert was taken to the hospital and operated on for the removal of his gallbladder. While under anesthesia, he was again healed—the obsessing entity or entities which had caused the tobacco habit were removed; and from the time he regained consciousness from the anesthesia, he has been entirely free of the habit. He has not smoked, touched, or even mentioned cigarettes; and once again, from that time on, the atmosphere in my sister's household has remained placid and calm, and free of obnoxious fumes!

CHAPTER XLIII

An Informal Talk to a Student (1964)

S - Dr. Norman, I notice of late people are beginning to talk of the concepts of Unarius, in a way?

T - Yes, people are beginning to talk about things and concepts that we have had in our lessons and books for years, and they believe them to be new ideas. They are toying with ideas and are trying to explore. You students have a great advantage over these scientists; you are more than a thousand years ahead of them on that score because you could take these things up and conceive them and will learn what they will be living by in the future. Yes, you have all the advantages; you have more than they have in all of their universities put together, all their high schools and all their grade schools. You have it right in those lessons and books of Unarius. That, in itself, is one of the greatest miracles that ever happened to this world—to have all that wisdom in those books.

S - I just feel sometimes that I am getting to understand these things more than even the scientists, and my, but it is a wonderful feeling.

T - Not only that, but you get tuned in to the whole creative universe, the entire Infinite Intelligence. You can tune into it because that is the way these teachings are constructed; and the books are put together that way so that it carries all this power with it. It makes it much easier to understand; and not only that, but regardless of how many times you read them, you will always find something new every time. This is unique; you cannot find that in any other books on this earth!

S - Yes, every time I read it, it keeps changing and adding to, and changing.

T - Yes, that's right because it is infinite in nature,

constructed from Infinite Intelligence. You simply cannot get it any other place. No, there is no end to it. Don't think you will ever come to any end of the wisdom contained in these various writings, for you will not. This is your path, your future.

S - I want to understand exactly how it is with energy, etc.

T - Well, I am going to get into it even more thoroughly in some book in the future. It is like the electricity that comes over the wires; in the generator you have two polarities here, so by turning a rotator that is wired a certain way, it creates a field of force between them and it changes these polarities back and forth from positive to negative. It is these positive and negative impulses that travel along the wire to make an alternating current; it is the information that it carries.

S - The alternating current?

T - Well, it switches phase; the energy goes from one side to the other and when it does that, it is positive or negative phase, yes, like the sine wave. What that means when it is translated so far as the generator is concerned is that you are switching from one pole to the other. These, of course, all follow magnetic lines of force, as they are around the earth. This is all part of this cosmic hysteresis, but that is a little beyond the point we are trying to make just now. The thing is, this electrical impulse that goes up and down carries the information. Your electric clock goes by that information. It rotates at a certain speed and keeps perfect time because it is synchronized to the generator in the power house which rotates sixty times per second and the motor in the clock follows the exact pattern of thought which the generator is transferring. In other words, it, too, rotates sixty times per second just the same as does the generator; it changes the polarities and it is synchronized, locked to it. You are synchronized to thousands of things out here in the outside world. For instance, looking at the garment over here that just fell down, what happens? You synchronize and lock into that; it is something that is familiar to you. You have had that experience before so you have the wave forms in your psychic anatomy and you can lock into it. Everything you see is a transference of energy wave forms that lock that—whatever it may be —into you as objectivism into your consciousness.

S - You mean it is like two transformers of wires; when energy rotates from one, it automatically oscillates into the other?

T - That's exactly the same principle, just like the electric clock I spoke of, for they have a little coil of wire in the clock and a rotor and an armature, and it rotates just as does the generator.

S - These thoughts you are now speaking, they are going to me?

T - That's right. I have generated certain energy that you cannot hear which is going into your psychic anatomy but is inaudible, for this will transcend you to the point where you can understand it better. That is a little secret that we old Boys have that the Pro's in the colleges do not have because we can paint the picture for you, in a sense of the word; it becomes much easier for you to understand.

S - And these words from you then become a part of me?

T - That's right.

S - And will they always be attuned to me?

T - Yes, they will oscillate in your psychic anatomy forever! Not only that, but if you tune in to that—if you know how to tune into this particular thing—it can assume an endless variety of forms of consciousness. It does not necessarily have to be just these words because it is intelligent. Through harmonics it can tune you in to anything in the universe, or the Infinite. That's right. Yes, we old Boys know all these secrets and that's why we come to the earth to try and help people who get into these thresholds where they want something beyond this world, or to learn how to sustain life in other worlds; and when they get fed up and sick and tired of all these materialisms, then we are the ones who present it to them in a scientific way—and a way which can he verified by every manner and means possible and can be demonstrated in your own way.

You can have your own miracles; you can see your own consciousness enlarge to a point where the next life in the higher worlds is not only possible but it is feasible; it becomes a reality to you—worlds where you can live without your physical body. I live without my physical body all the time, or at least most of the time. I could not live with it very long, only as a compromise. I have to operate my physical body entirely differently than you do yours. Mine is like when they manipulate these puppets on a string, more or less after a fashion. I am operating it by remote control; like the robot, I am twisting the dials and sending the impulses into it. That is the reason why I could not do what you did out there using so much physical strength when you tossed those huge boxes of books about like they were empty. There is no necessity for me to have this physical strength because I live beyond that. It is very necessary to you; you have enjoyment with it and it is the level upon which you, at the present, function. To me, I could take it or leave it; it would make no difference one way or the other. That's the difference between being on the emotional plane or not being on the emotional plane. I have a great many other things that take the place of that. I am cosmically attuned. I can do many things with the mind and live in many places and areas that are not possible for you to live in yet until you develop this consciousness, so therefore, you have to have this libido; this is your drive to keep you living here on this earth. Yours is just as necessary

441

to you as mine is to me. We do not get emotional—who is better or who is worse or any such thing—it is just the same as the sparrow that falls by the wayside. We know all of these things in consciousness; they all have a place in creation.

We would not do like these colored people are doing, forcing themselves on others and into conditions and into society with which they are unfamiliar and increasing a lot of strain, not only on themselves but also, upon people who do not want them—people who cannot see these things as we do. To me it is absolutely immaterial; it is irrelevant. People who do not want me around, I go and find another place; I'd not try and force myself onto them simply because it was legal to do so. When you begin to understand humanity and the position on the scale of evolution in which people are, then of course, there would not be all this squabbling and fighting.

People would live differently if they knew these principles of evolution. Any time that you institute a system or government which is based or predicated upon things of equality, you are going to get into squabbles; and yet, what else can they do? There really isn't anything else or compromise because the whole psychology of life is based on the survival of the fittest which mandates an equality with everyone else. It is a personal drive with everybody in the world today that he is at least equal to everybody else. It is the old rat race, keeping up with the Joneses; if they cannot do that, then they are very unhappy. And by the time they get to where they think they are equal with everyone else, then they are very unhappy until they get a little power over them and rule them and inflict their unrest, their own dissatisfaction, their own emotionalism onto the other people. That's the reason we have these things; so we have political leaders; we have priests in churches and a great many other things because there are the values of life that people have gone through in their evolution to this particular point in their life. But some day it is going to have to pass because there is always a forward motion; you are either going forward or you are going backward.

The present here is either a combination of the past or it has to be a combination of the future. People in this world cannot live by the future because they do not know what the future is. All they are doing is going back into their past and trying to make their future out of their past, which is silly and absolutely impossible because in the first place, the future had already been created infinitely. They can't do anything about it; they can't change it; they do not have the intelligence to look forward into the future and visualize through their consciousness that all or everything that they are, is the future. That is what Jesus meant when He taught "finding the Kingdom of Heaven Within", and when you can visualize the kind of future you want and make it a tangible reality in your life, then you have achieved the kingdom.

S - When you speak of two opposite forces, does this mean two forces traveling in different directions?

T - Yes, you could say that in a particular allegorical situation. Not only do we find moving forces in two directions but in many, but I think what you are referring to is a fourth-dimensional hypothesis. You have to visualize that here everything travels this way—it has a beginning and an end on this earth. There are no beginnings and there are no endings in the next world— the fourth dimension. Everything travels in cycles or circles but the entire intelligence, whatever it is, is carried in that circle. In other words, instead of having a chair, you have the consciousness of the chair which rotates the complete cycle which tells you everything there is about this chair on that cycle. Therefore, the chair could live forever because if there is no beginning and there is no ending to this cycle, what this chair is, it cannot perish; can it?

S - Like the Laser Beam which has so many frequencies?

T - Well, of course, that is quite different; that is only a sine wave transmission that has beginning and end; it is still but a third-dimensional proposition. You see, if you are a little ant and you start going around on the edge of that pool, you would never come to the end of it; would you? Well, that little ant would not need to go around that pool to find out what was on the other side if he could visualize the entirety of that whole pool in the concept of his mind; would he? He'd just sit out there in one place and know what the whole thing looked like; wouldn't he? Yes, that is fourth dimensional. We have to understand these things that way; everything is manifest cyclically, then there is no time or space.

S - They could encircle the whole universe and everything?

T - Well, yes, it is in and out; and for instance, you move your hand through what is called air and space, but it is not space at all—it is infinitely filled. Your hand cannot feel it because it is out of tune with it, just like your television set cannot tune in to A.M. radio stations. They are right there all the time but it is insensitive to them.

So how valuable it is when you begin to understand energy and see what it is. This world could be just a little kernel or grain upon another world—a world that people could not see. There could be worlds around on the outside of it or on the inside of it. People of another dimension could be living in this world and you'd never know that they are here!

For the present, we shall break contact. Goodnight.

CHAPTER XLIV

Further Discussion (1964)

There is only one way a person can attain morality and that is through himself, by being moral within himself and to realize his responsibility as a person, as an individual, as a creative expression or a beginning of intelligence. If all of these people out there knew that all of their acts of consciousness were so recorded that a man like myself could walk among them and point out to them—and which I have done for many, many years and with hundreds or thousands of cases, just as I did this afternoon—they'd soon change their ways, wouldn't they? It makes no difference whether the thought, act or deed or experience, whatever it was, was expressed years ago, I could go back with them thousands of years and point up these same things to them. I find out where all their incurable diseases stemmed from and they are healed.

S - Can they be cured?

T - Yes, indeed, we have many thousands of testimonials there in the files of these healings: cancer of the breast, of the cervix, incurable conditions, anything, any condition which you can name, and I do not consciously send a thought to them. I do nothing at all consciously or physically. They take up the lesson courses and many times we only hear indirectly that they have had healings. The healing takes place so naturally and normally, and the adjustments in their lives occur that often they scarcely remark about it, so naturally did it take place; and occasionally it must needs be brought to their consciousness that it once existed a few months or weeks back.

Like little Louise in New York who has had very

445

wonderful visions, and they all follow the same patterns, those who remain steadfast. It is very indicative. Many students see the Brothers of the Brotherhood of the Higher Worlds coming to them. These are developed people who have lived perhaps on this world or other worlds and they have gone on in their evolution where they no longer need a physical body. They come to them silently and without personal identification, but these students can see them. They are not clairvoyant or mediums but they can see them; they see them as Lights or smell their fragrances and see them other ways. They know that they are there. They have the miracles happen to them which, in itself is the proof.

S - Do you think that the spirit has a job to do, that it could be part of his responsibility of coming back and helping the earthman?

T - Well, in a sense of the word, that is a rather broad inclusion of many things; we could classify that —as the Yogi used to call it—karma. Here is the implication—a guilt complex, as they term it in psychology. It is the sum and total of all of the unrealized and unrequited things for which he may or may not be responsible, such as vicarious responsibilities, etc. This would leave a sense of guilt or a guilt complex; and so reincarnation, to a large degree, by earth people is mandated by that and by the fact, too, that this is the only way that they know. But principally, the further the person goes along the line and the more of this accumulation or psychic debris is accumulated, the more you have to discard.

S - Then there is the positive and negative for everything?

T - Yes, you see cancellation is a very scientific principle; we do it in electronics all the time. In other words, we beat two pulses against each other and it is a heterodyne, or you can cancel out even a compound number of pulses together. So in a cancellation of a psychic condition which had manifested as a material condition or a physical condition, we have to first integrate or suspend at least temporarily, to a certain degree, the oscillations of the conscious mind into the subconscious. We bring about a certain condition where we can interject certain oscillations into these beat frequencies into the psychic anatomy which cancel out the aberration. The person retains the residual; the person can still remember the experience psychically or even consciously but it no longer has the effect in a negative way; it does not manifest itself in a pernicious way. It is now in an "out-of-phase" relationship with the present.

S - Well, does not the person have to compensate somehow for his ill or wrong in some way in the future?

T - This is a very broad area and yes, this is true to a degree, but when people go on over to the other side, as it was so described by Dante in his attempt to portray the pits of hell, well, this is all psychic imagery. We say of murder, one would have a tremendous sense of guilt; this is a terrible hell in which they live. Now there are spiritual organizations like the Unariuns who go into these pits, just as I am here on earth, to sort of ferret out the people who could be helped at that time; and in ways with which we are familiar, we manage to lead them out to the point where they can begin to integrate their consciousness in another dimension where they can see the possibilities and try to reinstate themselves. It is a spiritual therapy. I have described it to some degree in the book, "The Voice of Venus". The healing wards are described. The earth scientists with their space probes have proven to a certain degree that "The Voice of Venus" is right; but it is a spiritual dimension, nevertheless. The psychic anatomies have to have help; they all have to be healed and given certain therapies sometimes when they have gone so far.

S - Those who have never been exposed to a higher learning—they are going to have to come back until they are ready or are exposed; would you not say so?

T - I doubt very much if there is any person who has lived on the earth who has not been exposed to higher learnings, for the one and simple reason is, the creation around him would make it so and he would not have progressed in his evolution without having had some of it. This is his personal Christ, his personal savior. We could say that even the aborigine, as we find him in the jungles, is still a human being to the degree that he has a psychic anatomy which can be his intercessor or his savior from these spiritual worlds.

S - Would you say that a person of that degree would come back, and if they have improved themselves to the level they are on, that they would be given a chance to obtain further learning to improve themselves, etc.?

T - Yes, in a general sense, not necessarily that they are being given a chance, that it is mandatory, or because they ask for it—not necessarily that we have executive forums over there and that they must attend; but this desire must always be expressed from or by the individual—that he feels it is something he must do within himself. This is the inspirational kind of consciousness which is at work.

S - You mean a spirit reincarnating has the choice?

T - Oh yes, always, and in fact, that is mandatory, we say in a sense of the word; there is no help ever extended until he first expresses his desire or wish for it. He cannot possibly be serviced until he expresses himself.

S - Would this soul or spirit know that it had made this choice of the problems that will come after he returned to earth?

T - He would not know about it consciously and to the degree in his new life that he would be able to say that he remembered things as you remember things that happened to you yesterday. It is an orientation of consciousness with which the person subconsciously brings himself into alignment as he goes along. He re-creates in some way, automatically and without his own conscious knowledge of doing so, facsimiles of previous experiences so that he can try to master them or overcome them.

S - In other words, we are where we are because of ourselves?

T - Yes, that's right. Now for instance, a woman came to me who had cancer of the left breast. I pointed out to her that during a lifetime in France during the Napoleonic wars, she was stabbed in the breast with a sword and it left a psychic scar there. The death was a terrible thing to her and that aberration in her psychic anatomy manifested itself as cancer in this present lifetime. When that was explained to her, it disappeared; not only that but her obesity, which was also a sense of insecurity, disappeared. So we had cancellation of the fear impinged.

S - Yes, that makes much more sense to me than just reliving it repeatedly; then it is actually a cancellation of the fear?

T - That's right; it is the working out. This is the big science of Unarius and when students are able to do this themselves with the aid of the Brotherhood, their negative shocks are dissipated and the fear goes. Any psychic aberration in the psychic anatomy is a fear—a fear of something or another—a fear of death or of loss. They leave great psychic scars in the psychic. These negations have to be cancelled out because these countless thousands of beat frequencies which are all disassociated with the normal functioning manner at the time when this shock happened to him, now they all have to be corrected and put back into their proper orbits, their proper beat frequencies and in their proper relationship. That is cancellation. When they relive this thing in the sense of the word that they have recaptured this experience, they then usually place themselves in the proper position in the cycle so that this can be done very quickly. We can interject then, the necessary beat frequencies into those which cannot be straightened out and reset the others which have been.

S - Does the person have to see these experiences himself or does it take help from the Brotherhood?

T - Most of the students do have to have help from the Brotherhood. We say any paranormal activity such as experience has always been projections to them. In the Brotherhood we have implementation; that is, we have scientific instruments, ray machines, projection machines, etc., and apparatus which are used to project these things into their consciousness or to prepare them while they are asleep. That may sound a little fantastic but it is already being done in recording machines now. Many types of schools teaching special interests use them now; the army uses them to teach soldiers foreign language. They can learn a foreign language in a fraction of the normal time with this added sleep teaching system. We do this on a more extensive scale. While people are asleep, their conscious mind is temporarily suspended in its oscillating process. Then we have the personality in the right position on the cycle, the energy has been planted there. The re-creation from out of their own psychic anatomy is most often used because there has to be the relationship with it to project the image into consciousness where they were reliving the scene; and when they do this, cancellation occurs.

S - Do the students only relive the unpleasant things?

T - Principally, yes, because they are only here for that one purpose. Now some very few people could remain in the higher worlds of learning indefinitely—as I have described in my books—for any number of years to study very comprehensively. It would mean nothing to them there, and to myself, the physical body is absolutely unnecessary. It has had its evolution. This is something with which we are all faced; we cannot escape it. We either go backwards and evolve into infinite consciousness or we continue on upwards. Consciousness does not destroy itself because we have to expand consciousness to the degree where there is realistic and a tangible relationship to anything. There is no destruction to anything; everything is construct-ively inclined because this is the principle of regenerat-ive creation. And yet, it is demanded by the individual as an expressive form with audio and inspirations as the most sublimated of all these infinite creations; that is, the individual is, we say, a person who can deter-mine his own course of evolution because God has to re-create Himself in so many dimensions. But the human is the one expressive element of mind and consciousness which bestows itself individually in consciousness in every human. The degree of expres-sion in which the Infinite bestows itself or manifests itself upon every human, the degree in which the Infi-nite works through every individual is relative; it is entirely up to the plane upon which the human lives. It is to a certain extent true with birds or things of the animal kingdom, but to them they have not progressed in their evolution where they have sustained the ego consciousness strongly enough, or the subconscious-ness, and brought back with them the things which they were in former lifetimes to the degree that the human does. Some people have had cats, dogs reincar-nate back to them.

That little lady there with you just stepped right from out of three thousand years of the past. Yes, her rapport and memories with us are of that long ago in Greece.

Well, Max, I cannot go very much farther here with

you, as so much goes out; it is the same principle as Jesus said when the woman with the issue touched him on the hem of his robe. He said, "Who touched me, for I felt virtue leave me?" You will see in the future, that many things will change with you, for you have, in a sense of the word, been fired from a cannon into the future. Your wife there is really on cloud nine. She has waited and worked a long time for this realization, for the bringing together of these cycles. She has been, as have many of the "oldtimers", in and out of the temples, the synagogues and places of worship, the holy schools, the cultural schools, from the steps of the great Acropolis and the great philosophers through antiquity and history—even to Atlantis and Lemuria and ancient civilizations. That is how all of these things are being stepped up with her; she knows this and so do I. These are all things that have been written by her and by her own hand, thought and actions; they shall be with her forever. I can read them and can tell her all about them because I am just like the radio; I can tune myself into it. I have developed this faculty of mind, the consciousness which people call clairvoyance.

S - I would imagine that a person on a higher level or vibration would be easier for you to read for?

T - Not necessarily, I have never made any lines of limitation. I have never found one for whom I could not read their past, and when I do, I will say I will go back to school and learn all over again. I can find a dishonest person or one who willfully refuses to acknowledge what I bring to him—or he may be transcended and unable to form a proper relationship with his past. I have had that happen, too, for instance, two sisters. I read for one and it was fine right on down the line. She remembered everything I brought to her of her past present lifetime, but when I read for her sister, she could not place a thing. It was all a blank. So I went back to the first sister and asked her to help her out and then she was able to recall the various recalls in her own life. They all fit perfectly. We shall temporarily discontinue.

CHAPTER XLV

Philosophy From a Most Advanced Being to Ruth 1956

Dear Sister: There is indeed much that happens to people in the spiritual worlds in lives in between earth lives which explains the differences perhaps in the way that they interpret life in their various different missions on the earth plane. The great musicians, the artists, poets—those who have added some luster to the otherwise earthly drab existence—these things are all correlated organizations or coalitions which have been started as spiritual movements in some other spiritual plane or plateaus of understanding.

By far the average person's understanding of life leaves much to merely suppose that these things happen in the reactionary stances of everyday living but it is not so, for no one becomes intelligent until he exemplifies a much higher degree of interpolation of the way of life but basically, from the spiritual plateaus of understanding. For life, in itself, as far as the earth is concerned, is merely shadows of that which has transcended and already transpired in the higher dimensions.

And so it is with all those who we might call great minds, or to those who are outstanding in an intellectual way, as they did not come by these things by studying books that were written in the earth man's ideas. They did not come by them by obtaining mastery over their fellow man with the sword or spear, or some other superiority of armament or weapon. They came by them by the junction and the union of intelligence from the higher spheres of understanding—the common pool of human wisdom which is gathered together in the Infinite Cosmos and reside as participating agents in the Infinite Mind of God, and thus become a wellspring from which all may draw.

And these are the factors which determine an intelligent person from a weakling, a reactionary—by one who travels as does the common traveler, who are only concerned with pacifying their stomach and physical needs or desires.

So, dear ones, may we again reemphasize the importance of your position in retrospection to us here in the spiritual dimensions. Position is no more or less than how it is used and the way it is used, for in a way, the Infinite Mind of God is subjective to the various interpretations or interpolations of how man wishes it to be used; and this is the determining element, for no man can call himself simple nor can he call himself good; but only in the way in which he uses his wisdom does he either trap himself in the labyrinth of his own mind or does he become a dynamic and moving force in the Infinite Cosmogony.

These truths in themselves are great differences and ones over which we should ponder. There is much we can draw on constantly, an infinite pool or storehouse of wisdom. It is timeless, it is vast and it is universal; and it becomes one, or all of us, as to just how this wisdom is interpreted. It can become a stone which bruises our feet, or it can become a lighting and an illuminating power in your life, which transforms and transcends all things with which it comes in contact; for such is the power which the Infinite has given the higher forms of His Creative Mind, which is sometimes referred to as man. For here again in each man God hopes to live again—God does live again and expresses Himself universally one to another.

But I am not speaking of the material man who is bound with the interests only of his intestinal tract. Such a man must journey in spiritual spheres of consciousness the things which are beyond the realm of understanding which is contained in that nest of cells which is called the human brain, and which in itself is only another organ of the human body and so subjected to the regular cycles of rebirth and decay, as are all things.

Yes, indeed, for each atom in itself goes through a metamorphosis and becomes another atom more highly compounded, more intricately conceived; it is so as tiny gyrations pulsating, which represent life. And yet again, the atom becomes an even more compounded function which your scientist calls nuclear reaction, I believe.

To us it is merely the remanifestation of Infinite Wisdom in a timeless, and perhaps even to you, a spaceless world for space only resides in the minds of infants. And when the inner mind is so evolved and becomes so conscious, it is indeed a participating element with the Infinite Understanding. It sees all and knows all things instantaneously. So likewise does it participate.

Sufficient to say, you may find food for thought in these few remarks and that, too, to some extent as far as the exterior or your physical world is concerned, could possibly be limited to the degree in which an attunement is made and the way in which the mind does become a channel. So these things must be delivered to you in the common metaphor which is acceptable to the human mind, to the one in which you oscillate, to the comings and goings and the gyrations of the vortexal energies which are impounded in the fabrication of your own true self, for these things you will truly understand.

But to walk with me in my own world would indeed be something which the little mind could not grasp nor could I find adequate words in your vocabulary to so substantiate the imagery of the pictures in that earth mind which would refabricate the tissue of your psychic self. This, in itself, would be a form of spiritual destruction and foreign to your nature. So be patient, be complacent and always be positive, for we can be with you only in the correct proportion to which you are thus attuned; for it is much easier, as Jesus would say, for the camel to pass through the eye of the needle than a materialist to get into Heaven.

So it becomes equally obvious that the mind must transcend the thresholds of materialism, and this it must do as an agency for attunement; for the personality to attain a higher degree of consciousness means a constant re-resolution, reorientation of innumerable facts of life. But above all, it means consciousness of things which exist far beyond the ordinary borders of human understanding. In other words, no limitations; there is nothing, and I repeat, nothing—and much more beyond that—than you will ever be able to possibly conceive or envision which does not already exist; or even anything that you could even ever hope for, does already exist—and always has! For those we might call Masters or Intellects, if I might resort to common phraseology, none of us has begun to approach anything which even resembles a terminating point, nor would we ever believe or could we ever conceive that an end is possible, for the moment we did we would find it, and we would stop.

Let us not be confounded with the word illusion, for illusion exists only in the mind of a person who is sterile in his contacts with the higher spheres of understanding. To a person who is conscious only of the reactionary stimuli as concerned with the physical appearances or appurtenances of the physical world do these things become imagery even more substantial and heavy than the graven statues which he has carved for himself and will sink him even deeper in the mire of his own subconscious.

So, dear ones, I am happy to have been with you

for a few moments this evening. I am also very grateful that we have two such devoted friends in the nether worlds as you two, for indeed God would become useless or finite and handicapped and thus become ungodlike if He could not be so expressed into all of the nether worlds.

We look forward to the day when you shall have complete spiritual emancipation, as you have already achieved partially this emancipation. And let us know positively that you will continue on, as your face is now turned unto the East, and that you are, as Mohammed would say, walking towards Mecca. And do not be deviated by the devices of the underworlds for there are many, as you no doubt know. As I leave you with a strong and positive bit of power which you can place, it has come to me through vibration something of a song, perhaps of someone who has succeeded in trapping a celestial object from a star and put it in his pocket.

In Tibet and China a long time ago, we had a pocket in our sleeve. Now we have capacities and other ways, but do so for such bits of Shining Radiant Light which I hope I can leave with you to help and to eliminate some of the darker moments which may still be unlighted or unillumined.

CHAPTER XLVI

An Inspirational Message

To Ernest and Ruth: To my children of the earth, I bid you greetings at your time at the quickening of the Spirit. We trust you will not be disturbed or dismayed at the hostility, anger and unrest of the many earth people, for these are great movements of transition; all shall come unto its own rebirth, unto the eye of the maker which is its creative substance.

The differences which the people of the earth find among themselves are as small shadows tossed about in the dawn and break of a new day.

Plentiful and spiritual abundance shall be the reward of those who have followed the path most faithfully, not that Truth and its virtues need rewarding, for it is sufficient unto its own luminosity to dispel all evil forces which would blur or darken its Radiance.

Just as it was prophesied, there is one among you who is the Comforter, which gives you the moral strength and courage to overcome, not as a person or doctrine or a kept covenant, but each person's own infusion of Light—the Wellspring of life.

There are, as you call Christians, among men who observe this as the week of the resurrection yet, mark not the time or place when life either dies or ceases to be. And how can anything be resurrected which has not died? And in this resurrection, let us be sure we have buried all of the old distrusts and hatreds of the past and as we rest from our labors, receive the resurgence of life everlasting and abundant.

This would indeed be much better than to glorify an ancient passion of blood, for as the wheel of life turns for each one, and as each spoke marketh the century of his coming and going, it is indeed well that he travels upon this wheel lightly—not overburdened with the desires and lusts which muddy the rim of his wheel. Better indeed it is for him to grow lilies of pure and whitened desire of spiritual attainment from the slime and ooze of his earthly world than to cover himself with the sackcloth and ashes of recriminations, for like vultures, all must roost in their own rookery and own time—and barren indeed is the desert where they seek their food; and if we must have wings, let them be those which will carry us high above the rocky crags and crevasses into the sunnier pastures where the fields are lush with newborn flowers.

The time upon the earth for any man is like a treadmill and each life a step when his tired foot must push the never-ending chain to each succeeding step, each one like its last yet more unyielding as the body grows tired and the shoulders are bent beneath a heavy load of karma. Must it be that such a man must use his tongue as his own whiplash and that the stripes upon his back are those he counts against himself? Even the jackal in the desert has a better lot than such a man. The vessel of life is but meant to temper the steel of character—not to destroy it, for he who heats the steel of life with the turmoil of passion, greeds, lusts and anxieties but takes from the metal that which makes it strong—and that it shall surely shatter unto a thousand pieces when immersed in the clean, cool freshness of a new life.

And he who maketh the bricks for the building of walls and cities knows that in their baking that equalness of heat must be maintained lest they break and become useless. Foolish indeed is the man who maketh of his life unto the measure of that of another; and only in living and creating his own life, can he become the artisan which will create something of rare beauty or a great destructiveness, for metal, like many things used by man, has no choice and it can become the plowshare or the sword.

And so, good children of the earth, and especially to you two who are constantly refreshing and filling the vessel from the inner life, and that even as the vessel is filled afresh does it become transmitted from the drossness of the earth into a rare and beautiful chalice, finer than the finest alabaster, for these Waters from the Inner Spring transform all things; nor canst they become muddied or tainted. For no man approaches this Spring unless he is freed from the mires of the earth and has cleansed his garments and anointed himself with the oil of consecrated desire; and these Inner Waters are not marked by cross or temple, neither are they held apart to but a favored few, for all mankind must drink from these Waters ere he perish from thirst on the desert of his own iniquities.

Like the plants and flowers and trees which taketh from the earth the things which are necessary to be combined with the sunshine and fresh air, it too finds within its own way, Waters which are not of the root or soil but which giveth its form even unto every generation. And so it is with every man.

But I see my time is getting short to be with you and the mind needs to be returned. We are most happy and grateful that we can be of service to you, for these are but mere words which I have uttered, yet they, too, carry the moisture from this Inner Spring.

Take good care of that which you have, nor canst see nor touch, the most precious of all possessions, for this is life and as such, is part of the Creator who, in that constant never-ending procession of cycles, large and small, meets with all things and dies not for a single instant.

And so let every man find his own resurrection, each unto his own time and place; but for you who truly walk in the Light, resurrection is always with you and in the giving of life, in thought and form and sub-

461

stance to the inert and drabness which is around you, do you become the resurrector; for to create is to be godlike and no man can do unto another which he cannot do unto himself.

And so let us create that which is the true resurrection, for as God lives He thus moves through all things and in the creation do you become part of the moving. Only a fool will destroy, for the destructiveness which he exerts against his adversary is not half so great as that which he wields against himself.

It has been said that if thou art smitten upon the cheek, turnest thou the other, yet it must truly be meant and intended that thou takest the force of thine adversary's blow and create from it some substance of life which will help him turn away from the destructiveness of his ways.

And that as these things are well said and intended, yet they are carried into the ears of babes and are uttered as their words. And so it is that I find evil in this hour and in the hearts of men who have followed in My footsteps, for verily did these things which were said and talked of on the shores of Galilee enter into the ears of babes and became their words. Yet, more than this, for whilst they said these things and talked much of that which was said, yet they grew up, not as men but as thieves carrying nothing in their minds but a guileful way to use those words, so that all would cast themselves down before their feet and worship them in their false temples and that they would glorify their hatreds of one man against another. And as they hold aloft the cross of crucifixion that as of that day and hour do they become, in turn, crucified to their own evil. Only through the lustful passions that goodness could be preserved into posterity, yet even so, the cock croweth three times unto each man and that he denieth himself before his neighbor; and his evil ways is but his voice.

(In writing His words, I, Ruth, felt it was He and instinctively expressed the thought.) ("Yes, ye knew me then.")

And now, do I come to you in what is but a moment of remembrance not unforgotten but remembered only for the wisdom which could be borne, not as a cross to Calvary but as an illuminating Light cast from the Vessel of Life with well-kept wick, kept filled from the Inner life to guide each man, each unto his own Mansion, unto his own Garden, his own winepress, wherein he could press the rarest of all vintages, from grapes gathered from all corners of the universe.

And so, dear ones, there is no separation, neither from this moment henceforth, shall all of us be ever at thy side, for the fruit of the past has been gathered and withered is the tree of that time, yet the fruit endureth and so again, it is the time of harvest and the time of storing away, for soon the tree shall wither even as it has done before; yet from the fruit and in the seed thereof springeth anew another tree, and let us find always that its fruit is richer and more abundant than otherwise borne before.

We rest—Selah.

CHAPTER XLVII

A Master Speaks on Mastership

They call us Masters, but we come only as humble servants; for Masters are only those who have learned of life and have ceased to be slaves of life, and instead have become servants of mankind. You would ask for identity and that you would call us by name; yet it would be that ye should call us better by the virtues which we can express. For love, service, and the beatitudes of the Infinite Mind are not called by name. Each one becomes unto the other and in becoming, adding unto the all, yet knowing not of each thing that it is called by name; nor is it known for its face or of the garments that it wears, but in the way in which it brings to each and every one its own invisible blessing.

And so that it should be that ye seek all of the virtues of life, seek them not by name, for if a man does become a Master, he is master of only one thing, and that is the mastery of himself. He who takes with him the name of his father, or of his country, or of his wife or children, or even the name of himself, takes with him a heavy burden—one laden with all of the things of the material world. For even the Infinite has no name and is not called as such, either in Heaven or in any of the netherlands. For everyone knows the Infinite by the virtues contained therein; and such of these things may be to each one, and whether he counts the lambs in his flock or that he may multiply his various blessings in many other ways, yet to each man these are, in his own way and manner of speaking, the virtues of the Infinite. Yet all of these things should pass from him, yea, even their names and of all things that they are called by, for each one exists unto its time and its place, and can neither serve nor be of benefit to anyone in the morrow when all things must again be accounted and all virtues must be realized differently, each in its own way.

Gather strength, dear ones, for the method of bringing you these things is, in itself, but poor tribute to all of that which is exemplified in the higher consciousness, nor can we measure out the Infinite as grains of sand or even as the treasures, for each of these things, too, as they are spoken in the words of flesh and earth, so be it that each man finds a way of measuring his own grains of sand and bringing to himself the treasures which he so desires. Yet even as he does these things he is, in all manner and form, much less than a suckling babe in the arms of his mother.

It is very difficult for a person to understand anything about Creation, or God, or man unless he understands energy, because everything always functions from one polarity to another. The dynamics of life, as far as they are concerned with the Infinite or man individually, collectively or the summation of all things, means that the dynamic interchange of thought, idea or consciousness between polarities is called positive and negative, that is, the oscillating or the sine wave motion or the cycular motion, whatever dimension it is that we are so concerned with—the only way that we can rationalize what God is. He is not a personality because He is Infinite, and in order to be Infinite He must be finite in all things, and that means, too, that God is also good and evil. That is very difficult for the average person to understand, and he cannot until he gets into interdimensional relationships and understands how energy functions, because what he is concerned with, as an individual, at any one particular time, is a certain given set of conditions under which he functions from the plane or dimension in which he (the individual) is presently incarnated. Therefore, in the commonly accepted term of positive and negative, if he is positively connected to the cycular movement or the dynamics of energy in all manifestations of energy around him, then he can say that those things are good; but if he gets on the other end of the cycle where consciousness or idea, or form, or any other interpolations are functioning from the negative end of the cycle, then he says that is evil; but he has not stopped to consider that it is just as necessary, so far as God, or the Infinite is concerned, to function with as the positive, because the positive could not function without the negative, or vice versa.

Neither have people stopped to figure that if they were under another given set of conditions as far as their own relationship was concerned, so that they were in a favorable set of circumstances with the negative end of these cycles, then the condition would be exactly reversed, and what they formerly thought was good was now evil and what they formerly thought was evil was now good, because everything was moving forward with them. They have not stopped to consider that so far as interdimensional relationship was concerned, what they felt to be evil in their interpolations or manifestations on the earth today—for instance, under any certain set of conditions means that could they see completely and abstractly into interdimensional relationships, they would see that what they call evil is actually the positive cycle for another set of cycular conditions which would remanifest in another interdimensional relationship as negative or evil; and that goes on and on ad infinitum.

What this all means is that this is the beginning of evolution as far as the earth man is concerned in any society which is apparently concerned at this time, and you will find that he is still in a comparatively crude or rough state of evolution; he is still very much of an animal; he is only on the threshold of beginning to learn. The first step he takes in learning is through the

reactionary dimensions, and that means that he is constantly (like the fireman who would put a fire hose
against the side of a burning building) reflecting subconsciously from any set of given thought patterns or
various other experience quotients in a psychosomatic
fashion from one to another, or from one childhood
to adulthood, etc; from wherever we include our psychosomatic science, these are only, in themselves, comparative relationships. But they do not in any sense of
the word mean that they are absolute, because man has
not yet, so far as his earth life is concerned, even to the
most highly advanced and most intelligent form of life
upon the earth, even closely approached an absolute
mental function. He cannot, because the absolute is the
Infinite Itself.

That which we refer to as mastership and various
other types of higher spiritual position means merely that the individual so concerned in that way has a
much broader horizon of the interplay of interdimensional relationships as one either combined with the
other, or that they are oscillating as positive and negative functions, one from another. That is why man has
become so completely confused; that is the reason why
there are today so many thousands of laws that the
average citizen of this country has to obey. There are
something like six or seven thousand laws, at least
theoretically, that he is supposed to obey, and many of
these laws he has no knowledge of whatsoever. He is
constantly breaking the laws without his knowledge or
without anyone else's knowledge. Therefore, we can see
the uselessness of such comparative values in life that
now we have to set up lines of demarcation and lines
of delineation whereby he is theoretically supposed to
function as an integral community in a nation; because
this means that when any person, or group of persons
constructed the law-governing agency, they are only
constructing to themselves certain lines of demarcation

and certain interpolations of what they conceive life to be, in a general reactionary sense or term, which they have incurred in past life incarnations. And it does not in any sense of the word mean that this same set of conditions or interpolations is correct for another group of people who are on a different elevation or who are functioning from another plane of life—or vice versa. And that is the reason there are so many laws— laws to circumscribe a certain function and other laws which can actually prevent that law from working— highly contradictory! As any lawyer can tell you, what is actually meant when it comes to a court battle is that it is not necessarily justice or fair play, but who has the strongest set of arguments!

And so man will never achieve peace or tranquillity on the earth, or in any earth world, so far as that is concerned, unless he can conceive much more infinitely and much more abstractly than he is doing now. He has to conceive the infinite function, not as law but as principle or principle function, because man has, so far as spiritual or metaphysical groups are concerned, used the term "law" rather loosely and in too broad a sense. There is no stretch of imagination that would say that God has laws, because God is both infinite and finite and maintains that infinity in all finite things, circumstances, conditions, and interdimensional relationships; and under such an understanding, we can easily say that if God had laws He would contradict Himself and would cease to exist. He would not only become His own judge and His own jury, but He would have to execute Himself.

That is the sum and total in a nutshell of what has confused not only the lawmakers, the jurisdictional agencies, the enforcement agencies of this country, but it has also confused the average citizen. It has confused the churchgoer, the Christian, the metaphysician, or the so-called spiritual interpreter of life, because he is always confusing the word 'law' with infinite function; and infinite function is, in itself, a perfection of imbalances which can only function as it does from polarity patterns, cycular patterns, and interdimensional relationships. It is very different from merely circumscribing a certain dimension of certain theoretical reaction as far as a group of people is concerned, to have a law which would regulate the reaction according to how it was so circumscribed by the concept of those who enacted the law and who were enforcing it. These, in themselves, are two different given sets of circumstances—and very often law enactment and law enforcement, too, are very different for the same law.

So to avoid confusion, if a metaphysical student is really going to understand the complete abstraction of the Infinite, he must first do away with that generally misconceived idea of law so far as infinite function is concerned, because there just are no laws so far as God is concerned. He has no laws; God is a function; He is a principle of all things, but He is no lawmaker or lawgiver. As far as the average individual is concerned, and God being so impersonal, God knows that every man is part of Him; He can be completely impersonal in regard to His relationship to every fellow man because He knows in the absolute and abstract, that man will either do one of two things: he will progress forward along a certain line of evolution in what can be called a predetermined set of positive conditions until he arrives at some position of mastership in what we might call a positive relationship to the given set of circumstances under which he reincarnated; or should he, at any time, deviate from that set of conditions and go into what people generally conceive as evil, he will progress along a certain plane of evolution into other dimensions or in relationships with other dimensions which are completely foreign to the way in which he started out.

Under the latter set of conditions, the person does not destroy himself, but he has to revert in a cycular fashion back to the origin of his birth; that is, the dawn or the start of his own reincarnations and to retrace his footsteps, so to speak, in a pattern of reincarnation which will lead him either from a new set of principles —as far as reincarnation is concerned—into another dimension, or that he follows his former pathway and now takes the right direction so that he again arrives at a positive relationship as a master with his originating set of reincarnating conditions.

That explains mastership; it explains why we have these so-called great planes where people are living, many of whom can be considered as masters and adepts, who are entirely evil as far as our way of life is concerned, simply because they are exercising interpolations of intelligence which are entirely foreign to what we conceive as our pattern of thought. We have arrived at these concepts from a given set of polarity patterns, and when we deviate from these or we see things which deviate from them, then they are necessarily evil; and they must be evil for one of a number of reasons. (See note at end of article.)

First, we can crudely say that they are not constructive; they could not be constructive to us because they could not function according to the cycular patterns and the various relationships which we have incurred through reincarnation—and there are other reasons, too. So far as the individual person is concerned, he passes on into that limitless limbo of timeless or voidless space ahead of him and occupies a position which is entirely foreign to the place of his birth, to the origin of his reincarnative cycle. He therefore is an evil person as far as we, in comparative analyses, can say; he is exercising these things as evil; he is still functioning however, so far as the individual's ego or id is concerned, with the various personality quotients or other extractions which have arrived more or less intact through that reincarnative pathway. But ultimately he will have to resolve back—and he will, by his own will and volition—to the place of his primeval birth, so to speak, and start the cycle all over again, and either reincarnate into a different set of conditions which will lead him into any one or another of the predetermined destinations, which he may have vaguely envisioned, or which may have been part of the life cycle which was most strong, or which was manifest as the greatest frequency relationship with many of the cycular movements of the life cycle.

It takes a person who has spent many thousands of years thinking along these lines to explain concepts as deep as these; we cannot simply acquire them overnight, or even in a lifetime. It must become something which has to be lived with and pondered over; it must be exemplified and worked with, and this given set of conditions must remanifest itself infinitely. That is one of the greatest and most confusing pitfalls that mankind has ever fallen into in his comparative analyses, because whenever these imbalances are so upset that he attempts to live by a certain set of reactionary principles which he has found effective in past lifetimes, then he is indeed lost, because as a functional human being, he must maintain a certain equilibrium, a certain balance with many dimensions of relationship. And if he does not, he is lost; he is going to have an unbalanced condition. (See note.)

In nature we see how infinite God is manifesting His balance in all natural wild species of plant and animal life—unless they are interfered with in some way, usually principally by agencies or groups of men —and through the ages of time, the earth has maintained a stable existence so far as plant and animal life is concerned. And that is simply done because of the same relationship there with what we call the balance

471

of nature which, in the higher sense, is maintained in the spiritual way. We cannot say for one moment that because a lion or any carnivore feeds on the herbivorous animals he is necessarily evil. His function, while it is destructive in nature, provides a very beneficial effect, because if the herbivorous animals were not destroyed and eaten by the carnivore, very soon they would overrun the earth and exterminate the plant life and the planet would be decimated.

That is a typical example of how we can misconstrue good and evil. Because something appears to us, under a certain set of conditions, as evil does not necessarily mean that it is so, because if we were functioning from another dimension of consciousness, that which we call evil could and most likely would appear to be good. It could be very constructive because it was moving with us in all our relationships to the present and the past life.

Note: It was the answer to that riddle that I knew had to be answered before I was satisfied. And I did not find it in any church. I found it on the work bench in the television shop; I found the secret for which I was looking. It was not really hidden from me all along because I have known all about it—known about it for perhaps hundreds of thousands of years. So I found that man, so far as the earth life was concerned, is stumbling blindly along the path. He does not have spiritual eyes, but at the same time through various relationships from lives which he has previously lived —as well as the intuitive guidance from the higher planes and channels, as well as his own ability to travel in his sleep state—and various other factors and even though he does not acknowledge these things or know anything about them—they have succeeded in creating for him some of the greatest miracles of his life, such as television, etc. People do not seem to realize these things; they do not seem to realize what a tremendous thing this really is, these various electronic gadgets and the biases with which they are surrounded —the radio and our communication systems—and how far science has gone in perfecting these contrivances as far as the material world is concerned.

This was made possible because in some way or another, man has reached through into the higher reaches of his spiritual self and obtained the answers to these things and constructed them. It is a very close parallel with the true creative principle of life; life simply could not exist in any other way. It just would not be possible for any man or any group of men, scientists or otherwise to construct a whole new set of physical laws on this earth that were different or contrary, or in some way out of reach of the realms of those principles which have been created by the Infinite Intelligence. It just could not be possible. All that man does—and he does not create anything—he only becomes conscious of something that has been there all along! He calls it discovering or creating something —but he does not.

He has only brought something into existence in another form or another state, for it has been there all the while. So is it not strange that he goes about patting himself on the back and deifies himself that he is the highest form of creation on the earth? Well, if he had a little insight and vision he would be very ashamed of himself in comparison, because he is not much higher on the scale of life than is the cow he milks or the dogs which bark at his door. He is not wise when we start comparing these things with that which we can see in the Infinite Cosmos which lies beyond the grave, or the so-called grave, which is the loss of the physical form. Man succeeds in awakening himself as far as his personal ego is concerned, so that he can carry himself into these spiritual dimensions; in the course of time and evolution and reincarnation, or whatever particular evolutionary pattern he wishes to follow, he will realize these things in the future day.

There have been men who have come from the higher spiritual dimensions to live upon the earth and tell of these things. But man could not understand them and he only wished to destroy them in one way or another. Jesus was one of them, and there have been others. It is one of the primeval laws under which man lives. It guarantees, in a sense of the word, that he is going to be safe as far as this world is concerned; for the future generations which follow on the earth will follow the same evolutionary pattern that he has found. That, in itself, is a direct tribute to the long-range intelligence of that Infinite Mind. For how else could man attain mastership, attain the individual stewardship of the Infinite Mind in the individual without passing through all the planes of Infinite Consciousness before he attains that?

So it is a wonderful thing to think about. In spite of all the stupidity, the ignorance, all of the things and ramifications which the material life involves, yet behind it all there is a very beautiful and wonderful infinite science where man can—in spite of all his sins, iniquities, shortcomings, and his stupidities—gradually climb the scale of the ladder of life. He destroys himself; sometimes he slides back down, but he always manages to recreate himself, bring himself back up, to go on. It would be contrary to conceive anything other than this way. Jesus was conscious of this principle as he said, "Even the sparrow which falls by the wayside was accounted for." He meant that simply because the very atoms in the sparrow's body were part of that Infinite Consciousness, not that anyone kept records.

The principle (law) of form or change from one energy to another is always a manifestation; even though it is so infinitesimally small with the Infinite Consciousness, it is all accounted for so far as the Infinite Mind is concerned. So is it not wonderful? Great Truths—things upon which to ponder! Yes, even in the most bestial content of any man's personality, there is one way that he can live through all of that and attain mastery over it—and you can say under those circumstances that there is such a thing as evil—for evil does the good thing unto everyone. It becomes good for having conquered evil. But how else could man become good if he had not so conquered? He would have no comparisons, no gauges, no platforms. He would simply be an inert vibrating mass of electronic protoplasm without identity. He must retain the idiom of every circumstance, of every experience, of every shock which he encounters, every evil; even though it is conquered or cancelled out as far as any repercussive effects or continuity in any future life is concerned, the idiom of that is contained or retained. He knows of those things, and that is all part of his progression into the Infinite, because after he has attained mastery over them in the reciprocating polarity patterns through which he has traversed, it is the structures, the forms of the spiritual self which have enabled him to live from the spiritual ego or id, in the spiritual dimension consciousness.

This food for thought is extremely deep and only for those who have the way and the means of reaching through. From the reactionary thought process, one would link himself to the basement. When he would turn the mirror of his mind upward, he would see the reflection of creation in all its grandeur, its magnitude of Infinity. He can live in that and breathe in it; he can manifest it into his consciousness, and that is the true way of life. Then his mind does not become something that is a slave unto every objectivism in his material world—that which he calls truth or manifestation, the power to concentrate, to realize upon some desired gains or some appurtenance, or some particular possession in the material world which is not creative—not in any sense. Man only becomes creative when he tunes himself upward or turns that mirror upward into that vast Infinite—that Cosmos. When he does that, that mirror not only shows him all of these things so far as his conscious life is concerned, but somehow or other those things can put life into his own life and put life into the lives of others with whom he associates. For there is no way or place in which those things would show upon the mirror of his mind which could be reflected from the surface which would be creative, because in Infinite Consciousness they are creative. And that is the way in which they live and regenerate themselves, for they are part of the Mind of the Infinite, and they can only be such; and those are the true Truths.

So how can we circumscribe through the mental processes of what we call the physical mind all that we need of this world and what we think is right for us? If we obtain power and mastery over the physical dimension to the extent that we realize the gain, the acquisition of some material wealth, we have not exerted mastership over anything, but we have become slaves to these things. That is not the true creative process of life; it simply means that when we have turned the mirror of our minds upward, it becomes something like the wires which bring electricity into our houses, or the pipe lines which bring the water into our homes; it becomes a channel for that Infinite Mind to flow through into our minds and the minds of the people about us, and that is the only way. That is called, "Finding the Father and the Kingdom of Heaven Within." That is Nirvana.

But actually it is the ultimate goal of everyone even though man knows nothing about it, and perhaps shall not for hundreds of thousands of years; yet there is something there that is part of that man—that Christ

Self. Jesus called it the "Comforter", that guiding ray, that beam that always draws him along his path of life, from one life unto another, through all kinds of sins and iniquities, sorrows and tears. We can become a craven coward or become a hero; it makes little difference because always that guiding light goes ahead and shows us the way.

THE JOINING

Part Two

Dear Ones: At this hour and in this place, I
again come to you.
And while I am of spirit, I knoweth not the
necessity of one hour or one place.
For surely in me, all hours, each is joined
in its proper place.

I come among you as one of you—a man
among men so that you knoweth of me
by name.
And my form yieldeth to thee—my body.
For surely as I am of this form and in this
place,
Yet I am not one of thee, but of spirit
And as such, I liveth not in the form or in
the flesh
But rather, the flesh liveth in me and
corrupteth me not.

For if ye should not see me thusly, how
should you know me, or how should you
call me if I am not known as a man and
only of spirit?
Then thine eyes yieldeth not my form,
neither does thine ears tell thee of my
name.

And so it was, many years ago, I was born
among thee
A Man among men, to yield to thee the
things of spirit,
Each in its hour and in its place.
For surely, if you knoweth of these things
and from the spirit, each in its time and in
its place,
Then ye knoweth of Me, for I am joined in
them, and, in them, they manifest to thee,
Each in its time and in its place.

So it must be thusly, the joining of all
things and their proper placement.
For, as ye cometh upon them, and your
eyes yield their form and your ears hear of
their name,
Then you knoweth of them and they, too,
become joined in thee.
And in thine future, you, too, become as
of spirit Joined in all things.

And as spirit, so ye too, may rest from
among men the conquering ideals and
ambitions to be, as they are, each one, a
citadel unto himself.
For, as he becomes a citadel, so is he
turned to stone

And he yieldeth neither the form nor the spirit nor will his ears heareth celestial music
Neither will his feet tread the pathways of the stars among those who have become spirit.
Yet, if I were to speak to thee of spirit, how would you know Me, or how would you know spirit if you know nothing of all things save that you have been in and, part of, this world, each one unto many lifetimes.

Man has not yet cometh to the time and the place where all these lives have yielded him naught but sorrow and pain.
For he is ever searching for that time and place, and that hour when he, too, is joined in all things and in all hours and in all places—
And he knoweth of them all, yet holding with all, the vision that here, too, must be a new beginning
A new place to withhold a new infinity.
And a searching and seeking, and a joining in the many ways of spirit so that it, too, yields more of its own self.
For, in these things, are born the essences of creation.

And, as the planets around their suns spin
in their mad galaxies of never-ending and
ceaseless motion,
So it is, in all creation, that these things,
too, must yield unto themselves, what
they are.
Not as they would be seen or as they
would be heard, but as they know of
themselves and how are they thusly joined
in spirit.

And so, as you ponder the many hours
ahead, and you are searching and seeking
and striving to join in spirit so that I would
have you remember me as such, having
joined in you, these common things which
I, too, have joined in spirit.
Not common to you, but uncommon to
all earth men.
Only in the principles of creativity do they
become ever apparent, do they become
the sustaining virtues of thy life.

And that you should not seek as other
men do, nor should you seek among them
for this joining of spirit and all the things
of which spirit is.
For surely you shall find none of it – for

they have not.
Each man must seek and search among the things of which he is
The treasures which he has stored in the after years to the things in which he has envisioned in his future
To his hopes, his aspirations and his ideals.
He must sift among the ashes of his experiences for the last traces of virtues which have been left by the fires of emotion.
He must ever be conscious that, in this world, there are many things which seek to destroy and to nullify all that he has thus joined.
For there is ever about him, the ways of men and their undoing, each one unto himself.
And in their hollow mockeries, their hypocrisies and their bigotries, they, too, are searching.
They, too, must find the erstwhile essences of spirit.
For, the longings in their hearts are truly born of spirit.
For are not all things thus created from it?
And are not all things its substance and itself?

Each thing, good or evil, so contrived, as each man seeth it in his own eye, becomes as naught to another man in his joining. For this joining washes away these traces of emotionalisms which yieldeth the taint of sin, of strife and of turmoil and naught is left save the pure golden grain of wisdom.

Thus, man cometh unto the world and he is one among the many denizens which dwelleth upon its face and he is nourished in its sustenances.
And he clotheth himself in its many forms and he diversifies himself in many other ways and thinks that it is all—
Yet, ever fearful that this passeth away, even so as he sees these things vanish from his eyes.

What then of the morrow? Are ye yielded up again unto the abominations of the earth world?
Will ye return to again wash thy pathway in blood and tears?
To the final unending, ending of thy life?

Or will ye seek, among the ashes of what you are, to gain these things of spirit, these essences, which have, in their many forms and manifestations, lived through all of the emotional tirades of thy existence?

Surely, then, this is the way of the joining. This is the way in which you, too, can again live and be joined in spirit.